MW00651405

Wind, Wings, and Waves

Wind, Wings, and Waves

A HAWAI'I NATURE GUIDE

Rick Soehren

A Latitude 20 Book
University of Hawai'i Press
Honolulu

© 2019 University of Hawai'i Press
All rights reserved
Printed in China

24 23 22 21 20 19   6 5 4 3 2 1

Library of Congress Cataloging-in-Publication Data

Names: Soehren, Rick, author.
Title: Wind, wings, and waves : a Hawaii nature guide / Rick Soehren.
Description: Honolulu : University of Hawaii Press, [2019] | "A latitude 20
   book." | Includes index.
Identifiers: LCCN 2018026799 | ISBN 9780824876616 (pbk ; alk. paper)
Subjects: LCSH: Natural history—Hawaii—Guidebooks.
Classification: LCC QH198.H3 S584 2019 | DDC 508.969—dc23
LC record available at https://lccn.loc.gov/2018026799

University of Hawai'i Press books are printed on acid-free paper
and meet the guidelines for permanence and durability of
the Council on Library Resources.

Design and composition by Wanda China

Cover photo: Keawa'ula (Yokohama) Bay, O'ahu, viewed from the
Ka'ena Point trailhead.

*This book is dedicated to Alan Ziegler and John Culliney,
two great scientist-authors who have inspired so many
to love and protect the living islands of Hawai'i.*

Contents

Preface

Scientists do not use the word *magic.* It just is not in our vocabulary. We leave the term to British authors who write fabulous books about witches and wizards. But you cannot write about the natural world of Hawai'i, and you certainly can't explore and learn about these amazing islands, without the feeling that they are special. Unique. Yes, magical.

The Hawai'i that often comes to mind may not seem magical. Crowded beaches, Waikīkī nightclubs, manicured golf courses? No. These places may hold their pleasures, but the natural world of Hawai'i offers so much more. Stare down an erupting volcano. Peer over the tallest sea cliffs on the planet. Trudge through snow in the morning, swim with green sea turtles in the afternoon, dine on food from a half-dozen cultures at sunset, then gaze upon the Milky Way. See the rarest birds on earth and listen to them sing. Snorkel in an alien world of shapeshifters, gender-benders, symbionts, and ancient beings. Listen to the whales sing. Sit in a forest and listen to nothing but the wind.

Hawai'i truly is a magical place. All it takes is a little bit of knowledge to recognize the magic and know where to find it. Let this book be your guide. Aloha.

Rick Soehren

Acknowledgments

It would have been impossible to write this book without the generous help and support of many people. For advice, assistance, encouragement, review of materials, the use of photographs, and other support, I am very grateful to: John Barnes at the Mauna Loa Observatory; Jim Darling at the Whale Trust; Jim Denny, author of *A Photographic Guide to the Birds of Hawai'i*; Arleone Dibben-Young; Dolphin Bay Hotel staff, and proprietor John Alexander; Larry and Suzanne Farwell; Aileen Feldman; J. B. Friday at the University of Hawai'i College of Tropical Agriculture and Human Resources; Roy Gal at the University of Hawai'i Institute for Astronomy; Edward Gomez at the Las Cumbres Observatory Global Telescope Network; Erika Heath; Norton Heath, U.S. Navy, retired; David Henkin at Earthjustice; Elia Y. K. Herman, state co-manager of the Hawaiian Islands Humpback Whale National Marine Sanctuary; Brenden Holland at the University of Hawai'i Hawaiian Tree Snail Conservation Lab; John Hoover, author of several fine books on Hawai'i's marine life; Frank Howarth, coauthor of *Hawaiian Insects and Their Kin*; Peter Jacobsen; Janet Leopold and the staff at the National Tropical Botanical Garden; Shannon Lyday at the NOAA Office of National Marine Sanctuaries; Ed Lyman at the Hawaiian Islands Humpback Whale National Marine Sanctuary; Michelle Murdock; Mike Opgenorth and the staff at Kahanu Garden; Shelley Paik at the Kaua'i Island Utility Cooperative; Whitney Peterson at the Pacific Islands Climate Change Cooperative; Marsha Prillwitz; Kalani Quiocho, Native Hawaiian cultural specialist; Tia Reber at the Bishop Museum; Nancy Reese and Dan Phillips; Scott Rowland at the University of Hawai'i Department of Geology and Geophysics; Tamara Sherrill and Whit Germano at the Maui Nui Botanical Gardens; Rob Shallenberger; Lloyd Soehren; Forest and Kim Starr of Starr Environmental; Don Swanson at the Hawaiian Volcano Observatory; Jennifer Waipa at the Kaua'i National Wildlife Refuge Complex; Ross Winans at the NOAA Pacific Services Center; Martina and James Wing, Manta Ray Advocates; Matt Young at the Macaulay Library,

Cornell Lab of Ornithology; Marjorie Ziegler, executive director of the Conservation Council for Hawai'i; and several anonymous reviewers. Any remaining errors in the book are all mine.

The professionals at the University of Hawai'i Press have been very helpful. I am grateful to: Nadine Little for her patience and encouragement; Masako Ikeda and Debbie Tang for taking up a big project midcourse; Cheryl Loe for ably and cheerfully bringing the project to conclusion; and Trond Knutsen for help with graphics and websites. Wendy Bolton did a fine job of copyediting for the Press, with a light and deft touch.

Finally, I am profoundly grateful to Jeanne Howe, who edited and improved the manuscript; to John Culliney for inspiration, hospitality, use of illustrations, and review of the entire manuscript; and to my wife, Marti, who was patient and supportive throughout a long writing effort.

1   A Land Like No Other

Introduction

Hawai'i is a special place. For its area, this string of islands holds more natural diversity than any other land on earth. From snow-capped peaks to erupting volcanoes to tropical forests to sandy beaches, shallow coral reefs to profound ocean depths, you can find it in Hawai'i. And these islands are so isolated, so far from every continent, that unique life has evolved to blanket the land.

Reminders of Hawaiian history are always nearby because these islands were swept from a traditional Polynesian culture into a thoroughly westernized U.S. territory, then into a society enriched by a diverse cultural mix—all within the span of a single human lifetime. Hawai'i is also a place of explorers. Polynesian explorers discovered these islands. Native Hawaiians are now exploring their ancient, nearly forgotten voyaging ties to other islands of Polynesia. Meanwhile, astronomers explore the universe from the tallest Hawaiian mountaintop, sacred realm of Hawaiian gods.

It is easy to lose sight of this special Hawai'i. It isn't promoted in tourist literature because you don't have to pay to experience it or hire someone to show it to you. Even lifelong residents may not fully realize what diverse wonders surround them. And yet, exploring the natural world of the islands is the best Hawaiian experience of all. You can see, hear, smell, feel, and taste extraordinary things that simply don't exist anywhere else on earth.

HOW TO USE THIS BOOK

Wind, Wings, and Waves was written to help you appreciate and explore the natural world of Hawai'i. Each chapter is devoted to one aspect of

FIGURE 1.1 Green sea turtles are common near Hawaiian shorelines. This turtle is trailed by a pair of sailfin tangs at Kahe Point on Oʻahu. (Rick Soehren)

nature in the islands and opens with some background on the topic. Then, each chapter after this one has a **Field Trip!** section describing places where you can experience nature for yourself. In the back of the book you'll find a table listing all these field trips by island to help you plan your itinerary. Finally, each chapter ends with **Learn More**, a list of my recommendations to help you find out more about a topic.

All of that may lead you to expect a book that is well organized and tidy, but nature is not tidy and refuses to be put into neat compartments or chapters. John Muir explained it this way: "When we try to pick out anything by itself, we find it hitched to everything else in the Universe." It is hard to learn about one aspect of nature without being drawn into other areas. The natural world is connected in thousands of ways we know about and probably tens of thousands of ways that we don't yet understand. Bottom line? This story of the natural world in Hawaiʻi jumps around a lot. There isn't any other way to tell it. So in nearly every chapter you'll find cross-references to other chapters and topics.

One theme, however, will come up over and over: Hawai'i is fragile. The land and its life have been harmed through actions taken either without full understanding of just how fragile this complex environment can be, or sometimes through greed or carelessness. The Hawaiian word *mālama* means "to take care of, care for, or preserve." As you explore, please exert *mālama* for this land so it will continue to be a beautiful and wondrous place.

Even little things matter. A lot of this care is just common sense, but here's one precaution that may not occur to everybody: clean your hiking shoes before you come to Hawai'i, between hikes, and when you travel between islands. Seeds can ride along snagged to a shoelace or stuck in dried mud in the treads of a shoe. One of Hawai'i's biggest environmental problems is the damage caused by species of plants or animals that were transported from someplace else. Don't add to the problem by spreading invaders.

This book isn't intended to provide detailed instruction on how to snorkel or what to bring on a day hike. Still, a few things really come in handy and are worth mentioning before you pack: **Polarized sunglasses** will reduce reflected glare and help you peer beneath the ocean surface. I'd never go near the ocean without them. **Sun protection** is especially important in tropical Hawai'i. A wide-brimmed hat, sunscreen lotion, and a rash guard shirt for snorkeling or swimming are all good to have. I've seen more than one visitor whose trip was ruined by a sunburn acquired on the first day of vacation. If you use sunscreen lotion in the water, make sure it does not contain oxybenzone, a chemical that may harm coral. Even tiny amounts may harm the reef; better to use a rash guard shirt to block the sun. And sunscreen is not just for the beach; at high elevation it may feel cool but there is less atmosphere to filter the sun's rays. **Binoculars** aren't just for birders. They are handy to have for observing other wildlife, marine mammals, smoldering volcanoes, even stars. **Walking sticks** are surprisingly helpful on steep slippery trails, and you can find collapsible ones that fit in a suitcase or daypack. They are so useful that people have offered to buy mine as I hiked along muddy trails. It is good to keep **a small flashlight** in your daypack, even if you don't expect to be out after dark; the sun sets more quickly in the tropics. Besides, you'll need one or two to use inside lava

FIGURE 1.2 History is never far away. These petroglyphs are at the Pu'u Loa petroglyph field in Hawai'i Volcanoes National Park on the Big Island. (Rick Soehren)

tubes. **A tote bag** will come in handy for carrying all your toys to the beach. And since Hawai'i has banned disposable plastic grocery bags, you can take your tote bag to the grocery store, too.

A few other things I always pack: plastic bags to protect my cameras during unexpected rain showers, a travel thermos so I can enjoy my Kona coffee all day long, and clothing layers for warmth and water resistance because you never know when a big mountain will call to you.

THE HAWAIIAN LANGUAGE

Hawaiian is an official language of the State of Hawai'i. Most place names, many street names, many common words or phrases, and most names for native plants and animals are Hawaiian. These names can be very difficult for visitors to remember and very intimidating to pronounce because they are so unfamiliar. A basic understanding of the Hawaiian language will be helpful in pronouncing and remembering these names.

The Hawaiian language was an oral one until missionaries and other westerners created a written Hawaiian alphabet consisting of just twelve letters. The five vowels are pronounced as follows: *a* as in *among; e* as in *bet; i* as in *machine; o* as in *hole;* and *u* as in *true.* (The vowels sound much like they do in Spanish.) Each vowel is usually sounded separately in Hawaiian pronunciation. The consonants *h, k, l, m, n, p,* and *w* all sound pretty much like they do in English except *w,* which is usually pronounced as a soft *v* when it follows an *i* or an *e,* and sometimes when it follows an *a.* The accent in Hawaiian words is usually on the next-to-last syllable and alternating preceding syllables. Words with five syllables are stressed on the first and fourth. The vowel pairs *ae, ai, ao, au, ei, eu, oi,* and *ou* are pronounced as single syllables with the emphasis on the first letter. Thus, *lei* is pronounced LEH-ee, not LAY.

You'll notice some Hawaiian words in this book are written with two symbols not used in English. One is the ʻokina (ʻ), a consonant in the Hawaiian language that looks like a reverse apostrophe and indicates a glottal stop or separation of sound as in the expression *uh-oh.* The other is *the kahakō* or macron, a line over a vowel to indicate emphasis. When an *a* is stressed in this way it is pronounced like the *a* in father; a stressed *e* is pronounced as in they. Hawaiian words and foreign language terms are in italics, except when they are used as place names. A good discussion of pronunciation and grammar is included in *The Pocket Hawaiian Dictionary.* See **Learn More** at the end of this chapter.

Yes, all of this may seem a little bewildering if it is new to you, but you will be glad for the pronunciation help when you want to tell your friends about the ʻiʻiwi (ee-EE-vee) you saw along the Puʻu ʻŌʻō (POO-oo OH-oh) Trail, the maile (MAee-leh) vine you saw growing in Kōkeʻe (KO-KEH-eh) State Park, or the heiau (HEHee-AHoo) you visited at Puʻu Honua o Hōnaunau (POO-oo ho-NOO-ah o HO-nah-oo-NAH-oo) National Historic Park.

One more intriguing twist: early spoken Hawaiian language was a little different from the Hawaiian in today's written form. When English-speaking missionaries wrote down the Hawaiian language as it sounded to their ears, they simplified or missed—and thus effectively erased—subtle differences in sounds. The Hawaiian language hasn't been the same since. How do we know what spoken Hawaiian sounded like in 1820? See chapter 8.

A word formed by imitation of a sound is said to be onomatopoeic, from the Greek term meaning "to make a name." Many Hawaiian words sound this way. One onomatopoeic Hawaiian word is *'ūlili,* the Hawaiian name for a bird whose English name is wandering tattler and whose call sounds like its Hawaiian name.

Other names are descriptive. Throughout the book there are translations of names for places, plants, and animals to help give a sense of what old Hawai'i was like and how early Hawaiians perceived their world.

Visitors may want to learn a few Hawaiian words, especially the terms commonly used by local people when giving directions: *mauka* means "toward the mountains," and *makai* means "toward the sea." These terms are much more useful than compass directions when you're on an island. Two other words that you'll see and hear a lot are *keiki,* the Hawaiian word for child, and *kama'āina,* which means "native born," or literally "land child." Businesses often give a *kama'āina* discount to customers who can show a Hawai'i driver's license.

FIGURE 1.3 High-elevation forests are home to native birds, plants, even insects. This is the Nature Conservancy's Waikamoi Preserve on Maui. (Rick Soehren)

BE CAREFUL OUT THERE

Finally, a word about personal safety. The field trips described in this book will take you out into nature. It is your responsibility to make sure you are adequately prepared for the conditions you may encounter, and that you are physically capable of the trips you decide to take. If you have doubts about your ability to hike a particular trail or snorkel at a certain beach, listen to your inner voice. Car break-ins sometimes occur at isolated trailheads and tourist spots. Don't leave valuables in your car. Leaving it unlocked may prevent a broken window. For the benefit of disabled readers, there are descriptions of conditions in many field trips. The table in the appendix includes additional information on access for the disabled, noting field trips that are completely wheelchair accessible and those that can be enjoyed by a wheelchair user, but are not completely accessible.

LEARN MORE

Many of the museums, parks, government agencies, and other resources mentioned in the book maintain websites. Web addresses have not been included because they tend to change too frequently to be useful for long in a book like this, but names and other descriptive terms in the text were chosen specifically to help you locate these websites using search engines such as Google.

Throughout the book, you'll see many recommended publications from the University of Hawai'i Press. Please don't think I'm shilling for my publisher. The university has done an exceptional job of publishing materials that are relevant to the natural world of Hawai'i. Outstanding books I've found by other publishers are also mentioned in the **Learn More** sections.

Each chapter lists books and other materials that are specifically relevant to that chapter. Listed below are some basic resources and some general references:

- James A. Bier, *Reference Maps of the Islands of Hawai'i* (Honolulu: University of Hawai'i Press, various publication dates). Even in a world filled with tourist literature maps and Internet maps, a good paper map can be indispensable. This series of maps, one for each main island (Moloka'i and Lāna'i are combined) depicts features relevant to this book: correct place names, *heiau* locations, major coral reefs, ages of recent lava flows. Excellent companions to this book.

- Mary Kawena Pukui and Samuel H. Elbert, with Esther T. Mookini and Yu Mapuana Nishizawa, *New Pocket Hawaiian Dictionary* (Honolulu: University of Hawai'i Press, 1992). This Hawaiian–English dictionary will help you understand Hawaiian grammar and translate Hawaiian words.
- Mary Kawena Pukui, Samuel H. Elbert, and Esther T. Mookini, *Place Names of Hawai'i* (Honolulu: University of Hawai'i Press, revised edition, 1974). Nearly every place name in Hawai'i tells a story or has a history. This might be the most interesting dictionary-format book you'll ever read.
- Alan C. Ziegler, *Hawaiian Natural History, Ecology, and Evolution* (Honolulu: University of Hawai'i Press, 2002). This is unquestionably a textbook. You can tell from its heft (hardbound, 496 pages) and its textbook price. But if you finish *Wind, Wings, and Waves* and you want to learn more, this should be next on your reading list.
- John L. Culliney, *Islands in a Far Sea: The Fate of Nature in Hawai'i* (Honolulu: University of Hawai'i Press, second edition, 2006). This is another hefty book (hardbound, 432 pages), but don't let that scare you off. This book describes many aspects of Hawai'i's natural world, and goes on to describe how human ignorance and greed are damaging the island environment. This book just might make you cry—and then take action.
- Sonia P. Juvik and James O. Juvik, editors; Thomas R. Paradise, chief cartographer; *Atlas of Hawai'i* (Honolulu: University of Hawai'i Press, third edition, 1998). This is a reference book and a coffee-table book in one. There's a lot of informative text in addition to the maps.
- A. Grove Day, editor, *Mark Twain's Letters from Hawaii* (Honolulu: University of Hawai'i Press, 1975). In 1866 Samuel Clemens was sent to Hawai'i by his newspaper employer, the *Sacramento Union*. This book is a collection of his letters originally published in the *Union* under his pen name, Mark Twain. It is part fascinating history, part commentary on the times, part droll Mark Twain wit. Once you have a little familiarity with the places Twain writes about, you'll find the book even more interesting.
- Isabella L. Bird, *Six Months in the Sandwich Islands* (Rutland, VT: Charles E. Tuttle Company, 1974 edition). Isabella Bird was way ahead of her time. In 1873 this remarkable Englishwoman traveled alone to Hawai'i and stayed six months. First published in 1890, her thirty-one long letters to her sister back home provide a glimpse of Hawai'i as it existed in a much simpler time. Like Twain's book, her letters are even more interesting when you have some familiarity with the places she describes.

2 In the Beginning
Volcanism and Plate Tectonics

Imagine an island that rises up from the depths of the sea. A magical place where wonderful plants and animals, unseen anywhere else on earth, live and evolve. An island that isn't rooted in place, but slowly travels across the sea like a sailing ship. And then this magical place, this ark with its precious cargo of unique plants and animals, sinks back below the waves. But it doesn't stop; this sunken island continues its journey along the ocean floor until it disappears forever into the inky depths of the deepest waters on earth. In its place, more magical islands rise from the sea, one after another. And more mysterious and wonderful plants and animals appear. Like some ancient doomed caravan, new islands with new life travel across the sea, one after another, for untold tens of millions of years and ultimately sink below the waves. You have imagined Hawai'i.

We'll get to the explanation of rising, sinking, traveling islands later in this chapter. Now let's start with a little information about the 50th state. Hawai'i is composed of eight main inhabited islands plus a long string of about 124 smaller and mostly uninhabited islands, reefs, and shoals collectively called the Northwestern Hawaiian Islands. Altogether these islands total just 6,423 square miles. Hawai'i ranks 47th in size among the states, larger than only Rhode Island, Connecticut, and Delaware. The largest island in the archipelago is the southernmost, called Hawai'i or simply the Big Island to avoid confusion with the state name. At 4,028 square miles it is larger than all the rest of the islands combined.

It is about 1,600 miles from the Big Island in the south to the tip of the Northwestern Hawaiian Islands: a bit more than the distance between San Francisco and Dallas, or London and Istanbul. It's even farther to other land. Honolulu is 2,400 miles from San Francisco. It's 3,850 miles to Tokyo, 2,800 to Anchorage, and 5,070 to Sydney. If you look at Hawai'i on a globe, all the continental landmasses would be at the very edge of your gaze. Most of what you'd see is water. Lots and lots of water.

And some of that water is very deep. The deepest ocean waters on earth are at the Marianas Trench in the western Pacific between Japan and New Guinea, reaching a depth of about 36,000 feet. The waters off Hawai'i can't quite compare, but they're still surprisingly deep, around 16,000 feet or three miles.

Hawai'i is mostly within the tropics. Geographers define the tropics as that area straddling the equator between the Tropic of Cancer at about 23 degrees north latitude down to the Tropic of Capricorn at 23 degrees south. These latitudes bound the area in which the sun will be directly overhead at some part of the year. The main Hawaiian Islands lie in the tropical North Pacific between the equator and the Tropic of Cancer. Many of the tiny Northwestern Hawaiian Islands extend north of the tropics.

Starting from the south, the main Hawaiian Islands are Hawai'i

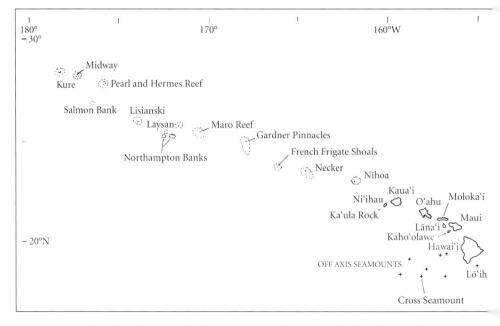

MAP 2.1 The Hawaiian Archipelago stretches from Kure Atoll in the northwest to Lō'ihi Seamount, erupting on the seafloor to the southeast. (Map drawn by John Culliney)

Table 2.1 The Main Islands at a Glance

Island	Population (2010)	Area (Sq. Miles)	People/ Sq. Mile	Max. El. (Feet)	Visitors (2016)
Big Island	185,079	4,028	46	13,796	1,550,046
Maui	144,444	727	199	10,023	2,640,175
Kahoʻolawe	0	45	0	1,483	—
Lānaʻi	3,135	141	22	3,366	63,338
Molokaʻi	7,345	260	28	4,970	60,367
Oʻahu	953,207	597	1,597	4,003	5,461,880
Kauaʻi	66,921	552	121	5,243	1,187,476
Niʻihau	170	69	2	1,281	—

or the Big Island, Maui, Lānaʻi, Molokaʻi, Oʻahu, and Kauaʻi. Two more main islands are not accessible to the public: Kahoʻolawe is off the coast of Maui and is dangerously littered with unexploded bombs from its decades of use as a U.S. military bombing target. Niʻihau, west of Kauaʻi, has been privately owned since King Kamehameha V sold it in 1864 and has been mostly closed to the public ever since. Its residents, nearly all of Hawaiian heritage, made up the only voting precinct in the state to reject statehood.

Stretching off to the north and west are the Northwestern Hawaiian Islands or, more poetically, the Leeward Islands. (*Leeward* is an old nautical term meaning away from the wind, in this case downwind from the prevailing trade winds that blow from the northeast.) Two of the islands at the very west end of the chain were strategic locations during World War II: Kure Atoll and Midway Atoll.

Farther north and west the chain continues with submarine mountains called the Emperor Seamounts. They no longer reach the surface, or perhaps never did. They stretch nearly all the way to the east coast of Russia, terminating at two deep sea trenches, the Kuril and Aleutian.

LATE TECTONICS AND HOT SPOTS

How did islands come to exist in the middle of a very deep ocean? For a long time, the prevailing idea of island formation was pretty simple:

it was theorized that a crack opened up on the sea floor, through which magma or molten rock from the hot liquid core of the earth was released. As new parts of the crack opened up, eruptions occurred and created new land. It was believed this crack ran from the northwest where the islands seem oldest to the southeast where Kīlauea (it means "spewing") Volcano is still erupting. Actually, there's one more volcano offshore: Lōʻihi Seamount is erupting and building an island. It is already more than thirteen thousand feet high when measured from the sea floor, but it's still more than three thousand feet from the ocean surface.

The idea of a sea floor crack was a pretty tidy theory, and it did a good job of explaining a line of islands that were progressively younger as you moved southeast. But all over the rest of the world geologists and biologists were making untidy observations they just couldn't explain: Why are there marsupials in South America and Australia, but virtually nowhere else? (I say virtually because there is one marsupial in North America, the Virginia opossum, and there are fossil marsupials in Antarctica.) Why are there matching mountain ranges in Ghana and Brazil? And the kicker, plain to any school kid who ever looked at a world map: why does the east coast of South America fit the west coast of Africa— pure coincidence?

The explanation takes us a long way from Hawaiʻi, but it is arguably the most important scientific revelation of the last 150 years: plate tectonics. The term comes from the Greek word *tektōn*, a builder. This theory holds that the earth's lithosphere—the cold, brittle outer layer of our planet containing the crust and a bit of the mantle layer below—is actually cracked into many big pieces or plates that all fit together. These plates are about 25–100 miles thick. Some plates hold continents, some hold oceans, some hold a mix. These plates move, in some places colliding, in other places pulling apart, and in still other places sliding along next to each other. But don't think of the plates as puzzle pieces that never change. These plates are growing along some edges. Plate material is lost at the opposite edge when it sinks back into the layer at the bottom of the lithosphere, called the mantle, or else it is pushed up to form mountains like the Himalayas. The new plate material often oozes out of the earth along undersea ridges. Plate formation in the middle of the Atlantic is pulling Africa and the Americas apart.

Plate tectonics theory would explain the distribution of marsupials;

they're found on separate modern landmasses that once were joined. And it explains the similar rocks and interlocking coastlines of South America and Africa. But what about the islands of Hawai'i? The theory does a good job of explaining island formation, too, with just one additional element: a "hot spot" in the mantle. At a hot spot, heat energy is conducted upward so strongly that molten rock punches right through the plate to the ocean floor as a volcano. The volcano eventually forms a seamount at the bottom of the ocean. And with enough energy and molten rock, this seamount grows until it becomes an island.

Most of the Pacific Ocean is located on one large plate, the Pacific Plate. Like all the plates that cover the earth's surface, it is drifting. And it turns out that the direction of drift is in precise alignment with the islands of Hawai'i, along a line from active Lō'ihi, Kīlauea, and Mauna Loa near the southeast tip of the Big Island to Kure Atoll in the northwest, a distance of about 1,600 miles. A similar pattern holds for the Emperor Seamounts that stretch nearly across the ocean. All the islands are in a tidy curving line.

As the Pacific Plate drifts, it pulls each Hawaiian island away from the underlying hot spot, cutting off the source of energy and signaling the end of the main eruption phase for that volcano or island. Scientists believe the Hawaiian hot spot is a column about 150 miles in diameter that likely extends all the way to the core–mantle boundary, some 1,800 miles below the surface. Currently the hot spot is feeding three very active volcanoes in the state: Mauna Loa, Kīlauea, and still-submerged Lō'ihi. Three less active volcanoes, Hualālai and Mauna Kea on the Big Island, and Haleakalā on East Maui, are still connected to the hot spot and will likely erupt again. Each volcano may stay connected to the hot spot for about a million years. Maui, where eruptions occurred as recently as the 1600s, is now pulling away from its energy source.

Would you like to know more about this hot spot? Well, you're not alone. Geologists would like to know more, too. We can't exactly go have a look, or even probe it with instruments. Remember, we're talking about something happening under 16,000 feet of ocean, under 100 miles of lithosphere, deep within our planet. And the Hawaiian hot spot is not the only one; there are something like twenty of these hot spots around the globe, apparently sitting in relatively fixed positions while the plates of the earth's surface glide around above them. Recent, very clever, research used shock waves produced by earthquakes to create an image of the hot spot column, something like a sonogram image of an unborn baby. Except the hot spot baby is 1,800 miles tall and spitting up lava.

For all the references to the hot spot that you see in tourist literature, guidebooks, and textbooks, you'd think we're discussing a concept as familiar as a grocery store. In fact, we are just starting to understand what is really going on. When it comes to explaining hot spots or a lot of other things in Hawai'i, there are plenty of theories but few definitive answers. Many times, the answer is "We don't know."

We Don't Know. This book explores a lot of the questions that will occur to you as you travel around the fiftieth state. Perhaps surprisingly, the most common single answer in the pages to come is "We don't know." Part of the magic of Hawai'i lies in its mystery. There is a lot about these islands and the life that blankets them that we don't fully understand. There is plenty of work for future generations of scientists.

Fortunately, geologists do know something about determining the age of rocks. The process is called radiometric dating, and it gives us a way to determine the approximate age of each Hawaiian island. The results are quite consistent with plate tectonics. The age of surface lava flows on the Big Island ranges from 0 to about 500,000 years old, on Maui from 750,000 to 1.3 million, on Lāna'i 1.3 million, on Moloka'i 1.75 to 1.9, on O'ahu 2.6 to 3.7, on Kaua'i 5.1, and on Ni'ihau about 4.9 million years old. The Northwestern Hawaiian Islands are even older, with Midway Atoll coming in at about 28.3 million. The seamounts beyond are predictably older still, from about 30 million just past Kure Atoll to 75 or 80 million years old where the chain is swallowed by deep-sea trenches.

Knowing the distance between the hot spot and distant islands such as Midway, and knowing the age of these distant islands, enables us to calculate the speed at which the Pacific Plate and the Hawaiian Islands are drifting. It is between three and four inches per year, a little faster than your fingernails grow.

Where the Pacific Plate is grinding against neighboring plates or sliding beneath them, there is friction. This friction causes earthquakes all around the edge of the Pacific Ocean. Volcanoes—very different from hot spot volcanoes—also form at the plate boundaries. The Andes mountain range of South America, the Aleutian Islands that form a "tail" on Alaska, Mt. St. Helens, Mt. Fuji, and many others are all part of this active perimeter that has earned the name "Ring of Fire."

Paradoxically, the same Pacific Plate that grinds at its edges and spawns volcanoes is also remarkably flexible, like an air mattress floating on water. The Hawaiian Islands are, in a sense, floating on this raft. These massive islands have been deposited on top of the earth's crust and they push the crust down a bit. Oceanographers can measure this effect: the ocean floor is pushed downward around the edges of islands, creating a trough around them. This seafloor arches a bit higher when you get farther away from the islands. The effect is most pronounced around the Big Island, where the Hawaiian Deep reaches roughly eighteen thousand feet, surrounded by the Hawaiian Arch. The arch rises two thousand feet above the surrounding seafloor, which averages sixteen thousand feet deep outside the Hawaiian Deep and Arch.

Tsunami!   When an earthquake shifts an undersea tectonic plate, it can push up an immense volume of water, resulting in a tsunami. A tsunami is a wave or series of waves, usually generated by an earthquake, that can travel long distances across water and inflict great harm when it eventually encounters land. Hawai'i is in the middle of the Pacific Plate, with seismically active plate boundaries in all directions. The islands lie at the bull's-eye of the planet's largest tsunami generator. That's why you will see signs pointing to tsunami evacuation routes near the shore and yellow tsunami warning speakers on telephone poles.

Hawai'i experiences a damaging tsunami about once every dozen years. The 2011 Fukushima earthquake in Japan caused a moderate tsunami in Hawai'i, sending a couple of feet of water through shops along the main street of Kailua-Kona on the Big Island. The same tsunami even did moderate damage to marinas along the California coast. More powerful tsunamis can be deadly, especially when they approach a coastline feature like a bay that funnels their power. Just such a bay exists in Hilo on the Big Island's east side. A tsunami in April 1946 killed 159 Hilo residents. Another in May 1960 killed 61 and devastated much of downtown Hilo. The town wisely refrained from rebuilding on this low ground. Today, the area is a huge grassy park. Nearby, just across the street from the bay front, sits the Tsunami Museum.

Geologists have coined a lot of terms to describe volcanic rock that you might find in Hawai'i—the vocabulary of hot stuff:

Magma is liquid rock still in the earth that has not been released from a volcano. When magma emerges, it's called **lava**. The magma produced at a mid-ocean ridge where new plate material forms, or emitted from a hot spot, has a particular chemical composition and is called **basalt** when it cools into rock.

Solidified Hawaiian lava flows are named according to their surface texture. The main determining factor is whether the lava was still hot and fluid when it stopped or whether it continued to flow even after it had cooled a bit and become viscous. Lava that stops flowing while still hot and fluid forms ***pāhoehoe***, solidified lava with a smooth surface that when it is buckled, produces a characteristic "ropy" surface. Lava that continues to flow even after it has started to cool becomes much more jumbled and flows in a tumbling way. It forms *'a'ā*, lava that has a very rough surface.

FIGURE 2.1 Two main types of lava meet: smooth ropy *pāhoehoe* and rough *'a'ā*. (Rick Soehren)

When fluid lava is ejected into the air and hardens, it may form tiny particles that can float on the wind called **ash**. In Hawai'i, ash is most commonly formed when the magma encounters water underground, forming steam, which produces an explosive eruption. Such an eruption can result in an **ash cone**. Over time, an ash deposit can become cemented together into a soft brittle kind of rock called **tuff**. Such a transformed ash cone is called a **tuff cone**, Diamond Head being a familiar example.

Fluid material ejected into the air can also form and harden into large rounded blobs called **bombs**. Western geologists have named two other types of ejected material after the Hawaiian deity of volcanoes, Pele: glassy rounded beads are called **Pele's tears**, and very thin strands are called **Pele's hair**. You can often find Pele's hair carried in the wind for miles from an active volcanic vent.

Often, this ejected lava produces **cinder**, usually porous and ranging in size from a pea to a grapefruit. A volcano will sometimes erupt to produce a **cinder cone**, a big hill that may have a crater at its peak.

When a lava flow cools on its surface while it continues to flow underneath, it can drain away downstream, resulting in an empty cave-like **lava tube**. Lava tubes can be ten feet or more in diameter, and many miles long. Want to explore one? See the **Field Trip!** section at the end of the chapter.

HE ISLAND LIFE CYCLE

Plate tectonics gives us the big picture of how the Hawaiian Islands were formed, but that is really only the beginning of the story. After an island is dragged off the hot spot it will exist for another thirty million years or so before it disappears below the waves again. During its formation and slow disappearance, all sorts of things happen to this Hawaiian island that will make it unique and one of the most wonderful environments on earth.

The life cycle of an island is a long, slow, continuous process. To describe and understand this process of island evolution, geologists have conveniently divided the process into about nine discrete stages. The first stage of island evolution is the **deep submarine stage**, when the hot spot first pushes magma through the crust and an eruption begins. The pressure may be so great in this deep ocean environment

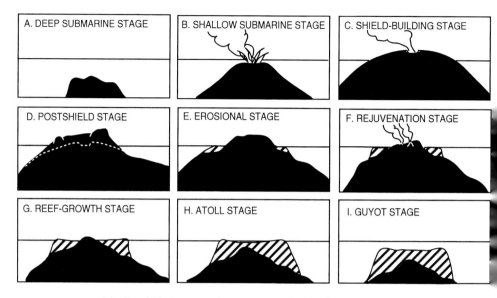

A. DEEP SUBMARINE STAGE	B. SHALLOW SUBMARINE STAGE	C. SHIELD-BUILDING STAGE
D. POSTSHIELD STAGE	E. EROSIONAL STAGE	F. REJUVENATION STAGE
G. REEF-GROWTH STAGE	H. ATOLL STAGE	I. GUYOT STAGE

FIGURE 2.2 Idealized life history of a Hawaiian island. All stages except B currently exist in the archipelago. (Figure by Keith Krueger, courtesy of Marjorie Ziegler)

that steam can't even form. Lōʻihi Seamount southeast of the Big Island is in this phase. How long will it take to reach the surface? We don't know, but if it grows at the same rate as volcanoes above the waterline, it might take another forty thousand years. Altogether this deep submarine phase may last a couple hundred thousand years.

The next stage is referred to as the **shallow submarine stage** or breaching stage. No islands in Hawaiʻi are currently at this stage. At this point the new undersea island is probably over the hot spot itself. When the growing seamount reaches within a few hundred feet of the surface, the weight of the overlying seawater is no longer enough to prevent steam from forming, and eruptions are explosive enough to shatter the new rock into fragments and even carry these fragments into the air. This forms a big unstable pile of material that may wash away in the waves and be replaced with new eruptive material time and again. During this phase the volcano may be roughly three hundred thousand years old.

Eventually our volcano grows large enough that eruptions are shielded from ocean water. New lava emerges and hardens before it comes in contact with seawater, and it forms an island. The volcano takes on a distinctive rounded shape that reminded early geologists of ancient battle shields, so they called this kind of hot spot volcano a shield volcano. Thus, this is the **shield-building stage**.

This shield-building stage is usually the most active period for the volcano because it is still directly over the hot spot. The volcano is a few hundred thousand years old when it begins this stage—its teenage years. Like most teenagers, it is growing rapidly and in spurts. The average growth rate is less than an inch per year, but single lava flows may be thirty feet thick. Perhaps 95 percent of the total volume of the volcano above sea level is built during this stage. Kīlauea and Mauna Loa are volcanoes in the early and later stages of shield-building growth, respectively.

And this growth is stunning. Hot spot volcanoes are the most massive mountains on the planet. The elevation statistics for Mauna Kea (the Hawaiian name means "white mountain") and Mauna Loa (long mountain), the two tallest peaks on the Big Island and within the entire state, are impressive but not world class at first glance. Mauna Kea tops out at 13,796 feet, with Mauna Loa just behind at 13,677. If you look at these numbers alone, the mountains seem no match for the world's tallest, Everest at 29,028 feet; the tallest peak in North America, Mt. McKinley at 20,237; or even the tallest peak in the lower 48 states, Mt. Whitney at 14,505.

But all these continental mountains have a head start: they rise from continental landmasses that are well above sea level. Hawaiian volcanoes start at the seafloor. And remember, they've pushed that seafloor downward because they're so heavy. There are three ways to measure the height of Hawaiian volcanoes: from sea level (the heights given above), from the level of the surrounding seafloor (over 30,000 feet), or from the weight-depressed seafloor directly beneath the big mountains. From this last perspective, Mauna Loa and Mauna Kea are both about 56,000 feet. Mauna Loa, slightly shorter but much broader at its base than its sister mountain, is the most massive mountain on the planet.

Hot spot shield volcanoes are different from continental volcanoes in more ways than just their larger size. Continental volcanoes tend to be conical rather than rounded like a shield. Mt. Fujiyama in Japan is a nearly perfect example. Another difference is the source of the lava: hot spot volcanoes are apparently fed by heat from deep within the earth's mantle, while continental volcanoes get their molten rock from much shallower activity at plate boundaries. Finally, continental volcanoes tend to have nastier dispositions. Think of the eruption of Mt. Vesuvius that buried Pompeii in AD 79 or the explosive eruption of Mt. St. Helens in 1980. Continental volcanoes often send plumes of volcanic ash thousands of feet into the atmosphere, a hazard to aviation because the gritty ash can clog jet engines and even melt inside hot engines. Hawaiian volcanoes certainly can be dangerous, especially for the foolhardy or ill-prepared, but they are not in the same league as some continental volcanoes.

During the shield-building stage, Hawaiian volcanoes experience something akin to growing pains: rift zones. You will hear the term a lot when you visit Hawai'i Volcanoes National Park. These are long fractures that radiate from the summit of the volcano. Sometimes eruptions occur along these fracture zones rather than at the summit of the volcano. Usually there are two rift zones on Hawaiian shield volcanoes, but sometimes more. Mauna Loa has two major rift zones: the southwest rift zone extends from the summit down toward Manukā Natural Area Reserve and South Point. The northeast rift zone, less distinct, ends near Kūlani (this means "like heaven" and—ironically—is also the name of a prison) south of Hilo. Look at the satellite image of Mauna Loa in figure 2.3; the rift zones will be obvious. Kīlauea also has two rift zones, a southwest rift zone and a very active east rift zone where the Pu'u 'Ō'ō vent has been erupting since 1983. 'Ō'ō is a traditional Hawaiian digging stick, which Pele used to dig this new vent. The vent was named by the people of the nearby village of Kalapana to honor Pele. She responded with a flow of lava that destroyed the village.

Eruptions also occur at the summit, where most shield volcanoes have a crater called a caldera that forms when a natural magma reservoir within the volcano drains and collapses. Kīlauea Caldera in Hawai'i Volcanoes National Park is one of the most accessible active calderas on earth. You can even stay the night at Volcano House, a hotel perched on the edge of the caldera, as Mark Twain did in June of 1866.

Kīlauea Caldera has been filled with lava flows at times in the past. Then, for reasons that we do not understand, magma drains from beneath the caldera. The top of the mountain collapses, creating a new caldera with more or less vertical sides and a jumbled floor. Eruptions then resume, and lava starts to fill the caldera once more. Occasionally smaller "pit" craters form in or near the caldera. Today, Halema'uma'u (fern house) Crater is a collapsing pit crater within the larger caldera.

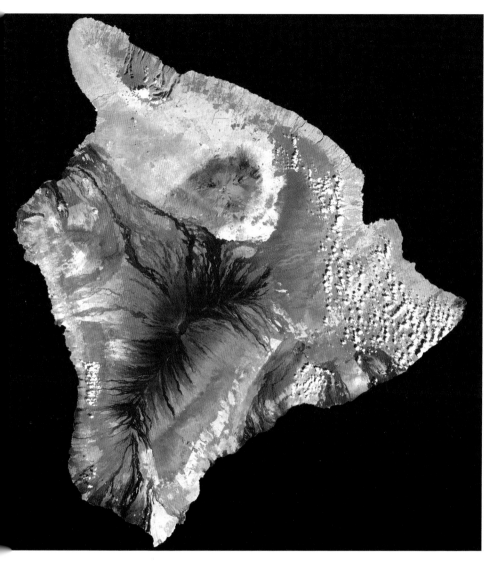

FIGURE 2.3 A 1999 satellite view of the Big Island shows prominent rift zones, the sources of many eruptions. (NASA Earth Observatory)

Kīlauea Iki Crater adjoins the caldera on its east side, and other pit craters are nearby.

When Twain visited the caldera in 1866 he saw a molten lava lake. In 1873 the intrepid world traveler Isabella Bird witnessed the same very active molten pool. There were periodic eruptions in Halemaʻumaʻu

Crater or the larger caldera for decades afterward. Some of the most notable lava flows were during 1919, 1921, 1959, 1971, 1974, and 1982. There were nearby eruptions along the east rift zone as well, with major flows deposited from 1969 to 1974.

Then in 1983 Kīlauea began a new phase of activity with eruptions occurring farther along the east rift zone at the Puʻu ʻŌʻō vent. These sometimes-vigorous eruptions have covered an entire village, cut off main roads, and added new acreage along the coast of the Big Island. For twenty-five years the caldera was relatively quiet, the most dramatic evidence of volcanic activity being the constant clouds of steam and sulfur dioxide emitted from vents along the caldera walls and cracks in its floor. Then in 2008 the slumbering Halemaʻumaʻu Crater stirred again, and a glowing lava lake once again formed within the crater.

In 2018, as this book went to press, Kīlauea entered a volatile new phase that prompted temporary closures of the national park and evacuations nearby. Magma found new outlets along the east rift zone, draining Halemaʻumaʻu and erupting in fissures outside the national park in populated areas of the Puna District. Any time this level of volcanic activity occurs, it may be too dangerous to visit some of the field trip destinations described in this chapter, including Lava Tree State Monument and Ahalanui Warm Springs County Park. In the old days Twain and Bird walked right up to the molten lava, so close that it burned their faces and melted their boots. Today the National Park Service and local authorities wisely enforce greater precautions. Be mindful of personal safety and check on local conditions before you visit the national park or the southeast corner of the Big Island.

All visible Big Island volcanic activity has been at Kīlauea since 1984, but Mauna Loa is still very much an active volcano. When it erupts it tends to pump out far more lava than Kīlauea. Eruptions from the northeast rift zone of Mauna Loa threatened the town of Hilo in 1881 and again in 1984.

In the **post-shield stage** the volcano has moved far enough from the center of the hot spot to reduce its supply of magma. The successive lava flows from the caldera and the rift zones no longer will be the most significant events shaping the volcano. In fact, the caldera itself may fill with lava and disappear entirely. Mauna Kea has entered the post-shield stage. Hualālai, the 8,271-foot mountain just *mauka* from Kailua-Kona, is well into this stage.

During this period, when the volcano is roughly 1.5 million years old, three dramatic processes shape the volcano or the island it forms. First, eruptions may start to occur near the summit of the volcano or along its flanks but not at the old caldera or along the rift zones. These little eruptions form cinder cones with craters at their peaks. These are not pit craters but bowl-shaped craters from which volcanic cinders have been ejected and deposited to form the surrounding slopes.

There are a lot of these cinder cones in the saddle area between Mauna Kea and Mauna Loa. From the highway they look like hills. Better vantage points are along the road up to Mauna Kea, leading to the Onizuka Center for International Astronomy and the higher summit area with its telescopes. From up on the flank of the mountain, look down into the saddle. It is littered with cinder cones. The most dramatic view is in late afternoon, when the setting sun places their craters in shadows.

The second process that shapes post-shield volcanoes, and sometimes younger shield volcanoes, is landslides. But not just any landslides; we're talking really big landslides, cataclysmic events. Remember the shallow submarine stage in the volcano life cycle that deposited a large unstable pile of material? Well, after a lot of shield building there is a very large mountain sitting on top of this weak foundation. The surprisingly common result is a big landslide (or more often, an undersea slide of material from the submerged flank of the volcano). These landslides sometimes cause nearly half the volume of a volcano to slump away. When all this material slides into the ocean, it can generate a huge tsunami, with the sliding material itself traveling more than a hundred miles along the seafloor.

Most of the Hawaiian islands have experienced these mega landslides. The nearly vertical windward face of the Koʻolau Range on Oʻahu, although quite eroded today, is not just a product of erosion. Nearly half of the ancient volcano that created this part of Oʻahu lost its foundation and slid seaward. A smaller but perhaps more dramatic slide formed the cliffs on the northern side of Molokaʻi. These are the tallest sea cliffs on earth, and the rubble field extends across the seabed a hundred miles north. Slides on the west coast of the Big Island may have resulted in tsunamis that carried reef fragments well up the flanks of Lānaʻi and Molokaʻi.

The third process affecting the volcano at this stage is subsidence.

The volcano has become very heavy, even with the occasional landslide diet that slims it down. This weight makes it sink, slowly deforming the plate and seafloor upon which it is riding. That's why the Hawaiian Deep, off the southeast coast of the Big Island, is the deepest area in Hawaiian waters. Post-shield volcanoes are sinking and shrinking.

If you've been keeping track of the island ages, you will notice that the age of the Big Island was given as 0 to 500,000 years, but then one of its volcanic mountains, Hualālai, was pegged at roughly 1.5 million. The larger number is age measured from the first seafloor eruption that may have continued for several hundred thousand years before reaching the ocean surface. Island ages are generally expressed as the age of the surface flows. Hualālai erupted as recently as 1801, and probably will again.

The next stages in the life of our volcano can overlap because several significant processes are all acting at once. These are the **erosional**, **rejuvenation**, and **reef-growth stages**. In the erosional stage our volcano loses even more of its mass, not through giant landslides but from the long process of erosion. Actually, a volcano starts to erode as soon as it is exposed to waves, rain, and other weathering. During its youth the volcano is growing much more rapidly than it is subsiding or eroding. Only in the erosional stage do the subtractive forces gain the upper hand and begin to diminish the volcano. Kohala Mountain at the northwest tip of the Big Island has entered the erosional stage, with deep eroded valleys such as Waipiʻo and Pololū along its northeast flank.

This erosional stage lasts a long time, from roughly 1.75 million years after a volcano first appears on the seafloor until it is more than five million years old and has traveled hundreds of miles from the hot spot. From Kohala north to Kauaʻi, the rest of the main Hawaiian Islands are in this lengthy erosional stage.

A dramatic example of erosion is Haleakalā (house used by the sun) "crater" on Maui. This feature near the summit of Haleakalā is not a crater or caldera in the volcanic sense. Rather, it is the head of two eroded valleys on Maui, Keʻanae and Kaupō. Erosion of these valleys has eaten all the way up into the former summit region of the mountain.

Perhaps the most dramatic example of erosion in all of Hawaiʻi is Waimea (reddish water from eroded soil) Canyon on Kauaʻi, sometimes called the Grand Canyon of the Pacific. Kauaʻi is about five million years old, so there has been a lot of time for erosion to carve out this great valley of the Waimea River.

During the long erosional stage a volcano continues to pull away from the hot spot, gradually severing its direct connection to the immense quantities of magma that allowed it to form and grow. However, long after a Hawaiian island has left the hot spot—the time gap can be less than a million years or over 2.5 million—it can produce a last gasp of scattered eruptions in the rejuvenation stage.

How does the volcano pull off this trick when it is no longer over the hot spot? One theory is that, as the old volcano glides away from the hot spot and is drawn across the hump of the Hawaiian Arch, the movement causes a small amount of melting. But rejuvenation eruptions can happen before, during, or after the volcano is dragged over the Hawaiian Arch, so this explanation can't be the whole story. In other words, we don't know.

Rejuvenation eruptions have occurred on Maui, Moloka'i, O'ahu, Kaua'i, and Ni'ihau, but apparently never on smaller Kaho'olawe or Lāna'i. The most recent rejuvenation flow discovered on Kaua'i is about half a million years old, occurring more than four million years after the island's formation. On O'ahu, rejuvenation flows range in age from about eight hundred thousand years to about forty thousand years old. Diamond Head, Tantalus, Koko Crater, and Hanauma Bay—familiar places on O'ahu—are all the result of rejuvenation eruptions.

Once rejuvenation eruptions begin, an island can experience them for over two million years, with long breaks in between. O'ahu may still be within this stage. The locations of rejuvenation eruptions are also unpredictable; they usually don't happen at a caldera or the site of any previous volcanic activity.

The third overlapping stage in our volcano life cycle isn't generated by geological forces like volcanic action or erosion. The reef-growth stage depends on organisms—corals and hard algae—that make their home and build their reefs on the shallow fringes of the islands. Like erosion, reef building starts early in the life of an island but doesn't become a significant shaping force for a while. Most of the reefs in Hawai'i are fringing reefs that grow where the land meets the sea. The classic barrier reef that grows offshore and protects a calm bay within is rare in Hawai'i. Around the main Hawaiian Islands, there are two barrier-like reefs. The landslide that occurred above Kāne'ohe

FIGURE 2.4 Diamond Head or Lēʻahi is a volcanic cone with a big central crater. A popular hike climbs from the crater to the summit. (Lisa Hoang/Shutterstock.com)

(literally bamboo husband; split bamboo has a sharp cutting edge, so the meaning is probably cruel husband) Bay on Oʻahu created an extensive shallow area ideal for reef growth. The outer portion of the reef acts like a barrier even though it didn't grow in classic barrier reef fashion. The oldest main island, Kauaʻi, has a true barrier reef: ʻAnini Reef near Princeville.

The reef-growth stage continues as long as there is some amount of volcanically produced island mass above water. A couple of the youngest of the Northwestern Hawaiian Islands, Nīhoa and Necker Islands at about seven and ten million years old respectively, are still at this stage. They are surrounded by shallow submerged platforms, the coral-covered foundations of islands that were once much larger.

Eventually, erosion and subsidence vanquish even the last nub of a volcanic island, leaving the barrier reef as a partial circle around the now-submerged volcanic island. This coral ring encircling a shallow lagoon is called an atoll and this stage is the **atoll stage**. Broken reef fragments may collect to form a low sandy island. In this way an atoll may form fairly substantial islands, sometimes several square miles. Midway Atoll, at about 2.5 square miles of land area, is an example.

The atoll stage can last a long time. Remember, Midway is over twenty-eight million years old. There is an elegant equilibrium between the corals growing upward through warm water toward the light they need (more about this in chapter 7) and the remains of the island subsiding ever deeper and drifting northwest into cooler water.

Eventually the cooler water slows the growth rate of the coral. The coral can no longer keep pace with the subsidence of the old island and the living reef is drawn deeper, where its growth is slowed even more. Finally, the coral dies and all that is left is a submerged island remnant with an elevated ring around its edge, like the parapet around some medieval castle. This is the **guyot stage**, and this type of sunken island is a guyot (pronounced something like gee-YOH).

The life cycle of our volcanic island is nearly over. At least our part of the story is nearly over; the submerged island may exist for another forty or fifty million years. It continues sliding along, carried by the Pacific Plate. It isn't alone; there is a whole submarine mountain range of ancient Hawaiian volcanoes gliding toward the edge of the Pacific Plate and its subduction zone. At the subduction zone our ancient island is drawn down into some of the deepest ocean on earth, eventually into the mantle of the planet. It's an eighty-million-year, four-thousand-mile journey that began at the Hawaiian hot spot.

We've been describing a series of islands, created by a hot spot that is pumping out prodigious amounts of lava. So you may have been wondering: if the Pacific Plate is moving at a fairly constant speed, and the hot spot is putting out so much material, why isn't there one continuous ridge-like island stretching from Kīlauea to Kure? Well, again...we don't know. Here's one theory: when the hot spot opens a conduit to the surface and erupts, perhaps it "sticks" to that volcano for a while, even as the volcano drifts away. Then the hot spot behaves like a sapling when you pull it over and let go. It springs back to its previous position. You can be sure the mechanism is a lot more complicated than this, but at least this theory gives us a plausible explanation for discrete islands instead of a long ridge.

This might leave you with the mental image of a conveyor belt with a hot spot factory popping out new islands at pretty regular intervals. This metaphor works, but only to a point. You see, the hot spot apparently doesn't produce magma at a constant rate, nor does it produce islands consistently. Many seamounts never grew large enough to break the ocean's surface, and there have been some big breaks in the conveyor belt, long periods when no new islands of significant size appeared. There's a big gap between Gardner Volcano (now Gardner Pinnacles) and Kauaʻi with only smallish islands such as Nīhoa in between. Why does this matter? In chapter 3 we will learn how these breaks in the conveyor belt have had a profound effect on island life.

Finally, we've been describing the rise and fall of Hawaiian islands as if the level of the surrounding sea remained unchanged. Nothing could be further from the truth. Sea level rise is a big issue today because human actions are largely responsible for a rapid rise, as discussed in chapter 13. In the past, there have also been drastic changes in sea level. During most of the last two million years, global temperatures and sea level have been much lower than they are today.

At the peak of an ice age 21,000 years ago, more of the planet's water was stored as ice, with much less in the oceans. Sea level was almost 400 feet lower than it is today. Shallow areas between today's islands were exposed: Maui and Lānaʻi were connected, and Molokaʻi

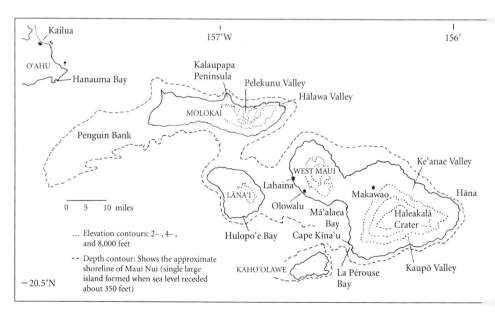

MAP 2.2 The islands of Maui Nui today, and the shoreline of a larger island that existed during the last ice age. (Map drawn by John Culliney)

was separated from them by—at most—a narrow and shallow channel. Moloka'i was nearly twice its present length because the shallow Penguin Banks west of the island were exposed. About 1.2 million years ago, before these islands entered the subsidence stage, Maui, Moloka'i, Lāna'i, and Kaho'olawe were all joined. This ancient mega-island is called Maui Nui, which translates to Big Maui. It was larger than the Big Island is today. This submarine bathymetry is shown in figure 2.5.

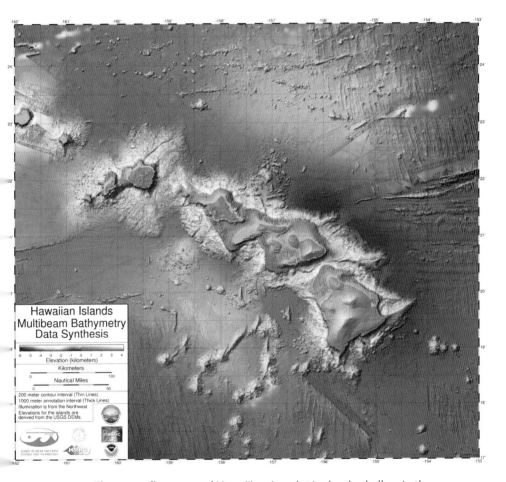

FIGURE 2.5 The ocean floor around Hawai'i varies a lot in depth: shallow in the protected waters of Maui Nui and the Penguin Banks west of Moloka'i, very deep off the Big Island where the weight of the large island pushes it down. (Paul Johnson and Dr. Brian Taylor, University of Hawai'i School of Ocean and Earth Science and Technology)

FIELD TRIP!

No matter where you are in Hawai'i, it's not hard to see some aspect of the life cycle of a volcanic island or evidence of geologic forces at work. Here are some of my favorite Hawaiian geologic wonders, island by island:

Let's start with the youngest island and proceed back in time. The **Big Island** consists of five volcanoes, including four that geologists consider active and one—Kohala—that is probably extinct.

2.1 HAWAI'I VOLCANOES NATIONAL PARK is the single best place in all of Hawai'i (maybe the world) to see geologic forces at work and learn about island formation. The centerpiece of the park is Kīlauea Volcano with its immense caldera and Halema'uma'u Crater inside the caldera. The park's visitor center, the venerable Volcano House Hotel, and the Jaggar Museum are all near the edge of Kīlauea Caldera. Since 1983 volcanic conditions in the park have been relatively stable. Occasionally molten lava would appear in Halema'uma'u Crater, but most of the active eruptions were a short way down the volcano's east rift zone at the Pu'u 'Ō'ō Vent.

Then in May 2018 the volcanic behavior of Kīlauea changed abruptly. The crater at Halema'uma'u filled with lava and overflowed onto the floor of Kīlauea Caldera. Just as suddenly, the molten pool drained away. The complex subterranean plumbing of the volcano found new outlets far down its east rift zone outside the national park where no eruptions had occurred for nearly sixty years. Lava poured from new fissures along this rift zone, destroying some seven hundred homes and covering local roads and highways.

Halema'uma'u, drained of lava, began to collapse in on itself. Each cataclysmic collapse produced a significant earthquake, damaging national park facilities and creating dangerous conditions around Kīlauea Caldera. The national park was forced to close indefinitely until the crater stabilized and facilities could be repaired. Eruptions like these have probably been common in the eighty-million-year history of the Hawaiian hot spot, but they are new and unprecedented for the geologists who study Hawaiian volcanoes today. One geophysicist commented that the scale of ground deformation and collapse was "just staggering."

That was the situation as this book went to press. Be sure to check conditions with the national park and the County of Hawai'i before planning a visit to the park or the southeast corner of the Big Island where recent eruptions occurred. Be sure to heed any safety closures or restrictions that might be prompted by increased volcanic activity.

Once the park reopens, your visit should begin at park headquarters, an easy thirty-mile drive southwest from Hilo. Along this road, you will be driving up the flank of Mauna Loa until you pass the town of Glenwood. Then you cross over to the much younger lava flows of Kīlauea.

The park has an excellent visitor center with good displays on the park's natural resources, a nice bookstore, and cheerful, enthusiastic staff. There are frequent ranger-led hikes and other programs, and excellent maps and brochures are available to help you see the park on your own. There are also plenty of safety warnings that you should heed. Molten lava, jagged *a'ā* along hiking trails, and noxious sulfur dioxide fumes are all hazards to respect and avoid.

The most profound evidence of volcanic activity visible in the park is Kīlauea Caldera. It is visible from many roadside turnouts. You can also walk to the caldera from the visitor center; a short path leads through the *'ōhi'a*-fern forest to Volcano House, the national park hotel perched on the caldera's rim. Walk through the hotel lobby to the crater rim path just outside the hotel. (Best late-afternoon end to a day of park touring: beer and *pūpū*, the Hawaiian word for appetizers, in the hotel bar.)

A short drive from the visitor center is the scenic Thurston Lava Tube, mecca for giant tour buses. Take the ten-minute walk down a steep paved path and concrete steps to the lava tube. It is actually a lava tunnel, because it is open on both ends. Then get away from the crowds. Take the one-mile out-and-back crater rim walk from the Thurston Lava Tube parking lot to the Kīlauea Iki trailhead lot. The trail hugs the edge of Kīlauea Iki Crater, which last held molten lava in 1959, and is easy to follow with the excellent map provided when you enter the park. If you're up for a more strenuous hike, you can descend to the floor of Kīlauea Iki. When larger Kīlauea Caldera is closed to hikers, the trail across the floor of Kīlauea Iki may be your only opportunity to walk across a crater floor, but be sure to heed any safety warnings. Look for native forest birds such as *'apapane*, *'ōma'o*, and *'elepaio* around the mouth of the lava tube and along the edge of Kīlauea Iki. You can see the red *'apapane* around the visitor center, too.

A drive down Chain of Craters Road within the park takes you past craters and across flows of *pāhoehoe* and *ʻaʻā*. A side trip out Hilina Pali Road will take you through rare dryland forest and *nēnē* (Hawaiian goose) habitat. The main road crosses lava flows from 1969–1974 before it makes a switchback down the Hōlei Pali, a steep slope that is evidence of past faulting events that dropped part of the volcano 1,500 feet. The most recent such downward faulting took place in 1975.

When eruptions from Mauna Ulu (growing mountain) between 1969 and 1974 buried parts of Chain of Craters Road, the National Park Service valiantly rebuilt. When the Puʻu ʻŌʻō vent started its long eruption in 1983 and covered the road, a visitor center, and most of the village of Kalapana, the Park Service threw in the towel and closed the road at the lava flow. In 2015 when flows nearly consumed the town of Pāhoa and a stretch of Highway 130, the buried section of Chain of Craters Road was rebuilt as an emergency escape route for residents of Pāhoa. Persistent lava flows severed it again a year later. When the 2018 eruption covered roads and eruption escape routes in Puna, Chain of Craters Road was rebuilt yet again. There's a message here: in a match between human endeavors and the volcano goddess Pele, Pele always wins.

Chain of Craters Road also passes the Puʻu Loa petroglyph field, one of the more extensive and better-protected petroglyph fields in the state. It is well worth a stop and a walk on the short rocky trail if the fumes from the east rift zone aren't too bad. Unfortunately the petroglyphs are almost directly downwind when the trade winds blow. Ask about air quality conditions at the visitor center before you take this walk.

Sometimes when trees stand in the way of an advancing lava flow, they leave long-lasting evidence of their former presence. If a lava flow surrounds a big tree trunk, the wood will cool the lava around the trunk. If the lava then recedes, the cooled lava remains standing, the tree trunk eventually decomposes, and a hollow lava tree stands where the old tree had been. If the lava does not recede, the decomposed tree leaves a hole in the lava flow called a tree mold. You can see tree molds in the park on the north side of Highway 11, just off Mauna Loa Road. Lava Tree State Park, perilously close to the 2018 eruptions, has the more dramatic lava trees. As this book went to press, the 2018 eruption threatened to cover these lava trees, so be sure to check the government website of the Lava Tree State Monument for current conditions before visiting. Interested in plants along Mauna Loa Road? See chapter 4. Birds and butterflies? See chapter 5.

There's another option for learning about the geology and biology of the national park: a nonprofit group called Friends of Hawai'i Volcanoes National Park. FHVNP conducts field seminars and private tours in and around the park.

2.2 AHALANUI WARM SPRINGS. This is a field trip destination that no longer exists, except as a fond memory and a painful lesson in the power of volcanoes. Until 2018, Ahalanui County Park on the southeast coast of the Big Island was the site of an ocean inlet with a partial seawall built to minimize tidal exchange of water. Volcanically heated spring water flowed to the inlet, making for a delightfully warm 90°F natural pool among the *hau* trees and palms. There were usually small fish in the pool since it was open to the ocean.

For months after the 2018 eruption began, beloved Ahalanui was

FIGURE 2.6 Ahalanui Warm Springs before it was covered by lava in 2018.

spared. At first, lava flowed to the sea at a point west of the park. Then other fissures along the east rift zone sent a river of lava flowing to the sea east of the park, cutting off all road access. The flows created hundreds of acres of new Big Island land. As this book went to press, the lava flow reached idyllic Ahalanui and filled the lovely swimming hole, extending the coastline of the island.

2.3 KAŪMANA CAVE. Want to visit a lava tube that is much less crowded than the famed Thurston Lava Tube in the national park? In the suburbs of Hilo look for Kaūmana Cave County Park. This is a publicly accessible lava tube that runs underground for over half a mile downslope from the entrance. You can travel a little ways upslope too, but this branch is more collapsed and difficult to traverse. To reach the park, take Waiānuenue Avenue *mauka* from downtown Hilo. At the 1.2-mile point veer left on Kaūmana Drive. The park is near the 4-mile point. Entry is free.

There are stern safety warning signs at the lava tube's entrance but basically you can waltz right into the gaping rocky cavern whether you are prepared or not, whether you possess common sense or not. You, of course, will be prepared. A bright flashlight and a backup are essential; I never venture very far without three. A strap-on headlamp works best because it always points where you're looking—much better than trying to scramble over rocks while holding a flashlight. Super-bright LED lights are worth the investment just for this little foray. A hard hat is advisable, but even a ball cap will provide a bit of padding against the inevitable head bump. Gloves will come in handy since you will find yourself scrambling over jumbled boulders that have fallen from the ceiling. Most of this rubble fell soon after the tube was formed during the eruption and the threatening flows of 1881, but there is always the chance that more rubble could fall. There is a constant drip from the cave ceiling and nearly 100 percent humidity in the cave. You will not avoid getting wet by wearing a breathable waterproof shell or rain jacket. It won't breathe enough to matter. Just wear a T-shirt and expect to come out drenched.

Starting to get the idea? It is great fun, reminiscent of Tom Sawyer's adventures, and worth a sweaty hour or two. However, this is a venture that is a bit strenuous, potentially dangerous, and should only be attempted by the well prepared. Even if you don't go inside, it is worthwhile to walk down the concrete staircase to the mouth of the tube and have a look. If this seems just a bit too risky to attempt on your own, tour operators lead walks into privately owned lava tubes in the Volcano area. In the past, the national park offered guided walks into a secluded lava tube near park headquarters. At press time, budget constraints had halted these walks, but check to see if they have resumed.

Kaūmana Cave isn't pristine by any means, although some of the amazing tube-adapted fauna of Hawai'i still lives in the farthest reaches of the cave. See chapter 5 for more information.

If you continue up Kaūmana Drive it will eventually merge with Highway 200, known as the Saddle Road because it traverses the "saddle" between Mauna Kea and Mauna Loa. This area is a natural wonderland that merits several field trips. For a description of the geology and botany, see chapter 4; for birding, see chapter 5; for astronomy, chapter 11.

Maui is home to two volcanoes, Haleakalā and West Maui, probably now extinct. Like the Big Island, Maui has a national park with outstanding geology.

2.4 HALEAKALĀ NATIONAL PARK. There are no active eruptions on Maui, although Haleakalā is almost certainly not done erupting. These days the major shaping effect is from erosion. If you've seen the tidy, round, vertical-walled Kīlauea Caldera then Haleakalā crater will seem messy by comparison. It's because the "crater" is really an erosional feature, formed as streams in the Ke'anae and Kīpahulu valleys and Kaupō Gap ate into the very center of the old volcano.

It isn't always easy to discern the boundary between adjacent volcanoes, but on Maui this is not a problem. From high turnouts along the road to Haleakalā you can look across a low isthmus to West Maui. The isthmus was formed from flows along the northwest and southwest rift zones of Haleakalā, spreading out to just touch West Maui.

Your first stop inside the park might be the park headquarters. It is more modest than the visitor center at Hawai'i Volcanoes, but the staff are no less helpful and there is a nice selection of natural history books. From there you have nearly ten miles of steep, paved switchbacks to reach the 10,023-foot summit at Pu'u 'Ula'ula (red hill), a visitor center, and an enclosed lookout cabin. It can be cold and windy at this elevation, so dress accordingly.

The crater offers a colorful panorama of young cinder and lava sloping away toward the far end of the crater, where erosion is washing the mountain down to the far side of the island.

The national park has great night-sky viewing. An area just inside the park offers excellent birding. It's easy to plan a trip that combines geology with botany, ornithology, and astronomy. See chapter 5 for advice on making this a combo outing.

2.5 ʻĪAO VALLEY. Maui's other volcano, extinct and eroded, is known as West Maui or the West Maui Mountains. The old eroded caldera region of West Maui is now partly within ʻĪao (cloud supreme) Valley State Park, just *mauka* from the town of Wailuku. Like Haleakalā, the West Maui caldera itself is eroded away. The walls of the valley are roughly the boundaries of the ancient caldera but much of the caldera material has been carried away by ʻĪao Stream. At its headwaters atop West Maui stands Puʻu Kukui, probably the second wettest spot in the state with over 380 inches of rain per year on average. ʻĪao Needle is the popular geologic feature of the valley. The "needle" is actually the highest point along a narrow ridge of basalt that has withstood erosion.

Park trails are paved, but many are narrow and steep and include concrete steps. People with limited mobility will still have good views of the needle. The valley walls block breezes, and runoff into ʻĪao Stream provides plenty of moisture, often making the valley oppressively humid. For a more comfortable picnic lunch, head back down the valley to Kepaniwai County Park just outside the state park. The county park is cool and shady, with picnic pavilions near the stream. It usually isn't crowded on weekdays.

2.6 CAPE KĪNAʻU. Maui's youngest lava flow formed Cape Kīnaʻu about four hundred to five hundred years ago. From Kīhei drive south and set your car's trip odometer to zero at the intersection of Wailea Ike (the road that comes down the hill from the end of the Piʻilani Highway, Route 31) and Wailea Alanui. Follow Wailea Alanui south through the tony Wailea development. At the one-mile point the road name changes to Mākena Alanui. Continuing south, you might want to stop at Mākena State Park. Take the first park entrance road you come to, at about the four-mile point, and park in the paved lot. From there, walk the broad sandy path through a *kiawe* forest to Oneloa (long sand) or Big Beach. It is a splendid expanse of sand with shade back among the *kiawe* (watch for thorns). The big geology feature here is just north of the beach. Puʻu Olaʻi (earthquake hill) is one of the largest and most prominent young cinder cones on Maui. It is visible from Wailea to West Maui. It is about one hundred thousand years old. There is a short trail over the tip of the cinder cone to Little Beach, where clothing is optional. Offshore is a young tuff cone, Molokini Islet.

Continuing the drive south you enter the ʻĀhihi-Kīnaʻu Natural Area Reserve at about the 5-mile point. At the 5.5-mile point you get to Maui's youngest lava flow and it is easy to discern: in this dry part of Maui there has been almost no weathering or erosion to soften the stark black ʻaʻā. The state of Hawaiʻi is struggling to strike a balance in management of the natural area reserve. The area was designated as a reserve so natural and cultural resources could receive adequate protection. The area has many archaeological sites, and stunningly high concentrations of reef fish. These attractions are popular with visitors and have led to overuse and degradation. For years all parts of the reserve past ʻĀhihi Cove and the nearby Dumps surf spot have been closed to the public to protect resources. You are allowed to drive through the reserve all the way to its southern border at La Pérouse Bay.

There's a great old story involving early explorers La Pérouse and Vancouver. They both mapped the coastline near the bay that bears La Pérouse's name. When people compared the La Pérouse map from 1786 with the Vancouver map made in 1793, they saw a new peninsula on the later map and deduced that a lava flow had entered the sea in the intervening years. But it probably isn't true. The La Pérouse map is so crude you really can't depend on it, and modern dating of the flow suggests it formed hundreds of years earlier.

Molokaʻi is a small island—fifth largest in the chain—formed by two volcanoes. The lower and older West Molokaʻi volcano is about 1.9 million years old, making it the oldest part of the Maui Nui cluster. Its highest point, Puʻu Nānā, is only 1,381 feet, too low to catch moisture carried on the trade winds. The volcano that formed East Molokaʻi is a bit younger at 1.75 million years, and taller. Kamakou, its highest point, is 4,970 feet. This is high enough to catch moisture, making this end of Molokaʻi much wetter.

2.7 SUBTRACTION AND ADDITION ON MOLOKAʻI. No, this is not arithmetic. We're talking subtraction of half a volcano by a landslide, and subsequent addition by rejuvenation eruption. Moloka'i boasts one of the most dramatic geologic features in Hawai'i, or anywhere on earth for that matter. The sea cliffs on its north shore are the tallest in the world, over 3,700 feet high. Their formation began with a swift and terrible event when the unstable offshore base of the north side of the East Moloka'i Volcano slumped, leading to collapse of part of the island. We know it happened quickly because the collapse sent debris across nearly one hundred miles of ocean floor.

It is hard to appreciate these dramatic cliffs from above, but you can get a sense of their height by viewing another geologic feature, the rejuvenation stage volcano that forms the Kalaupapa (flat plain) Peninsula. This point of land on the north coast was formed three hundred thousand years ago. It is much lower than the cliffs it abuts, only 405 feet high at its summit. You can see it from a clifftop lookout at Pālā'au State Park, at the end of Route 470 on the north side of the island. The peninsula is actually a tiny shield volcano. Look for the crater beyond the settlement of Kalaupapa.

There is another geologic feature at this park perhaps more popular than the stunning clifftop views, at least to teenage boys. Kaule o Nānāhoa is a very large phallic rock (Nānāhoa was a character of Hawaiian legend who abused his wife). Legend has it that the formation is completely natural and has not been shaped by human hands, but many visitors are skeptical. You can judge for yourself. The formation is up a short, steep, unpaved path.

O'ahu was formed by two fast-growing unstable volcanoes. One produced the Wai'anae Range in western O'ahu, including the highest point on the island, Mt. Ka'ala at 4,020 feet, now extinct. The second volcano on the eastern side may have started as a separate island, eventually filling the space that now forms O'ahu's central plain. Today the eastern Ko'olau Range exists as a long steep ridge, no longer recognizable as a volcano. It apparently had rejuvenation eruptions as recently as forty thousand to fifty thousand years ago, so it may not be done erupting. After contemplating the raw power of glowing Kīlauea on the Big Island, it might make you just a wee bit nervous to think that Honolulu's four hundred thousand inhabitants are living and working on a volcano that might still have some life left in it.

Some of this island's most interesting geological features also happen to be some of the state's most popular tourist sites.

2.8 DIAMOND HEAD. First stop on the Oʻahu volcanic tour is Diamond Head, or Lēʻahi (brow of the tuna, after its shape) in Hawaiian. Many visitors to Hawaiʻi know Diamond Head only from its familiar profile on postcards. They are shocked to learn that it is actually a round tuff cone with a broad, round, flat valley at its center. It is all the more dramatic because the U.S. military built fortifications into the mountain starting in 1908 and punched a convenient tunnel through the crater wall so they could drive into its center. Today you can drive through that same tunnel. From Kapiʻolani Park in Waikīkī follow Monsarrat Avenue around the *mauka* side of the crater. Here the road name changes to Diamond Head Road. Follow the signs into the crater where you can pay to enter and park. The military still uses part of the crater; the whole area is now the Diamond Head State Monument.

The most popular way to experience Diamond Head is to take the hike from the crater floor to the summit of Lēʻahi. It is short but steep: the rocky one-mile trail has a 560-foot elevation gain. The rock is called tuff; weathering has cemented the ash into this soft rock. The trail makes its way up the inside wall of the crater, giving you an up-close chance to see tuff. Near the top the trail passes through tunnels and dark spooky fortifications. The interiors are illuminated, but I bring a pocket flashlight just in case. From the summit you have great views of the crater, some of the other ash and cinder cones that dot the Honolulu urban landscape to the west, Koko Crater to the northeast, and of course Waikīkī just below you. By the way, Waikīkī means "spouting water" and it used to be a swamp.

Note that you are standing on the highest point of the crater rim. The irregular height is no accident. Trade winds were blowing when Lēʻahi was erupting, and the fine ash blew and built up this side of the crater wall.

Most of the trees you pass on the hike are introduced *kiawe* and *haole koa*. The most common bird is the red-vented bulbul, also introduced. From August or September through March or April, look for indigenous *kōlea* birds on the lawn. More about *kōlea* in chapter 5.

It can get pretty warm and very crowded on this popular hike. I like to enter the park soon after it opens at 6:00 in the morning—no heat, smaller crowds.

No account of Oʻahu geology would be complete without an explanation of how the tuff cone called Lēʻahi came to be called Diamond

Head. This rejuvenation eruption came up through layers of limestone formed by coral growth accumulated over a couple million years. The coral was pulverized by the eruption, and innumerable fragments mixed in with the volcanic ash. Rainwater percolating through the tuff dissolved the coral and formed calcite crystals. Early sailors discovered these crystals and hoped they might be diamonds.

There are two other big cones composed of cinder and ash on this side of the island that you can enter and explore. One is Koko Crater, home to a lovely and seldom-visited botanic garden. (See chapter 4.) Another cone formed right at the shoreline, and was partially eroded by the ocean. Today it is known as Hanauma Bay, one of the most popular snorkeling spots in the state. (See chapter 7.) Hanauma's cinder cone was formed about forty thousand years ago. Farther west, in the center of Honolulu, is yet another big cinder cone you can visit: Punchbowl Crater, home to a national cemetery.

2.9 PALI LOOKOUT. Another dramatic Oʻahu viewpoint is the Pali lookout, at Nuʻuanu Pali (cool height cliff) State Wayside park on the Pali Highway, Route 61 that connects Honolulu with windward Kailua. You will have to pay at the automated kiosk to park at the adjacent lot, but it is well worth it. (Plainclothes officers patrol the lot. Pay to park.) A broad ramp leads to the overlook. A thousand feet below you are the towns of Kailua and Kāneʻohe, the Mōkapu Peninsula with its Marine Corps Air Station, and Kāneʻohe Bay with its barrier reef. It is stunning. Visitors to the Pali Lookout usually face a howling wind. The predominant trade winds blow from the northeast, are lifted by the steep cliff, and pour through the notch at the lookout.

But never mind the splendid views or the startling wind. The most amazing feature of this lookout—something completely lost on most of the people who visit—is how it came to be. As you gaze out from this windy precipice, you are standing above one of largest landslides that ever reshaped the surface of the planet. Two million years ago, nearly half the ancient volcano that formed east Oʻahu suffered a huge collapse. All the mountain that once lay before you lost its foundation when the undersea flanks of the volcano collapsed in one cataclysmic event, sending rubble 120 miles across the seafloor. One chunk of the old mountain deposited on the seafloor is eighteen miles long and a mile thick. Geologists believe that the mountain was built upon a very unstable undersea foundation. When this undersea foundation collapsed, half of the volcano slumped. The lovely expanse of land on which Kāne'ohe and Kailua are built was at one time much higher, before the mountain's underpinnings went sliding off toward Alaska. While you're standing at this windy lookout, think about the volcano that isn't here anymore, to appreciate much more than most of the visitors around you.

On your way to the Pali lookout from Honolulu you can drive through an area of lush rain forest. Exit Highway 61, the Pali highway, at Nu'uanu Pali Drive, 2.4 miles *mauka* of the junction with the H1 freeway. This 1.6-mile stretch of road parallels the highway and eventually merges back on to it, giving you a good taste of jungly rain forest along the way.

2.10 ANCIENT REEFS. There's one final geologic feature to note on O'ahu, and it surrounds you everywhere on the island. O'ahu shorelines

FIGURE 2.7 Most of the big rocks at Shark's Cove are actually ancient fossil coral reef. (Rick Soehren)

experienced significant amounts of reef building about 125,000 years ago when the sea level was about 30 feet higher than today. When sea levels fell these reefs were exposed. These ancient exposed reefs exist on other islands, but they are particularly prominent and noticeable on Oʻahu. Some places to see the exposed reef include Pūpūkea (white shell) Beach County Park (also known as Shark's Cove) and Kahe Point Beach County Park (also known as Electric Beach). These are two of the best snorkeling spots on the island. Full descriptions are in chapter 7.

Kauaʻi is the oldest of the main islands at nearly five million years and the most eroded as a consequence of its age. It was long thought to be composed of a single large volcano, but now some geologists suspect that it may have formed from two. Besides erosion, as on Oʻahu and Molokaʻi, huge slumps have also shaped the Kauaʻi that exists today.

2.11 WAIMEA CANYON is the most dramatic example of erosion in all Hawaiʻi. Two routes approach the canyon. One, Route 550 or Waimea Canyon Drive, follows the canyon edge from the town of Waimea. A slightly better but less scenic road, Route 552, heads north from Kekaha and eventually merges with Waimea Canyon Drive. I recommend going up Waimea Canyon Drive for the canyon views, down Highway 552 for views of distant Niʻihau. Above the point where the two routes join there are several places to pull off the road and view the canyon, including Waimea Canyon Lookout at elevation 3,400 feet and Puʻu Hinahina, the highest canyon viewpoint at about 3,500 feet. If you want to see grand vistas instead of cloudbanks, it's advisable to visit the canyon early in the day.

As you gaze out across the canyon, you may notice that all the streams entering it come from the other side. This is because erosion had a lot of help forming this canyon: the western wall where you stand is the edge of a massive slump. In the distant past when Kauaʻi still had an active volcano, the eastern two-thirds of the island slumped. Subsequent erupted lava flowed toward the western slump wall, pooling and forming a nearly flat impervious plateau. Then millions of years of rainfall pooled on the impervious plateau, creating swampy conditions; eventually flowed downward toward the foot of the slump edge below where you stand; and was channeled along it toward present-day Waimea. The concentrated runoff produced a lot of erosion, chiseling out Waimea Canyon. This is an oversimplification; *Roadside Geology of*

Hawai'i and *Volcanoes in the Sea* (described at the end of the chapter) have good illustrated explanations.

The nearly flat, nearly impermeable plateau of basalt has its highest point at Wai'ale'ale, elevation 5,148 feet. Wai'ale'ale is one of the wettest known spots on earth, with an average of 422 inches of rain per year. The place name really fits; Wai'ale'ale means "overflowing water." This water can't soak in or drain away very well because of the flat basalt, and the result is the Alaka'i Swamp. The swamp and neighboring Kōke'e State Park are described in a chapter 5 field trip.

From the Pu'u Hinahina Lookout there is a short path to the Ni'ihau Lookout. If the air is clear you will be able to see the island of Ni'ihau in the distance. Tiny Lehua Island is just to its north (right). If the weather is very clear, you might also spot Ka'ula Rock, appearing just to the left of Ni'ihau. It is actually twice as distant from you as Ni'ihau and Lehua.

Kīlauea Point. There are some worthy geological sites north of Līhu'e as well. One of the youngest parts of the island—formed more than 1.5 million years after shield building—is Pu'u Kīlauea (spewing hill). It forms a small peninsula on the north shore of the island near the town of Kīlauea. Today the area is more famous for its historic lighthouse and the avian residents of the Kīlauea Point National Wildlife Refuge. (See chapter 5.)

2.12 Hā'ena Caves and the Nā Pali Coast. Sea caves can form when wave action erodes cliffs right at the shoreline. There are three great examples near the end of Highway 56, the Kūhiō Highway that follows the Kaua'i north shore. Near the end of route 56 is Hā'ena Beach County Park. Here the road passes the mouth of Maniniholo (traveling *manini* fish) Dry Cave. A mile farther is Hā'ena State Park. The road passes near Waikanaloa (water of the god Kanaloa) Cave, and a short overgrown trail leads to Waikapala'e (water of the lace fern) Cave. Both of these are wet caves, partially filled with water. Today none of these caves is still being shaped by wave action. They were likely formed when the sea level was a bit higher, and definitely before the barrier reef provided so much protection to this shoreline.

At the end of the road is the trailhead for the Kalalau Trail along the Nā Pali Coast. From the trailhead you can't see much, but if you hike just half a mile or so up the rocky trail, you will be rewarded with great views of the cliffs of the Nā Pali. Not surprisingly, Nā Pali means "the cliffs."

LEARN MORE

- Robert I. Tilling, Christina Heliker, and Donald A. Swanson, *Eruptions of Hawaiian Volcanoes: Past, Present, and Future* (U.S. Geological Survey General Information Product 117, 2010). A good introduction to Hawaiian volcanoes. This full-color, 63-page publication is available free online. Inexpensive print copies are usually available at the Hawai'i Volcanoes National Park visitor center.
- Richard W. Hazlett and Donald W. Hyndman, *Roadside Geology of Hawai'i* (Missoula, MT: Mountain Press Publishing, 1996). This book, part of a state-by-state series, gives you just what you'd expect: a non-technical explanation of Hawaiian landforms that you can see from the roadside while touring the state. *The* book for Hawaiian rock geeks.
- Gordon A. Macdonald, Agatin T. Abbott, and Frank L. Peterson, *Volcanoes in the Sea: The Geology of Hawai'i*, second edition (Honolulu: University of Hawai'i Press, 1983). Loaded with information on plate tectonics, volcanoes, and other forces that shape the islands. It has the length, heft, and price of a textbook, but is easy to read.
- Bill Bryson, *A Short History of Nearly Everything* (New York: Broadway Books, 2003). No, this isn't a book about Hawai'i; it devotes less than one page out of 544 to the islands. But it contains a great chapter on plate tectonics and the scientific revolution that brought this theory to wide acceptance. Also, it is arguably the best, easiest-to-read book on science history ever written. Read one page and you won't put it down.

3   You Can't Get There from Here

How Isolation Frames Island Life

Once upon a time a young couple from the mainland got hopelessly lost driving across the island in search of a hiking trail they had heard about. Eventually the visitors found themselves in the middle of the island with no idea which way to go. They came across an old farmer and asked for directions to their trailhead destination. The old fellow, like many elderly Hawaiians, had seldom traveled far from his farm. He started to direct the couple, stopped, changed his mind and began to describe a route in the opposite direction, stopped again, scratched his tanned, balding head, and furrowed his brow. Finally, he informed the visitors, "You can't get there from here!"

The joke is old but the punch line has been an apt description of Hawai'i's location for most of the last eighty million years: wherever you're coming from, you can't get here from there. People in today's world have difficulty comprehending Hawai'i's profound geographical isolation. Getting to the islands is easy today—by plane, it's less than six hours from Los Angeles, seven and a half hours from Tokyo. But what if you had to get here under your own power? You couldn't swim or row a boat that far. And you probably couldn't sail, unless you or somebody else built a boat, provided you with an array of electronic navigation equipment, preserved the food you'd need for a long sea voyage, made the containers you'd need for your water supply, and, well, you get the idea. It takes a lot of skill or help or luck to get to the most isolated chain of islands on earth.

 With just a few intriguing exceptions, successfully getting to Hawai'i intentionally and repeatedly has been a phenomenon limited to humans and achieved only in the last nine hundred years or so. This profound isolation, this vast watery buffer is what makes Hawai'i so unique. In turn, this isolation has made the island's plants and animals unique. But wait, you say, life in Hawai'i is abundant. Many of the plants and animals we see today are recent introductions, but even when the first humans reached Hawai'i these islands were already covered with plant and animal life—perhaps upwards of ten thousand species on the islands and in nearshore waters. So can it really be so hard to get to Hawai'i?

As a matter of fact, yes. First, this blanket of life didn't materialize quickly. As explained in chapter 2, it took millions of years for so many life-forms to accumulate. But time alone does not explain the plentiful Hawaiian life-forms. There are just too many. How did these isolated rocks become islands teeming with abundant life? It is one of the most amazing stories on our planet.

Every schoolchild in Hawai'i learns the basic ways that life reaches the islands: wind, wings, and waves. Every pioneering life-form that helped transform the islands from barren rocks to cradles of life arrived in one of these three ways.

Some life-forms were carried on the wind: the spores of ferns are so small that they can drift all over the world on the wind. Many plant seeds have winglike structures that help them float on the gentlest breeze (think dandelions). But wind transport isn't limited to plants. One of the neatest air transport tricks, and a remarkable example of tool making, is performed by many small spiders. They build hang gliders, spinning parachute-like webs that allow them to sail high into the atmosphere and travel great distances. It's called ballooning, and in the world of spiders it is a favorite way to disperse and find new homes.

Second, wings have carried

FIGURE 3.1 A Hawaiian happy face spider. T "face" is actually on its abdomen. (W. P. Mɩ

many species to the islands: insects, birds, even bats were probably blown away from continents during storms and ultimately found their way to Hawai'i. And wings can get you to Hawai'i even if those wings aren't yours: seeds, tiny bits of plants, and even snails have been known to stick to birds and hitch a ride. A more secure ride can be had if you travel inside the bird, accommodations enjoyed by seeds the bird ingests. Occasionally a bird will deposit an undigested seed from far away in an island location where conditions are similar to the seed's original habitat.

Finally, if you can swim or drift, ocean currents or sea breezes may carry you to Hawaiian shores on the waves. Waves would be the obvious method of transport for fish that inhabit shoreline coral reefs and freshwater streams, but the journey is not as easy as you might think; fish that inhabit nearshore waters need the structure that reefs and rocks and sandy ocean floors provide. Many of these creatures are weak swimmers, or they are garishly colored and quite visible to predators. They are as unlikely to successfully swim across deep ocean as you or I.

Plants sometimes arrive by water, too. Salt water kills most plants, but sometimes their seeds can withstand salt water long enough to drift to new lands and still be viable. Coconuts disperse this way, although apparently they never floated to Hawai'i on their own; there is no clear evidence of coconut palms in Hawai'i before humans arrived.

You might not even have to get wet as you ride the waves to Hawai'i. Tropical storms on continents often wash house-sized chunks of stream-side vegetation into the sea. For hundreds of years mariners have come across the implausible sight of upright trees gliding across oceans. These rafts of matted roots, soil, and vegetation can be veritable arks when it comes to bringing new life to isolated islands.

Natural air or water currents can help wayward life-forms find a new home. Hawai'i's dependable trade winds may bring seeds, insects, or even birds from the northeast, but the trades are not as big a supplier of new life as you might suppose. Why? For starters the trades are generated by the North Pacific high-pressure zone, which originates out at sea, not over North America. And the trades originate where the planet is cooler and drier. Any plant or insect arriving via trade winds might find warm wet Hawai'i too tropical to be a suitable new home.

Most wind-borne life that arrives in Hawai'i seems to come from the opposite direction, originating in warm wet Southeast Asia. As it happens, the high-altitude jet stream tends to dip through Asia each winter and then head straight for Hawaiʻi. The jet stream pulls warm air upward (sometimes over Asiatic lands) and drops cooler air over water (or islands). At altitudes up to forty thousand feet, with temperatures below freezing and speeds of over one hundred miles per hour, the jet stream is a wild ride. But for hardy life-forms that can survive two days on this roller coaster, it can be a ticket to paradise.

Below the waves, the currents are much more serene and more dependable. The North Pacific Gyre (from the Greek *gyros* or circle) is one of five big, roughly circular currents that sweep around the major oceans of the world. This current passes the Philippines, drifts northward by Japan, crosses the North Pacific, heads south along the coast of North America, then circles back westward, staying just north of the equator. This is the current that carried debris from Japan to Hawaiʻi and North America after the earthquake and tsunami of 2011.

This great gyre movement of water is slow and shallow, gliding at roughly half a mile per hour and carrying only the top three hundred feet of water or so. It is tempting to call the gyre a river of water passing through the sea, but it's a leaky river. Eddies and back currents tend to pull drifting materials into the center of the gyre, and winds can push any floating objects across and out of the current as well. The Hawaiian Islands are not perfectly positioned to receive the cargo of this gyre, but they are close enough to capture tons of floating debris and the occasional floating or drifting pioneer.

Five Gyres. There are five major gyres in the subtropical oceans of the world: North Pacific, South Pacific, North Atlantic, South Atlantic, and Indian. The gyres swirl around, catching up anything that floats near them, then dumping that floating stuff into the center of the gyre, where it remains. In this way, these five gyres have amassed the floating castoffs of an industrial world—largely plastics—into the five largest garbage patches in the world. The North Pacific garbage patch is well to the northeast of Hawaiʻi, but plenty of debris still washes ashore on to Hawaiian beaches. And this isn't just an esthetic problem. The debris entangles hapless fish, birds, and marine mammals. As the plastics weather and break down, they release chemicals, and marine life ingests the pieces of plastic. Ocean garbage is a global problem with no easy solution, but reducing, reusing, and recycling plastics and other materials can help.

But let's get back to wind, wings, and waves as the bearers of life in Hawai'i. A simple, alliterative answer—a little too simple, really. You see, hard as it is, getting to Hawai'i is the easy part. In the movies, desperate castaways are safe once they wash ashore on the beach of a tropical island. For plants and animals that complete the long journey to Hawai'i, the reality is far different. For continued survival, an arriving species must have everything it will need: the proper habitat, a dependable food source, and relief from predators and competitors. Oh, and one more thing: if your kind wants to stick around for more than one lifetime, you need a mate. For the overwhelming majority of plants and animals that arrive naturally on Hawaiian shores, the islands are not a paradise but a grave. Successful pioneers have accumulated slowly on these islands over the last thirty million years.

So, what did a newly formed island in the Hawaiian chain look like thirty million years ago while it was slowly accumulating pioneer species? In that distant time, Midway Atoll might have been a young island resting where Kīlauea erupts today. That would have been long before the Pacific Plate pulled Midway away from the hot spot on its course across the North Pacific. Midway was perhaps still erupting, but it had vast areas of cooled lava well above the reach of waves. There may have been ancient atolls far to the northwest, but their wave-washed land harbored little or no remaining terrestrial life, with no ready source of pioneering life for the young Midway.

A volcanic island in Indonesia called Krakatau (or Krakatoa) can give us a hint of how the procession of life arrives. Krakatau erupted explosively in 1883 and cleansed itself of every living thing. A series of scientific expeditions documented the return of life. The island is within thirty miles of Sumatra and Java, not nearly as isolated as Hawai'i. That meant new life arrived quickly. Within months the first spider ballooned in. Within three years there were ferns and some flowering plants. Four of the flowering plant species—no surprise here—were related to dandelions. A year later there were young trees, and by 1889 biologists found spiders, butterflies, beetles, and flies.

Individual plants and animals probably found their way to Midway's shore fairly frequently. We can guess this because wayward birds make their way to the Hawaiian Islands almost every winter, blown in by storms or just hopelessly lost. Generally, they linger awhile and then disappear. And so it was on ancient Midway; many arrived but few survived. Scientists estimate that, during the long course of Hawai'i's existence prior to human arrival, some new plant or animal has successfully colonized these islands at a witheringly low rate of once every five thousand years or so. Twenty-five hundred miles of open ocean is that much of a barrier.

The paradox is that there are many more species of plants and animals on the Hawaiian Islands than we would expect, given their isolation. There were over ten thousand island species when the first Polynesian voyagers arrived. What's going on here?

Before we can answer those questions, we need some background in biology, or more specifically taxonomy. What is a species? It is a fundamental concept for understanding Hawai'i's natural world, or any life on earth.

When explorers fanned out across the globe in the sixteenth and seventeenth centuries, they collected the new and unusual plants and animals they encountered. When these explorers returned home with their booty of biological specimens, museum keepers did their best to name and catalog the growing pile of life-forms. With little communication between museums, there was no consistency. The same plant in two different collections might end up with two different names. Some early scientists creatively lumped together animals according to their size, color, or whether they were terrestrial or aquatic, then asserted that such subjectively selected similarities showed that the animals were related. There was often little regard for more fundamental similarities in shape, structure, or physical attributes. As more travelers collected more specimens, the confusion intensified.

In the 1730s early taxonomists began assigning each living thing a two-word name unique to that organism, devising a system of binomial nomenclature that we still use today. The first word denotes a group of very closely related organisms—a genus (the plural is genera). The second word identifies a unique form of life within a genus—a species (the plural is species). By convention, the two words of an organism's name are italicized, but only the genus name is capitalized. There are additional levels of classification above the genus level, denoting larger and more diverse groups of related species. The main categories, starting with the largest, are domain, kingdom, phylum, class, order, family, and then genus and species. Today scientists use all these taxonomic levels, and sometimes additional ones, recognizing additional complexity among living things with categories such as subphylum, suborder, superfamily, and so on.

Let's use you as an example of this classification system. A taxonomist would place you in the domain Eukarya (organisms composed of cells with nuclei and mitochondria) kingdom Animalia (generally things we recognize as animals) phylum Chordata (having a central cord-shaped nervous system like a spinal cord) subphylum Vertebrata (bony animals with vertebrae protecting the spinal cord) class Mammalia (the mammals) order Primates (monkeys, apes, and humans) family Hominidae (the so-called great apes: gorillas, chimpanzees, orangutans, bonobos, and humans) genus *Homo* (humans and some of your extinct ancestors) and the specific name *sapiens* (from the Latin, meaning "wise or able to discern").

If this seems awfully complicated, that's because life on our planet is complicated, diverse, and abundant. How abundant? We don't know. There are nearly 1.5 million named, identified species. It is still relatively easy to "discover" new species—we've really only just scratched the surface of cataloging life on our planet. About eighteen thousand new species are described every year. And you don't have to trek off to remote places to find them; recently a new frog species turned up in New Jersey. Educated guesses about the total number of species on the planet generally put the number in the 8 million range, give or take a million or two. There's way more life than we've been able to find and count.

Let's consider just the bottom rung on our taxonomic ladder, the species. Often the distinction between two species is clear: your dog and your cat are different species. The classical definition of a species was a group of similar animals capable of breeding and producing fertile offspring. If two individuals were too dissimilar to manage this, then they must be different species. The classic barnyard example: a horse (*Equus ferus*) and a donkey (*Equus africanus*) can successfully breed, but their offspring, mules, are sterile. Thus, horses and donkeys are similar but distinct species.

The classic definition breaks down pretty easily: there are many distinct species that, in captivity, can interbreed and produce fertile offspring. So, new rule: a species is a group or groups of organisms that are "reproductively isolated" from other species in the wild. The reproductive isolation may be due to biological incompatibility like our horses and donkeys, physical separation such as two groups of lowland plants that evolve differences because they are separated by a tall mountain range, or behavioral separation such as Hawaiian fruit flies that have distinctive mating dances and only mingle with mates that know the correct dance steps.

Recently, our ability to read the molecular sequences of DNA has enabled us to identify similarities and differences among individuals and species. Now the challenge is to decide how much genetic difference must exist between two individuals before we proclaim them to be different species. Taxonomists fudge a bit by using terms such as *subspecies* and *races* to describe groups of individuals that vary from others of their species, but aren't different enough to warrant the title of unique species.

How does this variation occur? That's the perfect question to end our little digression about binomial nomenclature and digress again to a really interesting topic, sexual reproduction. We'll restrict ourselves to peering figuratively into microscopic cells and into the structure of chromosomes and DNA, where the really interesting part of sexual reproduction occurs (interesting to me, anyway; I'm a biologist).

We've classified you as a member of the species *Homo sapiens.* It's pretty clear that there is a great deal of variety within this single species. You are different from your neighbor (smarter and better looking, perhaps). Walk down the street in Honolulu and this genetic diversity is abundantly clear. Races from all over the world have come to Hawai'i, and have combined their DNA in innumerable ways. The Hawaiian language even has a word for it: *hapa,* or person of mixed blood.

Each individual carries a lot of diversity, too. You could have fifteen kids, and each one would look and act a bit different from the rest. That's because the DNA contributed by two parents can combine in a nearly infinite number of ways. Some of these combinations will be more fit than others. The slowest of your fifteen children isn't likely to be eaten by predators or starve to death because he is out-competed for food, but starvation or death by predators is just business as usual for most of the plants and animals on earth. That's survival of the fittest.

Over very long periods of time, diversity occurs in another way: random mutation. Usually mutations result in individuals that are less fit and who quickly die out. On very rare occasions, over hundreds or thousands of generations, mutations occur that benefit individuals. These mutations do not need to be visible changes. A mutation might alter an enzyme that allows some birds to metabolize nectar more efficiently.

Diversity among individuals of a species—humans, birds, bacteria, you name it—is both the product and the driver of evolution. If you harbor any doubt that evolution occurs, then you've come to the right place to see for yourself. There is not a better place on earth than Hawaiʻi to demonstrate the existence and remarkable power of evolution. This process has given rise to all the species of plants and animals unique to Hawaiʻi—literally thousands of them that occur nowhere else on earth—and many more that have been exterminated by humans or human influences.

Here's a real example. Let's go back in time about five million years. Kauaʻi is a young island sitting where the Big Island is today. Far to its northwest are older, eroding islands much like today. Similar to the process that occurred on Krakatau, a few species have traveled from those older islands to become established on the young Kauaʻi. Much more of the new life on Kauaʻi arrives from far-off continents. There are plants and flowers and insects and big colonies of nesting seabirds.

Meanwhile, in Asia, a very large flock of birds, similar to today's rosy finch, is migrating south in search of a wintering ground. It is stormy, and the flock rises to get above the weather and is caught in a low-dipping tongue of the jet stream. The birds are carried across the Pacific in icy hurricane-force winds. Most of the birds in this huge flock freeze, die, and drop into the sea. But quite a few of them, dozens or even hundreds, survive and are dropped by the jet stream into warm tropical air. They are very lucky birds indeed, for they drop directly on to Kauaʻi.

The birds are starving, and on Kauaʻi they find themselves surrounded by food. There are plenty of seeds, and they aren't even difficult to crack. There's little competition for the food supply, and few predators to dodge. The birds gorge, regain their strength, begin to breed, and soon establish a new population of birds on this Hawaiian island.

In time, Oʻahu also grows large enough to support plants and animals. Pioneering species from Kauaʻi and the older northwestern islands travel on wind, wings, and waves to colonize the new island. Our Kauaʻi birds have everything they need, and almost never cross water, but eventually a few make the crossing to the new island of Oʻahu.

Oʻahu eventually grows larger than Kauaʻi, with as many diverse habitats: rain forests, dry forests, shrubby grasslands, dunes. The pioneering Oʻahu birds are somewhat isolated from their Kauaʻi ancestors and over hundreds or thousands of generations they adapt to different conditions they've encountered. Remember, these birds possess genetic diversity so some offspring will do better in an unfamiliar habitat than others. Some offspring may have a stronger bill, perhaps, and be more successful at cracking certain seeds. Over time the Oʻahu birds become so different that when another Kauaʻi pioneer shows up, it doesn't recognize these Oʻahu birds as suitable mates. These Oʻahu birds are now physically and reproductively isolated; they have become a new species.

The sequence of speciation may happen in reverse, too. Some Oʻahu birds may return to Kauaʻi, keep to themselves, and in time evolve into another Kauaʻi species that is distinct from both the first Kauaʻi species and the Oʻahu birds.

A lot of time passes, and yet another huge island, Maui Nui, rises from the waves. There is now another island that the birds can colonize. For several million years, these birds exist on Kauaʻi, Oʻahu, and Maui Nui. They establish themselves on the Big Island as soon as it is habitable. Speciation can occur any time some birds make it across a channel that separates the islands, or when they exploit a different part of their diverse island habitat. Given enough time, this happens a lot. The number of bird species explodes, and they are all descended from that one flock of lost and hapless Asian finches.

Some species retain their stout seed-cracking bill. Others adapt to nectar-feeding and develop long, thin, curved bills that fit within the tubular lobelia flowers of the forest. Others become like woodpeckers (no true woodpeckers ever made it to the islands). This evolutionary process is called adaptive radiation: new species radiate from a common ancestor in order to adapt to a host of living conditions. Today we call these birds, all descended from a single ancestral species, the Hawaiian honeycreepers. The birds, like so many other Hawaiian plants and animals, are *endemic* to Hawaiʻi: they occur on these islands and nowhere else.

A note on timelines. Most scientists believe the ancestral birds first arrived on Kauaʻi. However, recent research on the arrival of the ancestral birds and on the age of Kauaʻi suggests that the birds came first. Perhaps they arrived on smaller, older, and less hospitable Nīhoa, nearly 150 miles northwest of Kauaʻi. It is very difficult to peer back in time with perfect precision.

How do scientists conclude that the finch-like ancestors of the

FIGURE 3.2 Honeycreepers evolved so many diverse forms that early biologists did not realize they are all closely related. (Original drawing by Aileen Feldman, courtesy of John Culliney)

honeycreepers have been in Hawai'i as long or longer than Kaua'i has been an island, or that other species such as *Hyposmocoma* moths arrived fifteen million years ago? They measure the rate of genetic change in island species over time, and compare these species with their genetically most similar continental relatives. The amount of genetic difference enables scientists to estimate how long their lineages have been apart. This procedure is often called a molecular clock.

Isolation and opportunity allow evolution to occur quickly on islands. Or at least quickly when you view the process in the context of an island's span of existence. When ducks and geese arrived on Hawaiian islands, some adapted to abundant food and nonexistent ground predators by losing their ability to fly. Other species retained the ability, and these flying birds colonized new islands as the islands appeared. And on each new island, flightless species then evolved. Even the Big Island, youngest in the chain, had plenty of time for flightless geese and rails to evolve.

This is the evolutionary magic of islands. Depending on the species, adaptive radiation can occur on a single island such as Madagascar or paired islands such as New Zealand. When there is an entire archipelago of islands, each with diverse habitats, the potential for new species increases exponentially. Darwin observed this phenomenon on the Galápagos Islands which lie 575 miles from Ecuador off the coast of South America.

When an archipelago happens to be the most isolated island cluster on earth, the result is the best example of evolution and adaptive radiation on the planet. And it helps that Hawaiian islands tend to be just the right distance from one another: too far for most birds or insects or floating seeds to go back and forth on a regular basis, but not so distant that no species ever make the channel crossings. In Hawai'i, a treasure house of unique life, the process has produced thousands of species that occur nowhere else on earth. For plants, birds, fruit flies, tree snails, reef fish, the process is the same and the result is the same: an abundance of unique life.

One interesting and puzzling little side note: after five million years or perhaps longer, descendants of those first pioneer finches still live on Nīhoa and neighboring Laysan. The Nīhoa finch and the Laysan finch are closer in appearance to the ancestral rosy finch than any of their honeycreeper relatives. They once existed on the main islands, but long ago died out. Their nearest genetic kin? The *palila,* which survives today only on the Big Island at the other end of the archipelago.

Just how rare an event was the arrival and survival of those finches? Scientists can get an idea by working backwards. For each group of related species in the islands, scientists try to determine how this adaptive radiation occurred. Modern gene-sequencing methods have helped immensely with this sleuthing. Sometimes, as with the finches, there was just a single founder species. In other cases, it appears that individuals of the same or closely related species arrived at two different times separated by thousands or even hundreds of thousands of years. In these cases, a genus or family of island species might have two founder species. By working backward on each genetic lineage, scientists have concluded that there have been fewer than one thousand terrestrial founder species that gave rise to all the native life on the islands.

If we make the imperfect assumption that these thousand species arrived over the course of the thirty million years that Hawaiian islands have existed then we conclude that these founder species arrived at a rate of one every thirty thousand years. For a long time, that's the calculation scientists used to estimate the frequency of successful pioneering events. The flaw in this reasoning, of course, is the possibility of breaks in the conveyor belt—those times when there might not have been a suitable range of habitats, especially mountain and forest habitat—to sustain all the species that previously arrived or evolved.

And that makes a big difference. During the time that the Gardner Pinnacles were a large island, comparable to today's Big Island, there were plenty of habitats to support many different species. And there were other high islands nearby. This happy time for island biodiversity occurred from eighteen million years ago to about eight million years ago. There existed a completely different set of "main" Hawaiian islands, sitting where the familiar main islands rest today.

Then the hot spot became less productive for a long stretch. The large islands eroded, subsided, and drifted away. The new islands that took their place were smaller and lower, offering much less habitat diversity. More than five million years ago the hot spot began a new age of greater productivity, forming Kaua'i and Ni'ihau and then continuing to pump out islands all the way down the chain to Lō'ihi. There is probably more land area in Hawai'i today than the archipelago has seen in thirty million years of existence.

Big gaps in island formation can have lethal consequences. An entire complement of island species evolved around what would have been the Gardner Islands. Then almost all this life was wiped out when only low islands remained, and finally, an almost entirely new complement of island life evolved again when the islands we know

FIGURE 3.3 The Gardner Pinnacles were once larger than the Big Island is today. Now they are eroded and have subsided to rocky islets. (Forest & Kim Starr)

today began to form. So it is not just the land itself that rises from the waves and disappears again. At least once before, an unknown number of species—perhaps ten thousand—evolved and then died out on ancient islands.

Modern genetic studies based on rates of mutation suggest that most of the plants and animals that are native to Hawai'i have existed on the islands for roughly five million years or less. They are almost all species of the "new" Hawaiian Islands. That means that the majority of our one thousand founder species arrived in the last five million years, not thirty million, increasing the rate of successful colonization to a relatively rapid rate of one surviving pioneer every five thousand years or so. Of course, this is an average, lumping together all types of plants and animals. The most frequent pioneers have been flowering plants whose seeds can travel by many means. Amphibians never made it to Hawai'i, and mammals successfully made the journey to these shores only a few times (bats and monk seals).

But there are a few intriguing exceptions: a handful of plants and animals that have been here far longer than the current islands have existed. Some damsel flies can trace their lineage back nearly ten million years. Hawaiian plants related to the familiar garden flower lobelia, with six genera of mostly rare or extinct species, arrived some fifteen million years ago. So did the *Hyposmocoma* moths, with four hundred species in the islands. The ancestors of some bird species—several kinds of 'ō'ō—arrived about the same time, making them the oldest endemic Hawaiian vertebrates. All these birds are extinct, the last one disappearing from Kaua'i forests about 1987. The most ancient Hawaiian species appear to be *Drosophila* fruit flies (fussy entomologists insist that they're properly called pomace flies). There are about eight hundred species, descended from perhaps two pioneering fly species. They can trace their family tree back for an astounding twenty-nine million years, to a time when the very first Hawaiian island emerged from the waves. Next time you see a Hawaiian fruit fly, show some respect.

There is one more special case of life reaching Hawai'i. It happens regularly, every year, almost like clockwork. We're talking migration, and there are about a dozen species that regularly perform this double feat of long-distance travel and pinpoint navigation. The migrants are waterfowl (ducks with chunky bodies and webbed feet) and shorebirds (more slender birds with long legs designed for wading in shallow water, and not much webbing between the toes). Some of the most common ducks include northern pintail and northern shoveler, known to Hawaiians as *koloa māpu* and *koloa mohā*, respectively. These birds winter in Hawai'i in small numbers, but the pintail's Hawaiian name hints that it was once much more common. *Māpu* means "to rise up like a cloud," apparently referring to flocks of ducks taking off from once-common Hawaiian wetlands. *Mohā* means "bright," referring to the shoveler's glossy green head. The most common shorebirds include ruddy turnstone and wandering tattler, known to Hawaiians by the onomatopoeic names *'akekeke* and *'ūlili*, respectively, and sanderling or *hunakai* (it means "sea foam," which the bird follows along the shoreline).

Now, go for a walk in a Hawaiian forest or park, or take a swim along the shore. Once you understand how all this life came to exist in Hawai'i, you will never see these islands in quite the same way again.

FIELD TRIP!

3.1 THE BIG ISLAND'S LONELIEST SPOT. If you want to get a feel for the profound isolation of Hawai'i, then South Point or Ka Lae (the point) on the Big Island is the place to go. It is the southernmost bit of land in the United States, and it points toward the biggest expanse of water on a watery planet.

From the Hawai'i Belt Road, Route 11, head south or *makai* on South Point Road. The junction is between highway mile markers 69 and 70. South Point Road is a bit narrow and rough, but it's paved the entire eleven miles to the point. About two miles from the highway you'll cross Kamaoa Road; continue straight. About a half mile farther you'll cross an area of *'a'ā*. This is a little tongue of lava that erupted from Mauna Loa's southwest rift zone in 1868.

At about four miles you'll come to a fork; keep right. You'll pass a couple of wind farms, including one with rusting abandoned windmills and a newer one still in operation. When you live on an isolated island and most of your electricity is generated by burning oil, wind energy is attractive. You will see evidence of relentless wind: some of the trees here are shaped like streamlined *bonsai*.

At about the ten-mile point is another fork; keep right. At the end of the paved road there is a rough lava parking area adjacent to seacliffs. During calm weather the daring or foolhardy dive into the ocean and then climb back up using the rickety ladders attached to the cliff face. I don't recommend it.

Look up the coastline toward Kona and you can see a spot on the coast where an escarpment—an abrupt cliff edge—meets the sea. You're on high ground with seacliffs; beyond the escarpment the slope into the sea is much more gentle. This escarpment marks the point where the southwest rift zone meets the coast; on the other side of the rift zone the land has slumped because of undersea landslides.

You're almost to the southernmost point. Continue on foot toward the navigational beacon (a light on a post). Next to it is a small *heiau*, an ancient place of worship, one reminder that this point has long been used by Hawaiians. A little farther on there is a low rock wall. It points almost due south, helpful for locating the southernmost tip of land.

Paradoxically, the ocean to your south appears vast and empty, but is filled with hundreds of islands, just tiny specks of land. These islands are way stations for birds that migrate annually and nesting grounds for seabirds that rarely visit land. They were stepping-stones for voyaging Polynesians who discovered and settled most of these islands over the course of thousands of years. If you sailed away heading due south you wouldn't hit land again until you reached Antarctica, some 7,176 miles away. But you'd pass by quite a few islands. Closest to Ka Lae is Johnston Atoll, 975 miles southwest and well off your due southerly course. About 1,225 miles south of Ka Lae you'd pass by Kiritimati or Christmas Island, but you'd miss it; it would be over the horizon, 100 miles to your west. Captain Cook made landfall on Christmas Eve 1777 and his name for the island stuck, even though Spaniards had visited the island 240 years earlier. During the Cold War, the United States and England tested about two dozen nuclear warheads on Christmas Island.

Another 144 miles and you cross the equator. Then about 1,725 miles along your route you'd come achingly close to Starbuck Island. If you were traveling on a masted vessel with a crow's nest, you might even see it, since it would be less than 14 miles off your starboard (right) side. Amazingly, this little speck of land was independently found by two different whaling captains, cousins Valentine and Obed Starbuck of the famous Nantucket whaling family. They both passed it during the whaling season of 1823.

Next you'd voyage past the Cook Islands, including Rarotonga, to your starboard, and the Marquesas and Society Islands, including

Tahiti, to your port side. Incredibly, you'd thread the needle; there are over a hundred islands in these groups, but you'd never see one, passing eighty-five miles from the nearest land. The islands are just too small, and the ocean is too big.

Then you would leave Polynesia and sail into the Great Southern Ocean, passing distant New Zealand far to your right and South America even farther to your left. And then there is no more land to your right or left; it is water all the way around the world at southerly latitudes. After more than seven thousand miles of sailing you would finally make landfall in Antarctica, the next firm ground south of Ka Lae.

Spying on the Neighbor (Islands). A main driver of speciation in Hawaiʻi is the Goldilocks proximity of the islands to one another—not too close and not too far. The result, repeated many times over, is that members of a species leave one island and colonize another. In time they evolve differently than their ancestors on the first island and form a second species. Then some of them return to the first island and they are too different from their ancestors in one way or another for interbreeding to occur. They continue to evolve away from their ancestors, becoming species number three.

The interisland distance is not perfect for speciation among all lifeforms. Seabirds fly great distances over water, so narrow island channels would pose no barrier at all. Water birds such as black-necked stilts are known to fly from one island to another. For other species, even the narrowest ocean channel is an impossible impediment to movement. Blind cave spiders are not likely to make such a journey.

What does this Goldilocks distance between islands look like? There are lots of places to see for yourself. Here are some with the nicest views.

3.2 Lānaʻi Lookout, Oʻahu. Follow the Kalanianaʻole Highway, Route 72, east from Honolulu. A little less than a mile past the entrance to Hanauma Bay you will come to the Lānaʻi Lookout. On a clear day, you can see Lānaʻi, Molokaʻi, and Maui. A map of the Hawaiian Islands helps you to identify them. Closest, appearing largest, and on the left is Molokaʻi. It may appear as two humps, with taller and more distant East Molokaʻi on the left, and West Molokaʻi to its right. Next is Haleakalā on Maui. It looks low because it is the most distant visible island. Finally, on the right, is Lānai. If it is not perfectly clear you may see only Molokaʻi, or no islands at all.

3.3 Mountaintop to Mountaintop, Big Island. From atop Mauna Kea, or nearly anywhere on the north-facing side of the Big Island from Waikoloa to Kohala Mountain, Haleakalā is usually visible. Look for a flat skirt of clouds with a mountain summit peeking out the top. Folks on Maui have a similar view, but they're seeing Mauna Kea. Sometimes they see a veritable parfait, with green slopes and white clouds and brown mountainsides and a snow-capped peak.

A few other lookouts are described in other chapters. Chapter 2 describes the splendid view of Niʻihau from Puʻu Hinahina on Kauaʻi. In chapter 8 one field trip offers a reach-out-and-touch-it view of Molokaʻi from lonely Shipwreck Beach on Lānaʻi. Chapter 13 describes the best vantage point of the islands that comprised ancient Maui Nui.

3.4 Any Big Lawn, August through April. This field trip could not be easier. Any island, any big lawn, any time of the year between August or September and March or April. What will you see? The *kōlea*, a little bird with huge abilities. Also known as the Pacific golden-plover, this pigeon-sized bird may be Hawaiʻi's best-known migrant. Unlike similar wading birds that seek out wetlands, this little bird prefers open grasslands. And we've created lots of open grasslands in Hawaiʻi: parks and golf courses. The result is that this bird can be seen in urban and suburban areas all over the islands.

Each bird is remarkably faithful to its own little patch of wintering ground, returning year after year. If you saw a *kōlea* last winter—or ten years ago—on the fairway of the 14th hole at the Wailea Blue course, chances are the bird you see this winter will be the very same individual. The *kōlea* that arrive in August are a mottled golden brown. By the time they are ready to depart for their breeding grounds the next spring most are in breeding plumage, sporting a black face and chest, edged in jaunty white.

The most amazing part of this bird's life history—scary, really—is its extreme annual migration. This bird breeds in western Alaska and Siberia. After breeding, the adults make a return trip, and the young make their first flight to Hawaiʻi or other islands in the tropical Pacific. Remember, these birds have legs made for wading in shallow water or standing on grass, and do not have webbed feet. This means it is nearly impossible to land and take off on water. You can probably figure out where this story is going: these birds have to fly nonstop from Alaska to

FIGURE 3.4 *Kōlea* with the black breast of breeding plumage in the spring, and regular plumage in the fall. (Rick Soehren)

Hawaiʻi, about three thousand miles, with nowhere to stop and rest. Dip into the water and you die. The flight takes three to four days. The birds' flight speed averages thirty-five miles per hour, but they occasionally catch strong tailwinds. At these times, they may achieve flight speeds of around one hundred miles per hour.

EARN MORE

- David Quammen, *The Song of the Dodo: Island Biogeography in an Age of Extinction* (New York: Scribner, 1996). A well-written and readable look (but long at over seven hundred pages) at the vulnerability of life evolved on islands. Hawaiʻi is mentioned more than a few times.
- Jonathan Weiner, *The Beak of the Finch* (New York: Vintage Books, 1994). Alas, this book is set in the Galápagos, not Hawaiʻi, but it provides a graphic description of how rapidly evolution can occur—measurable over only a couple of decades—when conditions are right and the process is unrestrained.
- Edward O. Wilson, *The Diversity of Life* (New York: W. W. Norton, 1999). Wilson lays a groundwork of evolution and biodiversity to set the stage for a description of human-caused extinctions and a call for better stewardship. There are a lot of examples, and the book is written in a very approachable, readable style. Wilson is an old-time naturalist and an articulate ambassador for life on our planet.

4   A Place for Everything
Hawai'i's Diverse Habitats and Plants

The dispersal of plants and animals to Hawai'i and their subsequent evolution and adaptive radiation may seem complex, but the distribution of plants on the islands is pretty simple and can be traced to just two primary factors: topography and Hawai'i's dependable trade winds. Botanists may quibble, and ecologists have devised at least a dozen different systems for describing plant communities, but unless you're a scientist, there are just two things you have to know: topography and the trades.

Let's start with the trade winds, or the trades as they are called, the fabled global subtropical wind patterns that aided sea captains along trade routes during the age of sailing ships. They occur on most of the world's oceans when warm air near the equator rises, is pushed north or south toward higher latitudes, and then sinks, creating winds. Because air at the equator is rising and thus leaving space below it for more air to rush in, trade winds blow from higher latitudes back toward the equator in a big atmospheric cycle. But the trades don't blow due south because the planet is spinning west to east beneath the rising and falling air masses, causing the trades to blow east to west. In Hawai'i the trade winds blow from the northeast.

The trades usually produce pleasant breezes, blowing at an average twelve miles per hour, and almost never exceeding twenty-five. Historically they have been pretty reliable, providing breezes in Hawai'i about 80 percent of the time in the summer. In recent summers they have been less dependable. They are less constant in winter when the atmospheric cycle that generates the wind drifts south, pushing the trades south of the islands. The trade winds carry moisture. If there were no Hawaiian Islands to catch this moisture, the open ocean in this region might receive about twenty-five inches of rain per year. When moisture-laden clouds blow over land they are lifted—and consequently cooled—by the topography. Thus, Hawai'i averages seventy-five inches of rain per year. But averages can be very misleading. The topography of the Hawaiian Islands, with volcanoes approaching fourteen thousand feet, creates a huge amount of lift. As clouds are blown by the trades on to the northeast shores of the islands, the clouds are lifted and cooled. This cooling decreases the clouds' moisture-holding capacity, and the moisture condenses into rain, a lot of rain. That's why the northeast or windward side of each island is the wettest. Most of the moisture is squeezed out of the air before it passes over the leeward side of the islands, so these downwind sides tend to be the drier parts—the rain shadow. It is no coincidence that most of Hawai'i's resorts are on the leeward sides of the islands; most people don't enjoy rainy vacations.

Flash Floods.   Many Hawaiian streams drain watersheds that are small and steep. This means that heavy rainfall in the mountains can drain into streams quickly, causing flash floods. Streams can rise with unbelievable speed, sometimes so fast that hikers are unable to escape a stream area. The only warning may be a thunderous roar from upstream, quickly followed by a wall of water. Hikers following streams or gulches must always be aware of the weather conditions not only in their present location but also above them in the watershed. If it has been raining hard above you, don't gamble with a streamside hike. Wait for another day.

Here's where it starts to get a bit tricky. Air that rises the farthest above the equator will cool and lose nearly all its moisture as it circulates north. Then this cold dry air gets warmer as it descends. Meanwhile, sunshine falling on the islands tends to heat surface air that contains much more moisture. This moist air rises and then cools. When warming dry air caps the cooling moist air, the result is an inversion layer—so called because it is the inverse of expected cooling that normally occurs higher in the atmosphere. This inversion layer traps moisture below it. The inversion layer can vary in altitude, but it's usually between five thousand and seven thousand feet. Like the trades, the inversion layer is more dependable in the summer.

Why is the inversion layer so important for weather and plants in Hawai'i? It goes back to topography. Some islands have peaks that are higher than the inversion layer: Mauna Kea, Mauna Loa, Haleakalā. When trade winds hit the side of the biggest peaks they drop their moisture along the big volcanoes' flanks, but are kept below the peaks by the inversion. When the trades hit lower islands, their moisture is squeezed out over the highest elevations.

And this makes a lot of difference. Rainfall at the summit of Mauna Kea is less than 15 inches per year, the same on Mauna Loa. Haleakalā is a bit lower and gets a bit more moisture, but still only 30 inches or less. By contrast, peaks below the inversion layer on other islands experience torrential rains: 337 inches in the northern Koʻolau Range on Oʻahu, 399 inches on Puʻu Kukui on West Maui, and reported ranges of 422 to 486 inches on Kauaʻi's Mt. Waiʻaleʻale. Waiʻaleʻale is reputed to be the wettest spot on earth, but there are spots in India and even on West Maui that may get more rainfall. In any case, remember to pack your rain shell.

When moisture is squeezed out on the flanks or peaks of the mountains, very little remains for the leeward side. The southern Koʻolau Range at Pauoa Flats receives 166 inches of rain per year, but four miles southwest in Waikīkī the annual total is 24 inches. Poʻipū on the south coast of Kauaʻi receives about 30. On Maui, leeward Lahaina and Kīhei receive less than 15 inches. I lived in Kīhei one winter, and it didn't rain a single drop all season.

The leeward Kona coast of the Big Island is a special case. Towering Mauna Kea and Mauna Loa are so effective at blocking trade winds that Kona has its own unique wind patterns. On summer afternoons, air over the west-facing mountain slopes heats in the sun and rises, drawing moist air from over the ocean. This is called convective uplift. The resulting cloud layer makes Kona the only spot in the state that gets more rain in the summer than the winter. These wonderful clouds also make Kona an ideal spot for growing coffee by providing the afternoon shade the coffee plants need. Coffee lovers everywhere are thankful.

The weather condition that most delights visitors and residents alike is snowfall. A few times each winter, on average, the highest elevations of Mauna Kea, Mauna Loa, and Haleakalā will receive a thin blanketing of snow, almost never deeper than a foot. Sometimes snowfall will occur at or below eight thousand feet, but it doesn't stick for long below eleven thousand feet. On clear days after a snowfall, expect to see people heading for Mauna Kea with skis or even boogie boards to get a taste of alpine sports.

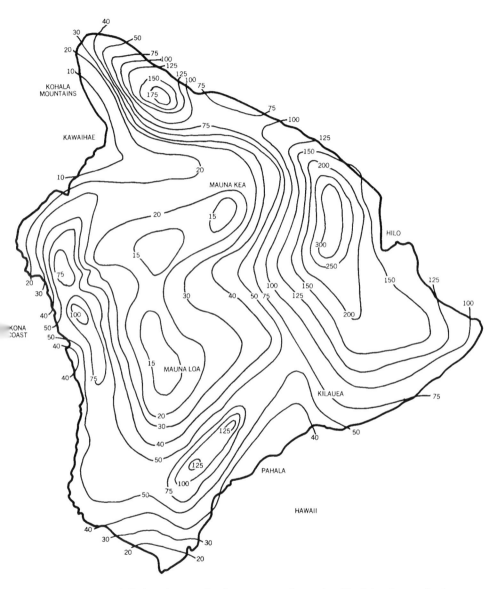

FIGURE 4.1 Rainfall distribution (inches per year) on the Big Island reveals the effect that big mountains have on the moisture-carrying trade winds. (Courtesy of National Tropical Botanical Garden)

Despite the occasional presence of snow on a few peaks, lower elevations in Hawai'i have relatively little temperature variation, especially compared to continental areas. That's because the islands are surrounded by the largest body of water on earth, and water temperature fluctuates much less than air temperature. The surrounding water moderates temperature variation on adjacent land. A couple of Honolulu climate factoids will bear this out: the average high and low temperatures during August, the hottest month, are 88° and 71°F, while the averages during chilly February are 81 and 63. The extremes aren't too extreme either: the record high temperature in Honolulu is 95°F, the record low, 52.

Hurricanes in Hawai'i. Sometimes the worst weather in Hawai'i comes during the summer. If conditions are just right—very warm ocean surface temperatures, a low-pressure system sitting just above this warm water, at five degrees from the equator to give it just the right spin—then a swirling storm system can form. If the system is weak it may become nothing more than a tropical depression or tropical storm, but if winds exceed 73 miles per hour, it is classified as a hurricane. Hurricanes are categorized by wind speed, from a Category 1 event with winds from 74 to 95, up to Category 5 with winds of at least 157 miles per hour.

Hurricane season in Hawai'i is roughly June to November, but only rarely do hurricanes actually pass over the islands; Hawai'i is a pretty small target in a vast ocean, after all. Most Eastern Pacific hurricanes pass to the east or south of the islands. The most destructive hurricane to hit Hawai'i in modern times was 'Iniki, which made a direct hit on Kaua'i in September 1992. With sustained winds of 130 to 145 mph it was a Category 4 storm, although it had wind bursts of up to 160 mph or more.

The storms called hurricanes in the Atlantic or Eastern Pacific are called typhoons west of the 180th meridian (just west of Kure Atoll) and cyclones in the Indian Ocean. When tropical storms or hurricanes form in a vast area north of the equator but south of Hawai'i, they are given Hawaiian names.

What do you do if a hurricane is headed your way? Turn to radio, television, or the Internet for advice and instructions from civil defense authorities, who generally have several days of advance notice. Visitors should also check with management of hotels or resorts. At the very least, try to stockpile a few days' emergency supplies: a gallon of drinking water per person per day, nonperishable food items in waterproof packaging, and fully charged cell phones and flashlights.

VEGETATION AND VEGETATION ZONES

There is no land on earth more sterile—literally—than a new lava flow. New islands that are not too isolated start to acquire life very quickly (see the discussion of Krakatau in chapter 2). When later arrivals displace plants established earlier, the process is called succession. It is a natural process that can happen quickly when a new lava flow is surrounded by Hawaiian forest, with various plant groups succeeding one another as pioneers on the new land. It happens whenever Hawaiian volcanoes erupt and cover the land with new lava.

Once the lava is cooled enough for steam to stop rising from cracks, rainwater will collect in depressions on the cooled stone surface. Bacteria and algae carried by the wind will start to reproduce in these pockets of water. Soon, mosses and lichens will arrive in the same manner and will germinate in shady damp crevices. It usually doesn't take long for Hawai'i's most adaptable tree, the '*ōhi'a lehua*, or simply '*ōhi'a* for short, to sprout on the mostly barren lava. '*Ōhi'a* seeds are very tiny and are easily carried on the wind. These "trees" will usually be very small in stature because of the relatively harsh environment, sometimes reaching maturity and blooming when they are only a foot or two tall. About the same time, small ferns called '*ama'u* will begin to sprout. The young fronds are reddish, which may protect them from the bright sun.

Lichens: They're Everywhere, and They're Strange. Hike around on a relatively young lava flow in an area that gets good rainfall, and you will probably see a mat of shaggy gray stuff growing on the rocks. It is lichen (LIKE-en), and during the first few years of a new lava flow's existence, it will be a dominant plant. Lichens are among the stranger life forms on our planet. It is not just one organism, but two different organisms living in symbiosis (an association between two organisms in which one or both benefit, in this case both). The structure of the lichen is provided by a fungus. Inside the fungus is an alga (plural algae) that photosynthesizes and provides energy for both the alga and the fungus. There are roughly twenty thousand different lichens in the world, and they can grow in almost any conditions.

Something else is happening on the aging lava flow: soil is forming. Weather and lichen break down thin edges of the lava. Organic materials such as leaves blow into crevices and decompose. This soil allows other seeds to germinate, and shrubs such as 'ōhelo and pūkiawe appear. Eventually, *uluhe* fern may carpet the lava flow, growing into a dense tangle that is three to even six feet high. The *uluhe* will shade out many shorter plants, but will hold decomposed organic matter and help build soil. This fern also forces trees such as 'ōhi'a to grow taller to compete for sunlight.

Eventually the trees win, and much of the *uluhe* is shaded out. Other ferns move in, such as the tree fern *hāpu'u,* accompanied by other trees and shrubs. The lava flow is now covered by a forest. As it grows shadier, mosses will cover many surfaces. Fallen logs will become food for fungi that break them down into ever-deeper soil. Under favorable conditions (not too wet, not too dry) *koa* will grow, eventually becoming

FIGURE 4.2 *Uluhe* ferns cover many younger open forest areas. (Rick Soehren)

150-foot giants with trunks more than 8 feet in diameter. This is a climax forest, the last stage in succession.

How long does all this take? Moisture from rainfall is key: a new lava flow on the windward side will support a complex mature forest within three hundred or four hundred years. On the leeward side, a flow of this age will still look fresh, perhaps colonized by a struggling *kiawe* tree or a clump of grass here or there.

Rainfall patterns and elevation—topography and the trades—together strongly dictate plant life. Vary these two factors and you get different groups of plant species, called vegetation zones. Visit a spot at the 2,000-foot elevation on the windward side of any island (well, not Kahoʻolawe; it tops out at 1,483 feet). It will either be raining, or the rain will have just stopped: this spot gets between 120 and 160 inches of rain each year. It is known as the rain forest vegetation zone, and that's exactly what you find: dense, nearly impenetrable tropical rain forest.

Follow the elevation contour around to the same elevation on the leeward side and the scene will be radically different. Here in the rain shadow it will be dry, because this spot gets only 30 inches of rain each year. You will be surrounded by open woodland, not dense forest. The open areas will be grassland or shrubby. It may be so dry that the trees had to evolve special coping mechanisms: some of them lose their leaves in summer to conserve moisture. This is the dry forest and shrub vegetation zone.

Of course there's one other factor that affects vegetation, and that's human activity. Since humans arrived in Hawaiʻi we have made radical modifications to the landscape. The early Hawaiians were industrious farmers who cleared huge swaths of lowland forest, especially in areas of moderate rainfall, in order to grow *kalo* (taro) and sweet potatoes. The remaining forest started changing at this time, too. A few of the plants the Polynesians brought with them (the so-called canoe plants we'll get to in chapter 8) spread into the forest. *Kukui* or candlenut is a good example. Western contact brought more land cultivation, ranching, and a flood of additional new plant species (more about them in chapters 9 and 10) that often completely replaced native species in the low rain forest and the dry forest—basically everywhere but some high wet areas.

Our hypothetical mid-elevation rain forest is probably heavily invaded by introduced tree species, unless it was cleared to grow

FIGURE 4.3 *Kukui* or candlenut tree is a canoe plant that is now widespread in Hawaiian forests. (Rick Soehren)

sugarcane. In that case, it's an abandoned cane field, since commercial sugar production has ceased on all the islands. Many forests were replaced by *kalo* and sweet potatoes long before western contact, and these crops were replaced by introduced pasture grasses or cane fields after westerners arrived. Today it is impossible to find any sizable area that is still completely in its natural undisturbed condition, and difficult to find any areas that are even close to undisturbed.

Botanists and ecologists have devised many different systems of naming and describing the various vegetation zones. Read too many botany books and the result could be confusion rather than enlightenment. In quite a few cases, their zone names and descriptions refer to the plants that used to live in the zone, not what you're likely to find today. This does not mean that all native species have been displaced. They are sometimes just a bit harder to find, and often surrounded by more recent arrivals. Figure 4.4 depicts a very simplified system of vegetation zones. It's the pattern that's important: vegetation varies

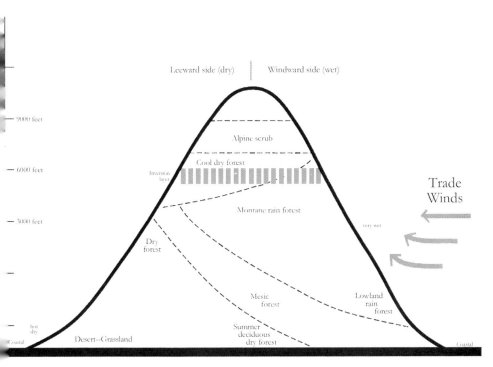

Leeward side (dry) | Windward side (wet)

9000 feet

Alpine scrub

6000 feet

Cool dry forest

Inversion layer

Trade Winds

Montane rain forest

3000 feet

very wet

Dry forest

Mesic forest

Lowland rain forest

hot dry

Coastal

Desert--Grassland

Summer deciduous dry forest

Coastal

FIGURE 4.4 Hawaiian vegetation zones. (By Michelle Murdock, adapted from *Hawaiian Insects and Their Kin* by F. G. Howarth and W. P. Mull)

according to rainfall carried by the trades and distributed unevenly by topography.

One more word about plants: in this book there is information about plants in four different chapters, depending on the plants' role in Hawaiian botany, history, and agriculture. This chapter describes *native* plants, those that occur in Hawai'i naturally and were not brought by humans. Natives can be either *indigenous* (naturally occurring in Hawai'i as well as other places) or *endemic* to Hawai'i (having evolved in Hawai'i and occurring no place else). This chapter also mentions some prominent *introduced* species brought by humans that occur alongside these natives. Introduced species are sometimes called *alien* or *exotic*. Chapter 8 describes *canoe plants* and their uses, those brought to the islands by the voyaging Polynesians. Chapter 9 describes plants introduced to Hawai'i later that changed the face of the land. Finally, chapter 10 describes plants that have figured prominently in Hawaiian agriculture.

Sound confusing? It can be. Here's some help sorting out native Hawaiian plants and others at natural areas around the islands.

Coastal areas, especially on the leeward sides of the islands, have been inhabited for a long time. When Captain Cook arrived in 1778 he noted villages and extensive farm fields in his descriptions of the land. But we really don't know what this **coastal** vegetation zone looked like before the first humans arrived. Our best clues come from well-preserved fossil pollen in lowland deposits, so distinctive that we can determine the plant genus or species that produced each pollen grain.

Despite the long history of modification, there are still some native plants to be found in coastal and lowland areas. Near the shore the most common and prominent native plant is the beach *naupaka* or *naupaka kahakai,* a bush with big shiny oval leaves and little white flowers that appear to be half missing. This plant is so hardy that it is used as a landscape plant by beach resorts. In more natural areas you might see beach morning glory or *pōhuehue.* It grows as a low trailing vine with funnel-shaped flowers in shades varying from pink to deep lavender, with a darker center. A little farther away from the shore you may spot the *'ilima,* a plant with yellow flowers that are popular for *lei* making. All three plants are indigenous to Hawai'i and are widespread on beaches of the tropical Pacific.

Several alien plants can grow in dry salty coastal environments. Casuarina or ironwood looks vaguely like a pine tree. Introduced from Australia, it is a common beach tree throughout the main islands. *Kiawe* (discussed below) is widespread and can also grow down to the beach. The canoe tree *kamani* and the vaguely similar false kamani, introduced later, both have big round-to-oval leaves and grow very near the water, where they provide welcome shade at some beaches.

Mangroves and pickleweed, two aliens found near the shore, are particularly troublesome for wetlands in Hawai'i. Mangrove trees, buttressed by their exposed roots, live at the edge of the water. They can grow as dense stands that crowd out other wetland plants. Most common is the red mangrove. You can see it at He'eia State Park on O'ahu's Kāne'ohe Bay. Pickleweed is a succulent shrub that fills shallow open water areas, displacing other plants and crowding out wetland birds. Look for it at Maui's Keālia Pond National Wildlife Refuge and on the Big Island at Aimakapā Pond in the Kaloko-Honokōhau National Historic Park.

FIGURE 4.5 Beach *naupaka*, with its half flower, is a common indigenous plant of Hawaiian shorelines. (Rick Soehren)

Legends of Half Flowers.   There are at least two Hawaiian legends that explain the unusual half-a-flower shape of the beach *naupaka* and a related *naupaka* that grows in the mountains. One story tells of lovers who quarreled. The woman took a whole, round *naupaka* flower and tore it in two, telling her lover she would forgive him when he brought her a whole flower. The fellow searched but alas, the gods had changed all the *naupaka* flowers into half flowers. Dejected, he died of a broken heart.

The other story tells of a mysterious and beautiful young woman who visited a village and hooked up with a handsome village man. Later he decided to return to his old girlfriend. The mystery woman, jealous and enraged, revealed herself to be the goddess Pele. She tore the two mortal lovers apart. The scorned goddess chased the man into the mountains, where sympathetic gods turned him into mountain *naupaka*. Then Pele chased the woman to the shore, where the gods turned her into beach *naupaka*. Now the lovers are forever parted, each forlornly bearing half a flower.

Farther from the leeward shore there probably used to be extensive forests filled with trees adapted to a dry climate that could survive on only thirty to forty inches of rain per year. Botanists think this **dry forest** zone might have been home to the most diverse plant communities on the islands. But these leeward slopes, up to about three thousand feet, were almost completely transformed by agriculture and ranching. Native species that once made up these dry forests are hard to find. This chapter's **Field Trip!** section describes a couple of places where you can see some of the trees and shrubs that used to be much more widespread. Today the most common tree of dry lowlands is the *kiawe,* a thorny tree native to South America, closely related to the mesquite tree of the southwest United States. It is so ubiquitous in lowland Hawai'i that many local people think it must be a native tree. In fact, every *kiawe* in Hawai'i is apparently descended from a single seed collected at the Royal French Gardens in Paris and planted at the Catholic Mission in Honolulu in 1828 by a French priest.

Where island slopes get more rainfall, about forty to one hundred inches per year, the forest is very different. This **mesic forest** is home

Mystery Plants of the Lowlands.   Scientists often study ancient pollen deposits to determine former plant inhabitants of a region. Pollen grains are often so well preserved in the mud of bogs that even after thousands of years they can be retrieved and identified. Pollen shapes are so distinctive that a trained eye can determine the genus of a microscopic pollen grain. When ancient pollen from coastal areas of Hawai'i was examined, scientists were puzzled. They found lots of pollen from the now very rare endemic *loulu* (pronounced low-lu) palm that survives only in a few isolated patches on the main islands and scattered groves on some Northwestern Hawaiian Islands. Even more mysterious, they found abundant pollen on O'ahu, Maui, and Kaua'i from an apparently completely unknown member of the pea family. Could a plant once this dominant really just disappear completely?

Eventually, both mysteries were solved. It turns out that *loulu* seeds are delicious if you're a rat, and rats immigrated along with the early Hawaiians. An onslaught of hungry rodents nearly wiped out vast natural groves of palms even before Hawaiians had cleared much land for agriculture. Some *loulu* palms survived in remote areas and on rat-free islands in the Northwestern Hawaiian Islands. A good place to see *loulu* palms today is the botanic garden inside Koko to three of the most iconic endemic trees in the Hawaiian forest: *koa* dominates this moderately wet forest, *ʻōhiʻa* grows very large here, and a few species of sandalwood were once quite common in these forests. *Koa* is one of the most well-known Hawaiian tree species. Early Hawaiians carved their dugout canoe hulls from giant *koa* logs. The largest known canoe had twin hulls, each measuring 120 feet long and 9 feet deep. Later, westerners recognized the beauty of *koa* wood and used it for furniture and paneling. Today it is still popular, but its use is controversial. There are a few *koa* plantations where the trees are getting large enough to harvest for lumber, but most *koa* comes from native forests and woodlands that have already suffered a huge amount of disturbance. This harvest of wild *koa* is an assault on the beleaguered Hawaiian environment, especially at high altitudes where endemic forest birds persist.

Koa trees have a little trick that helps them grow to be giants of the forest, large enough that an entire boat hull or two could be made from a single tree. For most plants, the lack of nitrogen in Hawaiian soils is an impediment to growth. But *koa,* like many other plants in the legume family, is a nitrogen fixer. That means *koa* has the remarkable ability to

crater near the eastern tip of Oʻahu. A handful of *loulu* species are the only native Hawaiian palms.

The case of the mysterious pea plant was harder to solve. The big break in this cold case came in 1992 when a couple of botanists doing a plant survey on Kahoʻolawe found two bushes growing on a rocky ocean outcrop where they were protected from hungry goats. The bushes were a species of plant the scientists didn't recognize. No one else did, either. The two plants were the only specimens of an endemic genus and species completely unknown to science. The botanists named it *Kanaloa kahoolaweensis.* When the pollen from this new species was examined, it had the same shape seen in the fossil pollen.

The mystery of the plant's identity was solved, but that leaves the greater mystery of how a plant once so abundant could be completely wiped out, save for two isolated specimens found on a big rock off Kahoʻolawe. We don't know, but here's one clue: the plant has proved impossible to propagate. Two seeds collected from the wild parent plants have germinated, but no further attempts to produce new seedlings have succeeded. Some necessary component of their reproductive cycle must be missing. With only a couple of aging plants surviving, we might not solve this last mystery before it's too late.

FIGURE 4.6 Typical appearance of 'ōhi'a, the darker tree on the left, and *koa*, on the right. Photo taken along the Pu'u 'Ō'ō Trail on the Big Island. (Rick Soehren)

make its own nitrogen fertilizer literally out of thin air. (To be precise, bacteria harbored in the roots of *koa* and other nitrogen-fixing plants actually perform this bit of alchemy.)

Koa trees have apparently existed in Hawai'i for a very long time. In her book *Hawaiian Heritage Plants*, Angela Kay Kepler points out that nearly fifty species of endemic insects have evolved to live on *koa,* more endemic species than are hosted by any other Hawaiian plant. She contrasts this with the coconut palm introduced by early Hawaiians; apparently not a single native insect evolved to live on it, although endemic insects that live on *loulu* palms will also use coconut palms.

One more tidbit about *koa* trees. Walk up to a big one and look among the branches for its leaves; you won't find any. As seedlings, *koa* trees have true leaves. The feathery leaves are compound, meaning they have many small leaflets growing from a center stem. When the tree reaches the height of one to about six feet, it undergoes a weird transformation: new leaf stems grow out flattened and sickle shaped, and no real leaves appear. These flattened, leaflike structures are called phyllodes and take the place of leaves on mature *koa* trees.

If you've ever visited a Hawaiian forest and seen *koa* trees, you're

FIGURE 4.7 *Koa* trees have true compound leaves as saplings. Later, they sprout flat, sickle-shaped phyllodes instead. (Rick Soehren)

probably scratching your head about now. Chances are, you've never seen one that was even remotely close to the size needed to make a huge canoe. And many *koa* trees don't even have a single main trunk, but instead branch out fairly close to the ground. These are not giants of the forest. What's going on? There are still *koa* trees large enough to be carved into big canoes, but most are growing in remote areas; a lot of the big trees in accessible areas have been cut. And if you damage the growing tip of a *koa* sapling, it responds by branching out. All the cattle, goats, and sheep introduced by westerners, even insects, have pruned a lot of *koa*. See chapter 9 for more on introduced species.

Another once-prominent tree of the forest has all but disappeared. It is sandalwood, and its story is a tragic one for the Hawaiian people and Hawaiian forests. Sandalwood or *ʻiliahi* is actually about half a dozen related species of endemic trees. Like the related sandalwood from India or China, it has wonderfully fragrant heartwood that can be used for furniture, small wooden goods, or incense. And like other sandalwood, it is very expensive. Westerners noted before 1800 that sandalwood was growing in Hawai'i and started trading for it with Hawaiian *ali'i* (chiefs). The chiefs, in turn, ordered their subjects into the mountains to cut the wood.

As the chiefs acquired more westernized tastes, they wanted more western goods. Traders obliged with another western concept: credit. The chiefs, perhaps failing to grasp the concept, ran up a huge amount of debt. The way to pay it off? Cut and sell even more sandalwood. During the height of the sandalwood trade, from about 1812 to 1830, chiefs forced their subjects to collect so much sandalwood that villages and farms were nearly abandoned. Men, women, and children were forced into the mountains to cut the trees. Even the roots of the trees were dug up for their fragrant wood. The virtual enslavement of the people didn't end until the supply of accessible sandalwood ran out. During this period the traditional Hawaiian way of life began to disintegrate as forests were stripped of sandalwood trees. Even today, these slow-growing trees are not common in Hawaiian forests.

One more detail about sandalwoods is they are the vampires of the Hawaiian forest or, more precisely, root parasites. The first roots sent out by a tiny sandalwood seedling are specialized to tap into the root system of other plants, preferably *koa*. The sandalwood thus supplements its own photosynthesis with nutrients from other plants' roots.

What's a *Kīpuka?* The term *puka* means "hole," and a *kīpuka* is a sort of hole in a lava flow: a patch of older land, usually vegetated, that has been surrounded by younger lava flows. They only exist on the Big Island, because on the older islands the surrounding lava flows have aged enough to "catch up" with the more mature vegetation of the *kīpuka*. Sometimes a *kīpuka* is a hill that has been surrounded by lava flows, such as Pu'u Huluhulu (shaggy hill) along the Saddle Road. At other times, a *kīpuka* will seem like a hole in a lava flow, because newer lava encircling the *kīpuka* is higher than the older ground. Just as islands fueled evolution and adaptive radiation, *kīpuka* probably stranded and isolated plants and animals and helped new Hawaiian species to evolve. Even today, *kīpuka* tend to be less disturbed than surrounding areas, and they harbor more native plants. The **Field Trip!** section describes visits you can make to *kīpuka*.

On windward slopes the uplift causes clouds to drop their moisture. From an elevation of a few hundred feet all the way up to the inversion layer, the result is rain forest that gets pelted with 120 to 450 inches of rain per year. In terms of vegetation, rain forest can be thought of as two different zones: the more pristine high-elevation **montane rain forest** dominated by native plants, and the highly disturbed **lowland rain forest** consisting almost entirely of introduced species. There is no sharp line between the two but native forest usually starts somewhere between 2,500 and 4,000 feet. Whether at high elevation or low, vegetation in rain forests is usually quite dense.

A prominent tree of undisturbed rain forest is the *'ōhi'a lehua,* often called simply *'ōhi'a.* Its blossom is called *lehua.* This tree flourishes where conditions are too wet to be ideal for the larger *koa* trees. In the rain forest the *'ōhi'a* can grow to a very large size, but its habitat is not limited to the rain forest. In fact, the *'ōhi'a* is one of the most adaptable trees anywhere. It grows from sea level to the tree line, in wet forests as well as dry woodlands. It is often a pioneer species, one of the first to take root in cooled lava flows. It can grow waist-high as a tiny stunted shrub or become a stately forest tree with a trunk diameter bigger than your waist. Kalōpā State Recreation Area near Honoka'a on the Big Island has some giant *'ōhi'a* trees.

Early Hawaiians held the *'ōhi'a* to be sacred, the abode of the god Kū. They used its wood mostly to carve temple images. Later, Hawaiians used the red *lehua* blossoms of the *'ōhi'a* for *lei* making. Westerners, when they arrived, put *'ōhi'a* wood to use as flooring and fence posts. The *'ōhi'a* is also vitally important to endemic forest birds. Honeycreepers feed heavily on nectar from *lehua* blossoms. More about this in chapter 5. Mature *'ōhi'a* and *koa* trees are shown in figure 4.6. Recently an introduced fungus has threatened *'ōhi'a* trees. (See chapter 9.)

Beneath the trees of the rain forest you will find ferns. Especially in the rain forests on the Big Island, magnificent tree ferns or *hāpu'u* grow as big as trees, topping out as high as 25 feet. Hawai'i is home to many fern species because fern spores can blow and disperse so easily and because wet windward environments are particularly conducive to fern growth. There are over 200 fern species in Hawai'i, including 125 that are endemic to the islands. Crater Rim Drive near Thurston Lava Tube in Hawai'i Volcanoes National Park is a tree fern wonderland.

FIGURE 4.8 *'Ōhi'a lehua* flowers bloom in Hawaiian forests, providing nectar for endemic honeycreepers. (Rick Soehren)

Gift from the Forest. The first Polynesian voyagers to settle in Hawai'i left their home islands not knowing where they would end up or what useful resources they would find at their new home. They skillfully transported a couple dozen plant species that they knew could provide them with food, fiber, and medicines. In the forests of Hawai'i they found many other useful plants such as *koa* and *'ōhi'a,* but the endemic Hawaiian plant more useful than any other was perhaps *olonā.* This leafy shrub of the nettle family has lost the stinging hairs of continental nettles. What it does have is an inner bark that produces the longest, strongest, softest fibers of any plant in the world. The Hawaiians treasured it, cultivated it, and used it to make everything from fishing nets to ropes to the twine for tying babies' umbilical cords. They considered it a minor deity. Westerners also appreciated the strong rope made from *olonā.* They used it for ships' rigging and harpoon lines. The Swiss imported *olonā* fiber to manufacture mountain climbing ropes until synthetic fibers became available in the 1930s. You can see hundred-year-old *olonā* fishing nets in the Bishop Museum.

Epiphytes—plants growing on other plants—are another feature of the rain forest. Lichens, mosses, and bird nest ferns can all be seen growing on the trunks or amid the branches of rain forest trees, particularly in the areas of highest rainfall. A rain forest is literally covered with life.

Lowland rain forest in Hawai'i is very different from the higher elevation native montane rain forest. Low wet areas were cleared by the early Hawaiians for growing *kalo,* bananas, and sugarcane. Later, these areas were among the first lands exploited by westerners for farming, grazing, and timber cutting. Early efforts to reforest the denuded land invariably relied on fast-growing introduced tree species. The fast growth rate has given the lowland rain forest an ancient look even though some dense forests were barren eroding hillsides just a hundred years ago.

Some of the introduced plants you see in the lowland rain forest will look quite familiar, perhaps because they are also growing on your windowsill at home. Pothos vine is commonly seen twining up the trunks of big trees. Another recognizable tree, known on your windowsill as a schefflera, grows here as the octopus tree, so named for its big, red, multi-armed blooms.

At high elevations, above the inversion layer in windward areas and near it on leeward slopes, is another kind of dry forest. *Koa* trees once again dominate in this **cool dry forest**. Other plants familiar from lower elevations also occur here, such as *'ōhi'a* and sandalwood. Here the forest floor tends to be more open than it would be in a rain forest, and this openness has aided invasion by exotic species. Flammable grasses such as fountain grass spread through the forest and create a fire hazard. Cattle once roamed wild in this high forest, munching away at anything they could reach, inhibiting forest regeneration by eating young saplings. In this way vast stretches of forest were converted to grassland dotted with lonely old *koa* trees.

On the highest peaks no trees grow at all. On Mauna Kea, Mauna Loa, Hualālai, and Haleakalā the cool dry forest gives way to **alpine scrub** of small shrubs such as *pūkiawe* and *'ōhelo.* Near the peaks even these plants are unable to withstand the lack of moisture, the rocky terrain with little soil, and the freezing wintertime temperatures. Plant life near these summits is limited to mosses, lichens, and a few hardy grasses.

It's a Thorny Issue.   Visitors to Hawai'i often hear that Hawaiian plants have lost their thorns and prickles because they never had to protect themselves from big grazing animals. The story has some truth to it. However, you will still need to be cautious, because there are plenty of thorns on some introduced plants. The widespread *kiawe* is a very good example, and it can grow right down to the beach, where you will be barefoot.

Some endemic plants do have thorns or prickles, perhaps because these plants just haven't yet had sufficient time evolving in Hawaii's isolation to lose their defenses. The *wiliwili* has thorns, and there is a prickly endemic poppy, the *pua kala* (*kala* means "spiny"). The *pua kala* has retained other defenses, too. It contains at least three narcotic agents including morphine. It also contains poisons, so don't be tempted to sample it. Finally, the Hawaiian raspberry, *'ākala,* has thorns, but they are sometimes soft to the touch; this plant seems to be in the process of letting down its defenses. There are Big Island field trips that will lead you to all three of these plants.

One thorny group of plants has puzzled botanists. The endemic genus *Cyanea* has apparently been in Hawai'i for a long time—long enough for at least seventy-three species of *Cyanea* plant species to evolve. About twenty of them, collectively known in Hawaiian as *hāhā*, share an odd trait. The young plants have prickles while they are growing, but for the most part the tops of the mature plants lack prickles on growth over three feet high. A possible explanation came to light when biologists discovered the remains of extinct flightless ducks and geese on most of the main islands (more about them in chapter 12). When the skeletons were reconstructed, it turned out that these browsing geese could reach and eat tender leaves only up to a height of about three feet. The *hāhā* still defend themselves against geese that browse no more.

One of the most famous plant groups in Hawai'i grows in this alpine zone: the silverswords. These plants are members of the sunflower family and are apparently descended from a common tarweed from California. These plants have been in Hawai'i about five million years. They are marvels of adaptive radiation, looking nothing like a tarweed or sunflower, and growing in extremely harsh environments. In Hawaiian they are called *'āhinahina,* (gray, silvery, or shining). In the Polynesian belief system, Hina is the goddess of the moon.

Most famous is the silversword that grows on Haleakalā on Maui. A very closely related silversword, perhaps a different subspecies, grows in very small numbers in one isolated patch on Mauna Kea. Another silversword species grows on Mauna Loa. It was long considered extinct until a few were discovered in the 1920s. There is yet another silversword that has evolved to exist in very different conditions, in the high bogs near the summit of Pu'u Kukui on West Maui. Other relatives of the silversword exist on Kaua'i: the *iliau* is a spindly plant, five to ten feet tall, with a tuft of narrow leaves at the top.

Silversword plants live for perhaps twenty years as a basketball-sized clump of narrow, hairy, silver leaves before they send up a flower stalk three feet high or more, with hundreds of individual flowers. And then they die. That is, if they live that long. Introduced goats are quite at home in the high, rocky regions where silverswords grow. If you're a goat, silversword plants apparently taste a lot like ice cream. That's why the silverswords on Haleakalā are uncommon and exist only within the fenced national park, why the Mauna Kea silverswords that once encircled the great mountain now cling to life in one tiny patch, and why the Mauna Loa plants were thought to be

FIGURE 4.9 The Mauna Loa silversword is less famous than its Haleakalā relative. You can see this silversword growing near the top of Mauna Loa Road on the Big Island. (Rick Soehren)

extinct until a few populations were discovered in remote places that even goats couldn't reach. Now these plants face a new threat: climate change. (See chapter 13.)

This virtual trip across the Hawaiian countryside has highlighted a handful of plants. However, we've really only scratched the surface; Hawai'i has over nine hundred endemic plant species. You could spend a long time mastering Hawaiian botany.

FIELD TRIP!

4.1 BIG ISLAND VEGETATION ZONE DRIVING TOUR. A drive over the Saddle Road from Hilo to Kailua-Kona will give you views of most of the vegetation zones in this chapter, and there's a lot of geology, archaeology, and wildlife viewing on the same route. You will pass through some isolated country with no services, so be sure to have a full tank of gas and bring plenty of drinking water and maybe a picnic lunch. Starting in Hilo near the mouth of the Wailuku River, take Waiānuenue Avenue *mauka*. A stop at Rainbow Falls along the river will give you a taste of lowland rain forest. From this park, backtrack a bit and head up Kaūmana Drive. You can make a stop at Kaūmana Cave near mile marker 4 on this route. (See the **Field Trip!** in chapter 2). Around the mouth of the lava tube there are some introduced plants, but much of the forest here is native *'ōhi'a* and *hāpu'u* fern.

A little farther up the hill, Kaūmana Drive intersects the main Saddle Road, Highway 200 at mile 6 on the Saddle Road. Continue *mauka* (right turn). As you leave the suburbs of Hilo you enter public forest reserve land. This stretch of the highway is in the rainiest elevation on the island, and you'd expect to see dense, ancient rain forest. Instead, there is a fairly open forest of small *'ōhi'a* and dense *uluhe* fern. Much of this area was covered in fresh lava by the eruption of 1855. On the dry side of the island, a lava flow of this age would be pretty barren. Here, it is well on its way to rain forest.

At mile point 22.4 there is a sign for the Pu'u 'Ō'ō Trail and a small rocky turnout. Along this trail you can cross the lava flows of 1855 and 1881, mostly over *pāhoehoe,* pass through some *kīpuka,* and see native forest birds. At this elevation, about 5,700 feet, you are well above the wettest zone. There are more *koa* trees here because it is a bit less wet. There is even a patch of the Hawaiian raspberry, *'ākala.*

(See **Field Trip!** in chapter 5 for complete information on the Puʻu ʻŌʻō Trail.)

Back on the Saddle Road, you can get a close-up view of a cinder cone at Puʻu Huluhulu. This vegetated cinder cone is on the south side of the Saddle Road at the intersection of the Saddle Road and Mauna Kea Road to the north and Mauna Loa Road to the south. The cinder cone is a post-shield eruption of Mauna Kea that was subsequently surrounded by flows from Mauna Loa in 1843, 1855, 1899, and 1935. Thus, it is a *kīpuka.* Part of the cone has been mined for gravel but the remaining hill contains older, well-developed soil with mature *koa* trees and a mixed understory of native plants and introduced grasses and pests such as German ivy (a vine with shiny dark green leaves). The hill is fenced to protect native plants from marauding feral goats and sheep. Notice the taller grass inside the fence, and the putting-green length grass outside. This will give you an idea of the impact of these hungry aliens. This *kīpuka* is a good place to see the native Hawaiian poppy, *pua kala,* with its prickly gray leaves and papery white blooms.

There is a parking lot, informational signs, and a hunter check station at the foot of Puʻu Huluhulu. Sometimes there is a supply of trail brochures. There are short steep trails to the top of the hill, elevation 6,758 feet. (The trail brochure describes a lot of birds and it is wildly optimistic; at this *kīpuka* you will never see all the endemic birds it lists. The Puʻu ʻŌʻō Trail is a much better birding spot.)

From the top of Puʻu Huluhulu, there are splendid views of the saddle area. There are also good views from the roadside. Mauna Loa is on the same side of the highway as Puʻu Huluhulu. Notice a lot of relatively fresh lava flows, interspersed with older areas that support dry forest. Near the parking lot, you can see a graphic demonstration of how young these flows are: from outside the gate to the *kīpuka* walk west (toward Kona) along the fence about a hundred yards. You can see a stone wall built in the late nineteenth century that has been mostly covered by the lava flow of 1935.

Across the highway, the lower slopes of Mauna Kea are mostly pasture. This area was probably mesic to dry open forest before a couple of centuries of grazing obliterated most of the trees. Many of the hills in this area are actually cinder cones. To get a good view of them, drive up Mauna Kea Road toward the Onizuka Center for International Astronomy into an area of alpine scrub. From a higher elevation, look

FIGURE 4.10 The endemic Hawaiian poppy *pua kala* still retains toxins for defense. Photographed at Puʻu Huluhulu on the Big Island. (Rick Soehren)

back into the saddle, littered with cinder cones. They are on both sides of Mauna Kea Road, and along the Saddle Road to the west. There are more on the northeast flank of Mauna Kea near the town of Waimea. Behind the Onizuka Center is a small fenced area where you can get a close-up look at Mauna Kea silversword. The Onizuka Center is also a great place for stargazing. (See chapter 11.)

Continuing on the Saddle Road to the Mauna Kea State Recreation Area, at mile marker 34 you will find restrooms and picnic tables. The elevation here is about 6,400 feet. Look up at the slopes of Mauna Kea just behind the recreation area to see one of the most unexpected sights in Hawaiʻi: evidence of glaciers. After miles of *pāhoehoe* and *ʻaʻā*, you may start to think that volcanoes have been the exclusive shapers of this geologic landscape. But during the last ice age, Mauna Kea had glaciers, and the evidence of their presence is still visible today. In Pōhakuloa Gulch above the recreation area there is gravelly rock that is more gray than the rest of the reddish slopes of the mountain. From this vantage point the gray material appears to be on top of the mountain, but it is not. These are glacial moraines, piles of gravel that have been ground and scrubbed beneath, and in front of, a slowly advancing glacier. A moraine is the classic signature of a glacier's current or former presence. And remember that Mauna Kea was still active when some of these glaciers existed.

The medieval sword makers of Toledo in Spain discovered the process of ice hardening. They would plunge a red-hot newly forged sword blade into ice water. Often the blade would crack and be ruined. But when it withstood the temperature shock, it hardened into the world's finest steel. There was no steel in ancient Hawai'i, but lava erupting into snow or massive glaciers underwent a similar hardening. This dense ice-hardened basalt was the best material the ancient Hawaiians had for making blades such as adze heads. One of the most famous ancient adze quarries in the islands is near the summit of Mauna Kea.

At Mauna Kea State Recreation Area the wind varies considerably in strength and direction throughout the day. In the morning it is usually calm. By early afternoon there is warm air rising from the sunny Kona coast—convective uplift—and the wind can be howling in this area. (That same rising air brings summer afternoon showers to Kona.) By dusk things have equalized and it is calm again. During the evening the cooling air sinks and the winds reverse direction, usually blowing more gently than during the day.

Don't be alarmed if you see army tanks rolling across the countryside or fighter jets dropping live bombs. South of the highway is the Pōhakuloa Training Area, a military reservation larger than the island of Lāna'i. Obviously, this area is closed to the public.

Continuing your drive along Highway 200 you will climb a little more to the summit of the Saddle Road, 6,632 feet, then descend rather quickly. Rainfall near the recreation area is only about twenty inches per year, and below you near Waikoloa on the coast it is about ten inches. By the time you descend to the Hawai'i Belt Road, Highway 190, you will be in very dry country. As you head downhill to the left toward Kailua-Kona on the Belt Road you will be on the leeward slope of 8,271-foot Hualālai and will encounter more moisture and greener vegetation, even outside irrigated areas. This is the result of the convective uplift discussed earlier. You can make a stop in dry forest at Pu'u Wa'awa'a. (See the **Field Trip!** in chapter 9.)

Ideally we would end our Big Island vegetation zone trip in the coastal vegetation zone, but there are few remnants of this zone along the Kona coast. Most undeveloped areas, such as the Kaloko-Honokōhau National Historic Park, support a lot of introduced *kiawe* and fountain grass. Native coastal plants are uncommon. One good place to see some is Puʻuhonua o Hōnaunau National Historic Park. (See chapter 8.)

4.2 Endemic Plants in Hawaiʻi Volcanoes National Park.

The main attraction in this national park is the erupting volcano. Elsewhere in the park there are lots of other fascinating things to see and you will have these areas of the park almost to yourself. Most of the sights on this field trip are along Mauna Loa Road, *mauka* of Highway 11 about two miles west of the park entrance. Kīlauea Caldera and most of the volcanic sights are *makai* of the highway.

The first stopping point on Mauna Loa Road is a side road just off the main highway, leading to a cluster of tree molds. They look like holes in the ground, but they are very special holes. They formed when lava surrounded big trees and hardened before the tree trunks incinerated. The results are molds of the tree trunks that once stood here. Note how big some of these trunks were—several feet in diameter. They were most likely *ʻōhiʻa* trees, far larger than any growing in the area now.

The next stop is about 1.5 miles up Mauna Loa Road at Kīpuka Puaulu, a forest *kīpuka* undergoing restoration. There is a 1.2-mile unpaved loop trail through the *kīpuka.* At the trailhead there is usually a supply of $2 trail guidebooks (twenty-six pages, full color) for sale with an honor-system cash box. The trail guide is so worthwhile that you should buy one in advance at the bookstore inside the park Visitor Center to make sure you have one. It will add a lot to your *kīpuka* visit. Along the path through the *kīpuka,* many native plants are labeled. Another species you are likely to encounter along this trail is the Kalij pheasant, a black or gray chicken-like bird with a big V-shaped tail. Sixty-seven of these birds, a native of central Asia, were introduced on the Big Island in 1962. They are now widespread.

You may notice that it isn't nearly as lush and green here as it is nearby around the town of Volcano, or near the Visitor Center in the national park. You are in a mesic forest, the transition between the rain forest vegetation zone below and the cool dry forest zone above.

After your stroll through Kīpuka Puaulu, continue up Mauna Loa Road. (Note: the road is sometimes closed beyond the *kīpuka* due to high fire danger.) The paved road climbs another 9.5 miles to the

Mauna Loa Lookout at 6,662 feet. It is very narrow and winding, so allot forty-five minutes for the drive to the top.

There aren't very many places where you can pull off the road, but you can at Kīpuka Kī, about 1.5 miles past Kīpuka Puaulu. A sign will let you know when you're there. At Kīpuka Kī you will be surrounded by *koa* forest. The understory plants beneath the big trees are not dense, so it is fairly easy to stroll among the *koa* trees. You are definitely in the cool dry forest zone now. Listen and watch for the *'elepaio,* a tiny endemic bird with reddish brown plumage, a white rump, white wing bars, and a cocked tail. This is a good place to spot them. (See figure 5.4.)

At the end of a long slow drive to the top of the road there are several rewards. You can hike the trail up Mauna Loa; it is only twenty miles and an elevation gain of seven thousand feet to the top. You can enjoy the view of distant smoking Halemaʻumaʻu Crater from the little stone pavilion. But the prize for plant lovers is just fifty yards from the end of the road along a rocky trail: a cluster of Mauna Loa silverswords. These plants are the descendants of a handful of survivors that existed at two remote sites in the 1990s. Since then volunteers and park staff have built fenced exclosures to keep hungry goats out and have propagated seedlings. Each plant lives roughly ten to twenty years. It will bloom once, sending up a flower stalk three to nine feet tall, and then the plant dies.

This concludes our trip up Mauna Loa Road, but there is more interesting plant life to see within Hawaiʻi Volcanoes National Park. The area between the Visitor Center and Thurston Lava Tube is a lush fern forest. The crater rim trail between Thurston Lava Tube and the Kīlauea Iki trailhead is a short easy stroll offering great views of the *'ōhiʻa* fern forest on one side, and Kīlauea Iki crater on the other. Finally, a drive down Chain of Craters Road and out narrow paved Hilina Pali Road will take you into fairly intact dry forest. This is also a good area to look for *nēnē.* (See figure 5.9.)

4.3 EAT AN ENDEMIC PLANT. High-elevation wet areas in Hawaiʻi Volcanoes National Park are home to the *'ōhelo,* an endemic shrub related to blueberries and cranberries. (Another endemic *'ōhelo* species occurs on Haleakalā, Maui.) You will see these shrubs around Kīlauea Caldera. They have oval leaves with finely toothed edges, tiny bell-shaped flowers in spring, and edible red or sometimes yellow berries from summer to winter. The berry, about a third of an inch in diameter, has a

FIGURE 4.11 *ʻŌhelo* berries are tart but edible. The little crown shape at the tip of the berry will help you identify them. (Rick Soehren)

crown-shaped structure at the end that can help confirm that you've got the right edible fruit. It is legal to pick up to a quart of berries per month for personal use in the national park, although seasonal closures on collecting berries may be established at park discretion to protect a food source for foraging *nēnē*, the Hawaiian goose. The berries are an important food source for these birds. If there is not a closure, eat a few and leave the rest for the birds. Don't confuse it with *pūkiawe*, a different endemic berry with prickly leaves often found near *ʻōhelo*. *Nēnē* like both berries, but people don't find *pūkiawe* palatable.

The *ʻōhelo* played an important role in ending the traditional Hawaiian *kapu* system of cultural or religious prohibitions. The system was first openly defied by Queen Kaʻahumanu in 1819 shortly after the death of King Kamehameha I, when she persuaded her son to eat with women, which was then a forbidden act. When angry gods did not strike him dead, some people began to question the *kapu* system, but others were too faithful or too afraid to violate its strictures. In 1824 High Chiefess Kapiʻolani, a converted Christian who would later become queen, traveled to Kīlauea to defy the goddess Pele and affirm her faith in a different god. *ʻŌhelo* was a plant sacred to Pele, and anyone who

FIGURE 4.12 *Pūkiawe* is a common endemic shrub and a food source for *nēnē*. (Rick Soehren)

wanted to eat the berries had to first throw some into the volcano as an offering, but not Kapi'olani. She threw stones into the crater instead, ate *'ōhelo* berries, and did not seem to incur Pele's wrath. Her actions shook the faith of many who still adhered to the *kapu* system, and accelerated the adoption of Christianity in the islands. (There is more information about Hawaiian culture and *kapu* in chapter 8.)

Around the town of Volcano, making *'ōhelo* berry jam is something of a cottage industry. The jam is seldom available outside of a few shops in Volcano Village, so look for it there during your visit.

4.4 A SILVERSWORD RELATIVE ON KAUA'I. The silversword relative on Kaua'i is called the *iliau* and it doesn't look anything like the other silverswords. It is tall, skinny, and green. A good place to see this plant and other endemics is the Iliau Nature Loop, a short 0.3-mile easy loop around an open flat area with many *iliau*. Several of the native plants along the trail are labeled. The trailhead is about 0.75 mile after the second 8-mile marker (there are two in a row as this goes to press) on Kōke'e Road. There is a paved turnout that can hold two or three cars on the roadside away from the canyon; the trail is on the canyon side.

Be careful crossing the road because drivers are paying attention to the scenery, not you.

There's another place in the area where you can see a few *iliau*, near the junction of Waimea Canyon Drive and Kekaha Road. Park off the road at the junction, walk down Waimea Canyon Drive about one hundred yards, and hike across eroding red dirt about fifty yards into the point of land between the two roads (away from the canyon). There are several *iliau* growing in this spot. And there's a really nice view of the island of Ni'ihau, too.

Botanical Gardens. Hawai'i is home to many unique endemic plants, and many of these plants are now rare in the wild. So you would hope and expect that there would be plenty of great botanical gardens where you could see these unique plant species. Sadly, this is not the case. There are some stunning botanical gardens that showcase tropical plants from around the world, but there are very few that do a good job of protecting, propagating, and displaying rare Hawaiian plants. Some of them also feature canoe plants, the couple of dozen plant species that voyaging Polynesians brought with them to Hawai'i. Here are a few gardens that are worth a visit.

4.5 KOKO CRATER BOTANICAL GARDEN, O'AHU. The City and County of Honolulu maintains several botanical gardens, including the manicured Foster Garden downtown, sprawling Ho'omaluhia Garden on the windward side, and Wahiawa Garden in the arid center of O'ahu. If you are interested in native plants, the garden in Koko Crater (a little past Hanauma Bay if you are coming from Honolulu) is by far the best one to visit. It isn't exclusively dedicated to native plants; you enter through an enchanting grove of plumeria trees with their fragrant five-petal blossoms. Other sections showcase plants of Africa and Madagascar. But there is a big section devoted to native plants including an extensive collection of *loulu* palms, *wiliwili* trees, *pili* grass that the Hawaiians used to cover their houses, endemic hibiscus, and more. The garden is almost never crowded. In fact, it is so lonely here that they have to post a guard to keep people from stealing the plants. Paths are unpaved and covered in mulch. Admission is free. It gets warm and sunny here, with only patches of shade, so early morning is the most comfortable time to visit.

To reach the garden from Honolulu, take the Kalaniana'ole

Highway, Route 72, east past Hanauma Bay. Turn *mauka* at the stop light on Kealahou Street, then left again on Kokonani. Follow this road past the stables to the end where there is a dirt parking area at the garden entrance.

The garden is located in a rejuvenation stage tuff cone usually called Koko Crater. Its old name is Kohelepelepe, and if you are reading this aloud to the children, this would be a very good time to send them into another room. You see, Kohelepelepe translates to "flying fringed vagina," and of course there's a legend behind it. Once upon a time Pele was lounging on the Big Island when the pig god Kamapua'a made unwelcome advances. Pele's sister Kapo decided to help, and Kapo had a most unusual ability, even for a deity: she had a flying vagina that she could send anywhere. She sent her vagina flying off to lure Kamapua'a away from Pele. The vagina flew to O'ahu, where it landed at Koko Crater, making the vaguely suggestive crater imprint that exists to this day.

4.6 LYON ARBORETUM, O'AHU. One of the most popular hikes on O'ahu is the relatively short hike to Mānoa Falls. The out-and-back distance is 1.6 miles, with an elevation gain of 800 feet. The trail passes through lush rain forest, although most of the plants are introduced species. You are rewarded at the end of the trail with close-up views of Mānoa Falls, streaming 160 feet down a lava face. Parts of the trail can be very slippery when wet, and it is usually wet; this area gets about 165 inches of rain per year. Bring your walking stick and your mud shoes.

What does this have to do with Lyon Arboretum? After visiting Mānoa Falls with its crowds of tourists and locals, get ready for some forest serenity. You can find it right next door at the University of Hawai'i Lyon Arboretum. The origins of the arboretum are a reflection of Hawai'i's environmental struggles. Back in 1919 sugar planters whose fields surrounded Honolulu were worried. Rampant feral goats and sheep, with a few cattle and horses thrown in for good measure, had denuded the hills above Honolulu. The forest sponge that held much of the runoff had been gnawed away by feral animals. The planters were worried about erosion, and even more about loss of their water supply. They employed Harold Lyon, a forester, to fix things. Lyon planted an experimental forest of tropical trees that ultimately became Lyon Arboretum. Some of his botanical choices were innocuous enough.

Others, like Albizia, have become forest pests or worse. His legacy was a lush wonderland of tropical plantings that is today known as Lyon Arboretum.

There is a requested donation of $5 per party, which allows you to park for free. You will be given a trail map of the 193-acre grounds. Keep in mind that some of the trails are mostly in the mind of the mapmaker; stay on the main routes or you may find yourself wandering and looking for civilization. The section devoted to native Hawaiian plants is disappointing, but the collection of canoe plants is very good, with a smartphone narration system. As a bonus, the arboretum is inhabited by a wonderful variety of birds including endemic ʻamakihi and three species of cockatoo. The cockatoos escaped (or were released by disgruntled keepers) when a small aviary/tourist attraction next door went out of business in 1994. Cockatoos are rather long-lived, but these birds may not be the original escapees: there are pairs that inhabit nest cavities in the big trees of the arboretum.

The arboretum and the Mānoa Falls trailhead are at the upper end of Mānoa Valley. To reach the area, take Punahou Street *mauka* from the H1 freeway or the city center. Punahou splits into Mānoa Road and East Mānoa; keep left on Mānoa. When you get to the confusing five-way intersection, stay on Mānoa and follow it to the top of the valley. Parking at the Mānoa Falls trailhead is limited to a relatively small private lot, where parking will cost you $5. To reach Lyon Arboretum, drive past the private parking lot and follow the signs. There is no Mānoa Falls trail parking at the arboretum. Bring insect repellent.

4.7 MAUI NUI BOTANICAL GARDENS, MAUI. This garden seems to have a lot going against it: an obscure location in Kahului; parking limited to the street, where there are no curbs or gutters; an odd facility that used to be a zoo (the weird little structures around the grounds are the remains of animal cages); and tenuous finances. What does it have? a hard-working staff, a dedicated group of volunteers who help with maintenance and propagation (they call themselves the Weed and Pot Club), and a location in the coastal vegetation zone where some of Hawaiʻi's rarest plants once grew. The result is a tidy little garden that offers the best collection of rare coastal and dry land plants anywhere. For people who want to see the nearly vanished plants that once blanketed lowland Hawaiʻi, this gem of a garden is the place to

FIGURE 4.13 Several species of *loulu* palm are Hawai'i's only native palm trees. These are at Maui Nui Botanical Gardens. (Rick Soehren)

come. They also maintain collections of virtually all known varieties of several canoe plants including *kalo* or taro (more than sixty Hawaiian varieties), bananas or *mai'a* (more than a dozen), sugarcane or *kō* (about twenty varieties), and *'awa* or *kava* (a dozen varieties). There is a modest admission fee, which includes a great full-color brochure with photos and identification information for nearly all the plants in their collection. Most of the paths through the garden are paved. For native plant lovers, this is one of the best gardens in the state. It is located at 150 Kanaloa Avenue in Kahului.

4.8 MCBRYDE AND LIMAHULI GARDENS, KAUA'I. The National Tropical Botanical Garden (NTBG) is an organization hampered by a misleading name. It was chartered by the U.S. Congress for tropical plant research, conservation, and education. But it is not an agency of the government and it can't rely on the steady funding of a government agency. Like other nonprofit organizations it relies on donations to support its important work. NTBG operates two public gardens featuring native plants on Kaua'i: McBryde on the arid south side of the island near Po'ipū and Limahuli near the end of the road on the lush north side. Both are extremely well-maintained gardens where you can see and learn about endemic Hawaiian plants and Polynesian canoe plants.

McBryde Garden has canoe plants paired with excellent interpretive signs and an extensive collection of native plants. There is also a biodiversity trail and a stream-side path among palms from all over the world. Sometimes volunteers staff a pavilion near the canoe plants, showing how they were used. This is not a showy garden of exotics, but a place to learn about natives and canoe plants in a beautiful setting, the Lāwa'i Valley. Next door is the NTBG Allerton Garden, a more formal setting with tropical plants from around the world. Garden tours depart from the visitor center located on Lāwa'i Road at the west end of Po'ipū. One tour includes a stop at the horticultural center, where rare plants are propagated. Tour reservations must be made in advance, online or by phone.

Limahuli Garden is located on the much wetter north shore, nearly at the end of Highway 56, the Kūhiō Highway. The garden has a section of canoe plants, with informative plant labels and an excellent booklet that is included with the cost of admission. There is also a large section of native plants, including a very ambitious section where the existing forest of introduced invasive trees has been removed and replaced with endemics, including some of the rarest plants on earth and some that are extinct in the wild. A walk through this section is sobering. At Limahuli the setting is the star: the narrow deep Limahuli Valley, with its ancient rock terraces built by Hawaiians to grow *kalo* or taro, surrounded by green crags.

There is an admission fee at the gardens, well worth it for plant lovers. Another unit of the National Tropical Botanical Garden is Kahanu Garden on Maui, described in chapter 8. Due to the steep terrain and unpaved paths, disabled access at all the NTBG facilities is poor.

Indoor Tours of Giant *Koa*. Nearly all the really big *koa* trees were cut for canoe building or, later, by westerners for fine woodwork. You can still marvel at the immense size of some of these trees and appreciate their beauty. You will just be doing it indoors, at museums, fine old buildings, and even tourist hotels. Here are a few places to appreciate *koa* wood products.

FIGURE 4.14 Limahuli Garden on Kaua'i's north shore has endemic plants, canoe plants, ancient *kalo* terraces, and great scenery. (Rick Soehren)

4.9 INDOOR *KOA* IN HONOLULU. 'Iolani Palace in downtown Honolulu was the official residence of Hawaiian royalty for a few short years from its dedication in 1882 until the overthrow of the monarchy in 1893. Then it spent a long inglorious period as a government office building until it was restored to its royal glory in 1978. You can reserve space on a tour, pay your admission, and marvel at *koa* woodwork such as the grand staircase. The downside, ironic in a couple of ways, is that the State of Hawai'i is fiercely protective of this palace of overthrown monarchy and its fine woodwork harvested from disappearing forests. You can't touch anything, and you will be asked to wear cloth booties to protect the wood floor. During your visit to the neighborhood, you can marvel at buildings constructed from coral blocks (see chapter 7) and look for adorable white terns nesting in the big trees on the palace grounds (see chapter 5).

Bishop Museum is just outside downtown Honolulu and is a much more satisfying place to see fine *koa* wood work. The main museum building, completed in 1889, is overflowing with *koa* staircases, paneling, railings, and display cases. And they encourage you to enjoy it,

Hawai'i's Diverse Habitats and Plants   **99**

touch it, run your hand along *koa* railings as visitors have done for over a hundred years—much more satisfying than the cloth bootie tour of the palace. There are a few million other good reasons to visit the Bishop Museum, but more about that in chapter 8.

4.10 INDOOR *KOA* ON THE BIG ISLAND. Hulihe'e Palace on the waterfront in the center of Kailua-Kona is a delightful place to visit, a tranquil respite from the shops and restaurants of the town. It gives visitors a peek into the mind-set of Hawaiian royalty at a time when they were rejecting the cultural (and woodworking) bounty of Hawai'i in favor of western styles and materials. It was built in 1838, not as a palace but as a home for a governor of the island who served royalty. Only later did it fall into the hands of royalty. In the late 1880s King Kalākaua remodeled the place to reflect his idea of appropriate royal surroundings. He removed flooring that was probably *koa* or *'ōhia* and replaced it with western materials. He used Douglas fir from North America—a soft wood that is inferior for flooring—and added purely decorative pillars of North American redwood. There is still some *koa* to be seen, including the staircase and many of the furnishings. The prize is a round dining table, seventy inches in diameter, with a tabletop made from a single plank of *koa* heartwood. Allowing for some sapwood outside the heart of the tree and a layer of bark, the living tree probably had a diameter of roughly eight feet.

After your visit to Hulihe'e Palace, stroll down to **King Kamehameha's Hotel** on the other side of the Kailua Pier. In the concourse adjoining the lobby you can marvel at the *Māhoe*, an outrigger racing canoe carved from a single *koa* log. Perhaps surprisingly, the canoe is not that old. The log was cut in 1976 on a private ranch on the flanks of Mt. Hualālai, which rises just behind the town. And here's the most amazing part: *māhoe* means "twin" in Hawaiian. A single log was big enough to make two identical canoes. The other one is in Tahiti.

Another Big Island location with fine *koa* and *'ōhi'a* woodwork is the **Mokupāpapa Discovery Center** in Hilo. (See chapter 12.)

There are a few other spots where native plants are protected and thrive. Two of these, **Ka'ena Point** on O'ahu and the **Waikamoi Preserve** on Maui, are described in chapter 5 because their biggest draw is birdlife. There are two Nature Conservancy preserves on Moloka'i that protect coastal plants and rain forest plants. They can be visited by guided tour one day each month, and the tours tend to fill up months in advance. Contact the Nature Conservancy Hawai'i for details.

LEARN MORE

- H. Douglas Pratt, *A Pocket Guide to Hawaii's Trees and Shrubs* (Honolulu: Mutual Publishing, 1998). Don't let the small size of this book fool you. It is remarkably complete and will help you identify many of the trees and shrubs you encounter in various vegetation zones. The text is narrative rather than a species-by-species account.
- Robert J. Gustafson, Derral R. Herbst, and Phillip W. Rundel, *Hawaiian Plant Life: Vegetation and Flora* (Honolulu: University of Hawai'i Press, 2014). Beautifully illustrated with 875 color photos, this book contains detailed descriptions of nearly two-thirds of Hawai'i's native plants. At 336 pages you won't carry it into the field, but will enjoy it as a wonderful reference.
- John B. Hall, *A Hiker's Guide to Trailside Plants in Hawai'i* (Honolulu: Mutual Publishing, 2004). This is a small book packed with information. Species descriptions are organized by vegetation zone.
- Michael Walther, *A Guide to Hawai'i's Coastal Plants* (Honolulu: Mutual Publishing, 2004). Lots of color photographs and information on good places to see native plants.
- Angela Kay Kepler, *Hawaiian Heritage Plants* (Honolulu: University of Hawai'i Press, 1998). A very readable account of the ethnobotanical uses of over thirty endemics and canoe plants.
- Donald R. Hodel, *Loulu: The Hawaiian Palm* (Honolulu: University of Hawai'i Press, 2012). Want to know about the endemic palms of Hawai'i? This is the book for you. Very readable, written by a palm lover, not a professional botanist.
- Katie Cassel, *Nā Pua o Kōke'e: Field Guide to the Native Flowering Plants of Northwestern Kaua'i* (CreateSpace Independent Publishing Platform, 2010). The profusion of plants in the rain forest at Kōke'e State Park on Kaua'i can be bewildering. This little book with color photographs of over seventy-five plants can help you identify at least some of the wonderful plants of the high-elevation rain forest. Available for purchase at the Kōke'e Museum.

5   Original Owners

Hawaiian Birds and Other Unique Creatures

The morning is clear. The thin mountain air is clean, perfumed with recent rain and the scent of a Hawaiian forest. As you hike among lush *kīpuka* filled with *'ōhi'a* and *koa* trees, Mauna Kea lies behind you, Mauna Loa looms ahead. The *'ōhi'a* trees are in bloom, red *lehua* blossoms bright against dark green foliage. And then you see a flash of red-orange among the red blossoms: an *'i'iwi,* one of the most beautiful of the endemic Hawaiian honeycreepers.

If you want to see amazing birds that are the product of extreme isolation and adaptive radiation, Hawai'i is the best place in the world to be. There's other extraordinary wildlife in the islands, for sure: humpback whales in the winter, or Hawaiian reef fish. But the birds are in a class by themselves.

What makes the endemic birds of Hawai'i so special? There are other places in the world where the whales and reef fish are just as stunning. And yes, there are other islands where isolation and time have resulted in amazing birdlife. The extinct dodo of Mauritius is an example; New Zealand's fuzzy flightless kiwi still survives; the finches of the Galápagos are famous. But Hawai'i still harbors endemic bird species that are remarkably diverse and—in a few cases—still fairly common, species whose ancestors have dwelled in Hawaiian forests for five million years. The profound and lengthy isolation, the extreme extent of adaptive radiation, and the ease of viewing put Hawaiian birds in a class all by themselves.

You don't have to go too far afield to see native birds—a high-elevation Big Island hike in the "saddle" area between Mauna Kea and Mauna Loa is an easy drive from either Hilo or Kona. And depending on the island and location where you're looking for birds, you might

encounter some other phenomenal examples of endemic life: giant dragonflies, iconic butterflies, incomprehensibly tiny land snails, even a bat—
all creatures that evolved in Hawai'i and occur nowhere else in the world.
Their stories tell of isolation, evolution, and adaptive radiation. Sadly,
they also chronicle habitat loss, pressure from introduced creatures, and
even extinction. We will get to the bad news in later chapters. For now,
let's take a look at the creatures that were Hawai'i's original owners.

BIRDS

In Hawai'i you can see some of the rarest and most amazing birds on
earth. That doesn't mean that every bird you see is a product of eons
of island adaptive radiation. Just as most of the plants you see in lowland areas are introduced, so are most of the birds you see in lowland
areas or around inhabited places. In fact, among the bird species you
can find in Hawai'i about half are ones that humans have brought from
somewhere else. This includes the ubiquitous mynas, the tame little
zebra doves that seem more numerous than people in Hawaiian towns,
and a host of others. These introduced species account for almost all
bird sightings because these are the birds that hang around our homes,
parks, and developed places.

Still, it is relatively easy to see native bird species that got here on
their own or are descended from the birds that arrived millions of years
ago. Just head for the places that Hawaiian birds call home. All you need
is a pair of decent binoculars, the trail essentials listed in chapter 1,
maybe a field guide from the **Learn More** list in this chapter, and you're
ready to go.

Well, not quite ready. First you have to decide which birds you
want to seek out. Endemic forest birds such as honeycreepers? Sea birds
that come to land mostly to breed? Or migratory birds that make the
journey of a lifetime and do it twice a year like clockwork?

Let's start with the birds that are generally called *endemic forest birds.* This is a catchall term used to refer to many small species
of endemic birds that generally dwell in relatively undisturbed forest
or woodland, usually at elevations above a few thousand feet. Many of
them are descended from the Eurasian rosy finches described in chapter 3. These birds have evolved in isolation for roughly five million years
and have become radically different from their rosy finch ancestors, and

Life Lists.   Many birders keep track of all the bird species they've seen. It is called their life list. Usually, an avid birder will subdivide this list: birds seen in North America, birds seen in a single big year, birds seen from home. These lists can be long. The most intrepid (and wealthy) birders travel the globe and accumulate lists of over 8,000 species seen or heard, out of perhaps a little more than 10,000 bird species in the world. A few birders scouring the lower 48 states have seen more than 800 of the 900 or so North American bird species.

In Hawai'i it's a different story. The number of different bird species to be seen is not huge—experienced birders on the mainland can see more species in a day than many Hawaiian birders see in a lifetime in the islands. The record for Hawai'i is 234 bird species seen or heard in a lifetime (out of a total of 317 species recorded in the islands), yet avid birders in California have seen 231 species in a single long day of birding! The total of 317 species needs a bit of explanation. It does not mean there are 317 species lounging around waiting to be counted on any given day. In some cases, a single hapless wayward bird from a far-off place makes landfall, birders from all over the islands dash to see it, and after a week, a day, or maybe just a few hours, it is gone. Quite a few other bird species on the list have not been seen in years or decades, and are likely gone forever. For the birds that breed in the main Hawaiian islands, make regular migratory visits, or just show up fairly frequently, the species total is a little over 100. Most of these birds are introduced, or are migratory winter visitors. Whittle the list down to endemic birds, and there are fewer than 20 species that you might be able to see. But they are amazing, and they draw birders from all over the world.

some, from each other. There are about sixteen species surviving today; when the first humans arrived in Hawai'i there were many more. These birds are called Hawaiian honeycreepers. Some of the most common species among them are indeed nectar feeders, but others have evolved to fill other ecological niches, feeding on seeds or insects instead.

Other pioneering birds gave rise to their own unique lines of endemic Hawaiian forest birds. At some point in the distant past, some thrushes made it to Hawai'i. They evolved into a handful of unique island thrush species. One of them, the 'ōma'o, is still common enough to be seen fairly easily if you know where to look. Birders from anywhere in North America will probably recognize it as a relative of the American robin. Another, the endemic 'elepaio, is a flycatcher whose ancestors probably journeyed from the islands of Polynesia a couple of million years ago.

The **Field Trip!** section will describe specific spots on several islands where you can look for these endemics. For now, we'll consider the forces that affect these birds' survival and dictate the ranges where they still occur.

Finding endemic birds wasn't always such a challenge. When the first humans arrived, these unique species were literally all over the place. But five million years without a whole lot of competition or predation tends to make species very vulnerable to outside forces like introduced competitors and predators, habitat modification, and disease. Today, our only clues to the former ranges of these birds are ancient bird bones deposited before the first humans arrived. Since human arrival, it has been one long story of retreat for Hawaiian endemics.

When early Hawaiians cleared land for their farms, the birds had to retreat. Polynesian rats that accompanied the first Hawaiians ate bird eggs and chicks, reducing safe nesting territory. Westerners introduced cattle, sheep, and goats that ate their way through a lot of the remaining habitat. Newcomers brought new bird species that competed with the endemics. But worst of all, the introduced birds carried bird diseases such as avian malaria and pox. The introduced tropical mosquito served as a vector or host, biting endemic birds and infecting them with diseases to which they had no immunity. Endemic birds survived mostly in high-altitude strongholds above the range of the mosquitoes.

Add it all up, and what home is left for endemic birds is relatively undisturbed natural areas that are high enough in elevation (generally 4,500 feet or so) to be above the range of tropical mosquitoes. Now take another look at the elevation figures in Table 2.1. Moloka'i, Lāna'i, and Kaho'olawe are too low to have any appreciable mosquito-free zones. O'ahu has limited areas near the tops of the Ko'olau Range and Mt. Ka'ala in the Wai'anae Range. Kaua'i is right on the cusp, with mosquitoes now entering the vast, flat Alaka'i Swamp that had been a stronghold for endemic birds. Only Maui and the Big Island have good-sized areas above the mosquito zone.

If you're planning a trip to see endemic Hawaiian forest birds, there are other considerations, too. On Kaua'i, the gateway to public areas where endemics might be seen is Koke'e State Park at the top of Waimea Canyon. Many of the forest roads are unpaved and rugged. In winter (the wetter part of a year-round wet season) the trails can be muddy, slippery, and unpleasant. Maui has vast forest tracts filled with some of the rarest birds on earth. Most of these areas are closed to the public, or access is strictly controlled. Birding opportunities are limited, and advance planning is key. On Oʻahu the endemic forest birds survive in very low numbers. But the good news is that the mountain trails where you might see them are generally well maintained and readily accessible from Honolulu.

What's the fail-safe option for seeing the most endemic birds and the greatest number of species? Head for the Big Island, where national parks and forest reserves with plenty of trails offer great birding, plus less-accessible areas where birding tours can help you see other species.

Four of the endemic forest birds you are most likely to see are *ʻapapane, ʻamakihi, ʻiʻiwi,* and *ʻelepaio.* Other endemics are rarer, and often dwell in less-accessible spots. If you spend more time in the forest or hire an experienced guide, there are at least half a dozen others on the Big Island, Maui, and Kauaʻi that you have a reasonable chance of seeing.

ʻApapane. This flashy crimson honeycreeper with black bill, wings, and tail is the most abundant, most widespread, and easiest to see

FIGURE 5.1 The *ʻapapane* is common on Kauaʻi, Maui, and the Big Island. (Jim Denny)

of all the Hawaiian endemic forest birds. It is a nectar feeder, its primary food source the *lehua* blossom of the *ʻōhiʻa* tree. It is medium-sized for a honeycreeper, about five inches in length. It lives on all six main Hawaiian islands that have forested areas meeting its environmental needs, absent only from Niʻihau and Kahoʻolawe. The presence of *ʻapapane* on six islands doesn't mean they are easy to see on all six. In fact, it is challenging to see one on Lānaʻi or Molokaʻi, and you need a bit of luck to spot one along forested mountain trails on Oʻahu. If you go to the right birding spots, you can depend on seeing this species on the Big Island, Maui, and Kauaʻi. Generally they are found above the mosquito zone, although they are sometimes spotted at lower elevations.

ʻAmakihi. Not a single species, but related species on different islands. These smallish (4.5-inch) honeycreepers are yellow-green. They have a dark bill, dark eyes, and a dark patch between the eye and bill (the area called the lore) giving the appearance of a little black mask. The *ʻamakihi* are more generalist in their diet than the *ʻapapane,* feeding on nectar, insects, and fruits. The *ʻamakihi* will even feed on nectar and fruit from introduced plants, a habit that sometimes draws them down into urban areas. Fortunately for these birds that venture into low elevations, the species seems to have some immunity to mosquito-borne diseases that are deadly to some other honeycreepers.

The *ʻamakihi* are birds in the midst of island-fueled adaptive radiation. Early explorers noted the presence of *ʻamakihi* throughout the main islands from Kauaʻi down to the Big Island. It didn't take long for naturalists to notice that the birds on Kauaʻi were different from those on other islands, with longer, thicker bills. By the late 1800s the Kauaʻi birds were considered a separate species of *ʻamakihi.* Subtle differences distinguish the *ʻamakihi* on other islands, too. This has caused perpetual squabbles among taxonomists and ornithologists: how many species of *ʻamakihi* are there? How many subspecies? What genus name should we give them? The Bishop Museum calls the whole business "tortured."

ʻAmakihi are second in abundance only to *ʻapapane* so they are pretty easy to find. The Kauaʻi *ʻamakihi* can be found in the wet forest around Kokeʻe as well as lower, drier forests nearby. The Oʻahu *ʻamakihi* is a little more difficult to spot, but you might see one along forest trails above Honolulu. On the Big Island *ʻamakihi* are very common in the wet and dry forests at higher altitude and have even established healthy

FIGURE 5.2 ʻAmakihi species are common on Kauaʻi, Oʻahu, Maui, and the Big Island. (Jim Denny)

populations near sea level in the southeast corner of the island. This is a very good sign, because it shows these birds have developed some resistance to mosquito-borne avian malaria. ʻAmakihi are fairly common on Maui, uncommon and hard to see on Molokaʻi, and they have disappeared from Lānaʻi.

Iʻiwi. The *iʻiwi* is perhaps the most striking honeycreeper of all. It is a brilliant scarlet-orange, with a very large salmon-colored bill. Black wings and black tail complete the ensemble. At six inches in length it is larger than other common honeycreepers and dominates them: an *iʻiwi* will readily shoo an *ʻapapane* away from choice *lehua* blossoms. Apparently the *iʻiwi* bill was designed with something other than *lehua* blossoms in mind: it is sized and curved perfectly to feed on the nectar of native lobelia flowers. Fortunately for the *iʻiwi,* it can feed on the nectar of other blossoms as well, since many lobelias are extinct or nearly so.

The *iʻiwi* has a name that's often mispronounced. The *w* is pronounced like a *v* (ee-EE-vee). A bit of historic trivia will help with the pronunciation. Charles Clerke, an officer on Cook's voyages, was the first westerner to write about the bird, noting in 1779, "the native name is *eeeeeve.*"

FIGURE 5.3 The *ʻiʻiwi* is fairly easy to see on Maui and the Big Island, uncommon on Kauaʻi. (Jim Denny)

The *ʻiʻiwi* is taxonomically simple: one species exists (or used to) on all the forested main islands. Why no island-by-island speciation? The bird is good-sized and a strong flier. Perhaps there was too much exchange of genetic material between islands for the birds to evolve into separate species.

Today the *ʻiʻiwi* is gone from Lānaʻi, nearly gone from Molokaʻi and Oʻahu, and hard to find on Kauaʻi. In 2017 it was listed as a threatened species. Sizable populations survive only on the two islands with large areas above the mosquito zone: Maui and the Big Island. The reason for this restricted and shrinking range seems to be the bird's total lack of immunity to avian malaria. One bite from an infected mosquito, and an *ʻiʻiwi* is doomed. Happily for birders, there are a few spots where these birds can still be seen. Spotting one is the birding thrill of a lifetime.

ʻElepaio. As with the *ʻamakihi*, there are different *ʻelepaio* species on different islands. These little birds stand out from the other endemic forest birds we've described in many ways. For one, they are not honeycreepers. They are in a family of birds called monarch flycatchers. They evolved from birds that arrived in Hawaiʻi in much the same way that the Polynesian voyagers made their way across the

FIGURE 5.4 *'Elepaio* species are common on Kaua'i and the Big Island. (Jim Denny)

South Pacific: by island-hopping their way east and north. Today there are genetically similar monarch flycatcher species in Polynesia and Southeast Asia.

The *'elepaio* don't look or act anything like honeycreepers, either. These 4.5-inch birds are rusty brown (Kaua'i birds are more gray) with a light-colored throat and belly. They often strike an endearing pose with their tails cocked up. These are cute little birds. They are insectivores, so they are usually found down below the blooming forest canopy preferred by nectar feeders, often at eye level for birders. And *'elepaio* are bold and curious little birds, so they often approach and scold quiet hikers and birders. Did I mention that this are cute little birds?

The *'elepaio* offer a classic case of island-fueled evolution, except for one thing. There's a big mystery plopped right in the middle of an otherwise perfect example of speciation. You can find *'elepaio* from Kaua'i in the north, continuing down through O'ahu, and at the southern end of the archipelago on the Big Island. The birds on each island are somewhat different from those on other islands. Taxonomists have classified each as a separate species. It's a textbook case, except for one thing. There's no *'elepaio* on any of the islands that made up Maui Nui. We can't blame human impacts for a recent extinction:

archaeologists tell us there's no record of an *'elepaio* ever existing on any of the islands of the Maui complex, despite the existence of abundant habitat. How did island-hopping birds just hop over Maui, Moloka'i, and Lāna'i? Scientists are at a complete loss to explain this. It is a source of immense scientific bafflement. Only the little birds themselves know the answer.

There's another thing these birds know, according to Hawaiian legend. It is said that the *'elepaio* is the earthly embodiment of Lea, the goddess of canoe makers. When men went to the forest to harvest a big *koa* tree in order to carve a canoe hull, the spritely *'elepaio* would guide them. If the bird spent a long time on a *koa* trunk, picking for insects, the canoe makers knew that it might have cracks and insect damage that would render it unsuitable for a boat hull. If the *'elepaio* spent little time on a *koa* trunk and moved on, the canoe makers could deduce it supported few of the insects that might weaken the wood. Their selection made, they could fell the tree to fashion a canoe.

Today you can still see *'elepaio* in the Hawaiian forest. They are very rare on O'ahu, but still fairly common in the right habitat on Kaua'i and the Big Island.

'Apapane, 'amakihi, 'i'iwi, and *'elepaio* are the most widespread and easiest to see of the endemic forest birds, but there are plenty of others to be seen by those that learn a bit about Hawaiian birds and their habitats. From the *'anianiau* of Kaua'i to the *'ākohekohe* of Maui to the *'akiapōlā'au* of the Big Island, Hawaiian forests still hold feathered treasure for birders who appreciate these very special birds.

Outside the forests there are other birding opportunities. Not surprisingly, Hawai'i is a hot spot for seabirds. The only real estate within thousands of miles is pretty desirable property if you're a seabird and you need a place to build a nest and rear your young. It's the one thing you can't do at sea. As a result, a dedicated birder has a good chance to see roughly twenty seabird species on or near the Hawaiian Islands.

The seabirds of Hawai'i are remarkably diverse in size, appearance, habits, distribution, and abundance. Even their attachment to the land is quite variable: some species never venture far from shore, while others leave the nest and may not touch land again for five or six years, when they're ready to start their own families. The viewing opportunities are diverse, too. To see some species, you need to get away from land. Birders who don't suffer from seasickness take pelagic trips to see birds that are rarely spotted from shore. Many seabirds breed on small islands just offshore of the main islands, and they can be viewed by telescope. There are even some protected areas where seabirds nest on the main islands, providing amazing birding opportunities.

Despite all the diversity, there's one thing that all the seabird species in Hawai'i have in common. They are incredibly, tragically vulnerable to many of the animal species that humans have introduced to Hawai'i and to other islands around the world. That's why offshore islets are favored by many breeding birds: no marauding rats, cats, or dogs. The remote islands of the Northwestern Hawaiian Islands are havens for nesting seabirds: some of these islands have always been free of human-transported pests, and on other islands the birds have rebounded after humans removed the pests that earlier humans introduced.

Here's a rundown of some of the seabird species that are easiest to see and identify from land:

Great Frigatebird or 'Iwa. The great frigatebird can often be seen soaring high over Hawaiian beaches. Look for a big black bird (females have a white chest) with bent wings and a long forked tail. The frigatebird's most remarkable habit is one of the ways it secures dinner. 'Iwa means "thief" in Hawaiian, and the English name refers to the fast eighteenth-century sailing ships called frigates that pirates used to overtake and plunder other vessels. Modern ornithologists use the term *kleptoparasite* for birds with this propensity. Call it what you will, the frigatebird sometimes steals its food from other birds such as red-footed boobies and wedge-tailed shearwaters rather than catching its own. Obscure trivia: the first western explorer to note this thieving habit was Christopher Columbus, who recorded it in the log of his voyage of new world exploration.

The frigatebird's remarkable ability to steal food is nothing compared to its sublime adaptations for soaring flight. It is more perfectly adapted for life on the wing than any other bird, a point reinforced by the many extremes in its physical form. It has the largest wingspan of any seabird commonly found in Hawai'i, seven feet, yet it weighs only about three pounds—about as much as a good-sized guinea pig. Its unusual skeleton is one way it keeps the weight down. A frigatebird has paper-thin, hollow bones, the lightest skeleton in comparison to wing length of any bird. It can soar for hours with nothing more than barely perceptible adjustments to wing position. Yet when it needs to maneuver quickly for fishing or theft, long wings and a huge forked tail make it an unparalleled aerial acrobat. Learning these acrobatics takes time; unlike other seabirds that abandon their young when the chicks are ready to fledge, frigatebird parents keep feeding their young for a year or more.

There's a cost associated with these superb adaptations. The frigatebird's legs and feet are so reduced in size that it can't walk and it can't swim. It will awkwardly drag itself into position to take flight.

When fishing, it dips only its long hooked bill in the water. It won't dive or settle on the water like some other seabirds.

Frigatebirds are commonly seen around the main Hawaiian Islands, particularly near Kīlauea Point on Kaua'i and the northeast side of O'ahu where they roost on Moku Manu Island. They don't breed around the main islands, but they nest on nearly all the islands of the Northwestern Hawaiian Islands. They usually stay within fifty miles of the islands, but some Hawaiian birds have ranged as far as the Philippines.

FIGURE 5.5 The great frigatebird or *'iwa* is built to fly—and steal other birds' food. (Jim Denny)

Where Are the Gulls? One of the big surprises for visitors to Hawai'i is there are no resident gulls. It sure seems like they would be at home, but in reality the conditions are all wrong. Gulls are scavengers, and they depend on shallow coastal waters. The islands of Hawai'i rise out of deep ocean and just don't have much shallow water area. And unlike many seabirds, gulls do not have special-ized salt glands to rid their bodies of the excess salt accumulated by life at sea; they need fresh water.

Still, a few straggling gulls do show up, mostly in winter. Most of them are immature birds that were blown to Hawai'i by storms or hitched rides on ships. Gull species most likely to turn up in Hawai'i include the laughing gull, Bona-parte's gull, and the ring-billed gull.

Laysan Albatross or *Mōlī*. The albatross is a bird that is fabled and labeled: fabled as the central creature in Samuel Taylor Coleridge's 1798 poem "Rime of the Ancient Mariner," and labeled a gooney bird by sailors who witnessed its clumsy movements on land. In truth, alba-trosses are some of the most graceful and impressive birds on earth.

There are at least thirteen albatross species worldwide, includ-ing two that breed in Hawai'i. The Laysan albatross is one of the most abundant seabirds in the state, with more than a million birds breeding in the Northwestern Hawaiian Islands, mostly on Midway and Laysan. A small number of birds nest at protected sites on the main islands, including Kīlauea Point on Kaua'i and Ka'ena Point on O'ahu, making these great **Field Trip!** spots. These birds exhibit no fear of humans or other animals; they can breed successfully on the main islands only in places where they are carefully protected from predators.

The Laysan is a very big bird. Although its wingspan of 6.5 feet is smallish for an albatross and shorter than the frigatebird's seven-foot reach, the Laysan albatross can weigh up to nine pounds, three times the weight of a frigatebird. That doesn't mean the albatross isn't grace-ful; it can glide over the waves and soar for thousands of miles in its search for food. In fact, Laysan albatross can range from one side of the Pacific to the other, and north to the Aleutians.

Laysan albatross mate for life, although if one bird dies the other will seek out a new mate. They perform an elaborate courtship dance that seems to strengthen their pair bond, and they produce one egg per year. Once the young bird fledges, it will be four or five years before it

FIGURE 5.6 Laysan albatross or *mōlī* spend most of their time at sea for several years, then come ashore to nest and raise young. These birds are at Kaʻena Point on Oʻahu. (Rick Soehren)

tries to nest, although it may visit the nesting ground as a juvenile. Perhaps it is observing its elders and learning the courtship dance. When the time comes to breed and nest, it will usually show up right where it was fledged. It usually takes a few years for young birds to get the hang of raising young, so an inexperienced bird may not be successful at raising a chick until it is nine or ten.

Remember the gyres and garbage patches described in chapter 3? The North Pacific garbage patch is right in the middle of albatross feeding territory. The birds can't always distinguish floating plastic from food. The tragic result is that they bring plastic back to the nest and feed it to their chick. The chick can handle a bit of plastic; it has to regurgitate other inedible things like squid beaks. But if it gets too much plastic and not enough food, the result will be starvation.

Scientists used to think that albatrosses might live as long as twenty years or more. That thinking was turned on its head when a nesting Laysan albatross banded on Midway in 1956 was recaptured in 2002. As of 2018, she was still returning to her spot on Midway, and still raising chicks. Since these birds usually don't nest until they're about five, she has to be about sixty-seven years old. Scientists have named her Wisdom.

Double Trouble. Scientists follow an arcane rule when forming the plural of some fish and bird names such as marlin, tuna, and albatross. The plural is the same as singular when referring to multiple individuals of a single species; add an *s* or *es* for more than one species. Here are examples: two Laysan albatross followed the charter boat while anglers on board caught three blue marlin. In Hawaiian waters, blue and striped are the most common species of marlins. Lucky birders might see black-footed and Laysan albatrosses.

In Hawaiian it is simpler: singular and plural words are the same, like one deer or two deer in English. One albatross is a *mōlī*, two albatrosses of any species are also *mōlī*.

White-tailed Tropicbird or *Koaʻe kea*. Visit any of the grand lookouts in Hawaiʻi that provide views over big holes in the ground, from Waimea Canyon and the Kalalau Valley of Kauaʻi to Kīlauea Caldera on the Big Island and chances are good that you will see white-tailed tropicbirds. These birds regularly soar around immense spaces in Hawaiʻi. Their bright white plumage makes them easy to pick out against the red dirt or green foliage. They look tiny when seen in such grand vistas, but they are good-sized birds with wingspans of three feet.

The white-tailed tropicbird gets its name from its most noticeable feature: two long, thin, streamer-like tail feathers that are longer than its body. What function do these bizarre feathers serve? We have no idea. It isn't a flashy male adornment intended to attract a female; both sexes have them. And just to make it all the more puzzling, there's a second less common tropicbird species in Hawaiʻi, fairly similar except that its tail streamers are bright red. You can probably guess its name: red-tailed tropicbird, or *koaʻeʻula*.

Why does a seabird spend so much time soaring over land? Again, we don't really know. It might have something to do with the bird's nesting preferences. Whereas most seabirds achieve nesting success only in places like the remote and predator-free Northwestern Hawaiian Islands, white-tails nest almost exclusively on the main islands. They build their nests on cliff faces where they are relatively safe from introduced predators such as rats and cats.

Hawaiian Petrel or *ʻUaʻu*. Most seabirds encountered in Hawaiʻi are wide-ranging. Among the birds we've just described, the great frigatebird and the white-tailed tropicbird are pantropical: they occur in the tropics around the world. Even the Laysan albatross, named for a Hawaiian island, nests in small numbers on islands in other parts of the Pacific. But Hawai'i does have some endemic seabirds. One of them is the Hawaiian petrel or ʻuaʻu.

The ʻuaʻu and some other petrels and shearwaters (a closely related group of seabirds) have a behavior that comes as a surprise to most people: they dig burrows in which to nest. In the past that was probably a pretty good way to keep a chick shaded and cool in the tropical sun. Unfortunately, the strategy proved disastrous once humans introduced rats and cats and mongooses to the islands.

At one time ʻuaʻu nested on all the main islands. The fossil record suggests that they were abundant in many lowland areas before the first humans arrived. By the early 2000s there were just a few small scattered breeding colonies on Kauaʻi and a larger colony nesting in Haleakalā Crater with perhaps 500 breeding pairs. The survival of the Haleakalā colony is attributed to predator-control efforts by the National Park Service and to the extreme conditions in the high-altitude crater that keep

FIGURE 5.7 Hawaiian petrels or ʻuaʻu usually come and go at night, but you can hear them calling in the darkness on summer nights near their burrows at Haleakalā on Maui. (Jim Denny)

predator numbers low. Those conditions are probably also at the edge of the birds' own tolerance, making it a struggle for them to survive.

The picture improved a bit in 2007 when, to their utter surprise, researchers investigating reports of scattered birds in the mountains of Lānaʻi discovered a colony as large as the one on Maui. Predator-control efforts began immediately.

It's hard to see an *uaʻu*. They can sometimes be seen from shore or on pelagic birding trips, but you have to know your seabirds pretty well because there are other superficially similar species out there. You can't wait by their burrow because the birds come and go at night. But

Political Football.   One of Hawaiʻi's endangered seabirds is threatened by a most unlikely peril: high school football games. The Newell's Shearwater or *ʻaʻo* nests in burrows in the mountains of Kauaʻi. When the chicks are ready to fledge, they leave their burrows at night and are naturally drawn to the light of the moon

FIGURE 5.8 A rescued Newell's shearwater is released. (Shelley Paik, Kauaʻi Island Utility Cooperative)

if you know when to visit their nesting areas you can hear them. Their Hawaiian name is onomatopoeic, that is, the name sounds like the bird's call. Once you hear it, I guarantee it's a sound you'll never forget. See the field trip to Haleakalā at the end of this chapter.

Our third category of birds is a varied group that goes by a lot of different names. These are birds that you find at the shore, at mudflats, ponds, or marshes, occasionally elsewhere. Some are ducks and geese, collectively referred to as waterfowl. The birds at the shore are sometimes called shorebirds, but they are also referred to as wading birds, waders, or wetland birds.

reflected on the ocean. It is a strategy that guided these seabirds to the water for perhaps millions of years.

Then development began to boom on Kaua'i, and the lights of hotels and shopping centers started to attract the birds. They would land on roads and parking lots. The ones that weren't run over would be easy prey for dogs and cats because, like many seabirds, they can't take flight from level ground. Eventually businesses began to shield lights when they could, and shearwater aid stations were set up around the island where residents could deposit any hapless birds that they found stranded.

Despite these efforts the bird's numbers are declining precipitously. Biologists are trying to establish new colonies at predator-free Kīlauea Point National Wildlife Refuge. They are also trying to further minimize night lighting, particularly from mid-September to mid-December when the young birds fledge.

And that's where the conflict comes in. School sports are wildly popular in Hawai'i, and autumn nighttime football games under the lights are an American tradition. Despite the danger to birds, Kaua'i County kept right on scheduling night games until 2010, when the county was found guilty of violating the Endangered Species Act and the Migratory Bird Treaty Act. Now most games must be played in the heat of the afternoon, and attendance has dropped. Parents and fans are upset. People have broken into ball fields at night and turned the lights on in protest.

It is a classic example of the difficulty we have in coexisting with the natural world around us. Understandably, the people of Kaua'i want to have high school football games at night, like every other community in the United States. The thing is, Kaua'i isn't like any of those other communities. It is the only place in the world with Newell's Shearwaters nesting in the mountains above football fields.

Birders, both local and mainland, are unanimously thrilled by Hawaiian forest birds and seabirds. When it comes to wetland birds, most of them migratory, it's a different story. Local birders are excited by the seasonal arrival of some additional avian diversity, but mainland birders tend to greet these ducks and shorebirds with a yawn. After all, many of them are pretty common back home.

Back home, yes. But there's a difference and it's a big one, between migrating on the mainland and migrating to Hawai'i. Many migratory species breed in higher latitudes like Canada or Alaska, and migrate south to warmer climates during the winter. If you migrate down the west coast of North America, you've got it pretty easy. Stop, rest, catch a snack any time you feel like it. On the other hand, if you migrate from Alaska to Hawai'i, your route takes you over 3,000 miles of inhospitable ocean.

The story of the Pacific golden-plover or *kōlea*, highlighted in a chapter 3 field trip, is a good example of this incomprehensibly difficult migration. This little bird is the most common, widespread, and visible of all the wetland birds in Hawai'i. It is so visible because it does not confine itself to wetlands. Its favorite habitat is open areas like lawns and grassy fields. It is commonly seen in parks, on golf courses, and along roadsides. And it's not too shy; these birds happily share their grassy areas with us humans.

Very few *kōlea* spend the entire year in Hawai'i. They breed in the Arctic from May to July, returning to Hawai'i in August for a long winter's layover. It is those trips to and from the Arctic that make this bird so impressive. You see, the *kōlea* doesn't have webbed feet like a duck or an albatross. Taking flight from water is nearly impossible. This bird makes nonstop flights between the Arctic and Hawai'i, twice each year. We complain about a six-hour airline flight, and this bird travels under its own power for three days straight.

There are far fewer wetland birds in Hawai'i than there used to be, because there are fewer wetlands. In Hawai'i, as in much of the rest of the United States, we have drained or degraded most of our wetlands. The Mānā Plain on Kaua'i? Seven miles of wetlands, drained in 1923 for sugarcane (and then abandoned). The big swamp at Waikīkī? I don't need to tell you what occupies that former wetland these days. (Waikīkī means "spouting water," an apparent reference to natural springs that used to exist in the area.)

The wetlands aren't all gone. Some are protected or have been restored in wildlife refuges and preserves. Visit one of these wetlands, and you'll see a lot of the same birds that you might see in California or other places where they spend the winter: ducks such as northern pintails, northern shovelers, lesser scaups, maybe the occasional American wigeon or green-winged teal. Shorebirds include sanderlings, ruddy turnstones, wandering tattlers, maybe a lesser yellowlegs.

For now we'll focus on some birds that are especially close to the heart of Hawaiian birders: the Big Four wetland species. They don't migrate, and they have all evolved various distances down the path to becoming endemic Hawaiians. All are considered endangered in Hawai'i due to the loss of habitat and other perils. Some of them look a lot like their mainland ancestors, but all are considered distinct species or at least subspecies.

The **Hawaiian gallinule** or *'alae 'ula* is very closely related to the North American common gallinule. These similar birds are considered subspecies. The *'alae 'ula* (*'ula* means "red" in Hawaiian) is a plump, mostly black, football-sized bird. Its most distinguishing characteristic is its bright red frontal shield (bill and forehead) with a yellow bill tip. In Hawaiian legends, the *'alae 'ula* brought fire from the gods to the Hawaiian people, scorching its bill in the process. Despite the *'alae 'ula*'s featured role in this ancient legend, some biologists believe its similarity to continental birds suggests a very recent arrival in Hawai'i, perhaps when early Hawaiians planted wet *kalo* fields and increased the bird's preferred habitat. Today it is most common on Kaua'i, with some birds on O'ahu; it is gone from the other islands.

The **Hawaiian coot** or *'alae ke'oke'o* is superficially similar to the gallinule, and the two species often occur in the same wetland habitats. It has a white bill and frontal shield (*ke'oke'o* means "white"). A small percentage of the birds have a red shield. Like the *'alae 'ula,* it is most common on Kaua'i and O'ahu. Unlike the moorhen, the *'alae ke'oke'o* can also be found on other main islands. It constructs a floating nest of aquatic vegetation. The *'alae ke'oke'o* is right on the cusp of specieshood. Early naturalists considered it a separate species, then it was lumped with North American coots, and finally split into a separate species again in 1993.

The **Hawaiian stilt** or *ae'o* is an endemic subspecies of the black-necked stilt of North America. It can be found on all the main islands. It feeds in shallow water or mudflats, so it is seen out of water a lot more often than the coot or moorhen. The *ae'o* is a tall very slender bird, looking formally dressed with a black back and white belly (figure 10.5). The elegant appearance is accented by its bright pink legs, nearly as long as its body. The *ae'o* has a trick to lure predators away from its nest and chicks: it will loudly feign injury, drawing away creatures that could endanger its young. And that's a hint that this bird hasn't been in Hawai'i all that long—until humans arrived, there were no ground predators.

Last of the four Hawaiian wetland birds is the **Hawaiian duck** or *koloa maoli*. This duck looks remarkably like a female mallard, and the species is descended from mallards. Recall that one hallmark of a species is a population that is physically or behaviorally isolated from similar populations and therefore does not interbreed. The *koloa* is a year-round resident of Hawai'i. Even when wild mallards were nearby, the mallards left Hawai'i at breeding time. Result: no interbreeding. Then people brought semi-domesticated mallards to Hawai'i that escaped and established nonmigratory, year-round feral populations around the state. Today, these feral birds are the greatest among a long list of threats to the *koloa*: interbreeding has resulted in a lot of hybrids, and very few pure *koloa* remain. Most of the pure birds are on Kaua'i.

One more wetland bird deserves mention: the **black-crowned night-heron** or *'auku'u*. Unlike the "big four" wetland birds already described, it is not endangered and is not genetically distinct from others of its species around the world. It may be fairly recently established, or perhaps frequent new arrivals keep the species from becoming genetically distinct in the islands. Look for this two-foot-tall gray bird with a black cap (juveniles are mottled brown) in wetlands around the state.

The last bird in this category is the most beloved by Hawaiians. It is the **Hawaiian goose** or *nēnē*. Despite being a goose, it isn't really a wetland bird. Many *nēnē* live and breed far from any ponds or marshes. In fact, they are gradually losing the foot webbing that their ancestor Canada geese display. The *nēnē* is endemic to Hawai'i, with sizable populations on the Big Island, Maui, and Kaua'i.

The *nēnē* has had repeated close brushes with extinction, and it really is a miracle that these birds survive today. The fossil record includes abundant evidence of geese in Hawai'i including some big flightless species reminiscent of the dodo (see chapter 12 on extinction). By the time Captain Cook arrived, Hawaiians had apparently devoured all but the *nēnē*. Early Hawaiians might have been on a path to save this bird; in addition to seeing wild *nēnē*, Cook and his men noted

FIGURE 5.9 The *nēnē* is Hawai'i's state bird and the only surviving endemic goose. (Rick Soehren)

that the Hawaiians kept domesticated *nēnē* (presumably protected from their rats and dogs). After western contact, new introduced predators and bird hunting took their toll. Early in the twentieth century the *nēnē* were clearly in steep decline. Recognizing that *nēnē* were easy to breed in captivity, the territorial government set up a captive breeding facility. Species saved? Well, no. In 1935, ostensibly to protect the captive flock from disease or disaster, the birds were split up and given to territorial senators and wealthy ranchers. Many suspected that it was a political decision, and it proved disastrous: all these birds died out.

In 1946 and 1947 a husband-and-wife team of biologists spent eighteen months scouring the Big Island for *nēnē* and found none, although they suspected that a couple of dozen geese might still be out there. These biologists called for a captive breeding program to commence immediately. Fortunately for the birds and for us, there were still some captive *nēnē* to start the program. Herbert Cornelius Shipman of Hilo, grandson of missionaries, great-grandson of a Hawaiian chief on Maui, had been keeping *nēnē* as a hobby since 1918.

Now you might recall that Hilo is one of those spots that is ideally situated to be destroyed by a tsunami. In 1946 much of downtown Hilo was leveled by a tsunami, and 159 people died. Most of the Shipman *nēnē*, kept at his coastal estate south of town, also perished in the disaster. But Mr. Shipman had recognized the dangers of putting all his eggs in one basket and had established a second captive flock at ʻAinahou Ranch, part of his vast landholdings. Once again the *nēnē* escaped extinction. (Perhaps coincidentally, *ʻainahou* means "new land.")

In 1949 Shipman sent two *nēnē* off to the Wildfowl Trust, a conservation organization in Slimbridge, England. The idea was to establish a captive breeding program far from the perils—natural and political—of Hawaiʻi. The program got off to a rocky start; the first two birds were both female. A male was quickly sent along. Shipman also provided birds for a government-sponsored breeding program at Pōhakuloa in the high saddle between Mauna Kea and Mauna Loa.

Eventually both of these programs produced birds for reintroduction. Today there are wild *nēnē* populations on several islands, but that doesn't mean this goose's perils are all behind it. The populations on the Big Island and Maui are supplemented with captive-bred birds because nesting success is not good enough to sustain the populations.

An accidental reintroduction has been more successful. Hurricane ʻIniki blew open a pen of captive *nēnē* on Kauaʻi in 1992. Kauaʻi had not been considered for *nēnē* introductions because the conventional wisdom was that the birds preferred the high, arid, rocky uplands that only existed on the Big Island and Maui. It turns out that *nēnē* had been forced up into these marginal habitats where the predator population was lower. Once the flock was loose on Kauaʻi—the only main island free of the introduced predatory mongoose—they got right to work breeding and occupying lowland areas all over the island.

It would be nice to conclude this *nēnē* story with a happy ending, but there's one more chapter that is just beginning. Biologists had long feared that mongooses could hitch a ride to Kauaʻi on the big barges that haul freight between the islands, and it appears that their fears have been realized. For several years there have been unconfirmed mongoose sightings on Kauaʻi. In 2012 grim confirmation came with two mongooses trapped near Līhuʻe. Authorities are vigilant for more mongooses and are making contingency plans for eradication. It appears the *nēnē* will have at least one more brush with extinction.

The best places to see *nēnē* include Kīlauea Point National Wildlife

Refuge and Haleakalā National Park (see **Field Trip!** information below). These geese are also fairly common at Hawai'i Volcanoes National Park where they sometimes graze on lawns (check the Kīlauea Military Camp lawn). They are common enough on Kaua'i that you might spot them on any golf course or pasture, especially on the east and north sides of the island. *Nēnē* are most active and visible from May to August. In fall and winter they are more secretive, pairing up and raising goslings. In spring they molt, losing their flight feathers; it's a good time to hide.

FIGURE 5.10 Three white birds you might see in Honolulu are from left to right: pigeon, white tern, cattle egret. (Rick Soehren)

What's That White Bird?   There are three prominent white bird species seen by visitors and residents in Honolulu and especially in Waikīkī. One is a white strain of the common pigeon, whose shape, size, and behavior will look familiar to a city dweller from anywhere in the world.

Another white bird about the same size nests in big city trees and flies around the tall hotels of Waikīkī. The white tern, or fairy tern as it is sometimes called, is a seabird and can be distinguished from a pigeon by the tern's long narrow black beak. In flight, white terns appear more slender than pigeons and almost never glide like pigeons do. Incredibly, urban Honolulu is the only place this seabird nests other than remote islands. Why? We don't know.

Finally, look for cattle egrets feeding on big lawns such as Kapi'olani Park. Egrets are the largest of this trio of white birds, with long legs and neck and a long yellow bill. Breeding birds have a rusty wash, and immature birds have a greenish-black bill.

It takes a bit of effort to see Hawai'i's native birds. Meanwhile, cities, towns, and the countryside are bursting with birds, nearly all of them introduced. The **rose-ringed parakeet** (figure 9.10), an escaped cage bird from India and Africa, is now common in Honolulu. The **common myna** was introduced to Hawai'i from India in 1865 in hopes it would eat insect pests. Now the birds are the pests. The **Japanese white-eye** or *mejiro* in Japanese is often camouflaged by its green plumage, but is quite abundant. The **Java sparrow** (figure 9.8) has elegant plumage of black, gray, and white, and sports a huge pink bill. The **red-crested cardinal** (figure 9.11) is a striking little gray and white bird with a red head. Brought from South America in the 1930s, it is now a common beggar at parks and picnic areas. (On the Big Island, look for a similar species without a crest, the **yellow-billed cardinal.**) The **common waxbill** (figure 9.7) is a tiny four-inch African import with a bill the color of crimson sealing wax. The **zebra dove** is nearly everywhere in Hawaiian towns. It is a very tame little dove introduced from Australia. The **gray francolin,** a plump brown bird

FIGURE 5.11 The common myna is widespread throughout Hawai'i. (Jim Denny)

FIGURE 5.12 The Japanese white-eye is common and widespread throughout Hawai'i. (Jim Denny)

FIGURE 5.13 The zebra dove is common and widespread throughout Hawai'i. (Jim Denny)

FIGURE 5.14 The gray francolin is uncommon on Kaua'i and O'ahu, common on other islands. (Stubblefield Photography/Shutterstock.com)

reminiscent of a small chicken, was introduced from India. It is the most common of three francolin species introduced as game birds. Its call, a piercing KEE-ka-ko, KEE-ka-ko, KEE-ka-ko, can often be heard early in the morning on Maui and the Big Island where the species is common.

Visitors to Hawai'i from North America will recognize many other avian introductions: northern cardinals, northern mockingbirds, house finches, house sparrows. Parrot fanciers will recognize the call of red-crowned Amazons. Hunters will recognize wild turkeys and ring-necked pheasants. Truly, the list goes on and on.

OTHER CREATURES OF THE FOREST

Beyond birds, it might seem like the wildlife viewing in Hawai'i is a bit limited. If you look more closely, though, there are a lot of native wild creatures in the islands. They are invertebrates: insects, spiders, snails, and more. They are everywhere from the beach to the summit of Mauna Kea, even living deep inside lava tubes, marvels of adaptive radiation. And before you dismiss them because "bugs aren't your thing," let me tell you about a few. I promise you will want to run right out and see them for yourself.

Hawaiian Happy Face Spider. Let's start with the invertebrate that has the best marketing campaign in the animal kingdom: the Hawaiian happy face spider or *nanananamakiki'i* (spider with a face image) shown in figure 3.1. It is a small spider; legs and all, it can dance around on a dime with room to spare. It is usually yellow or lime green. It gets its name from the distinctive red, black, and white happy-face pattern appearing on the back of some individuals (others just have black dots). This little spider is not much of a web spinner. It hangs out on the underside of leaves in wet forests, watching for the silhouette of its insect prey crawling on the upper side of the leaf. When the prey is close to the edge, the happy face spider reaches around the leaf edge for its meal. It can be found on Oʻahu, Maui, Molokaʻi, and the Big Island. Your best chance of seeing one is on the Big Island or Oʻahu, on the undersides of leaves in relatively undisturbed areas. You may need a magnifying glass to see its tiny happy face.

Kamehameha Butterfly. Would you like to know about all the endemic Hawaiian butterflies? It isn't a steep learning curve because there are only two: the Kamehameha butterfly or *pulelehua* and the Blackburn's blue or *koa* butterfly. (You might not want to tackle the moths; there are over 950 endemic species!) Your chances are better of seeing a Kamehameha butterfly because they are more conspicuous and a lot bigger than the Blackburn's blue butterfly (2.5 inches versus 0.5 inch). The trickiest part is distinguishing a native Kamehameha butterfly from several look-alike introductions that are closely related. See the **Field Trip!** section in this chapter for more information.

There's an interesting story about Thomas Blackburn, the English fellow for whom the Blackburn's Blue is named. All his life he was fascinated by insects. However, that fascination couldn't pay the bills, so he became a Protestant minister. In 1876 he secured a position working for the Church of Hawaiʻi and moved to Honolulu. For the next six years he spent his free time tramping around the Hawaiian countryside, collecting insects and sending them off to the British Museum. Nearly every one was a species entirely new to science. But here's the sad part: the endemic insects of Hawaiʻi have been displaced and killed just like island plants and birds. Today, entomologists can no longer find many of Blackburn's insects; some of the species he collected were never seen

FIGURE 5.15 (*left*) The endemic Kamehameha butterfly has a few white spots on the tips of its wings. In the male one or two spots are orange, not white. (W. P. Mull, from *Hawaiian Insects and Their Kin* by F. G. Howarth and W. P. Mull); (*right*) The closely related introduced red admiral has more white spots on the wing tip. (shenk1/Shutterstock.com)

again. In 1882 Blackburn moved to Australia, where he discovered more than three thousand additional insect species.

Giant Hawaiian Dragonfly. Hawai'i is home to the largest native dragonfly in the United States, aptly named the giant Hawaiian dragonfly but better known locally as the *pinao*. It has a wingspan of up to six inches, a bit larger than the 4.5-inch green darner dragonfly that is widespread in North America from Canada to Mexico and indigenous to Hawai'i. The *pinao* is widespread on all the main islands. It usually has a metallic green body with blue at the base of its long thin abdomen.

The *pinao* shares traits with many other dragonflies: it is a predator of other flying insects; it can move its front and rear pairs of wings independently, the better to hover and fly backwards as it catches its prey; and it lays eggs in or near water. The creatures that emerge are nymphs, flightless but just as predatory as their parents. The nymphs spend several months living in slow-moving streams, eating aquatic insects or even tiny freshwater shrimp before they metamorphose into adults. The nymphs are eaten by many introduced freshwater fish, so most successful *pinao* breeding seems to occur in smaller, high-elevation ponds and streams where introduced fish are absent.

The biggest challenge in spotting a *pinao* is distinguishing it from its close relative the green darner. Here is a way to tell them apart: the green darner usually has a very thin yellow or brown line on the leading edge of the wings, while the slightly larger *pinao* will have black on the wing edge.

Land Snails. OK, this next one may be a bit of a tough sell. Gardeners of the world loathe snails. In fact, most everyone feels some level of revulsion toward them, except perhaps the French. Nevertheless, some of the most amazing creatures that ever lived in Hawaiian forests are snails. These are not the plant-munching garden marauders you hate. Most of them have shells about half an inch long or less, sometimes much less (remember that their ancestors probably hitchhiked to Hawaiʻi stuck on some bird's leg). Some are tree snails, living up off the ground, subsisting on the fungi and algae that grow on leaves in the rain forest. Many are so colorful that the early Hawaiians made jewelry out of them. Later, children of the missionaries would go off into the forest and collect their beautifully patterned shells by the thousands, calling them little agate shells. In fact, they're in the genus *Achatinella,* which means "agate" in Latin.

At one time there were dozens or hundreds of species on Oʻahu alone, the product of explosive adaptive radiation and speciation. Sadly, most of them are gone now, victims of rabid collectors and misguided introductions of animals that like to eat snails. The rest are so rare that you might hike Hawaiian forests for years and never see any. One spot where you might see a tiny and rather drab brown native land snail is just above Honolulu. It's worth having a look if only because so many of its little snail brethren are gone forever. See figure 5.16 and the **Field Trip!** Section below.

Lava Tube Life. Finally, this very short discussion of Hawaiian terrestrial invertebrates would be lacking if we didn't mention the remarkable creatures that have evolved to live in lava tubes. These creatures were among the first species to make scientists consider how rapidly evolution might occur. They have evolved even on the Big Island, youngest in the chain. Most lava tube dwellers are blind because sight is an unnecessary waste of energy in the dark, so it seems unlikely that they could have evolved on an older island and somehow traveled and colonized newer islands. It appears that they have evolved from surface creatures time and time again, independently on every island. They are remarkably diverse: there are over two hundred species living in lava tubes, including insects, spiders, centipedes, and millipedes. At least seventy-five are so completely adapted to life in the dark that they cannot survive elsewhere. Some of them feed on roots that grow down through cracks in the lava tube ceiling; others live on fungi. There are predators in the dark, too. Hawaiian spiders living up in the daylight called big-eyed hunting spiders have evolved into lava tube forms with greatly reduced eyes. On Kauaʻi, one species has lost its eyes completely. Of course, it is known as the no-eyed big-eyed hunting spider. Even entomologists have a sense of humor.

I could go on and on about Hawaiian insect life. There are unique predatory caterpillars that ambush and eat other insects rather than munching placidly on leaves; and "rodeo" caterpillars that tie down native snails with silk for a meal of fresh escargot. There are hundreds and hundreds of species of fruit flies that recognize their own kind and figure out which flies to mate with by performing unique dances. There are little insects called planthoppers whose intestines loop up into their tiny heads, giving new meaning to the naughty colloquialism of having "the S-word" for brains. There are moths, lacewings, wasps, and flies that have all lost the ability to fly. Scientists have identified about 5,300 endemic insect species, and there are undoubtedly many more that we haven't yet discovered.

And finally, there is one terrestrial mammal besides humans that made the long journey to Hawaiʻi without outside help: the **Hawaiian Hoary Bat**. Before the first Polynesian voyagers came ashore, these bats were the only mammalian inhabitants of the islands' verdant hills and valleys. They weigh only about half an ounce—you could mail two of them for the price of a single first-class postage stamp. They're pretty much all wing, with a span of about a foot. They are a subspecies and descendant of the hoary bat that occurs over much of North and South America. (Hoary is an old term meaning white or grayish-white, referring to the white tips of the hairs on the bats' back and shoulders.) They can be found on the Big Island and Kauaʻi with a smaller population on Maui.

The Hawaiians knew them as ʻōpeʻapeʻa; it means "half a leaf," because an outstretched bat wing resembles half of a taro leaf. They eat insects using echolocation too high for the human ear to hear. Beyond that, we are not certain about the species. They seem to roost in trees and prefer forested areas. We think their numbers are greater in lowland areas where there are more insects. They like to feed over water and at forest edges.

Scientists thought the bat was rare and declining, so it was listed as an endangered species in 1970. With modern ultrasonic detection equipment we are hearing more bats in more places—perhaps a few thousand total—so they might not be quite as endangered as originally believed. Threats include pesticides and windmills. The bats also get snagged on barbed-wire fences, apparently because they stop echolocating for a few seconds and "fly blind" while they are eating insects on the wing.

ʻŌpeʻapeʻa seem to be fairly widespread on the islands where they occur, especially on the Big Island and Kauaʻi. Look for them at dusk over the shoreline or in clearings at the edge of forests. Hilo Bay and Kailua Bay on the Big Island are often suggested as good places to look for them.

FIELD TRIP!

5.1 KĪLAUEA POINT NATIONAL WILDLIFE REFUGE, KAUAʻI. If you want to see and learn about seabirds, Kīlauea Point is the best place in the state to visit. More than half a dozen seabird species can be seen depending on the time of year. Docents, signs, and a visitor center are available to help you identify the birds. You can even borrow a pair of binoculars (adult or child size), so you can get a better view. Oh yes, and you take it all in from one of the most scenic spots imaginable, a point of land jutting out from Kauaʻi's north shore, with a restored hundred-year-old lighthouse. In the waters below the point you might be lucky enough to see spinner dolphins, monk seals, or a humpback whale. Table 5.1 shows what birds can be seen at Kīlauea Point throughout the year.

Table 5.1   Seasonal Occurrence of Birds at Kīlauea Point

Species	J	F	M	A	M	J	J	A	S	O	N	D
Laysan Albatross (Mōlī)*	●	●	●	●	●	●	●	●			●	●
Wedge-tailed Shearwater (ʻUaʻu kani)*			●	●	●	●	●	●	●	●	●	
White-tailed Tropicbird (Koaʻe kea)	●	●	●	●	●	●	●	●	●	●	●	●
Red-tailed Tropicbird (Koaʻe ʻula)			●	●	●	●	●	●	●	●	●	
Red-footed Booby (ʻĀ)	●	●	●	●	●	●	●	●	●	●	●	●
Great Frigatebird (ʻIwa)	●	●	●	●	●	●	●	●	●	●	●	●
Hawaiian Goose (Nēnē)	●	●	●	●	●	●	●	●	●	●	●	●
Kōlea	●	●	●	●	●			●	●	●	●	●

...nes show presence of bird species at Kīlauea Point.
...ndicates birds that also breed at Kaʻena Point on Oʻahu.

The hillsides near the point, and Mokuʻaeʻae Islet just offshore, have been home to seabirds for perhaps millions of years. The introduction of rats, cats, and dogs put great pressure on these seabird colonies. This prompted the establishment of the Kīlauea Point National Wildlife Refuge here in 1985 and the completion of a predator-proof fence around a seven-acre part of the refuge in 2014. Protection of nesting areas has allowed bird populations to rebound, especially Laysan albatross and wedge-tailed shearwater.

Laysan albatross and wedge-tailed shearwater also nest at Kaʻena Point on Oʻahu.

At press time the refuge was closed on Sunday and Monday and open 10:00 to 4:00 other days. There is a modest admission fee. Access for the disabled is very good. The refuge even has an electric cart to transport mobility-impaired visitors up the 0.2-mile path from the parking lot and admission kiosk to the lighthouse.

5.2 SADDLE ROAD BIRDING SITES, BIG ISLAND. The high saddle between Mauna Kea and Mauna Loa is a wonderland. It is nothing like the stereotypical vision of Hawaiʻi. There are no palm trees, and even on the wetter windward side of the saddle the vegetation is not exactly lush. But if you want to see the raw evidence of volcanism at work, or native birds, or native plants, or more stars than you have ever seen in your life, then this is the place to come.

One of the best places in the state to see endemic forest birds is along the Puʻu ʻŌʻō Trail. The trailhead is at mile 22.4 along the Saddle Road. On this trail you have a chance to see as many as six endemic forest birds, some of them abundant. The trail is a bit rocky but mostly level and not difficult.

The name Puʻu ʻŌʻō translates to "hill of the *ʻōʻō*," an extinct endemic bird family. The species on the Big Island was last seen in 1902. Although you won't see an *ʻōʻō* here, you will have a very good chance of seeing other endemic birds. *ʻApapane* are abundant, *ʻamakihi*, *ʻiʻiwi*, and *ʻelepaio* are common, and you might see an *ʻōmaʻo*.

There is a small gravel parking area at the trailhead. Park carefully to leave room for other vehicles, and avoid rocky humps that could damage your car. The trail leads south from the highway for several miles. The best birding is in the first 1.5 miles or so, resulting in an out-and-back walk of three miles or less. The trail climbs over two low ridges of rough *ʻaʻā* in the first third of a mile. After that there is very little elevation change as the trail meanders across grasslands of old *pāhoehoe* flows and through or past several *kīpuka* with *ʻōhiʻa* and *koa.*

The bloom of the *ʻōhiʻa* trees can make a big difference in your birding success. There are always some *lehua* blossoms, and always some birds. When the trees are covered with blossoms, the nectar-feeding *ʻapapane* and *ʻiʻiwi* can be abundant. During seasons when the trees are blooming only sparsely, most of these birds will be elsewhere in search of nectar. At these times you might work to see an *ʻapapane* and you might not see an *ʻiʻiwi* at all. Summer and fall seem to be the seasons of least bloom.

Near the 21-mile marker is an area called Kīpuka 21. There is a paved entrance road heading north from the highway, leading to a big gravel parking area. The *kīpuka* is fenced, allowing native plants to regenerate. Many of the birds present on the Puʻu ʻŌʻō Trail can also be found here. When this book went to press, the fenced *kīpuka* was closed pending the completion of restrooms and an informational kiosk, but you can walk around the perimeter and peer inside. State officials hope it will open by 2019.

5.3 KAʻENA POINT, OʻAHU. If you want to get up close to a Laysan albatross and experience this bird's abject failure to fear humans, Kaʻena Point is the place to go on the main Hawaiian Islands. The albatross colony of a few hundred birds at this westernmost tip of Oʻahu is tiny compared to the million birds on Midway and Laysan, but those distant islands are off-limits. If you time your visit to coincide with the overlap in nesting seasons, you might be able to see both Laysan albatross and wedge-tailed shearwater at Kaʻena (see Table 5.1).

Kaʻena Point is a narrow arrowhead of land pointed almost due west. It can be approached from either the north or the south. The north side approach is often called Mokulēʻia because the paved road ends just beyond the beach of that name. The southern approach is called variously the Waiʻanae side (because you pass through this town on your way from Honolulu), Keawaʻula, or Yokohama Bay, names referring to the area where the pavement ends on the south side. This side of the island is economically depressed, and auto break-ins are more common here than on the north side. More than once, I've had police officers stop and advise against leaving my car unattended. On the other hand, the southern approach is far more scenic because it is mostly impassable to 4WD (four-wheel drive) vehicles, while the north side is a rutted wasteland of overzealous four-wheeling. The southern route follows the roadbed of an old abandoned railway, so the trail is mostly wide and level. However, there are a couple of spots where landslides have obliterated the wide trail. At these places you will need to follow a narrow hillside trail.

From either side it is a little more than three miles from the end of the pavement to the point, so you're looking at over six miles roundtrip either way. There are almost no trees on this arid leeward tip of the island, so sun protection and plenty of water are essential. (*Ka'ena* means "the heat.") Carry at least a quart or liter of water per person, preferably two. I try to be at the trailhead at dawn so the hiking is cooler and less sunny. Here's a tip: if you are planning to drive from Honolulu before dawn to visit Ka'ena Point, consider coming on a weekend. There might be a few more hikers sharing the trail with you, but you will avoid the horrible commuter traffic.

Laysan albatross and wedge-tailed shearwater have long tried to nest on this sandy point of land, but careless off-road vehicle drivers and marauding dogs, cats, and rats made nesting all but impossible. In 2011 authorities took advantage of the unique geography to build a nearly half-mile-long predator-proof fence across the tip of the island, protecting fifty-nine acres. The fence keeps out dogs, cats, rats, and even mice. The results have been nearly magical; populations of nesting birds are rising rapidly. Motorized vehicles are no longer allowed inside, so the dune ecosystem is recovering. The new fence also protects some plants and seeds that would be devoured by rats outside the enclosure.

Adult albatross are easy to spot in season, gliding low over the dunes or standing singly, in pairs, or in small groups, often doing the head-bobbing dance of pair bonding. The single chicks, hatched in late January or February, are more difficult to spot. They are dark gray and downy. Usually they sit beneath bushes to keep cool. When they come out, if they are motionless, you may mistake them for rocks.

While you're at Ka'ena Point, be sure to spend some time watching the shore. The rocky pools and tiny beaches at the point are good places to spot the Hawaiian monk seal. Because the point juts out into the sea, it is also a good place to spot other seabirds.

A few hundred yards inside the fence on the north side is a big rock known to Hawaiian people as *leina a ka 'uhane,* which translates to "leaping place of ghosts." It is said to be a point where souls of the dead would go to leap into the netherworld. In addition to the gates where the north and south trails pass through the predator-proof fence, there is a special gate just uphill from *leina a ka ʻuhane.* It was installed to ensure that souls coming down off the mountain could reach the stone to depart from the earth. When the fence was being planned, providing suitable access for souls of the dead was one of the larger issues to be resolved.

5.4 BIRDS AND MORE AT HALEAKALĀ NATIONAL PARK, MAUI. Most of the visitors who trek up the mountain to the summit of Haleakalā arrive early in the day, for sunrise, or at least as early as they can manage after a drive that might take two hours, depending on where on Maui they are staying. It gets so crowded that in 2017 the Park Service started requiring advance reservations to visit the park for sunrise. By mid-afternoon, the crowds are thinning. The visitor centers close well before 5:00. By late afternoon, you generally don't have to share Haleakalā with too many other people. And that's a good thing: there is less to detract from the quiet immensity of the mountain.

Here's my favorite Haleakalā itinerary. Have lunch down below. Pack a picnic dinner and lots of warm clothes and raingear. Head up the mountain, enter the park, and make a stop at Hosmer Grove just inside the park entrance. The elevation here is about 6,800 feet. Stroll the half-mile loop trail. Stop for at least twenty minutes at the gulch overlook, the farthest point out on the loop. This is the best publicly accessible place on Maui to see native forest birds. In over twenty-five years of visits, I have never failed to see *ʻapapane,* and only twice have I failed to see *ʻiʻiwi.* The twenty-minute duration of your stop at the overlook is important. You see, some honeycreepers including *ʻiʻiwi* make a feeding circuit, repeatedly traveling a loop through the forest that takes them to good feeding spots. If there is no *ʻiʻiwi* at the overlook when you arrive, there will almost certainly be one, or more likely several, passing through shortly. Other natives to watch for include *ʻamakihi* (often seen around the rain shelter at the campground where the loop trail begins and ends) and *ʻalauahio* or Maui creeper, a yellow-green bird similar to an *ʻamakihi.* They are most often spotted in the dense understory along the trail. Watch for *nēnē* in the grassy areas along the side road that leads from the park entrance to the Hosmer Grove area.

Now, while there is some daylight left, head to the summit area. Watch for *nēnē* between the entrance kiosk and the visitor center. You can stop at the visitor center just up the road from Hosmer Grove, but it closes at 2:45. Restrooms stay open later. Much farther up the road, there are three good spots for gazing into the crater: Leleiwi Overlook (elevation 8,840 feet), about 0.25 mile down a rough trail from its parking area; Kalahaku Overlook (elevation 9,324 feet), with a restroom and just a short hike up concrete steps and a trail to get to the overlook; and the near-summit visitor center (elevation 9,740 feet). You can check out all three and find a nice spot to enjoy your picnic dinner. My favorite is Kalahaku; it is usually nearly deserted at sunset, while the summit hosts hordes of visitors. If you do much walking around at these spots you will feel the elevation; the air is thin. Even in summer it will probably be cold and windy. Be prepared for intense sun, or fog and rain.

Then watch the sun set. It may set into a layer of clouds below you. Next, admire the stars and planets from one of the best vantage points in Hawai‘i (rivaled only by Mauna Kea and Mauna Loa on the Big Island).

Finally, if you are visiting during summer there is one more bit of magic that the mountain has to offer, and it's my favorite. The high steep crater walls are one of the last nesting refuges of the ‘ua‘u or Hawaiian petrel. These birds spend most of their life at sea, ranging across the entire Pacific. During nesting season from March through September they return to their nest burrows just after dusk and utter the calls that sound like their Hawaiian name. June and July seem to be the months when they are most vocal. To stand at the crater rim with billions of stars above, the lights of Maui twinkling below, and the calls of the ‘ua‘u echoing across the crater, is an utterly transformative experience. It just might keep you coming back to this high mountain again and again. The Kalahaku Overlook is a good place to perch on the crater rim and listen.

Nearby is the Waikamoi Preserve of the Nature Conservancy, adjacent to Hosmer Grove. This preserve is a stronghold of native birds and plants. The national park used to offer weekly guided walks into the preserve but discontinued them at least temporarily in 2016 out of concern that rapid ‘ōhi‘a death, a fungus that kills ‘ōhi‘a trees, might be spread there (see chapter 9). The Nature Conservancy continues to offer monthly guided hikes; see their website for more information.

5.5 KEĀLIA POND NATIONAL WILDLIFE REFUGE, MAUI. One of the best places in the state to see large congregations of wetland birds is this national wildlife refuge near the town of Kīhei on the western edge of the low Maui isthmus. As recently as 1965 this area had two hundred acres of wetlands. By 2002 only about seventy acres remained. And much of the refuge is composed of rectangular artificial ponds, a remnant of an ill-conceived 1970s catfish farm. Refuges like this one are vital to the continued existence of Hawai'i's wetland birds.

The refuge is home to breeding populations of two endangered wetland birds, the Hawaiian stilt or *ae'o* and the Hawaiian coot or *'alae ke'oke'o.* In winter these are joined by hundreds or even thousands of migrants including ducks such as the northern shoveler (*koloa mohā*) and northern pintail (*koloa māpu*). Other common wetland birds on the refuge include the Pacific golden-plover (*kōlea*), ruddy turnstone (*'akekeke*), sanderling (*hunakai*), and wandering tattler (*'ūlili,* a name that sounds like the bird's call). Frequently the refuge attracts rarities such as gulls.

The refuge has two areas open to the public: a boardwalk along coastal dunes and natural ponds, and a visitor center near the artificial Kanuimanu Ponds. The boardwalk is along Kīhei Road, Route 310 between mile markers 1.5 and 2.0, accessible only to southbound traffic. There are lots of interpretive signs to help you learn about the refuge and its inhabitants. The excellent visitor center and artificial ponds (where most of the birds can be found) are off the Mokulele Highway, Route 311, near mile marker 6. The boardwalk has excellent wheelchair access. The dirt paths around the ponds are also accessible during dry weather, but bumpy. There is very little shade, so bring plenty of water and sunscreen.

Be sure to check the visitor log for recent sightings. Some of the log entries are entered by hard-core birders who use alpha codes, four-letter abbreviations of birds' common names. Thus, black-crowned night-heron is BCNH, and Hawaiian stilt is HAST. Visitor center staff can interpret for you. At press time the refuge was open Monday through Thursday 8:00 to 4:00, closed on federal holidays. Hours seem to change frequently and the website may not be up to date, so call before visiting.

There's another wetland preserve on Maui, near the airport in Kahului. Kanahā Pond State Wildlife Sanctuary is my favorite place to spend a few minutes if I get to the neighborhood of the airport well before my flight departs. And it is a good place to see common wetland birds, sometimes *nēnē,* and occasionally vagrant birds blown to the islands by storms. The entrance, a small parking lot, and a pavilion (but no restrooms or water) are near the foot of the Haleakalā Highway, between the point where it merges with the Hana Highway and the intersection with Dairy Road. (It sounds more confusing than it is; a map will help.)

5.6 NATIVE PLANTS AND SNAILS ABOVE HONOLULU. Most of the mountain slopes above Honolulu were utterly denuded by introduced grazing animals during the nineteenth century, but a few pockets of native vegetation remain. The Kalāwahine Trail within the two-thousand-acre Makiki-Tantalus State Recreation Area follows the contours of Mt. Tantalus or Puʻu ʻŌhiʻa through a forest of mostly introduced plants, eventually leading to some natives including *koa* and *ʻōhiʻa*. The trail passes through an area where tiny native land snails can be seen, and in sunny patches along the trail one can often see the brilliant blue and green Blackburn butterflies flitting about on the foliage. The trailhead is on Tantalus Drive. To get there take Makiki Heights Drive to Tantalus Drive, and follow it uphill. Near the top you will cross a narrow bridge and then the trailhead will be on your left. It is adjacent to a private road, going uphill. There is parking on the right just past the trailhead. Note that older maps (including the Reference Map of Oʻahu published by University of Hawaiʻi Press) show this trail as the western part of the Mānoa Cliffs Trail and do not label it as the Kalāwahine Trail. The website for Nā Ala Hele, the State of Hawaiʻi Trail and Access Program, has a printable topographic map of the trails in this area.

A short fairly level walk—fifteen or twenty minutes at most—will bring you to an area of mostly introduced ginger along the trail where a colony of tiny endemic snails resides. They have no common name; the scientific name is *Auricullela diaphana*. Fortunately the snail area is marked with signs, or you would probably walk right by and never notice these very small snails. Fully extended, each snail measures less than a quarter inch from stalked eyeballs to tail. Two of them could slither around on a dime and be in no danger of touching the edge. They're not flashy. They're not colorful. But they remind us that life is dazzling in its diversity, and some of this diverse life survives even at the edge of a big city.

The trail can be muddy even in dry weather, and mosquito repellent may be necessary.

FIGURE 5.16 This tiny endemic snail was photographed along the Kalāwahine Trail above Honolulu. Approximately life size. (Rick Soehren)

5.7 BUTTERFLIES AND NATIVE PLANTS AT KĪPUKA PUAULU, BIG ISLAND. Most visitors to Hawai'i Volcanoes National Park are here for, well, the volcano. Mauna Loa Road, on the other side of the highway from park headquarters and all the current eruption activity, offers quieter diversions. Kīpuka Puaulu with its interpretive nature trail was described in chapter 4; this trail is one of the better places in Hawai'i to see native plants growing in their native habitat, even labeled so you know what you're seeing. This forest is also a good place to spot the Kamehameha Butterfly or *pulelehua* but beware: the closely related look-alike alien red admiral butterfly is also found in this forest. (See figure 5.15.) Caterpillars of both species use the native *māmaki* as a host plant. Finally, peek at the undersides of shrub and fern leaves in the *kīpuka;* you might see a tiny Hawaiian happy face spider (figure 3.1).

The *kīpuka* isn't a particularly good birding spot, although you will very likely see a big black chicken-like introduced Kalij pheasant. But there is some good birding just up the road at Kīpuka Kī. This area is fairly open and parklike, with a lot of big *koa* trees. This *koa* forest is a very good place to look for Hawai'i 'elepaio. They are most vocal, and thus easiest to spot, in the spring.

5.8 Birding at Kōke'e State Park. If you want to search for endemic forest birds on Kaua'i, Kōke'e State Park is the place to visit. There are a lot of other reasons to visit, too: great views of Waimea Canyon as you approach the park, vistas of the Kalalau Valley from inside the park, lots of endemic plants, many hiking trails, and a tiny museum and gift shop that has one of the best selections of books on Hawaiian natural history and culture that you'll find anywhere. There are also a couple of drawbacks. First, you won't see as many birds or as many bird species on Kaua'i as you would on the Big Island. Kōke'e and the adjacent Alaka'i Swamp are low enough that mosquitoes carrying bird diseases are starting to reach the area. The region took a direct hit from Hurricane 'Iniki in 1992, taking a toll on the birdlife. Second, many of the trails are very rugged or require a 4WD vehicle and good off-pavement driving skills to reach trailheads. The Pihea Trail is one of these rugged trails. The trailhead is at the end of the paved road at the Pu'u o Kila Lookout. The trail leads into some of the best publicly accessible birding areas on the island. But it is steep and slippery—hiking it is a full-body workout—and rain is common because you are near one of the wettest spots on earth.

One of my favorite trails at Kōke'e is the Awa'awapuhi Trail. The trailhead is at a small parking lot at the 17-mile marker on Highway 550. The trail heads downhill toward the coast, gradually moving from wet forest to mesic forest where you are more likely to avoid rain. Near the trailhead you may spot 'apapane, 'amakihi, and 'elepaio. There are lots of endemic plants (see **Learn More** in chapter 4 for a good plant guide). If you make it all the way to the end of the trail, you will have descended nearly 1,200 feet over a trail length of 3.1 miles. Your reward? Unforgettable views of a part of the Nā Pali coastline inaccessible by foot, and a 3-mile climb back up to the trailhead. Bring plenty of water.

With a 4WD vehicle and driving skill you can reach the trailhead for the Alaka'i Swamp Trail. The hiking is easy: the trail is fairly level, and much of it is on boardwalk across boggy swamp. This might be the best trail for seeing endemic forest birds. A longer drive on slick muddy roads will take you to the trailhead for the Kawaikōī Stream Trail, a fairly level trail that follows the stream for about a mile. Many people think it is the most beautiful streamside trail in all of Hawai'i. You can even combine parts of the Alaka'i Swamp, lower Pihea, and Kawaikōī

Stream Trails to make a great loop hike of about four miles—if you can get to the trailhead.

Even without 4WD you can drive to some of the best views in the park, near the end of the paved road. The Puʻu o Kila Lookout at the end of the road has a tiny parking lot that often is filled, with a viewing platform not accessible to the disabled. About a mile before the end of the road is the Kalalau Lookout. The views of the amphitheater-shaped Kalalau Valley and the ocean are nearly identical, but the Kalalau Lookout is more spacious and has good wheelchair access to canyon viewing areas and restrooms. Watch for *nēnē* on the lawns.

If you plan to hike at Kōkeʻe visit the museum first to buy a trail map. The State of Hawaiʻi no longer produces free trail maps for this state park. Museum hours are 9:00 to 4:30 every day. There is a snack bar open for lunch, very primitive cabins that can be reserved for overnight stays, a tent camping area, and a picnic pavilion.

LEARN MORE

- Jim Denny, *A Photographic Guide to the Birds of Hawaiʻi* (Honolulu: University of Hawaiʻi Press, 2010). This book has very good color photographs of most of the birds that can be seen in Hawaiʻi, with information on each species. It is a bit big to carry into the field, but it is the best reference for birders.
- Hawaiʻi Audubon Society, *Hawaii's Birds,* sixth edition (Honolulu, 2005). For decades this little book has been the reference of choice for carrying into the field. The sixth edition is getting a bit dated; a new edition is planned.
- H. Douglas Pratt and Jack Jeffrey, *A Pocket Guide to Hawaii's Birds and Their Habitats* (Honolulu: Mutual Publishing, 2013). Like other books in the series, this is a narrative rather than a true field guide with plenty of good information and great color photographs.
- Bird identification apps. Yes, there are apps that focus on Hawaiian birds. Content, quality, and availability can change rapidly, so you'll have to browse app stores for yourself.

6 A Whale's Tale

Whales and Other Marine Megafauna

One of the top contenders for most amazing nature experience in Hawai'i is pretty simple; it doesn't involve arduous hiking or special equipment. Just find a nice calm beach during the winter, preferably in the protected waters of Maui Nui. Swim out from shore, hold your breath, float on your stomach, and dip your head down into the water. That's it.

What's so special about this? ***You can hear the whales singing.***

Humpback whales make the long migration south from Alaska every winter. During their stay, the males sing their unique whale song. You may be able to hear the whales even when none are in sight; their voices carry for miles in the water. Their singing can be heard much of the time during the whales' peak winter abundance, throughout much of Hawai'i. And humpback whales aren't the only mammals sharing the water with us humans. Here's an introduction to Hawai'i's marine megafauna.

HUMPBACK WHALES

Every winter humpback whales migrate from their feeding grounds along the coast of Canada and Alaska, traveling 2,700 miles south to Hawai'i. They come to give birth in the calm, relatively shallow tropical waters and to mate. That's it. They don't seem to come to Hawai'i to socialize, although their social interactions in Hawaiian waters are very complex and not fully understood. And they don't come to eat. They feed on small schooling fish and shrimp-like krill in the summer up north and eat virtually nothing during their seasonal migration to Hawai'i.

Humpback whales are pretty easy to spot, for several reasons.

There are a lot of them: over twelve thousand of them visit the islands each winter. They're big: a full-grown humpback whale can measure up to forty-five feet and can tip the scales at forty tons. Finally, they are very active at the water's surface. They are mammals, so they need to come to the surface to breathe, but they also spend a lot of time at the surface thrusting heads, tails, or pectoral fins into the air, or leaping almost completely out of the water. They have been called the acrobats of the whale world.

What do we know about these creatures? Here are some basics. Their scientific name is *Megaptera novaeangliae*, meaning "big-winged New Englander." They are commonly seen off the coast of New England, and they have the largest pectoral fins (flippers or wings, corresponding to arms) of any whale. They got the common name humpback whale because of the way they arch their backs as they dive. Humpback whales, along with other whales and dolphins, are sometimes referred to as cetaceans. Their taxonomy is pretty complex, but basically they are all members of the taxonomic group Cetacea. Within this group (roughly equivalent to an order) there are separate suborders for odontocetes (toothed whales and dolphins), and baleen (filter-feeding) whales. The sperm whales of *Moby Dick* fame and the spinner dolphins described later in this chapter are odontocetes. Baleen whales include the gray whales commonly seen along the California coast and humpback whales around the Hawaiian Islands. Baleen whales draw huge gulps of water into their mouths and filter out food such as schools of herring or krill. The filter structure in their mouths is made of a hard black fingernail-like substance called baleen.

Humpback whales occur worldwide. Separate populations feed in the Arctic and Antarctic; generally, each population migrates to a shallow and warmer tropical or subtropical location during its respective winter to mate and give birth. Only a few subpopulations migrate to mid-ocean islands. Most winter in continental coastal areas.

Humpback whales are medium sized as whales go. Females are a little larger than males. They give birth to single young called calves that are ten to fifteen feet long and can weigh two tons. Their gestation period is nearly a year. By the time a juvenile whale reaches its first birthday it will already be upwards of thirty feet long.

We really don't know how long humpback whales live, and our best method of determining age is pretty crude: when scientists come upon a

FIGURE 6.1 (*a*) Breach: the whale propels itself rapidly almost completely out of the water, landing on its side with a thunderous impact. (Tory Kallman/Shutterstock.com); (*b*) Pec slap: the whale rolls on its side and slaps the water with its pectoral fin (like our arm). The sound can carry for miles. (Volt Collection/ Shutterstock.com); (*c*) Tail slap: the whale slaps its tail flukes against the water surface. Another loud behavior. (idreamphoto/Shutterstock.com); (*d*) Spy hop: the whale slowly raises its head vertically out of the water, sometimes turning, as if looking around at our world. (mikeledray/Shutterstock.com); (*e*) Peduncle arch: the whale arches its caudal peduncle (the part between the dorsal fin and tail) as it dives, usually indicating a deep dive, so the whale won't be visible for a while. (Ethan Daniels/Shutterstock.com); (*f*) Blow: this is the cloud of water vapor produced when a whale exhales at the water surface. (idreamphoto/Shutterstock.com)

dead whale, they try to extract the plug of ear wax that has accumulated over the whale's life and count the annual layers. A humpback whale's ear canal can be up to three feet long, so retrieving the entire length of this fragile column of wax is difficult, and the layers may not correspond perfectly to years of age. Guesstimates of life span range from forty years to eighty years or more, but wild creatures are constantly surprising us. In the 1990s Alaskan natives caught a bowhead whale and found stone harpoon points in its blubber—points that hadn't been used in over a hundred years. Then in 2007 Alaskans caught a bowhead and retrieved a steel harpoon point that was made about 1880. Old-time whalers didn't bother going after small young whales, so the whale was probably an adult when harpooned and around 130 years old when it was killed. Bowheads are larger than humpbacks and spend their lives in the coldest waters on earth, so they are certainly different from humpback whales in many ways. The point is, we really won't know how long humpback whales can live until we follow identified individuals from the time they are calves until they die. Come back in a hundred years—or longer—for an answer.

We can keep track of individual whales because of a fortunate trait: the pattern of light and dark color on the bottom of the tail is unique. Each time a whale commences a deep dive, the tail is thrust into the air and is visible for a few seconds. Today there is a huge and growing virtual library of photographs of whale flukes (each side of the broad tail is called a fluke), identified by date and location. Using this resource, researchers can track a whale throughout its life.

How many whales are there? An estimate of the worldwide population is about 100,000. In the North Pacific there are likely more than 21,000. More than 12,000 of these migrate to Hawai'i. Other North Pacific populations have breeding grounds along the coast of Mexico or the Philippines.

These population numbers are from 2015, and they represent a stunning comeback for the species. For a good part of the twentieth century humpback whales were a target of commercial whaling. They received international protection in 1966, but by then the hunt already had been mostly abandoned. The species was termed commercially extinct: the whalers couldn't find any more of them to kill. There may have been fewer than 1,000 left in the North Pacific. The first efforts to count the Hawaiian whales in the 1970s turned up a population between 250 and 600, but survey methods were crude and could have missed some. By 1980 there were 1,000 to 2,000 humpback whales wintering around the islands, and by the early 1990s about 4,000. Today that number has tripled, a remarkable recovery for a species hunted to the brink of extinction.

The whales' migration from their summer feeding grounds takes a little over a month. They don't all come at once. In fact, a particular sequence for their migration has been observed since the whaling days. The first to migrate are the females with yearling calves. Next come the immature whales. We're not sure when humpback whales reach sexual maturity, but it may be anywhere from eight to sixteen years old. After that come mature females without calves and then mature males. The last to make the journey are pregnant females that will give birth in Hawaiian waters. Why this particular order of age and sex? We really don't know.

We do know when the whales start to arrive and when they depart. In fact, the return of the first humpback whales each fall is cause for minor celebration. Usually people spot the first whales in October. The whales are very common from late December to early April, with the highest numbers in February and March. Whale sightings after May are unusual.

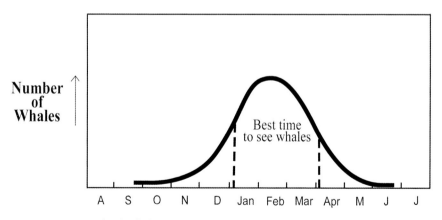

FIGURE 6.2 Humpback whales are in Hawaiʻi from October to May. During February and March they are most numerous. (Erika Heath, adapted from *Hawaii's Humpbacks* by Jim Darling; additional data from Hawaiian Islands Humpback Whale National Marine Sanctuary)

Why do the whales make this long annual round-trip? It is certainly warmer in Hawai'i, with a water temperature above 70°F compared to about 50°F at their feeding grounds. But the motivation doesn't seem to be energy conservation. It's a 5,400-mile round-trip—the distance from Los Angeles to London. And there's little food for them in Hawai'i. The whales would probably expend less net energy if they stayed in Alaska and ate all winter, even though their diet of small fish and krill is less abundant during the winter.

One guess is that the trip revolves around the birth of the calves. No one has ever witnessed a humpback whale birth in Hawai'i, but clearly the calves are born in Hawaiian waters. Mother and baby are vulnerable at this time and may prefer the relatively shallow waters of Hawai'i, only a few hundred feet deep, rather than waters that are thousands of feet deep at their feeding grounds. There may be fewer threats to the vulnerable calf in Hawai'i. There are toothy predators in Hawai'i,

FIGURE 6.3 Humpback whale mothers give birth in Hawaiian waters during the winter. (Ed Lyman, NOAA permit 14682)

including other cetaceans such as false killer whales and pygmy killer whales (more about these later), as well as tiger sharks, among the largest and most indiscriminate predators in the sea. But the pods or groups of killer whales back at their feeding grounds might be a bigger threat, and true killer whales are very rare in Hawai'i. Calf survival may be better in warmer water, too. Newborn whales don't have nearly as much insulating blubber as adults. Dropping your baby into Alaskan ice water just does not seem like a good idea.

Hawai'i appears to be the breeding ground as well as the birthing ground, which is why nearly every male humpback whale makes the annual journey. For females, the picture is a little more complicated. Occasionally females will remain in the north, but most females with yearlings migrate south. Female humpback whales sometimes give birth every year. Thus, some of the females that give birth in Hawai'i will head north nursing a two-ton baby and pregnant with its sibling. That is probably quite a strain (to put it mildly), and the average birth spacing is closer to every two years.

Just as no one has ever witnessed a Hawaiian humpback whale birth, no one has witnessed the whales mating. But the largest and most active groups of whales in Hawai'i appear to be unruly males pursuing females. There are a lot of mysteries associated with whale biology, but scientists have a pretty good idea what these excited males have in mind.

Although more than 12,000 whales make the annual journey, that doesn't mean there are 12,000 whales cavorting together in Hawaiian waters every February or March. Some whales will stick around for a few months, while others will spend only a few weeks in Hawai'i before starting the long trip north.

Pretty clearly, the migration is related to breeding and birthing. Males spend the most time in Hawai'i, three months or more. If you are a male humpback whale in Hawai'i, surrounded by potentially receptive females, why would you leave? Mothers with calves also spend well over a month. They have been observed swimming hundreds of miles up and down the island chain, as if mom is exercising junior before the long swim north. Females without calves spend the shortest time in Hawai'i, perhaps less than three weeks. If you came to get pregnant, and you got what you came for, why stick around and get harassed by all those males?

Where do the whales hang out while they're in Hawai'i? They seem to prefer relatively shallow water of about six hundred feet or less. And they favor the main islands over the Northwestern Hawaiian Islands. Thus, they might be seen almost anywhere around the main islands, and their habits make for good viewing. To provide an extra measure of protection for the whales in Hawaiian waters, the federal government and the State of Hawai'i co-manage the Hawaiian Islands Humpback Whale National Marine Sanctuary. The sanctuary boundaries include the areas where whales are most abundant. One part of the sanctuary always has the greatest concentration of whales, perhaps three-fourths of the whales present in Hawaiian waters at any given time. This is the shallow water of submerged Maui Nui, the area surrounded by Maui, Moloka'i, Lāna'i, and Kaho'olawe. The shallow favored area also extends

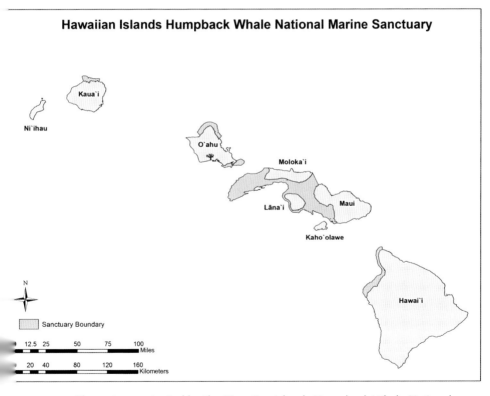

MAP 6.1 The waters protected by the Hawaiian Islands Humpback Whale National Marine Sanctuary are areas where your chances are good of spotting whales in season. (Graphic courtesy of Hawaiian Islands Humpback Whale National Marine Sanctuary)

Whalers in Hawai'i: A Mystery. One of the conflicts in Hawaiian history that is gleefully recounted by most historians is the famous friction that occurred between the staid Christian missionaries who first arrived in the 1820s and the bawdy, lecherous, rum-drinking whalers who made Hawai'i their favorite port of call every winter between roughly 1820 and 1860. If you assume the whalers were in Hawai'i to hunt Hawaiian whales, you would be completely wrong. In fact, there are virtually no records of these nineteenth-century whalers killing whales in Hawai'i. For the whalers, this time was a winter break to repair and restock their ships before heading north to the Arctic where they would hunt sperm and bowhead whales. But why risk your life in treacherous Arctic waters if thousands of whales are lounging around in some of the calmest, warmest seas on earth? Part of the answer seems to be that sperm whales were vastly more profitable to hunt. And there's human nature: once a whaling ship reached port at Lahaina, it was nearly impossible to keep the lonely, thirsty crew on board and sober. Intriguingly, however, it seems that there weren't any humpback whales in Hawai'i before western contact; the whales coincidentally started showing

over the submerged west end of Moloka'i, an area known as the Penguin Banks.

What about the singing whales? We call it singing, but it sounds—to our ears—like a series of moans and gurgles. We know that only the males sing, and that they usually sing only when they are alone. They may practice a bit at other times of the year, but nearly all the singing occurs during migration or in Hawai'i. The singing will often attract another male and when the two meet, the singing usually stops. Sometimes the two males will immediately part ways. Other times, they will go off together looking for females.

Scientists have recorded and analyzed these songs, and this is where it gets interesting and rather mysterious. All the males in a population sing the same song. That song is a particular series of sounds that usually lasts ten to fifteen minutes. The males will sing it over and over for hours. The favored singing posture is motionless with head down and tail up at an angle. During the course of a few years there will be subtle changes, like a slightly different arrangement of the song. Every singer seems to adopt the new arrangement at the same time. Different up roughly at the same time as the whalers. Whalers kept scrupulous records, and there are very few records of humpback whales in Hawai'i back then. By the 1840s Hawaiians started a few small-scale, shore-based operations to hunt the whales, but the whalers had to teach them how to do it. Hawaiians seem to have had no previous experience with humpback whales. Hawaiians did have a word for whale, *koholā,* but it apparently referred to any type of whale. There were at least half a dozen Hawaiian words or phrases referring to whale teeth and their uses, but humpback whales are baleen whales and don't have teeth. Any whale teeth in Hawai'i would have come from the occasional dead sperm whales that floated ashore. Sperm whales have teeth, and their three- to six-inch teeth made very exclusive ornaments.

All of this is a real mystery, even among historians and scientists. One theory is that—incredibly—Hawai'i was a more recent discovery for humpback whales than it was for humans. The shallow Hawaiian waters make perfect breeding grounds, but the whales used continental shore areas exclusively until some wandering whale discovered Hawai'i a little after the time Captain Cook happened upon the islands.

populations of whales each have their own songs. What does it all mean? There are plenty of theories, but we really don't have any idea.

Whale song brings us back to where this chapter started. Not only can you watch whales in Hawai'i, you can hear them, and without any special equipment. Their songs carry for miles in the water, so you may hear a whale song even when there are no whales anywhere in sight. You wouldn't want to be too close to a singing whale anyway. The sound at close range is about as loud as a good stereo turned all the way up. There are even reports that on rare occasions the whale song is so loud that you can hear it from shore. For advice on whale watching and whale listening see the **Field Trip!** section.

SPINNER DOLPHINS

Only one marine mammal in Hawai'i can compete with the humpback whales for visibility: spinner dolphins. Sometimes dozens of them at a time can be seen cruising along shorelines. They playfully "surf" on the bow wake of boats. They congregate near shore in quiet bays. And if all

FIGURE 6.4 Spinner dolphins are seen often off Hawaiian shorelines. (Marty Wakat/Shutterstock.com)

that isn't enough, they regularly leap straight out of the water, spin a few times, and plop back in. Their habits make them pretty easy to identify.

Spinner dolphins and humpback whales have a lot in common. Like whales, dolphins are warm-blooded mammals that nurse their young (which is something of an accomplishment when you're nursing under water and your baby doesn't have lips). They are both part of the same lineage that evolved from land mammals. Fifty million years ago their ancestors had hooves for feet like a deer, were somewhat doglike in appearance, and were starting to spend a lot of time in the water, like otters. About thirty-five million years ago the evolutionary transformation was more or less complete, and there were sixty-foot whalelike creatures swimming the seas. Coincidentally, this was roughly the same time that Kure and Midway were forming on the ocean floor, about where the Big Island is today. A cetacean's most closely related living terrestrial relative is the hippopotamus.

As with whales, there is a lot we don't know about spinner dolphins. One of the biggest mysteries is the population size of spinner dolphins in Hawai'i. They are pretty visible creatures, so you'd think we could get a good head count, but that's not the case. The best spinner dolphin census was done back in 2002. It came up with a figure of 3,351 spinners around the main islands and the Northwestern Hawaiian Islands. And it came with the acknowledgment that the figure was almost certainly wrong because the census was based on sightings from large boats that could not get too near shore—where lots of dolphins hang out during the day.

Spinner dolphins can be found around the globe in tropical and subtropical waters. Worldwide the population estimate is roughly 1.4 million, so Hawai'i's population is relatively tiny. There are four subspecies recognized. The Hawaiian spinners, *Stenella longirostris longirostris,* are part of the subspecies found around oceanic islands worldwide. In Hawai'i the dolphins dwell mostly around the main islands, with smaller groups near Midway, Kure, Pearl and Hermes Reef, and French Frigate Shoals.

Like whales, dolphins are highly intelligent, social mammals. Spinners are relatively small for dolphins, four to seven feet in length and 100 to 160 pounds. They have a beautiful tricolor appearance: dark gray on the back, blue-gray on the flanks, and a near-white belly.

Dolphin, Porpoise, or Whale? A common question is what is the difference between a dolphin and a porpoise? Mostly, it's the shape of the body. The word *porpoise* is derived from the Latin term *porcus piscus,* meaning "pig fish." Porpoises tend to be portly. They usually don't have the lean torpedo body of a dolphin. Most porpoises don't have the elongated beak common to most dolphins. Finally, porpoise dorsal fins are usually more triangular and squat than the hooked or curved fins of dolphins. The real test is tooth shape: porpoises have spade-shaped teeth while dolphins have conical teeth, though of course hard to see in the wild. There are about three dozen dolphin species in the world, and just half a dozen porpoise species.

What about dolphins and whales? Taxonomically, we can simplify by saying that dolphins are closely related to toothed whales, but they're in different taxonomic families. In general, dolphins are smaller and have more pronounced beaks than whales. When it comes to common names, things are haphazard. For example, the melon-headed whale that occurs in Hawai'i is actually in the dolphin family. And it isn't really whale-sized; it's usually only eight feet long or so. The killer whale is nearly whale-sized at up to thirty-two feet and eight tons. It's technically a dolphin, too—the largest member of the dolphin family.

Spinner dolphins have a predictable daily pattern of activity. They feed at night in groups that may number in the dozens or even hundreds. Their prey is small fish, shrimp, and squid, creatures that dwell in deep waters during the day but rise toward the surface and go closer to shore at night. Still, "toward the surface" is a relative term and spinners may dive to six hundred feet in search of food, which they find using echolocation. It's hard work, so they need to eat quite a bit to meet their energy needs, perhaps one organism every minute.

In the morning, usually between 6:00 and 9:00, the big pods of dolphins split up into smaller groups. These groups head for areas where they will rest until late afternoon. They seek resting areas that meet their exacting criteria: near shore, in protected fairly shallow bays, with a nice sandy bottom. Why so particular? The dolphins will enter a state that is somewhat akin to sleep, so they need a safe place. Nearshore waters in protected bays are more likely to be calm. Shallow water is less likely to be visited by big sharks, the dolphins' main predator. And the sandy bottom makes it easier to see approaching sharks when you're half asleep. The favored bays are used daily; they're well known to the dolphins and to people who watch them. See the **Field Trip!** section for a list of some.

For dolphins, the term *half asleep* is not just a figure of speech. It seems each dolphin actually does shut down half of its brain at a time, leaving the other half to stay awake and remain vigilant for sharks. They stop using their echolocation, too, perhaps a delphine version of "silent running," when a submarine keeps quiet to avoid detection by the enemy. In this sleep-wake state they swim back and forth slowly, occasionally surfacing for a breath of air. Getting your sleep isn't easy if you live in the ocean.

Around mid-afternoon, some of the dolphins will start to stir. They swim out toward open water, then back to their still-resting companions. They go back and forth until all of them are awake and ready to head out.

This time of day is often the best time to see big pods of dolphins cruising around within easy sight of land. It is also a good time to see them spinning. Why do they do it? We don't know. One guess: they're dislodging remoras, small parasitic fish that attach themselves to the dolphins' bodies. Another idea is that it is a form of dolphin communication. Finally, maybe they spin just because they can. It's fun.

As the sun sets and their prey is rising from the depths, they begin the hunt and their daily cycle starts over again.

Swimming with Dolphins: Pro and Con. A popular—and controversial—recreational activity in Hawai'i is swimming with wild dolphins. There are many tour operators, particularly along the Waianae coast of O'ahu and the Kona coast of the Big Island, who will take you out on a boat for a few hours, search for resting dolphins at some of the well-known bays, and let you snorkel and swim with them for a while. The practice is controversial because spinner dolphins are protected from harassment under the Marine Mammal Protection Act. The law does not specifically outlaw swimming with them, but any act of pursuit or annoyance that has the potential to change the dolphins' behavior is considered to be harassment.

Tour operators argue that they make sure customers are respectful and do not get in the path of swimming dolphins or even touch them. The operators point out that sometimes the dolphins, curious by nature, will actually approach the swimmers. Finally, they point to the hundreds of thousands of dolphins killed by commercial fishing operations and other threats (see the threats section later in this chapter). They argue that any impact they might have is insignificant compared to other perils faced by dolphins. People who take the tours often rave about the wonderful experience.

Marine biologists take a different view. They acknowledge the threats faced by dolphins and contend this is a powerful reason to give them all the protection we can. If dolphins are disturbed at their favored resting spots, they may move to less ideal locations where they will be more vulnerable. Visits by several boatloads of tourists every day eventually cause chronic stress and reduce the health of the population. Biologists also point out that some tour operators are more responsible than others. The bad ones will engage in practices like "leapfrogging" where the tour boat is positioned in front of swimming dolphins. "Look, they came to us!"

Even a tiny impact, multiplied by nine million visitors per year, can become overwhelming to a fragile environment. In the case of dolphin swims, I believe the risk of harming these beautiful creatures is just too great. Even though I would love to have the experience, I don't try to swim with dolphins.

What's the next best thing? There is a program called Dolphin SMART that sets standards for approaching and viewing dolphins by boat without entering the water. Book with a tour operator that complies with Dolphin SMART. You will see dolphins but will minimize the risk that you're harming them.

In 2016 the federal government proposed new rules that would keep boats and swimmers fifty yards away from dolphins. By the time you read this, new rules may be in place.

THE OTHER HAWAIIAN CETACEANS

Humpback whales and spinners may be the most visible of the cetaceans in Hawaiian waters, but they are certainly not the only ones. A handful of other cetacean species are seen occasionally, and a dozen more are rare but known to frequent Hawaiian waters. You are most apt to see two other dolphin species, bottlenose dolphins and spotted dolphins. Both species are larger than the spinners. Spotted dolphins range from six to over eight feet in length and can weigh upwards of two hundred pounds. Bottlenose dolphins are even larger, seven to twelve feet long and up to eight hundred pounds. Bottlenose are the most common dolphins in marine parks. They also tend to stay fairly near shore, so they are often seen from land or from boats cruising the shoreline. Spotted dolphins may be the most abundant cetacean in Hawai'i, but their favorite haunts are waters that are one to three miles deep. Both species bow ride; that is, they use the pressure wave created by a fast-moving boat to surf along while conserving energy. That's your best chance of seeing spotteds; watch for them bow riding in deep water during your channel crossings between islands. Bottlenose and spotted dolphins, like spinners, are darker above and lighter below, but the color gradations are not as sharp as they are in spinners. Adult spotted dolphins, as their name implies, have distinctive white speckles.

Most people never see any of the other less common Hawaiian cetaceans. You have to spend a lot of time on the water or be very lucky. Occasionally a tour boat watching humpbacks or spinners will encounter other whales or dolphins, and species identification may challenge the naturalists leading the tours. Some of the rarer species that live in Hawaiian waters include short-finned pilot whales, dwarf sperm whales, and false killer whales.

And then there are the beaked whales, so called because they are odontocetes that can grow up to twenty-three feet long with the beak-like rostrum (think nose) of dolphins. Until this century they were mysterious and rarely studied. We know of twenty-one species, mostly from studying carcasses that have washed ashore. There could be more species out there, yet to be described.

In Hawai'i there are three species of beaked whale; two, the Cuvier's beaked whale and the Blainville's beaked whale, have been the objects of intensive study this century. They are fifteen to twenty feet long. We still know practically nothing about these creatures, but scientists have fitted them with electronic tags that record their movement and the depth and frequency of their dives. The results are astounding and mind-boggling. These warm-blooded, air-breathing mammals have been tracked diving to 5,246 feet—just shy of a mile down. And they can hold their breath for over an hour and a half. They can make these deep dives day and night, every few hours. It appears that there are wide-ranging open ocean populations of both species, but also very small resident populations along the Kona coast. Even the resident populations are not easy to spot. They favor water several miles offshore and don't stay at the surface for long. Trained observers searching for them in areas where they are known to occur can go days without a sighting.

HAWAIIAN MONK SEALS

There's one more marine mammal you might encounter in Hawai'i: the endemic Hawaiian monk seal. Monk seals live throughout the Hawaiian chain, but the entire population of the species is not very large. In 2016, there were about 1,100 monk seals, with most of them in the Northwestern Hawaiian Islands and 200 around the main islands.

An adult monk seal is six to eight feet long, grayish brown, and weighs up to six hundred pounds. Females give birth to one pup at a time after gestation that is thought to be around eleven months. At birth a pup weighs twenty-five to thirty pounds. The mother will stay on or near land without eating for a month to six weeks to nurse and protect her pup. During that time she'll lose three hundred pounds while her pup will grow to about two hundred pounds. At that point she will abandon the pup. If the pup survives the first couple of years, it may have a life span of twenty-five or thirty years.

In modern times there have only been three species of monk seal in the world. The other two are the Mediterranean monk seal, with a scattered population now of only a few hundred, and the Caribbean monk seal. When Christopher Columbus visited the New World there were perhaps 300,000 of them. They were slaughtered mercilessly in the nineteenth century, and the last one was seen in 1952.

The Hawaiian monk seal probably evolved from the now-extinct Caribbean species. Recent research has shown that the two species diverged about 3.6 million years ago. At that time, there was no land bridge between North and South America. The seals probably traveled through an ancient Panama Canal. Monk seals tend to stay pretty close to land, since they feed on the ocean bottom. How did they get all the way to Hawai'i? We don't know.

Why are they called monk seals? No one is sure. The folds of skin around their necks may have reminded westerners of the folds of a monk's robes. Or it may have been the seals' reclusive, "monastic" behavior. Unlike other seals that congregate in big groups, monk seals tend to be solitary. You rarely see more than one at a time unless it's a mother with a pup. The Hawaiian name for monk seal is *īlio holo i ka uaua,* or "dog that runs in rough water."

With so few seals around the islands you'd expect seal sightings to

FIGURE 6.5 Monk seals like to bask on the shore. If you see one, give the seal plenty of space. (Rick Soehren)

be rare. It's certainly not an everyday occurrence, but when a seal hauls out on the beach to rest it attracts attention. Crowds tend to gather, and volunteers or government biologists usually set up signs to keep the curious from approaching too closely and spooking the seal back into the water. If you happen upon a monk seal and volunteers haven't yet erected signs, stay back 150 feet and don't get between the seal and the water. Ask others to do the same.

THREATS

Whales, dolphins, and seals are some of the most beloved wild creatures on earth and among the most threatened. Despite protections under U.S. law and international agreements, hundreds of thousands of marine mammals are harmed, harassed, or killed every year. How can this happen? There are a lot of ways. Some nations still hunt whales, although not humpback whales. The Japanese whaling fleet has killed about 7,500 whales in the last ten years. They claim it is all for scientific research.

Fishing can harm dolphins, too. Sometimes dolphins get entangled in fishing nets and drown before they can be freed. Fortunately, the problem is less severe than it used to be. Whales are occasionally entangled in fishing gear or discarded fishing nets. Humpback whales have been known to drag the floats and lines of fishing gear from Alaska all the way to Hawai'i. The Whale Sanctuary leads a daring effort to free whales from life-threatening entanglements and at the same time gain information to reduce the threat for other animals in the future. (This dangerous work is done by special permit; don't try it yourself.) Whales and dolphins can also be hit by boats; these injuries occur most often in places like Hawai'i where the water is crowded with boats and marine mammals.

One complicated, vexing, and deadly threat to whales and dolphins is sometimes euphemistically called "acoustic harassment." In plain terms, it is the naval use of sonar to detect submarines and other submerged objects. Why is it such a problem? Sonar generates underwater sound waves and relies on the reflection of these sounds to detect objects like submarines. To detect subs in a vast open ocean you need to generate extremely loud noises, hundreds of times louder than a jet engine. To whales and dolphins that use their own little clicking sounds as sonar to find food and communicate amongst themselves, naval sonar is excruciatingly loud, so loud that entire pods of whales sometimes beach themselves either to escape the noise or as a result of harm that the noise has caused.

The U.S. Navy has a huge presence around American coastlines where marine mammals tend to congregate, including Hawai'i. After initially denying there was a problem, the Navy has agreed to take some simple actions like posting lookouts for nearby whales and reducing the sound level when ships get too close to the marine mammals. Still, they acknowledge that naval training is responsible for hundreds of thousands of instances of harm or harassment each year. The Navy is funding the research of the beaked whales we are just starting to study. Apparently these whales are particularly vulnerable. Loud sonar causes them to alter their behavior quite suddenly. They surface quickly and get decompression sickness, more commonly known as the bends. The results can be fatal. If the U.S. Navy is using this sonar and belatedly—reluctantly—starting to consider its environmental impacts, navies of other countries are undoubtedly using it without any such precautions. Reducing these impacts is technically simple but diplomatically out of reach.

FIELD TRIP!

6.1 LISTEN TO THE WHALES. There are really only two tips you need for listening to whales. First, avoid extraneous noise. This means finding a spot where there aren't huge crashing waves, and where you can safely swim out to distance yourself from the sound of waves lapping on the beach. Remember that a lot of Hawaiian beaches have big surf and are not safe for swimming during the winter. Second, the whale song is much easier to hear if your ears are a bit below the surface of the water. Six inches minimum, a foot or two is better. The listening tends to be best in the protected waters of Maui Nui, surrounded by the islands of Maui, Moloka'i, Lāna'i, and Kaho'olawe, because the water is calm even in winter and the whales are concentrated in the area. You won't always hear whales singing, but their songs are audible much of the time during whale season.

6.2 WATCHING WHALES FROM SHORE. The great thing about whale watching in Hawai'i is that it often doesn't take a lot of effort. During whale season, just look out to sea from almost any vantage point and you might be rewarded. Of course, some spots are better than others. The whales tend to be more concentrated in the waters of Maui Nui, but they can be seen around all the islands.

One way for visitors to see a lot of whales is to book oceanfront lodging along Maui's west coast during the height of whale season. If you can afford to splurge for oceanfront, you may see fifty whales or more just by occasionally scanning the ocean while you lounge on your *lanai* (balcony or patio), sipping a beverage and reading a good book. You may also see pods of dolphins—dozens of individuals—cruising along the coast and occasionally spinning.

Other good viewing spots are peninsulas or points. A very popular West Maui viewing spot is Papawai Point. It's about three miles northwest of Māʻalaea Harbor near mile marker 8.5 on the Honoapiʻilani Highway, Highway 30. (For reference, the tunnel is a bit farther north, between mile markers 10 and 10.5.) There is a magnificent 240-degree view of the ocean. Logistics: the tiny parking lot at this lookout often fills up by midday. There is a lot of traffic on this highway, especially from late morning to late afternoon, so entry into the parking lot is easier when you are southbound and can turn right to enter. During whale season the Pacific Whale Foundation supports a whale information station at the point, staffed by a naturalist or volunteer.

Many of the spots that are good for whale watching are also places with other nature attractions. On Oʻahu, one of the best spots is Shark's Cove or Pūpūkea Beach County Park. This park offers interesting snorkeling in summer, but don't try it during the rough seas of winter on the north shore. See chapter 7 for more information on this spot. A couple other good spots on Oʻahu are the Lānaʻi Lookout (see chapter 3) and the Hālona Blowhole Lookout just to the north of the Lānaʻi Lookout. On Kauaʻi the best viewing is from the Kīlauea Lighthouse on the north shore (see chapter 5). On the south side there is good viewing along the coastline near Māhāʻulepū and the Makauwahi Cave (see chapter 12). On the Big Island the whales are concentrated along the Kohala coast. The stretch of coastline between Puʻu Koholā National Historic Park on the south and Lapakahi State Historical Park on the north (see chapter 8) is a good area for viewing. The Kalohi Channel between Molokaʻi and Lānaʻi is a whale highway. You can watch for them from the south shore of Molokaʻi or the north shore of Lānaʻi near the Pōʻaiwa petroglyphs (see chapter 8).

6.3 WHALE WATCHING BY BOAT. If you want a chance of getting very close to whales, a boat tour is the way to go. A lot of commercial tour operators offer whale-watching tours during whale season. Lahaina harbor is the epicenter of this business. Why? There are more whales off Maui than anywhere else, and the Lahaina waters are the most protected from the rough winter seas around other islands. Tip: the water tends to be calmest early in the morning, making early boat trips best for spotting whales on smooth water, and best for avoiding seasickness. Don't expect your boat to cruise right up to a whale; federal regulations prohibit boats and even swimmers from approaching closer than one hundred yards. Of course, whales sometimes approach boats.

These boat tours may also be the best way to get a close-up look at dolphins, who often bow ride. You may look down into the water from the front of the boat and see dolphins keeping pace with you.

Some tour operators are better than others. A tour operator certified by the Hawai'i Ecotourism Association is more likely to be knowledgeable and reputable.

6.4 OBSERVING DOLPHINS AT THEIR RESTING BAYS. Pods of spinner dolphins often use the same few bays for resting during the day. Seeing dolphins at these spots is never a sure thing, but you increase your chances by knowing where to look. On O'ahu, check Keawa'ula Bay (also known as Yokohama Bay) on the south side of Ka'ena Point. There are several bays used by spinner dolphins along the Kona coast. The most accessible are Kealakekua Bay (a favorite of snorkel tour boats), Hōnaunau Bay near Pu'u Honua o Hōnaunau National Historic Park, and Kauhakō Bay adjacent to Ho'okena Beach County Park. On Lāna'i dolphins are often seen at Hulopo'e Bay, where you will also find excellent snorkeling.

If you visit one of these bays, please refrain from approaching the dolphins. Don't swim or kayak out among them. Observe them from a distance of at least fifty yards.

6.5 SPOTTING THE ELUSIVE MONK SEAL. Compared to whale and dolphin watching, observing monk seals is a challenge. There are only about two hundred monk seals around the main islands, they are solitary, and their movements are not predictable. Your best chance to see one is when it has "hauled out" on the shore to rest and bask, usually on a sandy beach but sometimes on rocky shorelines. Among the main islands, there are more seals to the northwest, closer to the larger population in the Northwestern Hawaiian Islands, fewer to the south. Niʻihau may support a quarter of the seals around the main islands, but that privately owned island is off-limits for all who do not live there. The other monk seals mostly are around Kauaʻi, Oʻahu, and Molokaʻi, with just a few around Maui and almost none around the Big Island.

If you spend a week at the sandy beach resort of Poʻipū on Kauai's south shore, you have a fair chance of seeing a monk seal. By the time you see it, chances are good that a volunteer will have erected stakes and safety tape to keep the curious a safe distance back. On Oʻahu one of the most dependable spots is at Kaʻena Point (see chapter 5). However, you'll have a six-mile round-trip walk to get there, seals are hard to spot along the rocky Kaʻena shore, and they are not a sure thing. Sometimes they are seen from Kīlauea Point on Kauaʻi (see chapter 5) and near the Pōʻaiwa Petroglyphs at Shipwreck Beach on Lānaʻi (see chapter 8).

6.6 SPECIAL EVENTS, CETACEAN STYLE. Maui is home to two annual events that celebrate the presence of humpback whales. The events are organized by two nonprofit groups formed to study and protect whales. For over thirty-five years the Pacific Whale Foundation has been organizing the Maui Whale Festival, with multiple activities stretching from late January to early March. The highlight is a parade and free event held in mid-February in Kīhei, with live music and food trucks. The Whale Trust Maui has been organizing an event called Whale Tales for over a decade. It features a weekend of free lectures by whale scientists, plus receptions and other events centered in Lahaina. It is also held in mid-February, usually the same weekend as the competing festival. Why do two nonprofits with nearly identical goals hold separate events? Why don't they compare calendars? I'm afraid I have to fall back on this book's most common answer: we don't know.

The Hawaiian Islands Humpback Whale National Marine Sanctuary has a visitor center in Kīhei. There are displays on the sanctuary, the humpback whales, other marine mammals found around Hawaiʻi, and on the disentanglement program the sanctuary leads. Wheelchair access to the main display area is good. It is worth a visit if you're in South Maui. There is also a museum focusing on whales at the Whaler's Village shopping center in Kaʻanapali. It formerly centered on the somewhat grisly whaling past of Lahaina. A renovated museum, the Whale Center of Hawai'i, is being developed but had not opened as of early 2018. It will touch on the past, present, and future of whales in Hawai'i.

LEARN MORE

- Jim Darling, *Hawaii's Humpbacks: Unveiling the Mysteries* (Vancouver: Granville Island Publishing, 2009). This book is a gem. The author has done an outstanding job of communicating our scientific knowledge of humpback whales in a simple, well-organized way. The photos by Flip Nicklin are gorgeous. Highly recommended. All profits from the book support the whale research and education programs of the Whale Trust; Jim Darling is one of its co-founders.
- Brent S. Stewart, editor, *National Audubon Society Guide to Marine Mammals of the World* (New York: Alfred A. Knopf, 2002). This is a beautifully illustrated field guide to marine mammals, including descriptions of seals and sea lions, manatees, dugongs, sea otters, and polar bears, as well as cetaceans. Since it covers the world, only a few pages are devoted to Hawaiian species.
- Mark Carwardine, *Whales, Dolphins, and Porpoises,* Smithsonian Handbook (New York: Dorling Kindersley Publishing, 2002). A profusely illustrated introduction to cetaceans, including accounts of ninety-six species.
- Robin W. Baird, *The Lives of Hawai'i's Dolphins and Whales: Natural History and Conservation* (Honolulu: University of Hawai'i Press, 2016). Species accounts and conservation of the dolphins and whales encountered in Hawaiian waters, with lots of color photographs.

7 Ring around the Islands

Coral Reefs and Beyond

Ever watch kids come out of the water the first time they snorkel in Hawai'i? They're wide-eyed and sporting big goofy grins, wonderment showing in their faces because their world has just become much, much bigger. They've just visited the most complex environment on earth. Coral reefs have the same effect on the kid in all of us, although some adults may be too dignified to stumble out of the water giggling like six-year-olds.

If you take the time to learn the backstory of all the life you see while snorkeling, you will realize that this big, warm, welcoming aquarium is filled with organisms so strange and so far removed from our everyday experience that they are outlandish enough for a science fiction movie: armies of clones that build vast cities; highly advanced shape-shifters that change their form, color, and texture, making them nearly invisible when they don't want to be seen; symbionts that harbor other living organisms inside them to make their food; gender-bending creatures that can switch their sex seemingly at will; ancient beings that disappear and reappear; creatures that steal and use the weapons of other species, weapons they could not make for themselves; and simple farmers that tend the same little garden patches for twenty years. Welcome to a coral reef.

What makes a coral reef so special? Well, ask a real estate agent to describe the three most important features of a home: location, location, location. Most of the tropical ocean is empty. Take a boat one hundred miles off the Kona coast, dive in the water, and look around. Chances are you won't see a thing except deep blue sea. Food is scarce, so fish and other life forms are scarce. There's no structure at all to the environment, so there's no place to hide. The seafloor is miles beneath you in total darkness.

FIGURE 7.1 There is a lot going on at this Kona coast reef: the lobe coral has grooves made by snapping shrimp. To the left is a slate pencil urchin, in back is a rock-boring urchin, and in front, a small whitemouth moray eel. (Rick Soehren)

At the shoreline of an island, all of that changes. Rocks create structure, places where life can attach itself or hide. There is abundant sunlight all the way to the shallow bottom, so plants can photosynthesize, using light to make their own food out of water and carbon dioxide. And there are other nutrients that plants and animals need, deposited by runoff from the land. (A little runoff with its cargo of nutrients is a good thing; too much, and it causes problems. More on that later.) There is wave energy and tidal energy to circulate the water, helping some creatures to move about, and aiding waste disposal.

Life responds to this near-perfect environment in a big way. Just about every sort of plant and animal imaginable is represented here. They jostle for space, occupy every bit of exposed rock, and compete with each other, sometimes cooperating with the neighbors and sometimes eating them. A coral reef is one of the richest ecosystems on the planet. (That's why this chapter is so long.)

Remember the introduction to taxonomy and scientific naming in chapter 3? Taxonomy, the family tree of life, will come in handy now and will impart a bit of order here, because the variety of life is bewildering in its abundance and diversity. You can't always tell by looking whether you're examining a plant, an animal, or some remarkable combination.

CORAL

Let's start with the feature for which this ecosystem is named. The word coral can refer to three different things: the whole reef ecosystem; the coral head itself, comparable to a big apartment house; or the individual organisms that build and occupy the hard structure. Chapter 2 described the general distribution of coral: fringing the main islands, occasionally building barrier reefs, and forming atolls atop the ancient sinking islands to the northwest where the limestone of ancient reef may be thousands of feet thick.

When we talk about the coral head or the organism, the plural might be more accurate. There are about fifty species of reef-building corals in Hawai'i. Many of these are rare or very limited in the extent of

FIGURE 7.2 Finger coral. (John P. Hoover)

their growth. Just three species make up about 90 percent of the coral coverage around the main islands. Corals are members of the animal kingdom in the phylum Cnidaria (ny-DARE-ee-uh; the "c" is silent). Other members of the same phylum include sea anemones, jellyfish or sea jellies, and box jellies. Corals have been around for a long time. Their hard structures preserve well in the fossil record, and some are nearly five hundred million years old.

Different coral species grow different shapes of skeletons. The common and widespread lobe corals grow into big lumpy mounds; branching corals may look like heads of cauliflower or little leafless trees. Species grow at different rates—massive lobe corals grow less than an inch per year; more delicate branching corals can grow nearly four inches per year.

The living coral individuals, called polyps, all reside on the hardened coral skeleton that they secrete and build for themselves. Each polyp is a creature shaped like a bag that fits within the tiny chamber it has made for itself in the coral head. There is a single opening at the top of the bag and everything comes and goes through this single opening. Eating? Excreting? Reproducing? Everything enters and exits the bag in

FIGURE 7.3 Cauliflower coral. (Rick Soehren)

the same way. Biologist David Gulko likes to call this all-purpose body structure a mixed bag.

Polyps expand and multiply by cloning themselves. Each new clone, genetically identical to the millions of other occupants of its coral head, secretes a tiny hard cup of calcium carbonate—essentially limestone—in which it will live. When a polyp dies, a new clone will seal off its predecessor's chamber and will build a new one on top. That is how the reef grows. If you find a chunk of dead coral on the beach, you can see the little chambers.

Building the countless chambers that make up a massive coral head is an amazing feat for these tiny polyps, but they don't do it alone. Algae are growing inside the thin translucent bodies of these polyps, nourished by the polyps' waste products including carbon dioxide and nitrogen. The algae, in turn, photosynthesize and produce carbohydrates for the polyps. It's a neat trick called symbiosis in which two organisms enjoy a beneficial relationship.

Corals that harbor symbiotic algae are limited to species in shallow tropical or subtropical waters where they receive the ample light and warmth necessary for this symbiosis to be successful. Corals that grow in cold dark deep water without the aid of symbiotic algae grow at very slow rates. That's why you should think twice about buying coral jewelry. The red and black corals used for jewelry grow in water from 165 feet to nearly a mile in depth and are being harvested much faster than they can grow back.

What else do corals need? First, there has to be a firm substrate—rock—to attach to. You won't find a coral head growing on sand. And corals need clean salt water. Where Hawaiian rivers meet the sea there is invariably a break in the coral fringe because the corals can't tolerate the plume of fresh water or the load of silt that the rivers carry.

Coral polyps can clone themselves and secrete their stony coral heads for a long time. Such a colony may be hundreds or thousands of years old, or maybe more. How old? We really don't know. But we do know that corals don't just sit and grow in one place. If they want to disperse, to colonize new areas or new islands, they need a way to get around. Surprisingly, they have more than one way to go mobile.

A coral's primary dispersal method is through sexual reproduction. The individual polyps are fixed in place, so they engage in broadcast spawning. Eggs or sperm (or in many hermaphroditic species,

Symbiosis.   Life isn't easy on the reef. Sometimes you need a little help from your friends. That's what symbiosis is all about: an association between two organisms in which one or both benefit. The reef is home to perhaps more symbiosis than any other environment on earth. The most fundamental example is the relationship between algae and coral polyps; without this symbiosis the reef would not exist. Many other creatures make their home among the nooks, crannies, and structure of the reef and couldn't live without their symbiotic reef relationship. Most of the fish you see while snorkeling would not be there if it weren't for the coral that provides them with food and shelter. Other strange and wonderful symbiotic relationships exist between various reef inhabitants. Cleaner wrasses are small fish that set up cleaning stations. Dangerous predators will wait placidly while the little fish pick parasites off their bodies. Some crabs allow sea anemones to live on their claws, improving the food-gathering ability of both species. Carnivorous trumpetfish swim with schools of herbivores, waiting for them to flush other fish out into the open. Gobies are fish that live in the burrows of snapping shrimp and in turn warn the nearly blind shrimp of approaching danger. Just like in a human city, residents of the reef often depend upon one another.

both) are produced in the all-purpose sack and expelled into the water where fertilization takes place. As you can imagine, dilution becomes a big problem. How do the sperm and eggs find each other? For one thing, each species of coral seems to have its own spawning time. Millions of same-species polyps expel sperm and eggs synchronously. For finger corals, the magic hour takes place a couple days after the full moon, at about midnight. Rice corals do it a few days after the new moon, at about 9:00 p.m. This timing ensures maximum concentration of each species' eggs and sperm, and helps prevent interbreeding. How do they all synchronize their watches? We don't know.

If a sperm and egg find each other, they form a larva. Each of these larvae theoretically is capable of establishing a new coral colony, but most of the time, the larvae don't make it. A coral reef is filled with hungry creatures that eat by filtering water. Spawning time for corals is feasting time for their neighbors.

Any larvae that escape from the hungry reef will drift in the currents for a few days to a few months. Then, if they can find one, they settle on a solid substrate, become a polyp, and start a new cloned colony.

Is this how corals colonized isolated Hawai'i? Probably not. Some corals can exist in larval form long enough to drift to the islands, but most larvae can't survive long enough to make the journey from distant South Pacific coral colonies. So how did they do it? The answer seems to be a process called coral rafting. Coral larvae can attach to floating objects and raft their way to new homes. In the old days the raft might have been a chunk of driftwood. Today it can just as easily be an old ice chest or a stoppered bottle. Either way, a reproducing colony can raft to new island homes.

There's one more feature of corals and other Cnidarians that you need to know about, and it actually defines the whole phylum. It is a clue that corals—living rocks—are related to soft, nearly formless sea jellies. These creatures are equipped with something called stinging cells, but the term really doesn't do justice to the amazing structure that has evolved in these primitive creatures. A stinging cell is not like the passive spine on a blackberry branch. Each microscopic cell contains a long hollow coiled filament with a barbed point. When the cell's mechanism is triggered by prey that bumps it, or when the polyp senses the chemical signature of a nearby target, the cell fires its coiled filament and toxin is injected. Usually the filament doesn't stay attached to the coral polyp or sea jelly but the prey is immobilized and can be eaten. Each cell can fire only once, but the Cnidarian has thousands of them, and it can make more.

The stinging cells of corals are very tiny, some only about 1/10,000 of an inch long. If you put your hand on living coral you won't feel the stinging cells. The box jellies that occur in Hawai'i pack a much more powerful sting and can be quite painful. Even when jellies die and wash up on the beach, their stinging cells can still fire into your foot. The stings of the Portuguese Man o' War, a larger jellyfish-like Cnidarian that usually drifts in the open sea but can blow in toward Hawaiian beaches, are excruciatingly painful.

If the whole idea of stinging cells sounds amazing, here's one final twist that will boggle your mind. There are several species of sea slugs in Hawai'i called nudibranchs (pronounced NOO-duh-brangk) that feed on Cnidarians and have the remarkable ability to swallow unfired stinging cells and incorporate the unfired cells into their own flesh, where the nudibranch can fire them for defense. Some, like the blue dragon nudibranch, take the concept of reuse a step further. They incorporate

FIGURE 7.4 This box jelly washed ashore at Waikīkī. (Rick Soehren)

Box Jellies. The Cnidarians most likely to inflict their sting on people in Hawai'i are the box jellies. There are a couple of different species in Hawai'i. They get their name from the roughly cube-like shape their clear filmy bodies (called bells) take on as they swim. The most common species has a bell two inches across and about three inches long. Others measure about an inch by an inch. A tentacle up to two feet long, armed with stinging cells, trails from each bottom corner of the bell. Box jellies often show up on the leeward shores of O'ahu eight to ten days after the full moon, and they stick around for two or three days. Sometimes there are only a few, other months they are so numerous that beaches are closed. Spawning probably causes their carefully calendared presence, but we don't know for sure. It is so predictable that there are box jelly calendars posted online. Even dead jellies looking like little blobs of goo on the beach can fire their stinging cells.

The folk remedy for box jelly stings is to apply urine. Don't do it; there's no solid evidence that it does any good and it certainly adds insult to injury. Experts recommend that you douse the affected area with vinegar; it stops the stinging cells from firing. Use a stick or other tool to pull off any remaining tentacle. Some people are more sensitive than others to the burning pain. The pain usually goes away in a few hours, and the welts disappear in a few days. When in doubt, seek medical attention.

FIGURE 7.5 These yellow tangs are grazing on a rock covered with pinkish coralline algae. (Rick Soehren)

the Cnidarians' symbiotic algae into their flesh, too. Most nudibranchs are only a couple of inches long. Some are brightly colored and toxic; others generally stay out of sight.

Corals get some reef-building help from plants. Many of the colorful hard surfaces you see on the reef are not corals, but calcareous algae, sometimes called coralline algae. Like corals, they make calcium carbonate to serve as a sort of skeleton. Some look like shaggy little plants or coral heads. Others are flat creeping algae that can grow over rocks or dead coral. Often these are pink, lavender, or maroon. Other algae look more typical; you will recognize them as "seaweed." Many types of algae are picked in Hawai'i for food. They are called *limu* and are an important ingredient in *poke,* the popular raw fish dish.

VERTEBRATES OF THE REEF

Corals have relatives on the reef. In addition to the free-swimming or drifting jellies, sea anemones are part of the phylum. They usually live attached to hard surfaces. They got their name because they reminded early observers of flowers. Most of the anemones in Hawai'i are small compared to the six-inch-diameter giants that you can see on the west coast of North America. Sea anemone tentacles wave in the current, armed with stinging cells that can harpoon their prey of small fish and invertebrates. Like corals, anemones usually have symbiotic algae living within them. In other parts of the world, symbiotic anemonefish that are immune to stinging cells dwell within anemones. They do not occur in Hawai'i, never having made the long open-ocean journey.

The stinging cells of anemones are generally so small that you can rub your finger on one without injury. However, a few species of anemone relatives do produce powerful toxins, so you might want to keep your fingers to yourself.

Here's another remarkable symbiosis: the small Hawaiian pompom crab encourages little anemones to attach to its claws. Then it mops the sand with them. This helps the anemones pick up much more food than they could on their own, and the excess goes to the host crab.

Another big group of reef dwellers are the mollusks, phylum Mollusca, including nudibranchs as well as the familiar snails, clams, mussels, and oysters. Pearl oysters used to be common in some protected bays such as Pearl Harbor, but they have all but disappeared due to overharvest and degraded water quality. Pearl oysters need clean water; if you visit Pearl Harbor today you'll see that it is pretty murky compared to the water surrounding any thriving reef. In an unusual twist, Hawai'i is trying to grow filter-feeding oysters in Pearl Harbor—not to eat, but to help clarify the water. Oysters for human consumption are grown in north shore fishponds on O'ahu.

Some showy snails have also become rare on Hawaiian reefs due to shell collecting. The rarest and most beautiful, like the one-shelled cowries, can sell for hundreds of dollars to collectors. The Hawaiian limpet or 'opihi is a shelled mollusk that is collected for food. Its single flattened conical shell looks like a tiny sun hat. The best place to find these shells is on the beach near rocky shorelines, where people have discarded the shells after plucking out the tasty meat.

Many mollusks are herbivores, like garden snails. Others such as the cone snails are predators. Their coiled snail shells have a distinctive elongated cone shape. Where herbivorous snails have a rough organ like a cat's tongue to scrape algae, the cone snail has barbed teeth that are hollow and can inject venom. Those teeth are an excellent reason not to collect any shells that are inhabited. Besides, shell collecting is prohibited inside marine life conservation districts.

The most intriguing mollusks are creatures that bear little resemblance to their snail and clam relatives: squids and octopuses. Most squids tend to stay outside the reef in open water, although there are two species that live near shore. The Hawaiian bobtail squid is a two-inch-long nocturnal creature of mudflats and sandy areas. The bigfin squid, growing to about a foot in length, is occasionally seen near coral reefs.

Octopuses are very much at home on the reef. There are over a dozen octopus species in Hawaiian waters, including at least five that live in shallow water near the shoreline. They dwell among the cracks and nooks in the reef, and their long arms can search for other nook-dwelling prey such as crabs, shrimp, and shelled mollusks.

Octopuses were well known to the early Hawaiians, who appreciated the uniqueness of these creatures. In fact, one translation of the *Kumulipo* or Hawaiian creation chant relates that our universe is the latest in a long line of universes, each new one created when the previous universe was destroyed. According to this version of the chant, the octopus is the only creature to survive from the universe before ours—truly a creature from another world.

And why wouldn't we think the octopus is otherworldly? Anyone who gets to know these creatures has to be in awe of their abilities. They are shape-shifters. They have no skeleton, so they can contort into nearly any shape and squeeze through impossibly small openings. They have big brains—big for a mollusk, anyway—and eyes that are more complex than our human eyes. One species, the day octopus, occurs in Hawai'i and around the world. It averages about two feet from head to arm tip, giving it an arm span of nearly four feet. It hunts by day, so it needs good camouflage against larger predators. It can quickly change the color and texture of its skin in order to hunker down and disappear on the reef. The day octopus is smart, too. This species can solve puzzles and navigate mazes in the laboratory. In the wild, it uses tools, carrying things like discarded coconut shells for protection.

The eight arms of an octopus are amazingly sensitive and limber, the better to grasp objects and feel around for prey. The arms are lined with hundreds of suction cup appendages that enable it to hold on to objects with a glue-like force. An octopus can slither along on its arms, or it can travel via built-in jet propulsion, using a jet of expelled water to quickly escape danger.

The octopus has an amazingly sophisticated defense. When it feels threatened, it will turn its body very dark to give a predator a search image of a dark creature. Then it squirts a cloud of dark liquid we call ink and jets away. The confused predator goes for the ink cloud. But the ink cloud is more than just a false target. The ink sticks to the predator's eyes, clogs its nostrils and taste buds to disable sensory abilities, and may clog its gills to reduce oxygen uptake and thus the predator's ability to give chase.

Octopuses have three hearts. Whereas our red blood uses iron-based hemoglobin to transport oxygen, octopus blood uses a copper-based protein and is blue. In cool ocean conditions, copper works better than iron.

Octopuses don't live a long time. Different species have life spans of a few months to about five years. The big reason for a short life span is that they only breed once. After that the male wastes away and is gone in a few months at most. The female will fast and guard her clutch of eggs until they hatch, then she will die as well. Since they only reproduce once, they compensate with quantity. A day octopus may lay tens of thousands of eggs.

Another octopus species on Hawaiian reefs is the night octopus, an aggressive nocturnal hunter. It isn't huge by octopus standards, averaging about eighteen inches from its head to the tip of its outstretched arms, but it will take on big challenging prey. Like all octopuses it can deliver a venomous bite with its hard beak, the only bone-like thing in its body. If the night octopus realizes it has taken on too big a challenge and may lose the battle, it can intentionally shed an arm for the opponent to gnaw on while the octopus jets away. Later it will grow a new replacement arm.

Another species, the rock octopus, may have plans to evolve and take over the world. Much as our ancestors long ago emerged from the sea, this octopus can crawl out of the water on rocky shores to hunt for small crabs that commonly scuttle round on exposed rocks. Octopuses are amazing.

Octopuses have been prized as food since before western contact. In fact, the early Hawaiians made octopus lures from cowry shells that were functional works of art. Several different names are used for octopus. Local anglers often call octopuses squid. The Hawaiian is *he'e,* meaning to slip or slide. The Japanese is *tako,* and raw octopus is used in a dish called *tako poke.* Some people do not eat these creatures out of respect for their intelligence and abilities.

Despite centuries of hunting, it is still possible to see octopuses on the reef, especially in marine life conservation districts or other places where they are not hunted. The day octopus is seen most often, because it is out hunting during the same hours that snorkelers visit reefs. Remember that octopuses are masters of camouflage. It is usually possible to spot a day octopus only when it moves. You may be able to spot an octopus den, where an octopus will often retreat to eat its prey. Look for discarded bits of shell or exoskeleton that often litter the reef outside the den. This reef decoration is the origin of the term octopus' garden.

Another major group of reef invertebrates consists of sea urchins, seas stars or starfish, and sea cucumbers, all members of the phylum Echinodermata. Sea stars are not common in Hawai'i and many Hawaiian sea star species are active at night, so they are not prominent on the reef. The most common ones are typical five-armed stars that can be pink, blue, or spotted, about four or five inches in diameter. The one you'll most want to avoid is the descriptively named crown-of-thorns star, bristling with venomous spines. It can be red or green and grows to over a foot in diameter. It feeds on coral by pushing its stomach out through its mouth and digesting coral polyps in place.

Sea urchins, on the other hand, are among the most conspicuous invertebrates on the reef. They can grow to nearly a foot in diameter, sometimes are brightly colored, and often occupy fairly visible spots on rocks and coral heads. One of the most striking of the urchins is the slate pencil urchin. Slate pencil is an old name for the chalk used on blackboards, and the fat brick-red spines of this urchin look like sticks of chalk. They can live in protected niches or out in the open and are among the biggest of the Hawaiian urchins at a diameter of up to a foot.

Rock-boring urchins have the amazing ability to grind holes in the soft limestone of reefs, creating their own little home niches. A reef with a lot of these urchins looks like Swiss cheese. Rock-boring urchins can be either pale green or pale pink, sometimes darker. Their spines can puncture your skin if you press on them. Slate pencil and rock-boring urchins can both be seen in figure 7.1.

The urchins you really want to avoid are the spiny urchins, a few

FIGURE 7.6 The spiny urchin is one reef resident you definitely want to avoid because of its sharp, venomous spines. (Rick Soehren)

different species collectively called *wana* in Hawaiian (the *w* sounds like a *v*). One species is black or dark purple, and can grow to ten inches or more, although most are smaller. Sometimes *wana* have white or banded spines. These spines are needle-sharp. When you touch a *wana*, the spines inject painful venom, and they can break off in your flesh and cause infection. Among Hawaiian urchins *wana* are the most likely to grow in prominent spots on the reef where you might inadvertently bump one. Always exercise care when snorkeling around urchins. If surging water could push you into rocks where there might be urchins, stay away.

Sea cucumbers are relatives of the urchins and are quite common on Hawaiian reefs. They look vaguely like rotting cucumbers. Some have described them as sandy sausages. Most of them are sediment swallowers, meaning that they slurp up whatever they can find along the reef bottom and digest anything edible.

The crustaceans, kin to insects, are among the more successful invertebrates on coral reefs. They are members of the phylum Arthropoda, meaning jointed leg. Whereas insect members of the phylum have six legs, crustaceans such as crabs, shrimps, and lobsters have ten. One group of crustaceans, the barnacles, does not have readily apparent legs and its members look more like mollusks.

Shrimp are virtually everywhere on coral reefs, but they are usually inconspicuous. Most are no more than an inch or two long, and many are ghostly translucent. You really need to slow down and scrutinize small patches of the reef to spot them.

Even if you don't see any shrimp, you almost certainly will hear them. The constant popping or crackling you hear while snorkeling near a reef is made by snapping shrimp that are usually hidden away in cracks or under ledges. The snap is not what you'd expect; it is nothing like snapping your fingers. Each shrimp has one enlarged claw with a peg-like bump on one side that fits into a hole on the other side. This claw can close so rapidly that the peg and hole create a tiny jet of water that spurts out at over sixty miles per hour. That water jet causes a tiny air bubble to form in its wake. It is the collapsing air bubble that makes the sound. It creates a shock wave that—at close range—can be louder than a gunshot. The snaps stun prey and ward off predators.

On the other hand, a few shrimp species do go in for high visibility, as a way to bring in business. The cleaner shrimps set up little cleaning stations, and reef fish line up to give the shrimps an opportunity to pick off tiny parasites and bits of dead tissue. One of these species is the two-inch-long barber pole shrimp, so named because it has prominent bands of red and white around its body. Ordinarily a flamboyantly colored shrimp sitting out in the open would be quick and easy prey, but fish refrain from eating their beautician. This shrimp can even crawl safely into the mouth of a moray eel to clean between the eel's teeth.

There are crabs in the reef but they are hard to spot. Many are nocturnal, and they generally stay in the crevices where they are safer from predators and where more of their scavenged food tends to settle. Oddly enough, the best place to observe crabs is out of the water, where several species are common and quite visible. Look for thin-shelled rock crabs on rocky shorelines. The Hawaiian word for this crab is *aʻama.* They are mostly black, with bodies up to three inches across. They graze on seaweeds at the water's edge. On sandy beaches you may encounter evidence of two species of ghost crabs, so named because they seem to disappear like ghosts. You're much more likely to see their burrows than the crabs themselves because these creatures are most active at night. You may see fresh burrows during early morning beach walks, and you can even tell which crab species made the burrow by how it has been dug. Pallid ghost crabs are sand-colored crabs with a shell up to about an inch across. They are messy burrowers that throw sand out in a fan shape. They are sometimes seen at dawn and dusk. Horn-eyed ghost crabs are dark bluish in color, with shells up to about three inches across. They are mostly nocturnal, and they are tidy. They carry their excavated sand to a nearby mound. Their burrows vary in size, according to the size of the crabby occupant.

There are at least ten species of lobsters in Hawai'i but most do not have the familiar shape of North American lobsters. They usually lack big claws and some, the slipper lobsters, have very short antennae and legs. Lobsters have become rather uncommon in Hawai'i except at remote areas where they have managed to avoid hungry snorkelers and divers.

FISH OF THE REEF

The creatures that snorkelers usually notice in the water first are the fish. There are so many species, with such an array of shapes, colors, and sizes, that many people really never get past fish watching to see the other life on the reef. (That's why this chapter described most everything else first!) An observant snorkeler can easily see over a hundred fish species. And the colorful bounty goes beyond species count: some of these species exhibit such radical color and pattern differences between juveniles and adults or between males and females that early scientists mistook them for different species. Many snorkelers get overwhelmed by the diversity.

To avoid this, you need a little dose of taxonomy. By learning a few of the most common fish families and their characteristics, you will instantly know a fair amount about the diet and habits of individual fish you see, even if you don't know exactly what species you're observing. If you know that the new fish you spotted is, say, a member of the wrasse family, you will have an easier time looking it up and determining its species once you're out of the water. The book in your hands will help you identify fish families and a few of the most common species; see the **Learn More** section for some excellent fish guidebooks that will help you identify hundreds of additional species.

When a first-time snorkeler wades into the ocean on a sandy beach and dips her masked face into the water, the first fish she's likely to see is a member of the family collectively called **goatfishes**. Relatively few fish feed on sandy bottoms, and goatfish are the most visible. They get their name from their barbels or whiskers, which apparently reminded someone of a goat's beard. Most goatfish species grow to a maximum size of twelve to twenty inches, but many of the goatfish you see on reefs are smaller. When not scouring the sand for invertebrates, some goatfish form schools at middle depths between the surface and the bottom and may be seen over sand or rocky reef. Some goatfish species have the ability to change colors. The yellowfin goatfish that is common at Hanauma Bay usually resembles its close relative the yellowstripe goatfish shown in figure 7.7, but the yellowfin species can turn pink or red.

Some of the most noticeable fish on the reef are the **butterfly-fishes**. Fish in this family have bodies that are oval—or in some cases almost rectangular—in profile and are very laterally compressed (side to side). Most species are five to eight inches long. For most species, their most striking feature is their yellow, black, and white coloration, in distinctive patterns for each species. Most are carnivores, feeding on

FIGURE 7.7 Square-spot goatfish, also called yellowstripe goatfish. (John P. Hoover.)

FIGURE 7.8 Raccoon butterflyfish. (John P. Hoover)

small invertebrates or picking off coral polyps. Some species have very long noses for reaching into crevices. Many butterflyfish mate for life, and they are often seen in pairs. At other times, dozens of individuals of a single species will form a school—quite a sight.

Wrasses seem to be everywhere on the reef. And for good reason: there are more species of wrasses on Hawaiian reefs than any other family of fish. They are among the most variable of fish, too, although a few generalizations can be made. Most wrasses are elongated and oval in profile, like little torpedoes. Most species are between six and twenty inches in length. Nearly all have a dorsal fin (the fin on the back) that runs nearly the length of the fish but is not very tall, and a corresponding anal fin along the belly that is similar in shape to the dorsal fin. Wrasses come in just about every color and color combination imaginable. Males, females, and juveniles of a single species may all be different colors. All wrasses are carnivores and feed on a variety of invertebrates. Some eat other fish. Remember the cleaner shrimp? They have business rivals. The little four-inch cleaner wrasse, vivid purple and yellow, sets up a territory that is a cleaning station. Other species of fish will line up to get parasites picked off by the accommodating wrasse. In return, these customer fish don't eat the little wrasse.

FIGURE 7.9 Saddle wrasse. (John P. Hoover)

Sex Change. In the very strange and foreign world of a coral reef, perhaps no phenomenon is quite as surprising as the ability of many fish species to change their sex, seemingly at will. Some that do this the most are the wrasses and the parrotfish. Here's one way it works: among some wrasse species a dominant male will have a harem of females. His presence seems to inhibit any sex change among the females. If he is removed, the alpha female will immediately start acting like a male, herding the harem around. Within a few days, she grows to male size and changes to male color. And she stops producing eggs and starts to produce sperm. She is now a he.

Surgeonfishes get their name from the sharp, blade-like spines that protrude from each side of their bodies near the base of the tail. These spines are not dangerous to humans unless the fish is cornered or caught. Some surgeonfish are referred to as tangs. Surgeonfish vary in size from the convict tangs (*manini*) and yellow tangs at about eight inches, to some eighteen-inch species that are the size of platters. They are laterally compressed, so they're almost as thin as a platter, too. Coloration is quite variable, although many species show a lot of black with

FIGURE 7.10 Convict tang. (John P. Hoover)

FIGURE 7.11 Orangeband surgeonfish. (John P. Hoover)

some orange. Surgeonfish have very tiny scales, so they look velvety smooth. Most of them are herbivores, so many are found in shallow water where algae grow well. They often swim in schools. When dense schools of convict tangs move along the bottom feeding on algae, their movement often flushes out small fish or invertebrates. That's why carnivorous fish will sometimes follow the tangs, waiting for an easy meal. Vivid yellow tangs do not grow too large, so they are often caught for the aquarium trade.

Finicky Fecundity.   Most of the little saltwater fish displayed in home aquariums around the world are caught on coral reefs. It's a controversial practice because it reduces the number and variety of fish remaining on the reef, and many of the captured fish die prematurely. Why don't aquarists just breed these fish in captivity? Basically, we can't do it because the life histories and needs of reef fish are not well understood. The yellow tang is a good example. It is a prominent and highly visible member of the reef community, prized by hobbyists. By some estimates, 300,000 are netted out of Hawaiian reefs every year. After decades of trying, ichthyologists (fish biologists) are just learning to raise them in captivity. In 2016 researchers at Hawai'i Pacific University produced the first few hundred captive-bred tangs for the aquarium trade. Maybe hobbyists should stick with freshwater species that are more easily bred in captivity. Yellow tangs at home on the reef can be seen in figure 7.5.

Triggerfishes are named for a spine at the front of their dorsal fin that can be locked by the second spine in an upright position. This mechanism is used to wedge the triggerfish into a hiding place. If the second spine—the trigger—is depressed, the first spine can be released. When the fish is relaxed, the first spine is held close to the body and nearly disappears. Most triggerfish have an odd shape, something like a little football with a mouth on one end. Some of the most common triggerfish species can grow to ten to twelve inches in length, so in rare cases you may see one that actually is as large as a football. Most triggerfish are unfussy carnivores, consuming whatever bottom-dwelling invertebrates their strong jaws can crunch up. They are usually shy and will swim away if approached. However, a female guarding her eggs will charge and bite.

One triggerfish has the honor of being the Hawai'i state fish. This,

FIGURE 7.12 Wedgetail triggerfish or *humuhumunukunukuāpuaʻa*, the Hawaiʻi state fish. (John P. Hoover)

of course, would be the *humuhumunukunukuāpuaʻa*. It means "triggerfish with a snout like a pig." And it is a good example of why scientific names, unique to a species, are so important. The same Hawaiian name is used for two different triggerfish species. One is *Rhinecanthus aculeatus*, the lagoon triggerfish. The other is *Rhinecanthus rectangulus*, known variously as the wedgetail triggerfish, the wedge triggerfish, and the Picasso triggerfish. This species is the state fish.

Needlefishes are very long and thin, as their name implies. The species most commonly seen at snorkeling spots is the keeltail needlefish, which grows to about fifteen inches. These silvery carnivores sometimes escape a snorkeler's notice because they stay just under the surface, and most snorkelers are looking down. Another family of long thin fish that dwell at the surface includes the **halfbeaks**, so named because their thin lower jaw is much longer than their upper jaw. Long thin fish seen in the middle depths or near the bottom are usually **trumpetfishes** or **cornetfishes**. Both families eat other fish; because they are

FIGURE 7.13 Keeltail needlefish. Look for them just under the surface of the water. (John P. Hoover)

long and thin, they are nearly invisible to the prey they are approaching. Trumpetfish are stiff bodied and laterally compressed, making them most visible from the side. Cornetfish are more flexible as they swim, are compressed top to bottom so they are most visible from above, and have a thin tail filament. The Pacific trumpetfish is fairly common in Hawai'i. It grows to about thirty inches. Most are brown or black, but some individuals are bright yellow (the better to hide among a school of tangs or butterflyfish and wait for the school to startle prey). Cornetfish are bluish silver. They are usually about two or three feet long but some in protected areas like Hanauma Bay may be five feet long. Be glad you're too big to look like a meal to these fellows.

Damselfishes are usually not the first fish noticed by snorkelers because they are small, usually less than six inches and often only two or three inches in length. Once you notice them swimming just above the coral or in crevices, you'll realize that they're very common. Damsels are laterally compressed and oval to almost round in profile. They

FIGURE 7.14 Hawaiian sergeant. (John P. Hoover)

generally have big scales for such small fish, making them look scaly. Species of damselfish come in many colors, but most are drab. They can live a long time, up to twenty years. The most common damselfish, the Hawaiian sergeant, is yellowish green with five black bars running vertically down its sides. Most damselfish are herbivores. Some, like the Hawaiian sergeant, gather into schools and feed on planktonic algae, tiny plants that drift along in the water. The most intriguing damselfish are solitary fish that guard their own little territories where they "farm" algae. They ward off all other fish, whether they are herbivores or coral eaters. They pick out the undesirable algae species from their territory, and some even pick up small crown-of-thorns stars and move them off their "property." The unintentional result of this starfish removal is that damselfish territories sometimes harbor coral species that are scarce on other parts of the reef. Right now there are little damselfish that have been tending the same tidy plots of algae on the reef for twenty years, through hurricane and tsunami.

Swimming to Hawai'i. It seems like fish would have an easier time making it to isolated Hawai'i and establishing a new population than, say, little songbirds or trees or bugs. It is not necessarily so. All the fish you see on the reef live in fairly shallow water. They would be as out of place in mile-deep water as you or I. They would likely never be able to swim the long distance over deep water to reach Hawai'i. But their kids can! They aren't boastful parents; it's all about a fish's life cycle. Most of the fish that live on the reef will spawn there. When the eggs hatch, the tiny young are called larvae and they are very different in appearance and habits from their parents. They are usually tadpole-like, feeble swimmers that drift out to sea where they will spend weeks or months feeding on sparse plankton and growing. This stage of life can only last so long. Eventually the growing fish start to look more like their parents, and they need to find a suitable reef habitat or they will die.

This hit-or-miss lifestyle has produced a condition among island species called disharmony. It is a mismatch between the abundant taxonomic classes, orders, and families that exist in continental habitats, and the lower number that are established on islands, usually with some glaring absences. The fish families with the most representatives in Hawaiian waters, such as wrasses and moray eels, tend to have longer larval periods than other fish. Thus, their larvae have more time to make the long drift from Asia or the tropical islands to the southwest.

Moray eels are among the most exciting (or terrifying) fish on the reef for snorkelers to observe. They are snakelike in appearance, menacing with their toothy mouths agape, their necks pulsating, and their heads swaying. In fact, they are probably just breathing; most of their carnivorous hunting happens at night. Some species reach five feet in length, although most top out at two or three feet. Most come in shades of brown, black, or white and the patterns among some species are stunning: speckles, stripes, sometimes both. They are surprisingly abundant and may comprise 10 percent of the fish on the reef, but you won't see very many. Most of them are hiding in holes and crevices. That's why you should never stick your hand into holes, and why you should be especially careful snorkeling over rocks or coral in extremely shallow water where your face and other body parts are very close to the reef. Moray eels are generally not aggressive unless provoked, but you don't want to tempt them. (See figure 7.1.)

Parrotfishes are notable for many reasons. The big males of many species are among the largest and heaviest fish found in shallow reefs near shore, reaching lengths of up to two feet or more. They are generally shy and hard to approach. Parrotfish are long, stout fish with a rounded face, and teeth that are fused into a blunt beak-like mouth used for scraping coralline algae and coral. You can sometimes hear this scraping when you are snorkeling. The hard parts of algae and coral are broken down in the fish's gut and excreted as clouds of sand. A big parrotfish can produce a thousand pounds of sand per year this way. Among reef fish, parrotfish are the champions of the sex change. Depending on the species, young parrotfish may be a mix of males and females, or all females. These young are invariably drab, usually splotchy brown in this initial phase. Most never grow out of this phase. Later in life, some of the females will develop into a terminal phase. They turn into supermales and transform from drab to dazzling, turning brilliant blue-green in most species.

Some parrotfish make their own sleeping bags. At night they secrete a mucus bubble around themselves and sleep in it. Why do they do this? We really don't know, but one guess is that it traps their scent and makes them less vulnerable to night hunters like moray eels.

Uhu is the Hawaiian name for parrotfish. *Uhu* have been prized for food since ancient times. They are still one of the most popular fish in Hawaiian markets that cater to locals. This popularity has two downsides. First, big parrotfish are uncommon in areas where a lot of fishing takes place. You'll see a lot more of them in well-protected marine life conservation districts such as Hanauma Bay. Second, when you take most of the big herbivores out of an ecosystem, you run the risk

FIGURE 7.15 Bullethead parrotfish, colorful supermale and drab initial phase. (John P. Hoover)

of radically altering the balance. Some people believe that protecting more parrotfish would help Hawai'i manage the rampant overgrowth of marine algae that is occurring on some reefs.

FIGURE 7.16 The Moorish idol is the only member of its fish family. These were photographed at Beach House on Kaua'i. (Rick Soehren)

Fish without a Family.   One beautiful yellow and black fish that you might see on the reef is the Moorish idol. It looks vaguely like a butterflyfish, but it is not in the same family as the 130 species of butterflyfishes worldwide, including the nearly two dozen that occur in Hawai'i. In fact, the Moorish idol is notable because it has no other family members. Worldwide, there is exactly one species in the fish family Zanclidae. Moorish idols are widespread in the Indian Ocean and the Pacific. This is probably because they have an unusually long larval stage, which allows them to drift longer and disperse farther. They are often seen quite close to shore, visible even in murky water. You can often see them if you peer into the water from atop the sea wall either in Waikīkī near the aquarium or in downtown Kailua-Kona.

Porcupinefishes and **Pufferfishes** are two families of blocky-looking fish that have developed a range of unusual defense mechanisms including spines or bristles. Usually these spines lie flat against the body of the fish. When the fish are alarmed, they gulp water, which forces the spines to protrude at right angles, turning the fish into spiky spheres that are unpalatable to all but the most determined predator. And that determined predator has a surprise coming: most of these fish are highly toxic. People who eat them have died within twenty minutes. The toxin produces numbness, nausea, and paralysis of the voluntary muscles before death occurs. The fish do not produce the toxin themselves. It is produced by symbiotic bacteria that reside in the fish. Despite the toxicity, pufferfish are a delicacy in Japan, where they must be specially prepared by experienced chefs who remove poisonous tissues and serve the edible parts. The largest puffer in Hawai'i is the stripebelly puffer, olive drab and white, often a foot long, and often seen by snorkelers.

Relatives of porcupinefish and pufferfish comprise another blocky poisonous fish family, the **Boxfishes**. They cannot expand like porcupinefish and pufferfish. Instead, their scales have fused into a sort of hard exoskeleton. Only their fins, eyes, and mouths can move. Some of them can produce a mild toxic slime when stressed.

One more creature visits shallow reefs, a favorite of snorkelers and nature lovers: the **Hawaiian green sea turtle** or *honu*. The green sea turtle is a reptile species found around the world in tropical and subtropical waters. The turtles in Hawai'i form a distinct population. These turtles can grow to be over three feet in carapace (shell) length and weigh upwards of 250 pounds, although most of the turtles seen are somewhat smaller. Green sea turtles are fairly easy to spot around the main islands for two reasons. First, most of their diet consists of algae, so they spend a lot of time in shallow water near shore. Second, Hawaiian turtles have an unusual habit not shared with most other populations of green sea turtles: they come ashore to bask and rest. See figure 1.1 and check the **Field Trip!** section for good viewing spots.

Although green sea turtles are common around the main islands, very few of them lay their eggs on these islands. About 90 percent of the turtles make the five-hundred- to eight-hundred-mile swim up to the atoll known as French Frigate Shoals to nest in the sand just above the high-water line. Each female lumbers up on the beach at

FIGURE 7.17 A stripebelly puffer, photographed at "Two Step" near Puʻuhonua o Hōnaunau National Historic Park on the Kona coast. (Rick Soehren)

night, digs a pit that is wider at the bottom, like a flask (a remarkable feat when you are an aquatic animal digging a hole behind you using flippers!) and deposits about one hundred eggs that look like rubbery ping pong balls. The female covers the pit with sand and, her maternal duties completed, returns to the sea. She may nest two or more times during the summer nesting season. Then an amazing process takes place in the turtle nest. Turtles don't have sex-selecting X and Y chromosomes like mammals. Instead, the sex of the turtles is determined by the temperature in the nest. Eggs at the center stay warmer and generally produce females; those at the edge get cooler and are more likely to be males. After about sixty days the eggs begin to hatch. The first hatchlings will wait up to a day for others to hatch. When most of the turtles in the nest are ready to go, they'll dig their way out at night in a little flippered frenzy and scurry across the sand into the ocean. It is the most dangerous hour of their lives. They may be eaten by big ghost crabs or fall prey to birds on the beach if they don't make it to water by dawn. They are vulnerable to a host of big fish once they reach the water. The lucky ones swim out of shallow water into the deep ocean and disappear for about five years.

Well, maybe they don't actually disappear, but we have no idea where they go or what they do. It is one of the biggest mysteries in Hawaiian natural science. Young turtles rarely show up in fishing nets or in the stomachs of big predator fish. They are almost never seen by fishing boats or mariners. They are just…gone. It may be a long time before this mystery is solved.

After five mysterious years at sea, the young turtles return to the islands, often to the main islands rather than their birthplace in the northwest. They're twelve to eighteen inches long. It will be another twenty years or so before they are ready to breed. Then, their life cycle will begin anew. Most of them will make the long journey up to French Frigate Shoals, an atoll that they presumably haven't visited in about a quarter century, since the time they were an hour old. How do they find it, and how do they know they should return there? We don't know. A positive sign is that some turtles are now beginning to nest on the main islands, perhaps as they did before a millennium of hunting drove nesting turtles away from these shores. One spot where they've nested is Ma'alaea Bay on Maui.

A turtle's life span is another mystery. Until we have diligently tagged turtles for a long time, we won't know how old they can get. We think these turtles become reproductively mature at around twenty-four years old. When widespread tagging began in 1973, one female, number 6034, was first tagged on French Frigate Shoals. She was observed nesting every two to five years until 2011. That would make her at least sixty-two if she had been tagged during her very first nesting. In 2012 a storm destroyed the crude field station at French Frigate Shoals and regular monitoring was suspended, so we might not be able to track her in the future. But we know this: turtles live a long time.

Incidentally, green sea turtles do not get their name from the color of their shell or scaly skin, but rather from the color of their fat, a reminder of the days when they were commonly eaten, which was not so long ago. They were caught and sold in Hawaiian meat markets up until they received state protection in 1974. They were not listed as a threatened species under the federal Endangered Species Act until 1978. The turtles have made a remarkable comeback. During the first turtle survey at French Frigate Shoals in 1973 there were sixty-seven nesting females. In recent years the number has topped eight hundred.

When you observe green sea turtles at close range, you may notice tumors growing on their flesh. The condition is called fibropapillomatosis. It was rarely seen before 1985 but is now becoming more common among turtles in Hawai'i as well as in Florida and the Caribbean. The tumors seem to be caused by a virus, perhaps triggered by pollution. We don't know for sure. In some cases the tumors will shrink and the turtle will recover. In other cases the tumors get so large they interfere with feeding and the turtle dies. Do not confuse these tumors with barnacles, which may be seen growing on turtle shells or sometimes on flipper scales.

It is easy to tell a mature green sea turtle male from a female. When the male grows to nearly full size it will have a very long tail that extends beyond the tips of its hind flippers. The female's tail will only extend about as far as the edge of the carapace.

The Naturalist's Dilemma.   Many of the plants and animals in Hawai'i are rare, endangered, or nearly extinct. No responsible naturalist would advise people to go trooping off to view, for example, a plant that may have dwindled to fewer than ten individuals in the wild (this book guides you to good botanical gardens instead). Sometimes there is another reason why revealing a special natural spot is controversial: an influx of visitors can spoil a place for the people who live nearby, and the cumulative pressure of so many visitors can take a toll on native species. That's the case at Ho'okipa Beach Park on Maui's north shore just east of Pā'ia. It has long been a favorite surfing spot, and more recently a popular place for windsurfing. Then the social media world and some guidebooks advertised that green sea turtles regularly come ashore in the late afternoon to bask at the east end of the beach, except in winter when big surf washes away beach sand. Now, hundreds of tourists visit the beach every day to see the turtles. Some of these visitors do not respect the space of the turtles, the surfers, or the local families who are out having a picnic.

If you want to get a close-up dry-land view of big green sea turtles, Ho'okipa is probably the best place outside of the Northwestern Hawaiian Islands to do so. If you go, remember to be respectful of the animals and people who call this beach home. Set a good example and respect the fifteen-foot buffer space around the turtles that volunteers from the Hawai'i Wildlife Fund try to maintain. Better yet, volunteer or donate to help HWF efforts. Keep the aloha spirit.

There's another species of sea turtle that lives in Hawai'i, the hawksbill turtle or *'ea*. It is extremely rare, listed as endangered. This turtle nests on the main islands rather than the Northwestern Hawaiian Islands. There are fewer than one hundred nesting females. They nest mostly on remote beaches on the Big Island within Hawai'i Volcanoes National Park, with a few nesting at Ma'alaea on Maui, and other islands. You are likely to see dozens or hundreds of green sea turtles for every hawksbill. The two species can be distinguished by sight, especially if you are very familiar with the physical characteristics of the vastly more common green sea turtle. The hawksbill, as its name implies, has a more pointed beak than the rounded head of the green. Younger hawksbill turtles have a serrated edge on the shell, where shell scale points protrude. These edges may be worn smooth among older turtles. Greens have two big scales between their eyes, while hawksbills have four smaller scales.

BIG FISH BEYOND THE REEF

Marine life is concentrated at nearshore reefs where it is easy for us to view it, but of course life does not end there. The deeper waters beyond the reef have fewer nutrients, so the density of life diminishes sharply. At the top of the open-ocean food chain are the big predators, fish like tuna, marlin, and sharks. They are among the most fascinating and important creatures in the sea.

Sharks in Hawai'i are fabled, feared, and revered. They are also rarely encountered. Most snorkelers will never see one. In a state where millions of people are splashing around in the water, there are remarkably few shark bites, averaging about nine per year. Even fewer prove fatal to the human involved; there were only five shark bite deaths between 1980 and 2014. Many of the biting incidents happen to anglers who are in the water handling bloody fish. Most at risk are surfers, who spend quite a bit of time well offshore. The average snorkeler's chance of being bitten by a shark is far less than one in a million. And notice use of the term "shark bite" not "shark attack." Most encounters involve one or two chomps by the shark, and then it swims off. It is extremely rare for a shark to treat a human as a prey species, as a meal.

Shark Safety.   Shark bites are rare, but there is no point in pressing your luck. Here are some tips for avoiding sharks. Do not swim or snorkel at dawn, dusk, or at night. Some sharks come inshore to feed at night (but tiger sharks feed 24/7). Do not swim in murky water. Sharks hunt in these conditions because their senses allow them to find prey without seeing it. Do not swim near harbors or stream mouths. These are areas where nutrients can enter the ocean in the form of discarded bait or other things carried by streams that may attract sharks. Do not enter the water if you are bleeding or have an open wound. Avoid excessive splashing, because a shark might mistake it for an animal in distress, easy prey. Finally, don't let all of these tips frighten you. I have been swimming and snorkeling in Hawaiian waters for over a quarter of a century and I've never even seen a shark, despite trying.

Of course, the rarity of bites does not mean the sharks aren't there. Hawai'i is home to about forty-nine species of sharks and their close relatives, rays. They are all primitive compared to the so-called bony fishes already discussed; sharks and rays have a skeleton made of cartilage rather than real bone. Most of them are deep-water, offshore species, or incredibly rare, or both. One species was not discovered until 1976.

There are only about seven shark species likely to share space with humans. Three of them have names that hint at their nearshore habits: blacktip reef shark, whitetip reef shark, and gray reef shark. Blacktips and whitetips were encountered by early Hawaiians frequently enough to merit their own Hawaiian names, *manō pā'ele* (dark shark) and *manō lālākea* (white branch shark). The reef sharks are all relatively small sharks, averaging three to five feet in length, the largest being the gray reef shark that tends to stay in deeper water on the outer edge of the reef. It can reach seven feet. The remaining four species are mainly sharks of the open ocean, but they sometimes come inshore: blacktip shark, Galapagos shark, scalloped hammerhead shark, and tiger shark.

The last two are perhaps the most interesting. The scalloped hammerhead is well known for its weird hammer-shaped head, with eyeballs positioned out at the tips. Hawaiians called it *manō kihikihi* (shark full of corners). The head shape may be an adaptation that gives this fish lift as it swims. These sharks feed offshore, but in spring and summer females up to twelve feet long come into shallow bays such as Hilo,

Waimea, and Kāneʻohe to give birth. Some other shark species lay eggs, but each hammerhead female will bear between fifteen and thirty live young, about eighteen inches long, called pups. Kāneʻohe Bay on windward Oʻahu is a major pupping area for hammerheads. Females come into the bay in springtime and the pups are born between May and July. The females seem to eat little if anything while in the bay. Once they give birth they return to open water, leaving their pups to grow in the bay for several months. Incredible as it seems, this bay—so heavily used by humans—may host ten thousand young hammerhead sharks in the summer! The pups are not a threat to people. Disappointingly, they are hard for snorkelers to see because they tend to stay near the bottom in deeper parts of the bay, and they prefer murky water.

And then there is the tiger shark. If any shark in Hawaiʻi is going to kill you, it's this one. Hawaiians called this shark *niuhi.* It is one of the largest shark species found in Hawaiian waters, commonly reaching fourteen feet and occasionally growing to more than sixteen. They are slow to reach maturity and do not breed until they are ten or twelve years old. Then they make up for lost time; a really big female can give birth to eighty-two live young, each nearly three feet long. Young tiger sharks eat slow-moving fish, octopuses, and crabs. Adults eat anything they encounter. Some of their prey includes other sharks and rays, dolphins, turtles, and seabirds. Adults are apparently such eating machines that they have been found with all manner of inanimate objects in their stomachs. They are able to evert their junk-clogged stomachs, and begin eating all over again.

Tiger sharks are equipped with a sensory array that is really unimaginable for mere humans. They can smell blood or urine in the water from hundreds of yards away. (That's a good reason to use the restroom before you go snorkeling.) They can hear a thrashing fish from one hundred yards away. Their eyes are well developed; they can see in the dark as well as a cat, and their eyes are particularly adapted to look upward toward prey. And here is where it gets really interesting. Sharks have something called a lateral line. It is a sensory organ running up the sides of the fish and over its head. With this organ, sharks can feel subtle pressure changes in the water. They can use it to triangulate on a swimming fish in the dark or in murky water.

Finally, sharks have sensory pores on their faces called ampullae of Lorenzini. Strangely, the only other creatures on earth known to have these electroreceptors are a few other fish, the duck-billed platypus, and the echidna (a spiny anteater). These receptors seem to serve two very different functions for sharks: hunting and navigation. They detect the faint electric field that all living organisms generate around their bodies. It does not matter if a prey fish stops moving in the dark or in murky water or burrows into the sand, sharks will still know it is there. Electroreception also apparently serves as a very sensitive compass, allowing sharks to navigate throughout their feeding ranges. Tiger sharks in Hawai'i appear to have a home range that they occupy most of the time, with occasional forays far out to sea.

Sharks have cause to fear us more than we need to fear them. Early Hawaiians had reverence and respect for sharks but caught them and used big shark teeth for tools and weapons. The early western attitude was to kill sharks simply to display them as trophies, to gawk at their hulking form. Fear of sharks has prompted some ill-advised "management" schemes: between 1959 and 1969, Hawaiian authorities carried out shark research and control programs that killed over 2,500 sharks in Hawaiian waters. Similar programs continued into the 1970s. Some of those old attitudes persist now, and today sharks have even more to fear. Most sharks tend to grow slowly, live a long time, and produce few young. Such species cannot withstand too much fishing pressure, but by some estimates we kill over twelve million sharks worldwide every year for food, shark fin soup, fish meal, and dietary supplements. That is why many shark species are becoming less common.

Movies and other media have created a particular fear of great white sharks. They are very rare in Hawai'i. The wrong-headed shark culling programs that killed around 2,500 sharks included exactly five great whites.

Ichthyologists have had a jolly good time naming some of the other shark species that reside near Hawai'i. These include the shortspine spurdog, the viper dogfish, the spongehead cat shark, the mosaic gulper, the blurred smooth lantern shark, and the cookiecutter shark. This last one is a diminutive shark, no more than twenty inches in length. It feeds by opening its circular jaws wide and taking a round cookie-cutter scoop of flesh out of much bigger creatures, including other sharks, dolphins, and monk seals. Older beaked whales in Hawai'i look spotted from all the healed cookie-cutter bites on their flanks.

One other notable shark cruises through Hawaiian waters: the

FIGURE 7.18 Attitudes have changed a little since this tiger shark was caught at French Frigate Shoals in May 1937, but we still kill too many. (Norton H. Heath; taken aboard the USS *Neches*)

whale shark. At up to forty-five feet in length, it is the largest fish known. Among sharks, it is one of the most docile and harmless. A plankton feeder, it swims along with its huge mouth open, filtering krill, small squid, and fish. This shark is usually solitary and its whereabouts are unpredictable. On rare occasions divers and snorkelers on boats encounter one.

Your chances of swimming with a whale shark are very low, but take consolation in a similar and fairly dependable experience: swimming with huge manta rays. There are about nine species of ray in Hawai'i. These shark relatives are almost birdlike and essentially fly through the water with winglike fins. None are abundant, but under the right circumstances they can be lured close to observers. In the case of mantas, these filter feeders with widths of ten feet or more can be attracted by using lights at night to concentrate the plankton on which they feed. (See the **Field Trip!** section.) There are two smaller ray species that a snorkeler might encounter. The broad stingray has a maximum width of four feet and is most often seen blending in with sandy bottoms. The spotted eagle ray grows to seven feet in width, has a dark upper surface covered with striking white spots, and glides around over sandy areas looking for its prey of crustaceans and urchins. These two rays both have venomous tail spines that are used for defense. Neither species is very common.

Two other fish species of the open ocean are both prized by anglers and have amazing stories: the blue marlin and the yellowfin tuna. Blue marlin—*a'u* in Hawaiian—are perhaps the most prized and fabled of all game fish. Ernest Hemingway fished for them, and he wrote about them in *The Old Man and the Sea.* In the Atlantic and Pacific, sport anglers dream of landing a "grander," a marlin weighing in at a thousand pounds or more. These huge fish are invariably female; males are about a third the size of their mates. In Hawai'i, Kailua-Kona is the hub of recreational marlin fishing and is home to several marlin fishing tournaments each year. There is a small cottage industry among local people in Hawai'i making smoked *a'u* and selling it by the roadside.

Blue marlin are the largest members of a couple of related fish families collectively known as billfishes for their swordlike bills. Two smaller marlins that are sometimes caught in Hawaiian waters are black marlin and striped marlin. Other billfish include swordfish, sailfish, and spearfish. Billfish use their bills for hunting, but they usually do not stab the fish. Instead they thrash their bills while swimming through a school of prey fish such as small yellowfin tuna, then return to eat the stunned or injured. Blue marlin swim fast, over sixty miles per hour for short bursts. Blue marlin like warm water and are concentrated in tropical waters around the world. Seasonally they stray from the tropics, taking advantage of warm currents, and have been tracked migrating over nine thousand miles. Blue marlin numbers are dwindling due to intentional commercial fishing and inadvertent bycatch by longline fisheries. They are managed well in U.S. waters, but recreational anglers fret that eventually their hobby may be curtailed by necessary species protections. Want to check out marlin anglers with their catch? See the **Field Trip!** section.

Marlin anglers who head out from Kailua-Kona on chartered boats often come home with yellowfin tuna instead. In Hawaiian they are called 'ahi. As big marlins become scarce, some marlin fishing tournaments have added an 'ahi category to keep the competition lively, and fish in the one-hundred- to two-hundred-pound range are not uncommon. Yellowfin tuna are found worldwide in tropical and subtropical seas.

Phenomenal FADs. In the vast space of the open ocean, how do Hawaiian anglers find their fish? For generations, anglers have looked for flocks of diving, feeding seabirds such as red-footed boobies. Today, there are all kinds of high-tech tools like fish-finding sonar, but one of the most effective tools is decidedly low tech. It is called a fish aggregation device, or FAD. Basically, an FAD is just a buoy anchored in fairly deep water offshore. FADs provide a bit of structure in the otherwise featureless blue ocean. Fish seem to like structure, and they gather around the FADs. There are over four dozen FADs set up around the islands from 2 to 20 miles offshore, in water depths of 1,200 to 8,100 feet. Anglers know their GPS coordinates. Yellowfin tuna love FADs. These fast swimmers may range for 5 miles or more at night in search of prey, but many schools invariably make their way back to their home FAD precisely at dawn. We do not really know why they work, but Hawaiian fish and anglers love a good FAD.

Another kind of FAD is used by commercial ships fishing for tuna. They use a big net called a purse seine, like a giant net bag that is cinched around a school of fish. When objections arose to setting seines around pods of dolphins that are found with yellowfin tuna, the seiners started using drifting FADs. This is good for dolphins, but bad for all the non-tuna species that are attracted to FADs and get killed as bycatch, including turtles, sharks, billfish, and others.

Although yellowfin tuna are smaller than marlins, their abilities may be even more amazing. They have been described as "spawning and eating machines." A big female can produce millions of eggs every day during spawning season, but the spawning is nothing compared to the hunting ability of these predators. Tunas including yellowfins are perhaps the most perfectly adapted predatory fish in the sea. They chase down fish, squid, and crustaceans. They generally do not lose a chase with their prey because they have evolved every trick in the book of superpredators. They can swim at sustained speeds of twenty-eight miles per hour. Their bodies have weird sickle-shaped fins and rows of little finlets that serve to reduce drag and turbulence as they speed through the water. Whereas most fish shimmy through the water, tuna have a very tiny base of the tail, and when they swim only the tail moves back and forth. The body of the fish just glides through the water. Their sleek bodies even have little indentations where they can tuck their pectoral fins and the first of their two dorsal fins to further reduce drag. Their hearts are ten times larger than those of other similar-sized fish, and they have higher blood pressure, the better to pump more oxygen to their muscles. Compared to other fish, their gills have many times

FIGURE 7.19 Yellowfin tuna are popular among anglers and diners. This one was caught during a billfish tournament at Kailua-Kona on the Big Island. (Rick Soehren)

the surface area and can take in more oxygen. Tuna have way more red muscle than most fish, the better to swim fast for long periods. And they have one other advantage over the cold-blooded creatures that they prey upon. Tuna can control their body temperature, heating themselves to an astonishing 25°F or more above the surrounding water. This is a huge advantage, speeding up the internal chemical reactions that produce energy to power their torpedo bodies. You can call them efficient predators, but you can't call them cold-blooded killers.

Seeking Sustainable Seafood. The sea and its resources were once considered limitless. Today we know that even the ocean's resources, including its fish species, must be carefully managed or we risk depleting them to the point where they cannot rebound. Some species are managed better in some areas and worse in others. Some methods of catching fish result in an unacceptable amount of bycatch—that is, the other species that are caught by accident in pursuit of the target species. Even for farm-raised seafood, there are big differences in the amount of resources consumed and the amount of waste and pollution produced. How do you know if the seafood listed on a restaurant menu was sustainably caught or grown? Several organizations help consumers wade through all the information and provide guidance, but their standards range from rigorous to lax. One of the best is the Seafood Watch program developed by the Monterey Bay Aquarium, which offers regionally specific guidance that identifies best choices, good alternatives, and seafood to avoid. There are downloadable pocket cards on their website. Even better, they offer free smartphone apps. The apps are large so it is best to download and update them using a fast connection.

Compared to the impressive fish that live outside the reef, life upstream in Hawai'i's freshwater streams is pretty tame. Hawaiian streams are teeming with fish, but most of them are introduced. There are just five species of native freshwater fish, four of them endemic and one indigenous. They are all gobies or goby relatives, long thin fish with big heads. They are called 'o'opu in Hawaiian. The "giant" goby can get as long as fourteen inches; most of the others are considerably smaller. How did freshwater fish get to Hawai'i? The answer lies in these fishes' life cycles. They are amphidromous; that is, they lay eggs in freshwater streams and the newly hatched larvae wash out to sea. After a time, juveniles swim back into fresh water. That life history made it possible for larvae from an ancestor species to drift to Hawai'i.

Some of the freshwater Hawaiian gobies share a trait with marine relatives: the pelvic fins on their bellies are fused into a very functional suction cup. In the surf zone, this cup allows gobies to hold on to rocks. In streams it serves a more remarkable purpose. Many Hawaiian streams are punctuated by one or a series of tall waterfalls. Not a problem for the gobies. Their suction cups allow some gobies to climb up rocks and over waterfalls. And not just little rapids; some of these tenacious little fish have been collected upstream of 'Akaka Falls, a 442-foot cataract on the windward coast of the Big Island.

Hawaiian streams are also home to a couple of endemic freshwater shrimp called *'ōpae.* One of them is a champion climber like some *'o'opu* and can scale waterfalls. The *'ōpae* in streams grow to be two or three inches long. They have a tiny and very specialized relative, the *'ōpae'ula,* that lives in a very special habitat, anchialine (AN-key-ah-lin) ponds. These shallow coastal ponds have no surface connection to the ocean. They are fed by both fresh and salt water, making them brackish. Look for bright red, half-inch *'ōpae'ula* in anchialine ponds along the Kona coast.

FIELD TRIP!

There are enough good snorkeling spots in Hawai'i to fill a book. In fact, there are books describing snorkeling locations; see **Learn More**. Organized tours by land or boat can take you to many sites. Vendors who rent snorkel gear often provide a list or map of good places to visit. This section includes my list of some favorite snorkel spots around the state.

Snorkeling is second nature for people born and raised in Hawai'i. Many *keiki* (children) are comfortable in the ocean before they can even walk. But if you're a visitor to Hawai'i the snorkeling equipment and experience may be very foreign. If you try it without any advice or guidance you may not have a very pleasant experience: leaky or fogged-up mask, blistered feet from ill-fitting fins. For first-time snorkelers, a guided tour is a good way to learn how to use the equipment and visit a good snorkeling spot. There are a lot of tour boats that will take you out from places like Lahaina on Maui, Kailua-Kona on the Big Island, and the Waiʻanae coast of Oʻahu. There are also tours that will pick you up in Waikīkī and take you snorkeling at Hanauma Bay. You get personalized help because these tours are limited to six snorkelers for each instructor. Be sure to book a tour with an instructor; there are also cut-rate shuttle services that just dump you at the bay with snorkel gear. Once you get the hang of it, snorkeling is simple and very enjoyable. After one guided trip, you'll probably feel confident enough to snorkel independently (but always snorkel with a buddy for safety).

There are a few things to remember when you go snorkeling so that you don't have a negative effect on reef life. First, do not feed the fish. Feeding can change the fish community structure, leading to higher numbers of more aggressive fish. Second, look but do not touch. Repeated standing on coral can kill it. And some coral is very sharp and can cut you. You want to avoid touching other creatures like urchins because of their sharp spines. Do not try to "ride" a sea turtle or have it pull you through the water. This kind of harassment is a violation of federal law. Third, if you use sunscreen make sure it is waterproof so it won't wash off and leave an oil slick in the water. Make sure it does not contain oxybenzone, a chemical that is highly toxic to coral polyps and other marine life. Instead of using sunscreen, consider a tight-fitting shirt called a rash guard that will shield your torso from sunburn, or wear a dark T-shirt.

7.1 SNORKELING OʻAHU. Sometimes more people equals less nature. When it comes to snorkeling this principle does not necessarily apply. **Hanauma Bay** on Oʻahu offers some of the more enjoyable snorkeling in the state even though it probably greets more snorkelers than any other beach on the planet. Even if you like to experience nature in relative solitude, do not be dissuaded from a visit. Hanauma Bay has so much to offer that it is worth fighting (or avoiding) the crowds.

First, there is the geology. The nearly round bay is the eroded remnant of a rejuvenation-stage tuff cone, like Diamond Head. So, yes, you will be swimming inside a volcano! The shallower parts of the crater floor near the beach are covered with old fossil coral that died thousands of years ago when sea level fell. Now submerged again, this ancient coral is teeming with marine life. Then there's the natural beauty. The view from the visitor center at the rim of the crater— arcing crater rim, sandy beach, submerged coral, water grading from pale turquoise to deep blue—is splendid. And of course, the snorkeling. This is a marine life conservation district, and the fish are habituated to people, so the marine life viewing can be excellent. There are areas inside the reef suited for novice snorkelers, plus channels leading to the wondrous outer reef where experienced snorkelers can venture when ocean conditions permit. If you cannot identify something you see in the water, cheerful docents in a hut near the beach will try to help you with their library of marine guidebooks.

There are visitor amenities, too: restrooms at the crater rim and down below at the beach, an informative visitor center, a snack bar with a shady picnic area, lifeguards, showers, snorkel gear for rent, a shuttle service in case you prefer not to walk the steep road into the crater, and fat-tire wheelchairs available for use on the beach.

The only downside is the crowds. Upwards of three thousand people visit the bay each day the park is open, totaling more than a million per year. All those people tend to make the beach crowded. And they kick up sand in the water as they enter for snorkeling, reducing the clarity and visibility. They take a toll on the inner reef, where most snorkelers venture. But do not despair. The county now closes the park on Tuesdays every week to give the marine life a bit of a break. Parking is limited; the lot is often full by 9:00, and more motorists can't enter until the lot starts to thin out around 1:00. The county also requires visitors to attend a video or short lecture on personal safety and avoiding harm to the marine life. So things are better than they used to be.

Because of the crowds, people who visit Hanauma Bay may come away with wildly differing impressions of the place. It all comes down to timing. If you arrive late morning, you might be turned away because the parking lot is full. If you do get in, you'll stand in line in the hot sun for fifteen or twenty minutes, waiting to buy your entry ticket. By the time you get down the hill to the beach, there will be hundreds of people in the water, stirring up sand and making the visibility very poor. Here's how to avoid the madness. Plan to arrive shortly after the park opens at 6:00, certainly before 7:00. Most likely, there will be no one there to charge you for parking and no one to charge you for entry, although you will still get to hear the safety lecture. You can stroll right down to the beach and spread out anywhere you like (there is a tiny bit of morning shade beneath some *kiawe* trees).

If you are a novice snorkeler and stay near shore, you probably won't be dazzled by the marine life: a few fish, a little coral, maybe a sea cucumber bobbing along on the sand. More experienced snorkelers can venture to the outer reef through two channels that are marked with buoys. The outer reef is visited by relatively few people, maybe 5 percent of the bay's visitors. The marine life is abundant and varied, and the fish are accustomed to people. This outer reef area is one of the better snorkeling spots in the state. Do not attempt snorkeling the outer reef unless you are an experienced snorkeler and a good swimmer because currents through the two marked channels can be strong. If you are in doubt, consult a lifeguard.

If you arrive early, do exercise caution; lifeguards do not start work until 7:00. Also, allow plenty of driving time. Hanauma Bay is only about ten miles east from Waikīkī but the driving time from tourist hotels is at least half an hour.

Once you get some experience and gain confidence as a snorkeler, there are many other spots to explore. They may not have lifeguards and conditions may be more challenging. Two good Oʻahu spots that fit this description are **Kahe Point Beach County Park** (also known as Electric Beach) on the southern Waiʻanae coast and **Pūpūkea Beach County Park** (better known as Shark's Cove), a marine life conservation district on the north shore just north of Waimea.

Kahe Point does not look promising when you approach. Across the highway is a giant power plant, and the cooling water outfall is adjacent to the park. In fact, that outfall is a big reason the snorkeling is so good. The warm water bubbling up from the seafloor outlet is quite attractive to marine life. From shore you can spot the outfall because there is turbulence at the surface. There is little runoff on this leeward shore, so visibility is often very good.

Entry is via a narrow sandy beach bounded by the outfall structure on one side and an ancient fossil reef on the other. This tends to funnel wave energy, so you'll have to snorkel through some breaking waves. If the surf report predicts a south swell, entry will probably be too intimidating, and the visibility won't be optimal. Be sure to take a look at the extensive fossil reef that stands many feet above the water, formed about 125,000 years ago when the ocean was about thirty feet higher than it is today.

To reach Kahe Point from Honolulu, take the H1 freeway west about twenty miles, just past the Koʻolina resort. Where the highway approaches the coastline, you'll see the beach park across from the power plant. Unfortunately, car break-ins and theft sometimes occur at this park.

At Pūpūkea Marine Life Conservation District, much better known as Shark's Cove, the marine life is habituated to people and relatively abundant because fishing is restricted in this protected district. And like Hanauma Bay it is very popular, so plan to arrive early to avoid crowds. Unlike Hanauma Bay, there are few amenities: just parking, restrooms, and showers. There is no lifeguard, and entry involves an awkward scramble down a hill over rough rocks including massive chunks of ancient reef. Visibility is often good but seldom crystal clear because this spot is along the relatively wet north shore of Oʻahu. That means runoff and organic material are carried into the nearshore waters. The underwater topography is exciting, with a jumble of giant boulders and caves.

Adjacent to the cove is an extensive area of shallow tide pools. If you are reluctant to snorkel, put on a pair of reef shoes and wade around the tide pool area for a look at tiny fish and other marine life.

Shark's Cove is a seasonal snorkeling spot. In the winter, the famous giant surf of the north shore makes entry here a deadly proposition. Always exercise caution and study conditions very carefully before entering the water. And finally, don't let the name Shark's Cove put you off. Sharks don't seem any more numerous at this park than at most other snorkel spots. You will probably never see one.

Getting to the park from central Honolulu involves a forty-mile drive and a somewhat confusing maze of roads in central Oʻahu. Take H1 to H2. Follow it north until the freeway ends on the outskirts of Wahiawā. At this point you have several route choices. I like to drive through Wahiawā, past the Kūkaniloko Birthstones (see chapter 8), turn right on Highway 99, and head to the coastal town of Haleʻiwa. Take the bypass to avoid the town. Head northeast on the coastal Kamehameha Highway. Less than a mile past Waimea Bay where the road curves inland you will come to Pūpūkea Beach County Park, the formal name for Shark's Cove. There is a big grocery store just *mauka* across the highway. The place names all have stories: Wahiawā means "place of noise." Before the area was filled with city sounds, it is said that you could hear the rough winter seas from this inland town. Haleʻiwa means "house of the ʻiwa or frigate-bird." Waimea means "reddish water," colored from silt. Pūpūkea means "white shell." Kūkaniloko was an ancient Hawaiian chief.

Most beaches near Waikīkī are poor for snorkeling because the sandy bottom does not offer any structure for reef life. But at Kaimana, or Sans Souci, Beach, the last public area east of the Waikīkī Aquarium, you will find a protected beach with a rocky reef offshore. It is not world-class; there is little coral, the water can be murky, and there is a lot of introduced algae. Still, the fish are plentiful and it is really your only snorkeling option in Waikīkī. Between Kaimana and the aquarium is the Natatorium, a crumbling abandoned saltwater swimming pool. Just west of the Natatorium is an inviting ramp leading down into the water. You can snorkel here, but the surf tends to surge into this area, and there is a very unnerving drop-off about forty feet from shore.

7.2 SNORKELING MAUI. One of the most dramatic snorkeling spots in West Maui is also one that has the most people around it: **Black Rock** on Kāʻanapali Beach. There are persuasive reasons to get here early: if you are not staying nearby and have to drive, free beach access parking spaces are limited to about a dozen cars near the north end of the Kāʻanapali Parkway. Once these spots are gone, you have to pay handsomely to park at Whaler's Village shopping center, a long walk away.

Water entry is usually easy: just pad down the sand and slide into the water. (Big waves, more common in winter, can make entry a bit challenging.) The waters around Black Rock are an ecotone, or boundary between two distinct habitats: in this case, the sandy bottom and the rocky perimeter of Black Rock. If the water is calm enough, you can snorkel out around the tip of the rock. My favorite winter pastime at Black Rock is to swim out about as far as the rock juts out, dip my head down, and listen to the whales singing.

Black Rock holds a very important place in traditional Hawaiian beliefs. It is said to be a point where souls of the dead would go to leap into the netherworld. Geologists look at it and see a five-hundred-thousand-year-old rejuvenation cinder cone, part of West Maui's last gasp.

About five miles south of Lahaina near mile marker 14 is an informal but wildly popular snorkeling spot called **Olowalu** (many hills). There is a long sandy beach shaded by *kiawe* trees, and no facilities. The area has an extensive and very shallow coral reef. Sometimes the water is murky, especially when a south swell shoots up through the channel between Maui and Lānaʻi. The farther out you snorkel, the clearer the water.

The coral at Olowalu seems particularly susceptible to bleaching.

When corals are stressed, the polyps expel their symbiotic algae, turning the coral head a ghostly white. Corals can recover from bleaching events, but they are often fatal; the polyps starve without the nutrients from their algae. A rise in water temperature is often the cause of bleaching; abnormally warm ocean temperatures in 2014 and 2015 caused significant coral die-off at Olowalu. Climate change may cause much more bleaching and coral death in the future.

7.3 Snorkeling Lāna'i. This small island does not offer much in the way of snorkeling choice, but makes up for it with quality. Along the island's south shore are two adjacent bays, Mānele and Hulopo'e. Mānele Bay is all business: the ferry from Maui docks there. At Hulopo'e Bay next door, it is all pleasure: the snorkeling at **Hulopo'e Bay** is very good. And it is convenient, too. The beach park and good snorkeling are walking distance from the ferry dock. At the far end of the beach at Hulopo'e Bay is the lavish Four Seasons Resort Lāna'i. This snorkeling spot has almost everything: restrooms, showers, picnic tables in the shade of big *kiawe* trees, very easy water entry from a sandy beach, relatively few people, protected water in the bay, water clarity that is usually good to excellent, fairly abundant aquatic life (it is a marine life conservation district), occasional visits from turtles and dolphins. All in all, it rates right up there with the best snorkeling spots in the state. The underwater topography slopes down to about twenty feet deep, then levels out for a long way, to the mouth of the bay. The only thing missing is a concession stand. Bring everything you need in the way of food, drink, sunscreen, and gear.

7.4 Snorkeling Moloka'i. Most of the protected south coast of Moloka'i is silty or muddy and offers poor snorkeling. There is one bright spot: snorkeling at **Murpheys Beach** near the east end of the island. This spot is located just after the 20-mile marker (often obscured by vegetation) along Kamehameha V Highway, Route 450. There is no sign for Murpheys Beach, just a little space to pull off the road with a sandy beach visible through a break in the vegetation. If you reach a point where the highway ascends a rise to a big paved turnaround spot with a view of a little islet called Moku Ho'oniki, you went too far. Murpheys Beach is so shallow that you can only snorkel during a moderate to high tide. Clarity is surprisingly good considering the shallow depth and the generally muddy Moloka'i south shore. The area is protected by a long outer fringing reef, so the water is calm. There is a surprising abundance of coral including lace coral. There are also lots of fish, which is a surprise considering how many people go fishing on Moloka'i. It is easy to dismiss snorkeling on Moloka'i because of the relative lack of good spots, but this beach is worth a visit.

7.5 SNORKELING THE BIG ISLAND. Can a snorkeling spot get loved to death? Maybe so. The coastline near Kailua-Kona does not offer many good snorkeling opportunities. **Kahalu'u** (diving place) **Beach County Park** near the southern end of town is one of the best. A bay keeps the water calm, and the remnants of an ancient fishpond serve as an additional breakwater. There are a lot of fish and a big variety of marine life. There are also a lot of snorkelers, and they have been hard on the environment. People who have visited the bay for years or decades notice the decline in numbers and variety of marine life. These days, volunteers set up education stations to help snorkelers minimize their impact. For beginning snorkelers it is a good calm place to gain experience and confidence. The park has free parking, restrooms, showers, gear rental, and often a food truck.

A popular snorkeling spot known as **Two Step** is located just north of Pu'uhonua o Hōnaunau National Historic Park. The place gets its name from a natural rock formation like two big steps at the water's edge that make entry easy even though the water is too deep to stand. The abundant coral at this spot was hit hard by the coral bleaching event in 2014 and 2015, brought on by warm water temperatures. Most of this coral has died. Only time will tell how well the area recovers. Still, the water is extremely clear most of the time and snorkeling is pretty good. There are no facilities except a portable toilet, no sandy beach, and almost no shade.

To reach Two Step, take the driveway into the national park. Just before you get to the big parking lot, turn right on to narrow one-way Hōnaunau Beach Road toward the boat ramp, and there you are. There is a small private parking lot across the beach road where you may have to pay to park. Bring a stack of small bills.

7.6 SNORKELING KAUA'I. There is some very good summertime snorkeling along the north shore of Kaua'i, but in the winter the surf along the north shore can make the water dangerous. ʻAnini Beach, between Kīlauea and Princeville, may be the all-around best: long sheltering barrier reef, plenty of parking, plenty of shade, and beach park amenities like restrooms and showers. During calm seas, Kēʻē Beach (pronounced KEH-EH) offers more interesting snorkeling and an idyllic location at the very end of the road. There are showers and restrooms. Parking is abundant but inadequate for this spot's popularity, best to arrive early. If the seas are rough, lifeguards probably will not let you into the water. A legendary north shore snorkel spot is Tunnels Beach, protected by an encircling reef. You won't see a sign (residents like it that way), there is no public beach park, and there is almost nowhere to park along the highway. What to do? Park at Hāʻena Beach County Park, where there is no sheltering reef (not Hāʻena State Park farther west near the end of the road) and stroll northeast along the beach to Tunnels.

At almost any time of year except during strong south swells, south shore snorkeling at Kolopa (Beach House) Beach near Poʻipū can be rewarding. There is fairly easy entry. The water is shallow, no more than seven feet deep even fifty yards from shore. The area is protected somewhat by the adjacent peninsula occupied by the Beach House restaurant. The fish here must get fed a lot because they are very tame. The coral is still recovering from the battering it took in 1992 by Hurricane ʻIniki and from continual trampling by careless snorkelers. The water clarity is only moderate. There is public parking and a restroom across the street, although the signs make it look like private condo parking. To the east on the other side of the Poʻipū resort area, Poʻipū Beach County Park is nearly always calm, good for beginning snorkelers.

7.7 AQUARIUMS. Even if you can't go into the water, you can enjoy Hawaiian reef life thanks to two fine public aquariums: the Waikīkī Aquarium operated by the University of Hawaiʻi, and the Maui Ocean Center at Maʻalaea Harbor near Kīhei on Maui. The Waikīkī Aquarium is a compact facility at the edge of the beach in Kapiʻolani Park. It specializes in marine life of Hawaiʻi and the tropical Pacific. A free audio guide provides a huge amount of information about the displays. Friendly docents are on hand to answer questions. There is a touch pool for the kids. Right outside the aquarium you can see free-swimming reef life from the sea wall. Some guidebooks are dismissive of this facility;

don't believe them. It is a gem of an aquarium. There is an admission fee. It is open every day of the year except Christmas and the date of the annual Honolulu marathon in December. Wheelchair access is good.

The Maui Ocean Center is newer, bigger, and more commercialized than the Waikīkī Aquarium. It focuses on marine life of Hawai'i, including sharks and sea turtles. Displays are very well done. There is an admission fee. It is open every day. Wheelchair access is good.

7.8 SWIM WITH MANTAS. There are not too many opportunities, even for divers, to get a close-up look at big pelagic open-ocean fish. The larger the fish, the fewer of them there tend to be. But there is one way to see and swim with very large ocean creatures where they are induced to gather along the Kona coast of the Big Island: snorkeling or diving with huge manta rays. It can be the experience of a lifetime.

Here's the backstory: years ago one of the big resorts pointed lights at the surf so guests could see the waves breaking at night. The lights attracted "clouds" of zooplankton, tiny larval creatures of many species only about an eighth of an inch long. This concentration of plankton attracted the mantas, very large filter feeders that consume plankton. At first, only a few adventurous SCUBA divers went to watch the show. Now it has become a major tourist attraction for the Kona coast.

These are not stingrays; mantas are harmless majestic creatures. But they are very large: some have a "wingspan" of ten feet or more. They're closely related to sharks but have very tiny teeth. There are two spots near Kailua-Kona where big lights dependably attract plankton and mantas. One is near the Sheraton Kona Resort & Spa at Keauhou Bay, the resort whose lights originally attracted the mantas. It is located at the southernmost end of the Kailua-Kona resort area. The other spot is a cove very close to the Kona airport, just north of Keāhole Point.

Many tour operators offer nightly trips for certified SCUBA divers and snorkelers. You board a tour boat, usually at Honokōhau Harbor, just before sunset. The boat will then head north toward the airport. (A few operators operate out of tiny Keauhou Harbor; the boat ride to the viewing area at Keauhou is only a few hundred yards.) Once at the manta site, everyone is educated about proper etiquette before they glide into the artificially lit water, and for most people that moment is the only scary part. The fear passes quickly as serene mantas pass silently underneath you. Divers sit on the bottom in about thirty feet of

FIGURE 7.20 Snorkeling with huge mantas is a thrilling and humbling experience. (James L. Wing)

water with lights shining upward, while the snorkelers float at the surface, usually holding on to handles on tethered rafts so they don't drift away. Over 90 percent of the time, mantas will appear. At times only one or two will show and other times there could be twenty or more. For nearly an hour, you watch these huge majestic creatures glide around you while they feed, sometimes only inches from your body. In addition to the mantas, there are also schools of fish that come to feed on the planktonic marine life.

If you don't like the idea of jumping off a boat into the ocean at night, you can still see the mantas. Some companies offer a "ride along" option where you stay on the boat and have an above-water view. The Sheraton has a viewing balcony below their big lights, and it's open to all. Sunset cocktails and dinner at the adjacent open-air restaurant, followed by manta viewing, makes for a very pleasant evening. If you watch from land at the Sheraton, here's a tip: your viewing will be more successful after the boats head back to port. The resort lights will then draw the mantas closer to the shoreline where it will be easier to see them from the viewing area.

All in all, manta viewing is likely to be one of the most memorable wildlife experiences a person can have. You can schedule it for any night of the year, weather and surf permitting, and it is just about certain that a manta will appear. So what's the downside? The activity has become wildly popular, so there are a lot of boats concentrated in the two small areas each night, and there are a lot of people in the water. All of this activity can result in inadvertent harm to the mantas. A manta has been entangled in a diver's float line and an eager tourist pointed his underwater camera at the gaping mouth of a manta and lost it inside the creature's mouth. Unfortunately some visitors touch the mantas as they swim by, wiping away the creatures' protective film and exposing them to greater risk of skin infection.

How do you minimize the potential harm your manta viewing might cause to you or the mantas? Sign on with a responsible tour operator. Many, but not all, of the operators have agreed to abide by voluntary Manta Tour Operator Standards. These standards are intended to increase the safety of the manta rays and the human observers. The list of compliant tour operators is sometimes referred to as the Manta Ray Green List. Also, look for a tour operator that is certified by the Hawai'i Ecotourism Association. As this book goes to press, the State of Hawai'i is considering regulations to maintain safety for visitors and protect mantas.

Finally, remember that jumping into the ocean after sunset in the vicinity of big boats, big mantas, and big crowds of tourists is not without risk. If you choose reputable tour operators, they will look out for your safety, but don't depend entirely on them. Ask questions, make sure you are prepared, and if something doesn't seem safe to you, don't do it. The activity has a stellar safety record, but it is always prudent to do your research and schedule with a well-established, well-equipped, and ecologically conscious activity provider.

7.9 BIG FISH FROM SHORE. There's one other way to see big pelagic fish, short of going out and catching them yourself—attend the weigh-in for a fishing tournament. One of the oldest and biggest is the Hawaiian International Billfish Tournament held each summer at Kailua-Kona. During the weeklong tournament, charter boats bring anglers and their marlin and yellowfin tuna to the Kailua pier downtown each afternoon at 4:30. Depending on the luck that day, the catch can be impressive. Dates are variable; check the tournament website for details.

7.10 CORAL FROM SHORE. Yes, you can see and touch coral without ever getting your feet wet. During the nineteenth century, coral was used as a building material. Workers would go out on to shallow reefs, dive to twenty feet or more, and cut blocks of coral limestone using axes. The 'Iolani Barracks, on the grounds of the historic royal palace in downtown Honolulu, is a particularly fine example dating from 1871. Across the street, the Kawaiaha'o Church dating from 1842 has more rough-cut blocks. (The name Ka-wai-a-Ha'o means "water of Ha'o," a Hawaiian chiefess who bathed in a natural spring near this spot.) In Lahaina at the southwest corner of the waterfront square (with a huge banyan tree planted in 1873) there is a small reconstruction of one corner of the fort built here in 1832. These blocks are red because they were buried in the red dirt a long time, and discarded when the fort was disassembled and moved in 1850. Why did Lahaina need a fort? Missionaries imposed rules on the whaling fleet, prohibiting Hawaiian women from swimming out to the ships. Lonely and disappointed sailors lobbed a few cannonballs at the town.

FIGURE 7.21 The 'Iolani Barracks, on the grounds of 'Iolani Palace in downtown Honolulu, is constructed from coral blocks. (Rick Soehren)

LEARN MORE

- John P. Hoover, *The Ultimate Guide to Hawaiian Reef Fishes, Sea Turtles, Dolphins, Whales, and Seals* and *Hawai'i's Fishes: A Guide for Snorkelers and Divers* (Honolulu: Mutual Publishing, 2014 and 2007). Both these books are well written and feature great photography. The first covers turtles and marine mammals as well as nearly every fish on the reef: 396 species. The second book is slimmer and depicts 265 of the common reef fish, plus it has descriptions of good snorkeling spots on the four largest islands.

- John P. Hoover, *Hawaii's Sea Creatures: A Guide to Hawaii's Marine Invertebrates* (Honolulu: Mutual Publishing, 2012). Like Hoover's other books, this one is well written and beautifully illustrated with color photographs.

- John E. Randall, *Shore Fishes of Hawai'i,* revised edition (Honolulu: University of Hawai'i Press, 2010). Randall is one of the world's foremost authorities on tropical reef fish, and a skilled underwater photographer. His book describes 372 species, with color photographs.

- David Gulko, *Hawaiian Coral Reef Ecology* (Honolulu: Mutual Publishing, 1998). If you want to understand how the reef ecosystem works, buy this book. It is the size of a coffee table book, has the content of a textbook (it is for marine science classes from middle school to community college), and is as easy to read as any tourist guide.

- Susan Scott, *Exploring Hanauma Bay,* revised edition (Honolulu: University of Hawai'i Press, 2013). If you are planning a visit to Hanauma Bay, this book will greatly enhance your visit. It is packed with advice for everyone from first-time snorkelers to old hands. It also includes information about many of the more common species you will encounter at Hanauma Bay.

- Mike Yamamoto and Annette Tagawa, *Hawai'i's Native & Exotic Freshwater Animals* (Honolulu: Mutual Publishing, 2000). Describes the handful of native species and the mind-boggling array of introduced creatures found in Hawaiian streams and reservoirs, all illustrated with color photographs. Anyone who has spent time in an aquarium shop will see a lot of familiar faces.

- Gerald L. Crow and Jennifer Crites, *Sharks and Rays of Hawai'i* (Honolulu: Mutual Publishing, 2002). Pretty much everything you wanted to know about sharks, including descriptions of sharks found in Hawaiian waters. There are color photographs of all the species but—given the challenges and dangers of photographing live sharks—many of the photos depict preserved specimens.

- Craig Thomas, M.D., and Susan Scott, *All Stings Considered* (Honolulu: University of Hawai'i Press, 1997). There are a lot of things in the ocean that can hurt you. This book describes over fifty of them, including background, symptoms, and first aid. Fascinating and useful for avoiding injuries. Some of the color photographs are pretty grisly.
- Fish identification apps. Yes, there are apps that focus on Hawaiian reef fish. Content, quality, and availability can change rapidly, so browse app stores for yourself.

8 Landfall

The First Hawaiians

Captain Cook was puzzled when he made landfall in Hawai'i in 1778. This accomplished explorer had filled in the last big black hole in western maps of the eighteenth century, charting a constellation of previously unknown islands across the Pacific. But he couldn't figure out how Polynesian people traveled as far as Hawai'i. It wasn't hard to imagine primitive canoe travel among the closely spaced islands of the South Pacific, but Hawai'i was just too distant. The Hawaiians paddled out to Cook's arriving ships in hundreds of canoes, but they were mostly tiny fishing boats, not big seafaring craft. How did these people get to the most isolated place on earth, and where did they come from?

The mystery of origins continued for over 150 years, with all kinds of outlandish ideas proposed: Polynesians came from South America; the islands of Polynesia are the mountaintops of a great sunken continent; Polynesians descended from the Lost Tribes of Israel. It is a wonder nobody invoked space aliens.

Finally, in the twentieth century archaeologists in Hawai'i began to solve the puzzle. In the deepest and earliest layers of their archaeological digs at ancient village sites, they found artifacts such as bone fishhooks similar to those excavated in the Marquesas, an island group 2,100 miles to the southeast. More recent layers showed influences from Tahiti in the Society Islands, 2,700 miles almost due south of Hawai'i. So the *where* was starting to be understood. The *how* was still a mystery.

By 1970 theorists were divided into two polarized camps. One camp believed that Polynesians, with their stone-age technology, could not possibly have found specks of land like Hawai'i except by happy accident. In their view, a hapless group of Marquesans must have drifted off to sea and were saved when they just happened to hit Hawai'i.

And then a few hundred years later, a group of lost but very fortunate Tahitians—"waifs of storms"—must have been saved from starvation at sea when they happened to drift to Hawaiian shores.

The other camp, made up mostly of Hawaiians and other Pacific Islanders, heeded the stories and chants of their elders. They believed that the Tahitians had sailed back and forth between Hawai'i and the Society Islands for hundreds of years but had long ago ceased the epic canoe voyages between island groups.

The disagreements got pretty strong and pretty personal. Maybe it is just my perception, but it seems like there might have been an undercurrent of racism in there, too. Sociologists and historians scoffed dismissively at the idea that Polynesians could navigate the vast Pacific without compass or sextant. Among the most vocal (and mocking) was Andrew Sharp, a New Zealand historian. His writing is peppered with provocative statements. In 1961 he wrote: "deliberate navigation to and from remote ocean islands was impossible in the days before the plotting of courses with precision instruments," and "neither the Polynesians nor any other people in the Pacific performed the feats of deliberate long voyaging and colonization with which they have been credited."

He asked rhetorically, "Why do so many people hanker so determinedly after the notion that the Polynesians sailed to and from remote islands by deliberate navigation?" He answered his own question: "people who cherish this belief do so for unconscious emotional rather than scientific reasons."

About the same time, a fellow with a most unusual personal history was articulating a very different view. David Lewis was born in England to a Welsh mining engineer father and an Irish physician mother. The family moved to the South Pacific when David was a boy, and his unconventional father enrolled him in a native school on Rarotonga in the Cook Islands. Here the little boy heard tales of the great voyages of the Polynesians: legends of trips made long ago, and stories of the voyaging that still took place.

Lewis grew up to be a well-educated physician like his mum, but the sea always called to him. He retired early from doctoring to sail a catamaran around the world. In the South Pacific, he relied on ancient traditional navigation methods to guide his boat across the 1,600 miles of open ocean between Rarotonga and New Zealand. He missed his intended port by just 26 miles. This feat got him the funding to spend years crisscrossing the South Pacific, humbly asking old navigators from across Polynesia to share their knowledge.

These Polynesian voyaging techniques had been handed down through generations and were often well-guarded secrets. Little boys selected to be groomed as navigators were immersed in the old ways from an early age. However, by the middle of the twentieth century there was little interest in the old ways. The last of the navigators knew they must share their secrets or the knowledge would die with them and be lost within a generation.

The humble Lewis, who had spent his boyhood on Rarotonga, was just the person to compile this ancient knowledge. And he was just the person to make a public case for the veracity of Polynesian voyaging: he was well educated, articulate, an approachable writer, and white. (Actually, he was a study in contrasts: humble, reckless, studious, swashbuckling, and a legendary womanizer, but we're getting off topic a bit.) In 1972 he wrote a book describing all he had learned from the navigators. He was an expert sailor, now a knowledgeable navigator, and perhaps just a little proud. He titled his book *We, the Navigators.*

Still, the reality was that no traditional navigators had sailed the vast distance between Hawai'i and the fabled homeland of Tahiti for at least hundreds of years. Did Polynesians really navigate such long trips with precision? Could they? In 1973 a small group in Hawai'i set out to answer whether it could be done. Calling themselves the Polynesian Voyaging Society, they audaciously gathered the scant remaining knowledge about big double-hulled voyaging canoes, ancient vessels similar to big catamarans. They went south and west across the Pacific looking for a navigator. On Satawal Island, a tiny speck of an atoll and home to just five hundred people, they found Mau Piailug, one of the navigators interviewed by Lewis.

Back in Hawai'i they built a voyaging canoe, the *Hōkūle'a* (star of joy, referring to Arcturus, a guiding star for navigators). On May 1, 1976, under the guidance of Mau Piailug, they raised a great winglike sail and set out for Tahiti. Mau Piailug navigated using mental star charts memorized during his childhood, the position of the rising and setting sun, the direction of ocean swells, the formation of clouds, and the flight of birds.

Thirty-three days later, having followed the shortest possible route for a wind-powered vessel, they sailed into Papeete, Tahiti. Seventeen

FIGURE 8.1 Canoes greet Captain Cook at Kealakekua Bay. (Original engraving by John Webber, official artist on Cook's voyage to Hawai'i)

Canoe Design. Hawaiian canoes came in two basic types. Small boats used for fishing or short-distance transportation carried one to a few people, with a single hull and an outrigger or float jutting out from one side for stability. Larger canoes had two hulls with a platform between them, like a narrow catamaran. They could carry dozens of people for short distances. These big boats were used for voyages between Hawaiian islands, including transporting war parties. Both forms exist today. Many canoe clubs paddle six-person outrigger canoes, and many double-hulled canoes have been built to demonstrate Polynesian wayfinding.

thousand people—half the island's population—turned out to greet them. That legendary voyage sent ripples of pride across Polynesia and launched a cultural reawakening. Hawaiians, sometimes disparaged in the past as the descendants of hapless stone-age castaways, had proved to be in fact heirs to the greatest seafaring tradition on earth. With ancient knowledge of their oceanic world, all Hawaiians needed to navigate the greatest ocean on earth was wind, wings, and waves.

The clarity of hindsight shows us that this wayfinding ability should not have been such a puzzle; the clues were all there. Captain Cook could communicate with the Hawaiians who greeted him because they used many words that Cook had learned in Tahiti. Cook had encountered an old navigator in the South Pacific who was able to map out many of the islands of Polynesia, even those the old man had never visited; clearly he came from seafaring people. Hawaiian villages enjoyed the same larder as islands more than two thousand miles away: *kalo,* sweet potatoes, bananas, coconuts, chicken, pigs, dogs. Inadvertent castaways rarely have the foresight to pack so many provisions. Early Hawaiians consistently maintained that their oral traditions—they had no written language—told of their origins in Tahiti and of back-and-forth voyages. Even the name of the channel between Lānaʻi and Kahoʻolawe hinted at a knowledge of Pacific geography. This channel happens to point to the southwest, toward the center of the Polynesian islands. Its name, Kealaikahiki, means "the way to foreign lands."

Put all these bits of information together and the story of Hawaiian origins becomes much clearer. In the fifth century AD the seafaring Polynesians were ascendant, mounting voyages that spread across the Pacific, discovering and colonizing islands as they went. (Those who chafed under the dismissive early views of Hawaiian culture might point out that in the fifth century western civilization was anything but civilized. The Roman Empire collapsed during that century, Europe was mired in the Dark Ages, and the Renaissance wouldn't dawn for another thousand years.)

Then, sometime around AD 400—give or take a few centuries—this great seafaring people made their longest and most perilous voyage of discovery. They sailed 2,100 miles north from the tiny cluster of islands known as the Marquesas. Their double-hulled sailing canoes crossed the equator for the first time and sailed onward to discover and settle the most remote land in the vast Pacific, Hawaiʻi.

The peaceful Marquesans had Hawaiʻi all to themselves for about seven hundred years. Then around year 1100, voyagers from Tahiti in the Society Islands arrived. The more aggressive Tahitians quickly made the islands of Hawaiʻi their own. Eventually, Hawaiian legends would recall the *Menehune,* or little people of ancient times—probably the displaced Marquesans.

For roughly two hundred years thereafter, these great navigators and sailors made long sea voyages between the islands of Hawaiʻi and the Society Islands far to the south. And then the great voyages stopped. Why? We don't know. One idea is that the Hawaiians had simply used up most of the *koa* logs that were big enough to make great voyaging canoes. That theory really doesn't hold water; early western visitors saw several double-hulled canoes ranging from seventy to over a hundred feet in length. Even if *koa* was depleted, big logs of cedar, spruce, and Douglas fir from mainland forests occasionally drifted ashore and were prized for canoe building. Perhaps Hawaiian culture had matured to the point that Tahiti was no longer viewed as a superior cultural homeland.

For whatever reason, the cultural influences of Tahiti ceased, and early Hawaiians continued to develop one of the most complex societies in the Pacific. They formed an intertwined system of religion and governance. They built ambitious stone structures. They were industrious farmers. Their dozens of huge fishponds made them the most accomplished aquaculturalists (fish farmers) on earth. Their population swelled to at least two hundred thousand; some estimates put the number far higher. And they waged minor wars over territory, within and between islands, almost constantly.

It is beyond the scope of this book to describe in detail the early Hawaiian society, religion, and way of life. Instead, this chapter focuses on the physical evidence of their culture that has survived to this day. Western influence over nearly two and a half centuries has obliterated a lot that the early Hawaiians developed, yet signs of their long presence on these islands are everywhere.

Let's start as the Polynesian voyagers did, on a big double-hulled sailing canoe. We don't know what motivated these individuals to set off from their homelands—war, overpopulation, curiosity—but they were clearly prepared to be pioneers. They brought literally everything they would need to begin life in a new and foreign land. Table 8.1 lists the items that might have stocked a voyaging canoe. Piecing together the cargo list of ships that sailed roughly 1,500 years ago is difficult. Perhaps not all the plants came on a single voyage. Some listed plants may be indigenous to Hawai'i. It is quite possible that the voyagers brought certain plant species, only to find them already growing on their new island home. For example, botanists long thought that Polynesians had brought *hala* to Hawai'i, until the distinctive impressions of *hala* fruit were found in million-year-old lava flows on Kaua'i.

The plants that were brought to Hawai'i aboard ancient voyaging canoes are commonly referred to as canoe plants. Many of them are still grown in Hawai'i today: *kalo* or taro, banana, sugarcane, sweet potato, breadfruit. Some of them have escaped cultivation and naturalized so

Table 8.1 Ship's Manifest for a Voyaging Canoe

On Board	Purpose
Navigator	Trained from childhood, he guided the canoe to its destination
Crew, passengers	Up to about 20 people were the crew and founders of a new population
Pigs (*pua'a*)	Food
Junglefowl (*moa*)	Food
Dogs (*'īlio*)	Food
Banana plants (*mai'a*)	To be planted for food
Breadfruit plants (*'ulu*)	To be planted for food
Sweet potatoes (*'uala*)	To be planted for food
Taro (*kalo*)	To be planted for food
Coconut palms (*niu*)	To be planted for food, fiber
Sugarcane (*kō*)	To be planted for food, medicinal and ceremonial uses
Bottle gourds (*ipu*)	Used as containers, musical instruments
Polynesian arrowroot (*pia*)	Medicine, food
Turmeric (*'ōlena*)	Medicinal and ceremonial uses, dye
Kava (*'awa*)	Medicinal and ceremonial uses
Indian mulberry (*noni*)	Medicine, dye
Paper mulberry (*wauke*)	Bark used to make cloth called *kapa* or *tapa*
Ti plant (*kī*)	Leaves used for house thatching, rain capes, food storage, etc.
Candlenut (*kukui*)	Lamp oil, dyes, ceremonial and many other uses
Shampoo ginger (*'awapuhi kuahiwi*)	Hair conditioner, medicine, scent

smoothly into the forests of Hawai'i that you would swear they have been growing on these islands forever: shampoo ginger is a common sight in moist forests, and the silvery green leaves of *kukui* trees line many gulches in low to medium elevations.

Once the big canoe made landfall, its passengers probably sought out windward valleys as the first places to settle. These places offered

On Board	Purpose
Alexandrian laurel (*kamani*)	Wood for bowls and platters, dye, medicine
Hau	Light wood for floats, outriggers, medicine, may be indigenous
Elephant's ears (*'ape*)	Medicine, dye, famine food
Kou	Wood for bowls and platters, dye, medicine, indigenous
Portia tree (*milo*)	Wood for bowls and platters, dye, indigenous
Bamboo (*'ohe*)	A thin-walled bamboo used for musical instruments, knives, tools
Mountain apple (*'ohi'a 'ai*)	Food, medicine, dye
Yams (*uhi, pi'a, hoi*)	Three yam varieties; oddly, *hoi* is poisonous unless carefully prepared
Screwpine (*hala*)	Leaves woven into mats, indigenous
Pa'ihi	Food, medicine, may be indigenous
Auhuhu	Fish poison
Polynesian rat (*'iole*)	Stowaway or food
Land snail	Stowaway
House gecko	Stowaway, may be indigenous
A few weeds	Stowaways
Canoe repair kit	Woven cord, *hala* for sail repair, tools
Fishing tackle	Used to troll for fish during the voyage
Stone hearth, *niu* shell	Coconut shells burned to cook food
Food and water	Enough to supplement 20 people for about 40 days

ideal conditions, including fresh water for drinking and irrigation, deep soil for planting, and easy access to the ocean where streams punctuate coral reefs. Waipi'o and Pololū Valleys on the Big Island have probably been home to Hawaiians from the earliest days of settlement. There have probably been villages lining O'ahu's Kāne'ohe Bay for nearly as long. Hanalei Valley on Kaua'i was likely an early center of population,

The Sweet Potato, the Chicken, and the Wayfinder. How far did Polynesians range during their voyages of discovery? What were the limits of their world? We may never know for sure, but there is circumstantial evidence that their seafaring spanned the entire great Pacific. When Captain Cook explored Polynesia, he saw people growing sweet potatoes everywhere he went, including Hawai'i. Intriguingly, the sweet potato, like corn, tomatoes, tobacco, cocoa, and peanuts, is a plant that originated in tropical South America. Sweet potatoes are spread by tubers or vine cuttings that don't hold up to salt water, so they probably didn't float to Polynesia. Significantly, Polynesian names for sweet potato include 'uala in Hawaiian and 'umara and kumara in other Polynesian languages. On the west coast of South America, native Quechua words for sweet potato include umala and kumara. This suggests face-to-face trade. There is no maritime tradition among the Quechua or their neighbors, so South Americans probably didn't do the sailing. It seems quite possible that Polynesians voyaged all the way to the Americas.

And there's more. Some researchers have examined the DNA in ancient chicken bones on the west coast of South America and concluded that their ancestors were Polynesian junglefowl. This finding is in dispute but it adds to the circumstantial evidence. And the genes of Polynesian bottle gourds seem to contain traces of South American gourd DNA. And, although the significance is hotly debated, the canoes and fishhooks of the Chumash tribe in coastal California bear an uncanny resemblance to Polynesian canoes and fishhooks.

An alternative explanation is to dismiss the Chumash connection as coincidental and point to early Spanish explorers. They visited western Polynesia via the Indian Ocean around 1500. Then, sailing around the globe in the other direction, they could have bartered Polynesian chickens for sweet potatoes on the Atlantic coast of South America. Finally, they might have returned to Polynesia with sweet potatoes. There are problems with this theory, too. As early as 1532, the Spanish explorer Pizarro found plenty of chickens in Incan cities in Peru, all the way across South America on the Pacific side. It seems unlikely that native Americans transported chickens across the continent that fast.

Did Polynesian voyagers reach America? It is a mystery that may never be solved. Nevertheless, several lines of evidence suggest that Polynesian voyagers were trading chickens for sweet potatoes in South America around AD 800, about the same time the Norse were poking around Labrador and Newfoundland.

and it is still a center of fairly traditional *kalo* farming. *Kalo* plants bear a starchy rootlike corm that is peeled, cooked, pounded, and fermented to make *poi,* the traditional staple of the Hawaiian diet. You may be more familiar with the term *taro,* the name of this crop in English and other Polynesian languages.

It didn't take much time for the early Hawaiians to start using their environment to suit their needs. Where they moved stones either to clear land for farming or to build structures, the rockwork often survives today. Many Hawaiian valleys still harbor the remnants of stone terraces constructed for agriculture. Limahuli Valley on Kaua'i is an excellent place to see them. From the air, keen-eyed observers can still scan arid grasslands of North Kona and see hundreds of rows of rocks stacked when ancient farmers cleared miles of land. The scale of farming was so large that it amazed early western explorers; early accounts invariably comment on the extensive agriculture.

Rock structures weren't limited to the land. Early Hawaiians became masters of aquaculture. The most common type of fishpond was constructed along ocean shorelines in shallow water where a curving rock wall could be built to enclose acres of water. A few of these ancient ponds have been restored. The remnants of dozens more lie in shallow coastal water where they can still be seen from the air. The south shore of Moloka'i, offering some of the best shallow conditions, is lined with ancient and restored ponds. There are others in Kāne'ohe Bay on O'ahu.

It may seem odd that early Hawaiians, surrounded by coral reefs teeming with fish, would go to the extraordinary effort to build fishponds. But fishing tackle wasn't easy to come by: every hook had to be hand carved, every line painstakingly woven. And then you caught one fish at a time. You could spend weeks weaving a fish net to catch more fish at once, but you had to take great care not to damage your net on sharp coral or rocks. Fishing in the open ocean was impossible during stormy weather. Fishponds offered protected waters where many fish could be grown and then netted quickly. The system obviously worked well; nearly every suitable stretch of shoreline had a pond.

While many stone structures were purely utilitarian, the most prominent structures were those built for religious purposes. They are called *heiau,* and there are hundreds of them across Hawai'i. *Heiau* were more than just religious sites. For early Hawaiians, religion and governance were inseparable. The ruling class, the *ali'i,* were advised by

FIGURE 8.2 Early Hawaiians built dozens or hundreds of fishponds. A few, like He'eia Pond in Kāne'ohe Bay on O'ahu, are being restored. (Rick Soehren)

a high-ranking class of priests, the *kāhuna. Ali'i* and *kāhuna* conferred regularly, so royal dwellings were usually close to the *heiau* where the *kāhuna* worshipped and acted as intermediaries with the gods.

Some *heiau* are ruins like Keaīwa Heiau on O'ahu, its rocks mostly pilfered for later construction. Others have been restored to a semblance of their original appearance, including several located in national historic parks or state parks along the Kona coast. Some *heiau* are tiny, consisting of just a small platform. At the other end of the scale is Pi'ilanihale Heiau in Kahanu Garden near Hāna on Maui. It is the largest stone structure in all of Polynesia, so big that it looks more like a rocky mountain than an ancient temple.

The *ali'i* ruled in something of a feudal system. Until Kamehameha I used his keen strategy and western weaponry to overcome his enemies and unify all the Hawaiian islands in 1810, each island had been ruled by an independent chief. Even under Kamehameha's rule, each island was governed by a single chief who acted like a governor. Below the chief of an island in the hierarchy were lesser chiefs who controlled regions called *ahupua'a*. Each *ahupua'a* provided its residents access to a full range of resources from big *koa* trees in the forest, to lowlands suitable for agriculture, to shorelines teeming with fish. The common people who worked the land supported the chiefly and religious classes above them through taxes paid in the form of crops, fish, and the like.

The modern science of watershed management has a lot in common with the early Hawaiian concept of *ahupua'a:* using and caring for the land, the sea, and all their resources as a system, recognizing that actions upstream affect conditions downstream. In addition, the *ali'i* sometimes placed a *kapu* or prohibition on use of certain resources such as barring the harvest of fish species during their spawning season.

These approaches have led many people to believe that early Hawaiians were great protectors and stewards of the natural environment. The reality is a little more complex. Hawaiians managed their resources very carefully for the purpose of feeding a large and necessarily self-sufficient population. But the natural world suffered at their hands: a lot of native lowland vegetation was displaced by agriculture, and many of the birds the Hawaiians encountered were quickly eaten into extinction. (More on this in chapter 12.)

The *ali'i* were believed to be descended from, and answerable to, the gods. A crowded pantheon of gods and minor deities controlled their world, and these gods could be offended by human missteps. Any natural phenomenon that the Hawaiians could not explain was ascribed to actions of the gods. The four major gods and some of the realms they controlled were Kū (politics and warfare), Kāne (male power of procreation, irrigated agriculture, fresh water), Kanaloa (the ocean and voyaging), and Lono (nonirrigated agriculture, fertility, peace, and harvest). Other deities included Pele (the volcano goddess), her sister Kapo (she of the flying vagina), and Laka (goddess of the dance). *Heiau* were dedicated to certain gods. At a *heiau* dedicated to Lono, ceremonies might be conducted to ensure fertility of crops. The early Hawaiians developed a complex society that was maintained through rules intertwined with religion and social hierarchy. *'Ōhelo* berries grew near the volcano, so you had to throw some into the crater as an offering to Pele before you ate any. Commoners could not approach the top *ali'i* too closely. The punishment for stepping on the shadow of a high-ranking chief was death.

Despite all the rules imposed on Hawaiian people by their chiefs, life was not totally grim. In fact, the Hawaiian calendar included an extended celebration each year. From roughly November to February, a celebration called the *makahiki* would take place. Wars would cease, men and women danced the *hula,* and competitive games were held. The *makahiki* followed the harvest, and commoners would offer animals and crops to the god Lono. The chief of the island would gather the offerings in Lono's name and distribute the goods to the other *ali'i* and *kāhuna*. There was a ritual involved in this collection. The chief would travel around the island in a clockwise direction, stopping at each *ahupua'a* to gather offerings. The chief's arrival was advertised by his attendants, who carried a tall pole topped with a carved figure and a crossbar supporting a sheet of white *kapa* cloth, the versatile fabric that Hawaiians made from the bark of the *wauke* or paper mulberry.

It was during the *makahiki* that Captain Cook returned to Hawai'i in November 1778, after spending the previous summer in an unsuccessful Arctic search for a sea route from the Atlantic to the Pacific. His masted ships with their huge white sails rode the tradewinds from the northeast, stopped briefly at Maui, sailed on and rounded South Point at the tip of the Big Island heading clockwise, and anchored at Kealakekua Bay. Thousands of Hawaiians came out to greet their god Lono. The mistaken identity was understandable. After a few weeks of being treated quite literally like a god, Cook headed north. When a broken mast forced him to limp back to Kealakekua Bay the next month, the *makahiki* was over and the mood was different. Cultural misunderstandings turned into squabbles that escalated rapidly. The British shot and killed some of the Hawaiians. They, in turn, killed Cook. Curiously, the Hawaiians afterward asked Cook's lieutenants when Lono would return.

Particular prohibitions or *kapu* were imposed on women. For example, women could not dine with men, and they were prohibited from eating certain tasty foods such as bananas, pork, and shark meat. Women generally held a lower position in society than men of the same class. This may have been one factor that allowed the Hawaiian religion to crumble and fall. When Kamehameha I died in 1819 his twenty-two-year-old son Liholiho took his place as Kamehameha II. The favorite among Kamehameha I's twenty-one wives, Ka'ahumanu, saw her power and influence slipping away to a successor who was not of her blood. Claiming that she voiced the will of her dead husband, she proclaimed that she would share power with the young Liholiho. But her proclamation was not enough. The *kapu* system kept her out of the *heiau* where political and religious decisions were made. She was not afraid of breaking *kapu*. She had done it many times: eating pork and shark, sleeping with other *ali'i*. And she had seen many foreigners violate these strictures and suffer no ill will of the gods. She persuaded the malleable young Liholiho to break *kapu* in a very public way by dining with women.

The gods took no notice, or if they did, they didn't show it. Suddenly, the religious rules that bound Hawaiian culture were all suspect; the fearsome power of the *kāhuna* evaporated. Liholiho, probably at the goading of Kaʻahumanu, ordered all the *heiau* in the kingdom desecrated to emphasize their sudden shift from temples to rock piles. The conversion was not universal; five years later when the Christian convert Princess Kapiʻolani taunted Pele and ate *ʻōhelo* berries at the doorstep of the volcano goddess' realm, there were faithful who were sure she would be struck down. Kapiʻolani's action was itself an effort to further dispel the old beliefs.

When Christian missionaries arrived in Hawaiʻi just six months after Liholiho's seminal dinner, they had no idea just how lucky their timing was. They brought a new god to fill the void that had just been created, and Christianity swept the islands. Does that mean the old belief system was gone forever? No. Before the advent of proselytizing missionaries the Hawaiians had worshipped many gods. Even the converted had room in their minds for more than just one true god. In 1881 eruptions from Mauna Loa threatened the town of Hilo, and a day of Christian prayer had no effect. The desperate townspeople summoned Princess Ruth Keʻelikōlani, descendant of the Kamehameha family and adherent to the old ways. A formidable presence at over six feet tall and 440 pounds, she traveled to the hills above town and prayed to her gods. Within days the flow stopped and the town was spared.

If there was ambivalence over the public practice of religion, then attitudes surrounding another side of the early Hawaiian belief system were even more complicated. Liholiho threw into question the public side of Hawaiian religion with its *heiau, kāhuna,* and many *kapu.* But there was, and is, another side of this belief system—a private family side. Early Hawaiians believed that the force powering the universe, *mana,* was hereditary. It flowed from the gods or *akua* to the ancestral spirits or *ʻaumakua* to living parents, the *mākua.* Just as the gods could control the physical world, esteemed ancestors possessing great *mana* could exert control over the world of the living. A family's *ʻaumakua* were usually invisible and would be given a resting place in the form of a small shrine in the home. Occasionally *ʻaumakua* might take possession of a living creature and help the family. One family's 'aumakua might take the form of a shark to herd fish into the family's nets, while another family's ancestral spirit might appear as an owl to guide them across unfamiliar territory.

The public repudiation of ancient religion by their king did not prevent Hawaiian families from continuing to hold to their private beliefs. Respect and reverence for the 'aumakua continued more or less unabated. Families showed respect for their 'aumakua by sharing food with them. Food might be placed on the family's altar, or at a *heiau*. The family would also show respect by refraining from harming the animal whose form their 'aumakua might take. Even today, it is not uncommon to see offerings at *heiau* in Hawai'i. Because many families' 'aumakua took the form of sharks, efforts to kill sharks around swimming beaches are still controversial and opposed by some Hawaiian families.

Heiau and other stone structures withstand the warm wet climate of Hawai'i very well, but they are not the only surviving physical remnants of early Hawaiian culture and life. Throughout the islands there are petroglyphs: drawings or symbols scratched or carved into rock. Sometimes it is hard to know how old the petroglyphs might be. In other cases the images include sailing ships or Hawaiian names. These were obviously created sometime after western contact.

Many stone implements have survived: elegant *poi* pounders used to mash *kalo* into a paste for *poi*, adze heads made of the hardest basalt, fishing weights, and more. Objects made from wood or plant fiber are rarer. Original canoes and the *pili* grass houses of Hawaiian people were exposed to the weather and have mostly disappeared. There are life-size recreations in the Bishop Museum (see the **Field Trip!** in this chapter).

Treasured household goods have fared better. Wooden bowls were utilitarian works of art. They were carved from single large blocks of wood, some of them unimaginably large and nearly impossible to reproduce today because there are very few native trees of sufficient diameter. These bowls were heirlooms handed down through generations. Any cracks that developed over time were skillfully patched with inlaid wood. Many of these bowls are now in the collections of museums.

Among the rarest and most valuable artifacts are feathered capes and cloaks. These were made for the highest *ali'i*. Captain Cook was given one, apparently while the Hawaiians still believed he was the

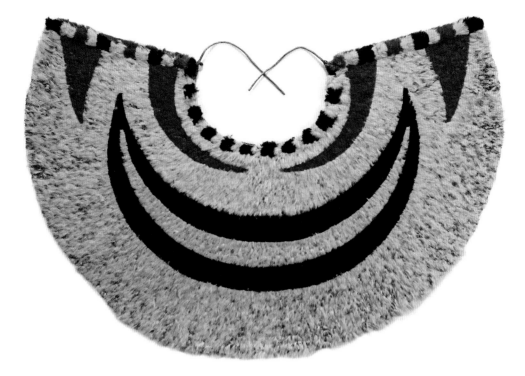

FIGURE 8.3 This feathered cloak belonged to Liliʻuokalani, Hawaiʻi's last queen. It is one of the last cloaks made with feathers of now-extinct birds. Yellow and black feathers are from species of ʻōʻō, honeyeaters that are all gone. The red feathers are from ʻiʻiwi, a honeycreeper that still survives. (Hal Lum and Masayo Suzuki, Bishop Museum)

embodiment of Lono. These garments were extremely labor-intensive to produce. First, *olonā* plants were harvested and made into strong twine. The twine was knotted into a mesh that served as the backing for the garment.

Meanwhile, bird hunters would gather feathers of the desired colors: yellow and black from species of ʻōʻō or *mamo* and red-orange from ʻiʻiwi. It is commonly stated that Hawaiians were careful stewards and would pluck just a few feathers from each bird and then release the bird back into the forest. Well, yes and no. Each ʻōʻō had only a few bright yellow feathers, so these birds could be plucked and released. The ʻiʻiwi is mostly red-orange. Some early western observers reported seeing bird hunters returning from the forest with hundreds of dead ʻiʻiwi. It is likely that the birds were plucked and then eaten.

The feathers were gathered into tiny bundles, and the bundles were sewn on to the *olonā* mesh in elaborate geometric designs. Capes covered just the shoulders, while cloaks were long enough to cover a man's body nearly to the ground. Yellow was the most prized color, owing to its rarity. A full-length cloak might be made from hundreds of thousands of feathers, plucked a few at a time from each captured *'ō'ō*. Today, all the species of *'ō'ō* are extinct—killed off not by careful feather plucking, but the heavy impacts of westerners later on.

Beyond the tangible remnants of Hawaiian culture, there are the intangibles: things like language, and *hula,* and the chants that served as the repository of knowledge and history for a people without a written alphabet. Paradoxically, the missionaries that came to Hawai'i starting in 1820 helped preserve Hawaiian language by writing it down, yet tried their best to stamp out much of the culture, like the *hula.* Women dancing around half naked was incomprehensibly lewd and vile to early nineteenth-century sensibilities. Fortunately, Hawaiians were irrepressible: they adopted the written alphabet to help preserve their history and their chants. The *hula* survived, too. Today it is a joyous and expressive demonstration of Hawaiian culture.

It was the missionaries who devised a written alphabet as described in chapter 1: five vowels and eight consonants including the *'okina* or glottal stop. Anyone who reads old historical accounts of early days will see phonetic spellings of Hawaiian names, and they often don't match modern spelling and presumed pronunciation. For example, figure 8.1 is an engraving made by the artist who accompanied Cook. He titled it *A View of Kealakekua in Hawai'i* but his phonetic spelling was *A View of Karakakooa in Owhyee.* Similarly, Kamehameha was sometimes written phonetically as *Tameamea.* Even today, native speakers on Ni'ihau pronounce a *t* rather than a *k.* Clearly there were regional variations or subtleties of pronunciation that were not adequately captured by the missionary alphabet.

Thanks to missionary schools, many Hawaiians learned to read and write Hawaiian. Some of them wrote down chants and oral histories. Many of these were secret and private, but western culture was swamping Hawaiian life so quickly that stories needed to be written down before they were forgotten and lost. It was in this spirit that in 1889 King Kalākaua obtained a copy of his family's genealogical chant, written in Hawaiian. It traced his family's descent not only back to human ancestors but all the way back to the creation of the universe, all neatly summarized in 2,102 lines of chant. After Kalākaua's death the first full translation into English was made by his sister the deposed

Loss of a Nation. For most of the nineteenth century, the Kingdom of Hawai'i was a sovereign nation. It had stood as a unified entity since Kamehameha I brought all the islands under his control in 1810. The kingdom quickly established itself by adopting the diplomatic and governance customs of other countries. The kingdom's rulers visited foreign nations: Kamehameha II and his wife traveled to England in 1824 (where they both died of measles). The kingdom forged foreign treaties with several European nations and the United States. The Hawaiian nation became a constitutional monarchy with the adoption of a constitution and establishment of a legislative body.

In 1889 Queen Lili'uokalani ascended the throne upon the death of her brother King Kalākaua. She would be the last nineteenth-century ruler of this sovereign nation. By 1893 western immigrants and their descendants held most of the land, wealth, and power in Hawai'i. A group of sugar planters and merchants overthrew the monarchy, imprisoned the queen, and asked the United States for annexation. President Grover Cleveland observed that "the lawful government of Hawai'i was overthrown," and refused the annexation request. The rebellious group waited until there was a new administration in Washington. President William McKinley approved annexation in 1898.

Today there are Hawaiian sovereignty efforts among people of Native Hawaiian descent, but many different views of what form this sovereignty should take. This brief history is obviously much simplified, but good to know if you are in the nation, then territory, then state of Hawai'i.

Queen Lili'uokalani while she was imprisoned in 1894–1895. The chant is called the *Kumulipo*. It means "beginning in deep darkness."

The *Kumulipo* is more than just a genealogy; it is a historical, literary, and spiritual treasure that very nearly did not survive to our time. It describes the genesis and place of the Hawaiian people in the cosmos of sky, land, sea, people, and gods. The *Kumulipo* is full of allusion, nuance, and double meaning. Different translators have interpreted the text in wildly different ways. For example, chapter 7 of this book related that one translation of the *Kumulipo* identifies the octopus—*he'e* or slippery one—as already present when the universe is created: "the octopus is present as observer of the process." A later translation comes up with a completely different meaning, and the octopus is gone: "Darkness slips into light." Although the text of the *Kumulipo* was saved, some of its depth and meaning may have been lost.

FIELD TRIP!

8.1 BISHOP MUSEUM IN HONOLULU. If you visit only one museum in Hawai'i, Bishop Museum is the one to see. The museum bills itself as the premier place to experience the history, arts, and culture of the Hawaiian people. It is the largest museum in the state and the top natural and cultural history institution in the Pacific. Bishop Museum was founded in 1889 by Charles Reed Bishop in honor of his late wife, Princess Bernice Pauahi Bishop, the last descendant of the royal Kamehameha family. Its original purpose was to house the extensive collection of Hawaiian artifacts and royal family heirlooms of the princess. Today the museum's collections are huge, containing over a million artifacts, more than 22 million plant and animal specimens, and documents and photographs about Hawai'i and other Pacific island cultures.

The original stone buildings include the Hawaiian Hall. In this multistory Victorian hall you can trace Hawaiian history through artifacts including *pili* grass houses and full-size canoes, fishnets woven of *olonā* and still serviceable after a century, a rotating collection of magnificent featherwork garments, and everyday objects like wooden bowls and implements. Even the hall itself is a museum piece. Built with lavish woodwork of *koa,* it shows how artifacts were displayed during the Victorian era (the displays have been updated, and they're excellent).

Cross the garden of endemic and canoe plants and visit the Science Adventure Center for the antithesis of the staid old Hawaiian Hall. You can walk or slide through a lava tube, control submersibles on a coral reef, and even watch rock melt at volcanic temperatures. Worth a visit for adults, and wildly exciting for the kids.

A planetarium, a section for rotating exhibitions, interpretive talks, a café, and a nice gift shop round out the museum's campus. But that's not all. The museum's website is worth exploring, too. It contains a lot of information on the natural and cultural history of Hawai'i: species accounts of birds, photos of artifacts, monthly star charts, and much more. The museum's campus is located on Bernice Street, near the intersection of the H1 freeway and the Likelike Highway, Route 63. There is an admission fee. Open every day of the year except Christmas. Wheelchair access is good.

8.2 CANOE PLANTS. The plants brought to Hawai‘i by early voyagers are everywhere in the islands, but it is hard to find places where they are labeled so you can learn to identify them. Here are a few of the better canoe plant gardens:

Lyon Arboretum, O‘ahu. This arboretum affiliated with the University of Hawai‘i has an excellent collection of canoe plants. You can use your smartphone to listen to recorded information about the plants marked by special signs. And you are surrounded by lush gardens in the rainy hills above Honolulu. See the **Field Trip!** in chapter 4 for more information.

McBryde and Limahuli Gardens, Kaua‘i. These two facilities of the National Tropical Botanical Garden both have excellent collections of canoe plants. See the **Field Trip!** in chapter 4 for more information.

Maui Nui Botanical Gardens. Early Hawaiians had many varieties of *kalo* or taro that could be grown in a range of conditions from water-filled patches called *lo‘i* to dry upland sites. This garden has taken on the task of serving as a repository and source for these old varieties, roughly five dozen of them. They have examples of other canoe plants, too. See the **Field Trip!** in chapter 4 for more information.

Kahanu Garden, Maui. See below under cultural sites.

The physical evidence of early Hawaiian habitation is everywhere on the islands and it is diverse: *heiau*, petroglyphs, fishponds, and more. Here are a few of the outstanding sites on each island. A note on visiting these sites: they are places of historical, religious, and cultural significance. Some are still in use. Visit with the respect and humility of a guest. Do not climb on cultural sites or take stones. Wrapping a rock in a ti leaf is not a traditional offering; please don't do it.

8.3 O‘AHU CULTURAL SITES. O‘ahu seems to have fewer good examples of cultural sites than other islands, perhaps because it is harder to preserve these sites in the face of a burgeoning population. One of the most intriguing is also the easiest for tourists to visit, because it is on the beach at Waikīkī right next to the police station: **Nā Pōhaku Ola Kapaemāhū a Kapuni,** also called the Wizard Stones or the Stones of Life. Hawaiian legend tells of four great healers who came from the Society Islands sometime around the year 1300. Their fame spread as they dispensed miraculous cures. Before they returned to their home island of Ra‘iātea they asked that four large stones be displayed to remember them, two near the hut where they slept and two at their favorite bathing places. They imbued the stones with great *mana*. Today all the stones are gathered at one spot.

Another group of stones has an even more interesting story. The **Kūkaniloko Birthstones** are near the geographic center of Oʻahu, just outside the town of Wahiawā. The birthstones are a cluster of half-buried boulders at a spot that was reputed to have great *mana*. Pregnant women of the chiefly class would come here to give birth to ensure that their babies would also have great *mana*. Today the stones are arranged haphazardly and some may have been added when sugar planters cleared surrounding land. It is believed that they were originally arranged in two rows of eighteen stones flanking Kūkaniloko, the birthing stone itself. Thirty-six chiefs would occupy the stones and bear witness to the royal birth. There are other stories that the site was a celestial observatory or a navigational training school with stones formerly arranged like a map of Polynesian islands. To reach the site from Honolulu take H1 to H2. Exit on to the Kamehameha Highway at Wahiawā, drive through town, and cross the bridge. The next stoplight you come to will be Whitmore Avenue to the right; the birthstones are down a short dirt road to the left.

In the Koʻolau Mountains above the town of ʻAiea is **Keaīwa Heiau State Recreation Area**. The namesake *heiau* is not very impressive; many of its stones have been carted away over the years. It was apparently a *heiau hoʻōla,* where healers were trained. The park's main attraction is a lovely 4.3-mile loop trail that climbs gently through a forest of introduced plants into a mix of introduced and native vegetation including *ʻōhiʻa* and *koa.* The park is one of the better places on Oʻahu to see native birds including *ʻamakihi* and—rarely—*ʻelepaio.* Early morning visitors will hear and may see a flock of a hundred or more red-crowned Amazon parrots leaving their forest roost.

The largest *heiau* on Oʻahu is **Puʻu o Mahuka Heiau** (hill of escape) overlooking Waimea Bay on the north shore, and it has quite a history. It is said to have been constructed by the *Menehune,* and some parts of the *heiau* complex date to the 1600s. It is a *luakini heiau,* dedicated to Kū and used for human sacrifice. In 1794 the explorer George Vancouver sent three men ashore at Waimea Bay to seek fresh water. Hawaiians killed them, and at least two became offerings at this *heiau.* (The preferred human sacrifice was a captured enemy warrior of the *aliʻi* class because he would have great *mana*. Apparently these sailors met the requirements.) A year later Kamehameha I conquered Oʻahu, and his high priest carried out ceremonies here. If you visit, keep in mind that the *heiau* is still in use; it is not uncommon to see offerings of food or money here. To reach the site, head *mauka* on Pūpūkea Road where it joins Kamehameha Highway just north of Waimea Bay. The wonderful snorkeling spot at Shark's Cove is nearby (see chapter 7).

Just inland of Waimea Bay in the valley of the same name is a cultural attraction called **Waimea Valley**. It is a historic and cultural park owned and operated by the Office of Hawaiian Affairs, a state agency established to manage land formerly owned by Hawaiian monarchy, preserve Hawaiian culture, and protect native Hawaiian rights. The valley includes a restored *heiau*, gardens with native and canoe plants, and extensive walking trails. Those who walk three-quarters of a mile up through the paved park paths will reach Waiheʻe Falls, a favorite swimming hole. Whether your interest is plants, cultural sites, or just a walk through shady forest, this is a very pleasant spot. There is an admission fee. The park is open daily except Thanksgiving and Christmas. The park can provide golf cart rides to the waterfall; most areas of the park are wheelchair accessible, but some paths are steep. Special cultural events are held throughout the year.

8.4 BIG ISLAND CULTURAL SITES. The Big Island is rich in history. The west coast of the Big Island has the largest concentration of major and easily accessed archaeological sites in the state. If you want to visit *heiau* and see petroglyphs, this really is the place to come. From north to south the major sites include:

Lapakahi State Historical Park, 45 miles north of Kailua-Kona and 12.4 miles north of the harbor town of Kawaihae, contains ruins and a few restored structures from a fishing village that existed here for more than six hundred years, until it was abandoned in the late 1800s. A brochure available at the tiny office or online describes twenty numbered sites along the self-guided 1-mile unpaved loop trail. There is no water and very little shade, and no access for the disabled except the office. The brochure asks you to stay on the trail, but I have seen snorkelers entering the gorgeously clear water near numbered site seven. A nice low-key place to visit.

Puʻu Koholā Heiau National Historic Site, 33 miles north of

Kailua-Kona and just at the south edge of Kawaihae, protects one of the last major *heiau* built in Hawai'i before western influence changed island life forever. This *heiau* is one of the most significant in Hawaiian history, too: Kamehameha I built it in 1790–1791 after a prophet said the king would unify all the islands if he built the great temple. And it is big, measuring 224 feet long. It is believed that the stones used in its construction came from Pololū Valley, 20 miles away, and were passed hand to hand by thousands of men pressed into service. A fence and signs keep visitors from approaching too closely. This park has the best visitor center and interpretive videos of any of the leeward Big Island sites. Disabled access is very good.

Kaloko-Honokōhau National Historical Park, just north of Honokōhau Harbor between Kailua-Kona and the Kona airport, is a mixed bag. There is limited park development and interpretation, but the area offers more variety to a visitor than any of the other historic sites in the region: *heiau*; Kaloko Fishpond, with an impressively restored seawall; petroglyphs; 'Aimakapā Fishpond, where native and migrant wetland birds can be seen; anchialine ponds; trails shaded by the *kiawe* forest; and Honokōhau Beach, a very pleasant recreational beach at the south end of the park by 'Ai'ōpio Fishtrap, where green sea turtles often beach and bask.

There are three access points to Kaloko-Honōkohau. The tiny visitor center is easily accessed directly from the first, Queen Ka'ahumanu Highway, Route 11. The center is a masterpiece of poor design and poor location: plunked down in the middle of harsh *a'ā*, opening toward the highway instead of the sea, and lacking traditional design elements that would catch breezes. Two other park access points are tricky. The second, a rough road to the northern end of the park including Kaloko Fishpond and a shady picnic area, branches off the highway, but you can only turn in if you are driving southbound. This road is barely passable for passenger cars. Third, the southern (and my favorite) part of the park is reached by turning off the highway on the road toward commercial Honokōhau Harbor, taking the first right turn, then curving around to the left past dozens of dry-docked boats (you'll think you must have taken a wrong turn) to an insignificant gate and sign at the northern edge of harbor property. A short unpaved path through the *kiawe* leads to beach, ponds, and *heiau*. Trees offer some shade until afternoon, and a restored canoe house provides shade all the time. Portable toilets are nearby. There is a petroglyph field a few hundred yards north; get a map from the visitor center to find it. This little beach at the south end of the park is one of my favorite spots in the Kailua-Kona area. It's a great place to watch the sun set, and often you will share the sand with a basking turtle or two. If you plan to linger after sunset, be sure to take a flashlight to get back to your car. Among park locations, only the visitor center has access for the disabled.

Puʻuhonua o Hōnaunau National Historic Park is off the Māmalahoa Highway, Route 11, about twenty-two miles south of Kailua-Kona. This park was the first established along this coast, in 1955, and for good reason. It preserves one of the few remaining *puʻuhonua,* or places of refuge, among the six to eight that once existed on the Big Island and perhaps three dozen statewide. A *puʻuhonua* has no single comparable institution or place in western society today. It was a location where *aliʻi* lived, where *kāhuna* tended religious temples, where the *mana* of the powerful was so concentrated that it could purify wrongdoers. Under the severe social order of pre-Contact Hawaiʻi, those who violated a rule or broke *kapu* were sentenced to death. However, if you could make it to a *puʻuhonua* before you were caught, you could be cleansed of your infraction.

There is a nice small visitor center with classic 1970s interpretive sculpture and frequent interpretive talks. The park brochure describes sixteen sites along a self-guided walking tour. Access for the disabled is good; paths around the site are sand, but balloon-tire sand wheelchairs are available for use. Green sea turtles are frequent visitors to the royal canoe landing cove in the park. Right next to the park is Two Step, a snorkeling spot hit hard by coral bleaching (see chapter 7). To reach the park, take Highway 11 to Highway 160, between mile markers 103 and 104. Drive four miles *makai* to the park.

In addition to the parks already described, there are two extensive petroglyph fields on the leeward coast of the Big Island in the Waikoloa area. They are close to one another and are both accessed from resort areas, but the feeling you get at the two sites is completely different. The **Waikoloa Petroglyph Preserve** can be reached by heading *makai* on Waikoloa Beach Drive near mile marker 76 on the Queen Kaʻahumanu Highway, Route 11. Follow the road to the intersection with Pohakulana Place and park in the shopping center parking lot on your right, near the gas station. Follow the old King's Trail that parallels Pohakulana (part of the historic trail is now a paved sidewalk) north to the rugged loop trail through the petroglyph field. The petroglyphs range in age: some seem quite ancient while others include names and dates from the 1860s. Unless early Hawaiians invented the happy face, there are some petroglyphs that are quite recent. While touring the field you will always be within sight of resort condos.

The **Puakō Petroglyph Archaeological Preserve** is a little more than a mile north of Waikoloa via the highway. Take Mauna Lani Drive *makai,* turn right at the big traffic circle, and follow the signs to the end of the road at Holoholokai Beach Park. The transition will be startling when you drive from the ultra-manicured grounds of Mauna Lani to the dry old *kiawe* forest beyond. There is parking at the beach park but no beach, just rocky shoreline—the few pockets of sandy beach on this young rocky shoreline are surrounded by the resorts. A rugged trail through *kiawe* forest leads to the petroglyph field. The petroglyphs are protected from your footsteps by a simple wood rail fence. All the glyphs here seem old; there are no names or dates. The round-trip walk to the petroglyphs is about 1.6 miles, just enough to keep casual visitors away. In the early morning you will likely have the place all to yourself, with only the sounds of the wind in the *kiawe* branches and the cooing of zebra doves.

The best times to view petroglyphs is when the sun is low in the sky and creates shadows that highlight the petroglyphs; it really does make a difference. The Waikoloa field can be visited at any time, but the trailhead for the Puakō field is in a gated beach park that is open from 6:30 a.m. to 6:30 p.m., making summer late-day viewing impossible. My favorite way to visit Puakō: bring a picnic breakfast to enjoy at the shady oceanfront picnic tables before or after a morning walk.

One of the oldest and best-preserved petroglyph fields in Hawai'i is the Pu'u Loa petroglyph field in Hawai'i Volcanoes National Park. (See chapter 2.)

Kamehameha built Pu'u Koholā Heiau in an effort to consolidate his control of all the islands. There are many legends, some of them contradictory, about his earlier life. According to one variation, he signaled his great future with a feat of strength when he was a teenager. There is a great block of stone now resting in front of the Hilo Library along Waiānuenue Avenue, called the **Naha Stone**. It is said that only a future king could budge it. Young Kamehameha was able to turn it over. You can visit the stone and form your own judgment.

8.5 CULTURAL SITES OF MAUI NUI. Maui doesn't have as many impressive *heiau* as the Big Island, but it does have the most impressive *heiau* anywhere: **Pi'ilanihale Heiau.** It is the largest *heiau* in all of Polynesia, so large that it looks more like a mountain than a temple. It is located within **Kahanu Garden,** a branch of the National Tropical Botanical Garden, near Hāna in wet, windward Maui. The garden has a modest ethnobotanical garden of canoe plants and the largest collection of breadfruit trees in the world: a huge grove with 300 trees of 120 varieties. Breadfruit or *'ulu* is one of the canoe plants, but it was never as prominent in Hawaiian life as it was in other parts of Polynesia. To reach the garden, take 'Ula'aino Road *makai* from its junction with the Hāna Highway, Route 360, at the 31-mile marker. The first half mile of the road is paved, the last mile is fairly well-maintained gravel. Just before you reach the garden there is a stream crossing. Do not attempt to cross when the water is high (the garden will be closed anyway). At

FIGURE 8.4 Pi'ilanihale Heiau at Kahanu Garden on Maui, half surrounded by dense forest, is the largest *heiau* in all of Polynesia. Note road and house at left for scale. (Courtesy of National Tropical Botanical Garden)

the entrance kiosk you can get a free brochure with your paid admission or purchase an informative booklet. Get the booklet. After a white-knuckle drive out the narrow, winding, cliffside Hāna Highway, the garden is a wonderfully serene change of pace.

There are some very fine petroglyphs near Olowalu in West Maui. To reach the **Olowalu Petroglyphs**, take the Honoapiʻilani Highway, Route 30, toward West Maui. At the 15-mile marker pull off at the Olowalu General Store and drive around it to a big old silver water tank in back. Take the semi-paved road *mauka* past the water tank for 0.4 mile where the pavement veers to the right to join a parallel road. Continue straight on gravel another 0.1 mile to a prominent red cliff face where the petroglyphs are located. Several of the seventy petroglyphs are large and dramatic. You can't get too close because the glyphs are up on the cliff face; binoculars help. This area is cared for by the Olowalu Cultural Reserve, a nonprofit group working to protect the *ahupuaʻa* of Olowalu and maintain traditional cultural practices.

Molokaʻi is renowned for its fishponds. Nearly the entire south shore of the island was once lined with fishponds, at least fifty-four of them. Most are now in ruins, their walls knocked down below the waves. One that is restored and visible from the public road is Aliʻi Fishpond. It is just west of One Aliʻi Beach Park on the Kamehameha V Highway, Route 450 at about mile 3.5.

Molokaʻi is also home to one of the most unusual cultural sites in the state, **Kaule o Nānāhoa.** It is a very large phallic rock that is said to be a natural formation. (See chapter 2.)

Lānaʻi is home to one of the most secluded publicly accessible petroglyph fields in the state, **Pōʻaiwa Petroglyphs** on the island's north shore. The area is near a very prominent shipwreck, so it is sometimes called Shipwreck Petroglyphs. To visit the petroglyphs, drive north from Lānaʻi City on Keōmuku Road until the pavement ends. Turn left in your 4WD vehicle and follow the unpaved road to the end, about a mile and a half. The last few hundred yards are especially sandy. When you get nervous driving, pull to the side of the road at a firm wide spot and walk the rest of the way. At the end of road is a stone sign that says *Shipwreck Beach.* Walk about a hundred yards farther along the trajectory of the road to the concrete foundation of a navigation beacon. From the foundation, look *mauka* and you should be able to follow the trail another two hundred yards or so to a shady little gulch where a few petroglyphs are located. I can't explain it, but this is one of my favorite places in the whole state.

Look up the beach another half mile or so and you will see the shipwreck, a World War II barge made of concrete that was intentionally scuttled on the reef after the war. This channel is infamous among mariners for its treacherous conditions. Trade winds funnel between Maui and Moloka'i, and when vessels emerge from the wind protection of the islands in either direction they are caught by surprise. The result is a veritable ship graveyard.

8.6 KAUA'I CULTURAL SITES. Kaua'i still has quite a few cultural sites, including ceremonial *heiau* that are not well preserved and utilitarian sites that are still in use. The largest concentration of ceremonial sites is called the **Wailua Complex of Heiau**, located along the big Wailua River near its mouth on the eastern side of the island. The Wailua *ahupua'a* was a center of political, religious, and social life before western contact, and the area still has many cultural sites, including some you can visit. At the mouth of the Wailua River is Hikinaakalā Heiau. *Hikina a ka Lā* means "east to the sun" or "rising sun," and that's about all we know about this ancient site. It must have been important: only some foundation stones remain, but these are impressive. After it was abandoned in 1819 most of the stones were taken away. At one time a house and sweet potato garden existed within its perimeter. Today it is within Lydgate State Park. To reach the *heiau* take Leho Drive where it loops *makai* from the Kūhiō Highway just south of the mouth of the Wailua River. Then head *makai* on Nalu Road where it branches off the loop road and drive to the end. The *heiau* sits on a promontory just at the mouth of the river.

Additional Wailua cultural sites are a bit inland, high above the deep river valley. Some are difficult to find (despite what some guidebooks say) but a few are right along Kuamo'o (backbone) Road, Route 580, which runs roughly parallel to, high above, and just north of the Wailua River. Less than a quarter mile up this road there is a turnout on the left at Holoholokū Heiau. This was a place of refuge (see the description of the Big Island's Pu'uhonua o Hōnaunau National Historic Park above). *Holoholokū* means "to run and stand"—exactly what violators of *kapu* did when they wanted to get to this *heiau* to be absolved. Walk a few yards up the road to a royal birthstone (see the description of O'ahu's Kūkaniloko Birthstones above). About a mile up the road is a busy tourist stop at 'Ōpaeka'a Falls. After you view the falls, take the marked walkway to the lookout on the other side of the road for a great view of the Wailua River Valley below you. It is easy to understand why Early Hawaiians chose to live here. Finally, leave the tourist crowds behind and walk back down the road a couple hundred yards to Poli'ahu Heiau. Not too much is known about this *heiau.* It is large and has a commanding view of the river valley below. For these reasons, some have suggested that it was an important *luakini heiau.* Poli'ahu is named for the goddess of snow; literally it means "garment for the bosom," referring to a blanket of snow. This is intriguing since freezing temperatures have only been recorded at the highest elevations on Kaua'i, and then only rarely.

Another ancient site on Kaua'i is perhaps the most interesting archaeological site in Hawai'i, **Kīkī a Ola** or the **Menehune Ditch**. *Kīkī a Ola* means "container acquired by Ola." According to legend, Chief Ola ordered the *Menehune* to build a stone-lined water ditch. In typical *Menehune* fashion they completed the task in a single night. What's so puzzling about this ancient irrigation ditch is the stones. Nearly every other stone structure you see in Hawai'i—or anywhere else in Polynesia for that matter—will be built of rough, naturally shaped stones. Kīkī a Ola is made of carefully shaped stone blocks. Who made these blocks? Why are they used only here, for a common ditch and not a *heiau?* We don't know; it is a complete mystery. Want to see these mysterious ancient stones for yourself? The small remaining section of ditch is along the Waimea River, just upstream of the town of Waimea on the south coast of Kaua'i. Just before the 23-mile marker (22.9) on the Kaumuali'i Highway, Route 50, take Menehune Road *mauka* from the highway. It is the second road heading *mauka* west of the Waimea River. Follow the road for 1.3 miles through a working-class residential area. Where the road climbs the levee and the Waimea River is visible, there is a swinging footbridge over the river. At the foot of the bridge is a short remnant of the ditch right next to the narrow road. There is no parking at the ditch site, but there are wide places in the road nearby where you can park. Be sure to look at the cliff face above the ditch. The unusual surface is pillow lava, which forms under water. During an ancient eruption on Kaua'i when sea level was higher, this area was a swampy backwater of the Waimea River.

Hanalei Valley has been home to *kalo* farms for centuries and it still is today. For more information see chapter 10.

You may think of salt as the cheapest seasoning in your cupboard, but in the past, and for many people in the world today, it is an essential preservative. Fresh fish will keep for a day or two if you have a refrigerator, a few hours if you don't. Salt the fish and dry it, and you have a protein source that you can keep for a long time. Pre-Contact Hawaiians made salt in small stone depressions, and they also made it in huge quantities at the **Hanapēpē Salt Ponds**. When whaling ships came on scene, salt became a valuable trade item. Today, Hawaiian red salt is a gourmet condiment and it is still produced at these red dirt ponds. The area is adjacent to Salt Pond Beach County Park in the town of Hanapēpē. To reach the ponds, take Kaumuali'i Highway, Route 50 to Hanapēpē, turn *makai* at the 17-mile marker and follow the signs to the park; the ponds are right next door.

8.7 *HULA.* When Christian missionaries arrived in 1820, they quickly clamped down hard on Hawaiian dance known as *hula.* To them, it was lewd and shocking. *Hula* went underground for half a century until King David Kalākaua ascended the throne in 1874. He valued all aspects of Hawaiian culture and did what he could to resurrect and preserve it. Bringing *hula* back out of the shadows was something of a personal crusade for him. Today *hula* is one of the most practiced and celebrated of Hawaiian arts. The state's biggest *hula* festival is called the Merrie Monarch Festival in Kalākaua's honor. It is held each spring in Hilo.

Today there are two main styles practiced by male and female *hula* dancers of all ages: *kahiko* or ancient style and *'auana* or modern. There are many *hula hālau* or schools throughout the islands (and the world, for that matter). The literal translation of *hālau* is a long house for canoes or hula instruction. The *hula* demonstrations at tourist luau and shopping centers may or may not be authentic. Look for a demonstration by a *hula hālau.* My personal favorite venue for *hula* is a stone *hula* platform overlooking Kīlauea Crater near the visitor center at Hawai'i Volcanoes National Park. Periodically *hula hālau* perform there, including an annual festival each July. Ancient *hula* performed at an ancient site, among the *'ōhi'a* trees and the singing *'apapane,* with steam curling out of Halema'uma'u Crater at your back. It doesn't get any better. Check with the Volcano Art Center (adjacent to the visitor center in Hawai'i Volcanoes National Park) for a schedule of presentations.

LEARN MORE

- Van James, *Ancient Sites of O'ahu: A Guide to Hawaiian Archaeological Places of Interest* (Honolulu: Bishop Museum Press, 2010). Descriptions of fifty sites around the island, their purpose, and how to reach those that are publicly accessible. A great resource for anyone who wants to see the cultural heritage of O'ahu. The same author has three similar volumes describing sites on the Big Island, Kaua'i, and Maui, Moloka'i, and Lāna'i, all published by Mutual Publishing.
- Patrick Vinton Kirch, *Feathered Gods and Fishhooks: An Introduction to Hawaiian Archaeology and Prehistory* (Honolulu: University of Hawai'i Press, 1985). This very readable book takes you from general descriptions of Hawaiian origins and settlement to detailed descriptions of some sites.
- David Lewis, *We, the Navigators: The Ancient Art of Landfinding in the Pacific*, second edition (Honolulu: University of Hawai'i Press, 1994). David Lewis's personal journey of navigational research.
- Martha Warren Beckwith, editor, *The Kumulipo: A Hawaiian Creation Chant* (Honolulu: University of Hawai'i Press, 1972). This is the most widely available translation of the ancient genealogical chant.
- Sam Low, *Hawaiki Rising: Hōkūle'a, Nainoa Thompson, and the Hawaiian Renaissance* (Honolulu: University of Hawai'i Press, 2018). The inspirational story of modern voyaging by ancient methods, told in an engaging and personal style.

9 Let Me Introduce You

New Life Comes to the Islands

In the spring of 1866 Mark Twain set foot in Hawai'i for the first time. He looked around and offered this as his initial observation on the fauna of an island paradise: "I saw cats—Tom cats, Mary Ann cats, long-tailed cats, bobtail cats, blind cats, one-eyed cats, walleyed cats, cross-eyed cats, gray cats, black cats, white cats, yellow cats, striped cats, spotted cats, tame cats, wild cats, singed cats, individual cats, groups of cats, platoons of cats, companies of cats, regiments of cats, armies of cats, multitudes of cats, millions of cats, and all of them sleek, fat, lazy, and sound asleep."

Twain's cat statement speaks volumes about introduced species in Hawai'i. Many visitors, back then and now, have been surrounded by introduced species and hardly have glimpsed a genuine Hawaiian species. The abundance of cats in 1866 Honolulu is a good example of what happens when you put adaptable plants or animals in a pleasant environment: they breed like crazy.

We distinguish between species that made it to Hawai'i on their own—indigenous or endemic species—from those brought to the island by humans. The newcomers we call introduced species, or sometimes alien or exotic species. When an alien species spreads rapidly and causes problems, we call it an invasive species. Hawai'i is full of them.

It seems like nearly every group of travelers to arrive on Hawaiian shores has brought species with them, starting with the first Polynesians. Captain Cook was next. In the log of his voyage, in his entry for February 2, 1778, he writes that he went ashore in a small boat with new species: "I went myself with the pinnace and launch…taking with me a ram-goat and two ewes…and the seeds of melons, pumpkins, and onions; being very desirous of benefiting these poor people, by furnishing them with some additional articles of food."

In the centuries since, this trickle of new species has become a torrent. Often the introductions are well intentioned; sometimes they are accidental. Occasionally life, when it is plunked down in a new environment, doesn't behave the way we expect. It escapes, it grows wild, it eats the natives or finds other ways to wreak havoc.

The list of introduced species is long and varied: ants, African snails, aquarium fish, avian malaria and avian pox, butterflies, cane toads, cats, cattle, coqui frogs, earthworms, eucalyptus trees, fountain grass, geckos, goats, *kiawe* trees, lantana bushes, marine algae, mongooses, mosquitoes, myna birds, orchids, parrots, predatory snails, sheep, strawberry guavas, turkeys, zebra doves. If none of those are strange enough for you, add to the list Australian rock wallabies, Brahminy blind burrowing snakes, and South American poison dart frogs. These are just a few of the species established in Hawaiʻi.

Just how many species of plants and animals have we introduced to Hawaiʻi? We don't know. There are so many that it is nearly impossible to count them all. Even if you did, your total would be wrong almost immediately. By some estimates, a new species arrives every day. Estimates of total alien species range from 4,000 to over 10,000. And that's just on land; there are more in the water. We've loaded up these islands with a huge, strange, and troublesome cargo.

What makes introduced species any different from those that arrived on their own by wind, wings, or waves? Sometimes there's no difference at all. Some canoe plants brought by voyaging Polynesians might also have been growing naturally on the islands before humans arrived. That's the case with *hala,* maybe with coconuts too. Many times, the new introductions are pretty benign. Nobody is afraid that pineapples will start growing wild and take over the islands.

But often, intentional introductions were selected specifically because they were hardy or aggressive or extremely cosmopolitan in their diet, or had other traits that made them supercompetitors. Goats will eat practically anything, so they're a good animal to have with you if you're a British sailor headed toward uncharted and unknown islands where the pickings may be slim. *Kiawe* trees are hardy and will grow in the most unforgiving climates. The small Indian mongoose is a vicious little predator and seems like a natural choice to eat a profusion of rats. Lantana is a lovely landscape flower that thrives on neglect. Common mynas are persistent hungry birds that you'd think would happily eat pesky armyworms. When the giant African snails introduced as a food item get out of hand, solve the problem by introducing the cannibal rosy wolf snail to eat them. The list goes on and on.

Even when a new introduction isn't a supercompetitor, it may be living alongside island species that lost their competitive edge evolving in blissful isolation for millions of years. The Japanese white-eye is a spritely little bird introduced from its homeland in the late 1920s. It is pretty adaptable, feeding on fruit, nectar, and insects. By some accounts it is now the most abundant bird in the islands, occurring from dry lowlands to high rain forests, relying on the same food sources as the beleaguered native birds.

Sometimes, island species just aren't equipped to deal with introduced predators. Ground-nesting seabirds have no idea what a rat is. They will sit peacefully on a nest while rats scurry right up and chew on eggs or the nesting birds themselves. Endemic forest birds will behave pretty much the same way. And rats have been brought to Hawai'i over and over again, for a very long time. The first was the **Polynesian rat.** Among the plants and animals brought by the Polynesians, it is one of relatively few that have caused trouble in Hawai'i. It is a fairly small rat species, now largely displaced by later introductions. The **Norway rat** has been in Hawai'i since the first European ships arrived. The **black rat** or roof rat is more widespread than the other rat species and does the most damage to native species. But the Polynesian variety may have done significant damage before the arrival of its more successful rat brethren. It ate birds and their eggs, insects, and seeds. Ecologists examining ancient pollen and evidence of early Hawaiian agriculture have concluded that the Polynesian rat may have leveled vast forests of native *loulu* palms even before Hawaiians burned the lowlands for agriculture. The rats managed this huge ecological shift by eating palm seeds. When an army of rats eats practically every seed, a palm forest can disappear within a few hundred years. Apparently that's just what happened.

Captain Cook's **goats** were probably the first animals introduced by westerners (along with the fleas these goats and their owners undoubtedly harbored). Cook left three goats on Ni'ihau in 1778 and possibly others on the Big Island in 1779 shortly before his death. In 1792 Vancouver brought more goats but noted in his journal that the Hawaiians already had them. From this early start, goats have gone on to be one of the most destructive animals ever brought to Hawai'i. They

FIGURE 9.1 The introduced gold dust day gecko is the most visible terrestrial reptile in Hawai'i. It is common in gardens. (Rick Soehren)

Geckos: Indigenous or Introduced? The presence of geckos in Hawai'i is a mystery. They're a familiar sight around Hawaiian homes: the chunky little tan reptiles walk on walls around the porch light at night, eating insects and chirping like crickets. It is generally believed that most of them came to Hawai'i as stowaways. Four species (out of at least eight now present) may have voyaged with the first Polynesians, others arriving later. But don't underestimate these little creatures. They have a skill that is very valuable for a pioneering species: parthenogenesis. A single female gecko that rafts to an island on a big floating mass of vegetation can lay eggs and hatch clones of herself. These parthenogenic geckos can reproduce and exist as a clan of females until a male arrives to provide genetic diversity and *y* chromosomes, whether he shows up a year or several millennia later. In this way, geckos have occupied many of the islands of Polynesia. Indeed, three of the gecko species that arrived with Polynesians or even earlier exist in Hawai'i as populations of females. They've been surviving without males for at least 1,500 years.

Today, most geckos seen around homes are common house geckos, a species that arrived only in the last century. They probably hitched a ride with military equipment shipped back from Pacific islands after World War II. An even more recent arrival is the gold dust day gecko. Native to Madagascar, this beautiful escaped pet is aggressively displacing other geckos.

escape from captivity. They climb almost everywhere. They eat almost anything. When they have a choice between eating introduced plants armed with defense mechanisms like thorns or a bad taste or eating relatively defenseless endemic plants, they'll selectively munch down the natives.

When Hawai'i Volcanoes National Park was established in 1916, park staff realized that goats were destroying native plants. They allowed periodic goat hunts to reduce numbers, but the remaining goats always replenished the population. In 1969 staff fenced off small areas to see how native plants would recover in the absence of hungry goats. The results were more than startling. Familiar native plants indeed rebounded, but in addition park botanists discovered entirely new Hawaiian plant species—plants whose seeds may have lain dormant for as long as 150 years, since before the goat onslaught. And they realized that probably other seeds had perished in that long interval, seeds from plants thus driven to extinction by hungry aliens. The Park Service knew they had to eliminate every last goat.

By erecting fencing around successive portions of the park and removing goats from each section, biologists eventually removed every single goat. How many goats were removed? We don't know, because only the larger efforts were documented. Between the time serious control efforts began in 1927 and the time the last goat was gone in 1984, the number of animals removed from the botanical wonderland of the park was upward of 120,000 goats. A similar effort involving forty miles of fence removed goats from Haleakalā National Park by 1990.

Even today large herds of goats run loose in Hawai'i. They are a common sight along the western part of the Saddle Road on the Big Island, and you can also spot them on the ridges at Kōke'e State Park and Waimea Canyon on Kaua'i where they gnaw back a lot of vegetation.

If any animal can compete with the goat for the title of worst enemy of native habitat, it is the **pig.** Whereas goats prefer drier areas of forest and woodland, pigs like it wet. They are everywhere in wet Hawaiian forests, rooting up the soil, leaving wallows where mosquitoes can breed, knocking over tree ferns to munch on them. One reason they dig is to search for tasty earthworms, another introduced species. The Polynesians brought pigs with them, but as far as we can tell these first pigs didn't do much damage to native forests. The Polynesian pigs were small and apparently stayed close to human habitation. When westerners brought larger European pigs to Hawai'i, the Polynesian and European varieties produced hybrids that quickly went feral and have been destroying habitat ever since.

As with goats, fencing is the best way to protect forests full of native plants from pigs. It is hard, expensive work to erect long fences through dense Hawaiian forests, but it seems to be the only solution. Fences protect the Nature Conservancy's preserves, including Waikamoi Preserve adjacent to Haleakalā National Park. In 2015 more than three miles of fence were erected to protect high elevation forest on Kaua'i.

Cattle are another domestic livestock introduction that went feral and did great damage to Hawaiian forests. They were first introduced by Vancouver in 1793. The following year he gave a few to Kamehameha I and suggested that they be released and allowed to build up their numbers for at least ten years. A royal *kapu* was placed on the cattle, and their numbers increased dramatically. By the 1820s there were probably

FIGURE 9.2 Cattle have grazed on one side of this fence near Volcano on the Big Island, while the other side is relatively undisturbed. Much of Hawai'i was exposed to this kind of grazing pressure for over a century. (Rick Soehren)

more cattle in the islands than people. For the next fifty years Hawai'i supplied beef and hides to much of the world and hardly put a dent in the cattle population.

Sheep were introduced in 1791. They didn't go feral and produce large wild herds like cattle and goats at first. One theory why not is that packs of feral dogs kept the sheep numbers down. Eventually sheep farmers controlled the wild dogs. Some sheep escaped and were adaptable enough to form large and damaging wild herds. Then in 1954 the Territorial government, encouraged by hunters, made things worse by releasing wild European **mouflon** in Hawai'i. Mouflon, sometimes called Mediterranean bighorn, are the wary, wild sheep of Corsica and Sardinia, and can jump fences as high as six feet. Mouflon (*Ovis musimon*) breed with feral sheep (*Ovis aries*) to produce offspring that may be worse for the unique Hawaiian environment than either parent: fecund, wary, and hard to contain.

You can spot sheep and mouflon, sometimes in huge herds, along the Saddle Road on the Big Island, especially on the drier leeward side.

FIGURE 9.3 Mouflon sheep were intentionally introduced as a game animal. They interbred with feral domestic sheep, and have been destroying habitat ever since. (Rick Soehren)

Axis deer, native to India, are another problematic introduced game species. Visiting dignitaries from Hong Kong gave eight of them to Kamehameha V in 1867. They were released on Moloka'i, and their numbers quickly increased. Later they were introduced to Lāna'i and Maui with the same result. Residents have conflicted feelings about axis deer. On the one hand, they are cute little deer that retain their fawn-like spots for life, and they are prized by hunters. On the other hand, they harm native forest, drive rare endemic plants ever closer to extinction, and are hard to exclude from sensitive areas because they jump fences.

An alien species doesn't have to be as big as a barnyard animal to be destructive. Some of the smallest—insects and even microbes—can be just as deadly to endemic species. In 1826 the whaling ship *Wellington* prepared to sail from San Blas, Mexico, to Hawai'i. The sailors filled their water barrels in Mexico and inadvertently scooped up the larvae of a tropical **mosquito.** Upon arriving in Lahaina the foul water barrels were rinsed and filled at a local spring, releasing mosquito larvae and condemning Hawai'i to suffer forever from another introduced pest.

But the story gets worse. The introduced mosquito can act as a vector (transmitting organism) for the bird diseases **avian malaria** and **avian pox**: the mosquito sips a bit of blood from an infected bird and transmits disease to the next bird it bites. These diseases may have existed in Hawai'i for a long time in migratory waterfowl, or may have been introduced with pet birds in the 1800s. Continental birds generally have immunity to these diseases. Without a vector—the mosquito—there was no way for the diseases to be transmitted to the endemic birds that had little or no immunity. Today tropical mosquitoes are widespread in the lowlands of Hawai'i, ranging up to about 4,500 feet. Some native birds like the *'amakihi* have some immunity and can coexist with disease-carrying mosquitoes. Others like the *'i'iwi* have no immunity at all; one bite from an infected mosquito and the bird will die. That's why you will probably never see an *'i'iwi* at or below 4,500 feet.

Occasionally landscape plants escape cultivation and invade wild lands. Culinary and ornamental gingers escaped into the forest, just as shampoo ginger escaped from the gardens of early Hawaiians. **Lantana,** a hardy flowering shrub native to the West Indies, can now be found throughout the tropics. **Princess flower** or *Tibouchina* bears stunning purple flowers on plants with velvety leaves in the garden. When it escapes to the wet forest it grows in thickets twelve feet high and crowds out natives. The **banana poka** vine was supposedly planted to hide an unsightly outhouse. Today it climbs forest trees and smothers them. And there are plenty more plant invaders.

Food plants usually don't escape from cultivation and grow wild. Hikers occasionally come across old Hawaiian banana groves buried deep in the forest, and there is some wild sugarcane remaining from the years when sugar production was big business, but these plants are not invasive. In a few cases, introduced fruit trees have become invasive. One of the worst is **strawberry guava**, imported from Brazil in 1825. It is a fruit of minor interest when it grows in your garden. But when it flies out of your garden, courtesy of some fruit-eating bird that drops the seeds in the forest, packaged with some nice fertilizing guano, it grows into a dense stand that excludes every other plant. You end up with a nearly impenetrable monoculture of guavas.

Hundreds of thousands of acres of Hawaiian forest harbor strawberry guavas, and this plant continues to spread. In an effort to slow it down, ecologists identified a biocontrol agent: an insect from the guava's home range in Brazil that forms galls on new guava shoots and slows their growth. The insect attacks only strawberry guava and one closely related plant species. Intentional release of a new organism is controversial, especially in a highly invaded place like Hawai'i. The potential release was studied and discussed for fifteen years. Finally, in 2013 the insect was released. Time will tell how effectively it slows the spread of strawberry guava.

While modern efforts at biocontrol are studied carefully nowadays, this wasn't always the case. Hawai'i has plenty of troublesome species that were released to control other introduced species. The **small Indian mongoose** was imported to control rats in sugarcane fields. But rats are nocturnal, mongooses are diurnal (active in the daytime) and mongooses prefer birds and their eggs. The mongooses ate a few rats, but not enough to make a difference. Until recently Kaua'i was the only island that had no mongooses, but for years there have been scattered reports of mongoose sightings. In 2012 two mongooses were trapped on Kaua'i, and reported sightings are on the rise. It doesn't look good for a mongoose-free Kaua'i.

FIGURE 9.4 The mongoose was intentionally introduced to eat rats. It has taken a terrible toll on birds, especially ground-nesting species. (Rick Soehren)

Sugar planters gave rat control another try in 1958, introducing the **common barn owl.** These night hunters do eat rats and introduced **house mice,** but they also hunt in woodlands where they prey on little forest birds.

The sugar growers made several other wildly careless introductions, hoping to control insects: **giant toads** or **cane toads** from Puerto Rico (turns out their poisonous secretions can kill pets) and **predatory wasps** (that have migrated up into the forest where they attack native caterpillars).

When **African armyworms** became a plague in the middle of the nineteenth century, the **common myna** (figure 5.11) was imported from India. This was no solution; the armyworms remained a problem for another thirty years, and mynas have become ubiquitous in Hawaiian towns and cities. They stay mostly in the lowlands where there aren't too many native species left to harm, but they can be a pest in the city. When mynas aren't paired up to nest and raise young, they roost in big flocks—big, noisy, messy flocks.

Cattlemen introduced **cattle egrets** (figure 5.10) in 1959 to control insect pests in pastures. Today the egrets themselves are the pests, eating the chicks of Hawaiian stilts, robbing prawns from aquaculture ponds, and causing potential airstrike hazards around airports where they like to congregate in open fields.

Perhaps no wrongheaded biocontrol story is stranger or sadder than that of the snail. It starts back in 1936, when the **giant African snail** was intentionally introduced to Hawai'i as a food item by the Japanese. Today it isn't a popular food item, but it certainly is a familiar garden pest. And it can get big: mainland visitors out for an early morning stroll on wet resort lawns are often shocked to see snails with three-inch shells slithering around. In 1955 the **rosy wolf snail**—a cannibal species that eats other snails—was introduced from Florida in an effort to reduce numbers of the huge African snails. However, the wolf snail

FIGURE 9.5 The giant African snail was introduced as a food species, but is now just a garden pest. And, ewww, that's my hand! (Rick Soehren)

only grows to about two inches. It will take on small African snails, but it prefers the smaller endemic snails. In fact, it has likely eaten some endemic snail species into extinction.

Hawai'i has no native amphibians because they are generally pretty delicate creatures whose porous skin doesn't travel well in salt water. But Hawai'i is now home to **bullfrogs** and **wrinkled frogs** and cane toads and more. One of the most recent amphibian introductions is the least glimpsed and yet most noticeable to people: the **coqui frog** from Puerto Rico. They aren't seen very much because they live up off the ground in bushes and trees, they are active mostly at night, they are drab brown, and they're usually only about an inch or two long. But the males have huge voices. Their call is similar to their name: ko-KEE. These tiny frogs can belt out their call at up to ninety decibels. And they are prolific; they can reach population densities of at least eight thousand frogs per acre. Apparently they arrived on the Big Island in the 1980s in shipments of tropical plants. Today Hilo is crawling with them, and they are successfully hitching rides to the other islands.

Visitors to Hawai'i get the impression that the authorities are vigilant about screening for alien species. Airline flight attendants distribute a "Plants and Animals Declaration Form" from the State Department of Agriculture. Passengers are required by law to fill it out. It

Strangers in Paradise. Here are some of Hawai'i's stranger introduced species:

In 1916 a private zoo in Honolulu had three brush-tailed rock wallabies. Dogs tore into the tent where the wallabies were kept and killed one, but a male and a female scampered up into the rocky hills of the Kalihi Valley. A hundred years later there is still a population of perhaps one hundred of them hiding out on rugged private land.

In 1932 the Territory of Hawai'i thought a good way to control mosquitoes in the Mānoa Valley of Honolulu would be to import 206 little frogs from the jungles of Panama. Not just any frogs, but green and black poison dart frogs. Yes, the frogs that secrete the poison used by South American natives to arm the tips of their blow-gun darts. This turned out to be another failed introduction: these frogs prefer ants, not mosquitoes. The pretty inch-long frogs still live in the wet forest, where they come out during or after rainfall. They are safe to handle if you catch one, but you should wash your hands afterward.

You hear this statement all the time: "There are no snakes in Hawai'i."

says so on the form, in red letters. Passengers must declare any fresh fruits or vegetables, cut flowers, seeds, soil, or live animals, as if someone smuggling animals is going to break down and confess when presented with a form. Meanwhile, whole boatloads and planeloads of plants and animals—everything from cattle to cut Christmas trees—arrive at Hawaiian ports where beleaguered inspectors, hampered by inadequate budgets, struggle to find pests that might be hiding amid the cargo. It is like looking for a needle in a haystack, and some aliens get through. When agriculture officials doubled inspection staff for a sixteen-week blitz at the airport in Kahului, Maui, they found as many pests as they usually find in a year's worth of inspections at all Hawaiʻi airports and harbors combined.

There is one alien creature for which officials are particularly vigilant: the **brown tree snake**. It is not established in Hawaiʻi, but it has hitched a ride and been intercepted several times. Native to Australia and the Solomon Islands, this snake was accidentally introduced on Guam around the time of World War II. The snake is mildly venomous but not deadly. It has no natural enemies on Guam, and the island's birds are not evolved to deal with arboreal snakes like this one. By the 1990s snake populations had reached a creepy-astonishing twenty per acre (about the size of a football field). Most of Guam's native

Wrong. Even most residents don't know it, but there is an introduced snake in Hawaiʻi: the Brahminy blind snake. Many garden enthusiasts see them and mistake these harmless snakes for the earthworms they resemble. They are brown, live in soil, and get no longer than six or eight inches. They have tiny vestigial eyes but they are blind, relying on other senses to find their prey of termites and ants (two other groups of species introduced to Hawaiʻi). These snakes are the most widespread terrestrial snakes in the world. They can hitch rides in potted plants (they are sometimes called flower pot snakes). In fact, they probably arrived in Hawaiʻi with landscape palms from the Philippines. Like some geckos and skinks, these snakes are parthenogenic, so a single female can establish a new population. These snakes take parthenogenesis to a whole new level: the whole species is unisexual, and no male has ever been found. The strangeness doesn't stop there. These snakes are anatomically odd, too. Perhaps to accommodate their slender shape, they do not have a left lung or a left ovary.

forest birds have been killed off by the aggressive snakes, along with ground-nesting seabirds, some lizard species, and even a species of fruit bat. Without the birds, insect populations have increased dramatically, and agriculture has been hit hard by insect problems. This reptile doesn't just cause grief for the birds. It climbs power poles and shorts out the lines, making power outages common. It will even go after sleeping babies. The snake has had a big negative impact on tourism.

There is a lot of commerce between Guam and Hawai'i, and the snakes like to climb and hide in aircraft wheel wells and cargo bays. Nearly a dozen snakes, living or dead, have been intercepted over the years. Keeping this snake out of Hawai'i is a high priority for state officials.

One invader is nearly invisible. About 2010 residents of Puna on the Big Island noticed that many of their 'ōhi'a trees were wilting and dying. The culprit? A fungus that causes a disease called rapid 'ōhi'a death. In seven years the fungus killed trees across 75,000 acres on the Big Island and shows no signs of stopping. Loss of 'ōhi'a trees would radically alter Hawaiian forests and spell disaster for the creatures that dwell there. It may be only a matter of time before the fungus arrives on other islands. This is a very good reason to wash your boots and clothes between hikes and when moving between islands. Experts recommend disinfecting hiking gear with a 70 percent alcohol solution.

And now, back to the cats that opened this chapter. Today they are even more abundant than they were in Twain's time. By some estimates, there are eighty thousand feral cats on O'ahu alone. As hunters, they are a big threat to native birds, including forest birds and ground-nesting seabirds. In addition, they carry a protozoan that causes toxoplasmosis; the disease is transmitted when rain washes cat feces downstream. This disease has killed *nēnē*, red-footed boobies, and other Hawaiian birds, and has infected endangered monk seals. Spinner dolphins may be at risk, too. Of course, cats pose similar threats anywhere they form feral populations or hunt outdoors. That's why bird experts recommend that cats should be indoor pets.

FIELD TRIP!

9.1 Kapi'olani World Tour. Visitors from all over the world fill Waikīkī's Kapi'olani Park. Not tourists—the plants and the birds and even an invasive alga just offshore. During a stroll through the park, you might encounter representatives from every continent except Antarctica. I recommend an early morning walk around the perimeter of the park. It is about 2 miles (2.2 if you also go around the zoo). One place to start is the Queen Kapiʻolani Garden on the *mauka* side of the park at the corner of Monsarrat and Pākī Avenues. There is a small free parking lot adjacent to the garden with the entrance on Lēʻahi Avenue. (There is also plenty of free parking along Pākī Avenue, where you can start your walk. Some other lots, like the one at the zoo, charge a fee, and other street parking is metered.)

The tiny Kapiʻolani Garden isn't really in the same league with botanic gardens in chapter 4, but it does have a modest collection of endemic plants, and some are labeled. Take a look *ʻewa* (away from Diamond Head) from the garden up Pākī Avenue. Monkeypod trees along both sides of the street form a shady tree tunnel. Native to Central and South America, these trees are among the most popular ornamental

FIGURE 9.6 The monkeypod is one of the most popular landscape trees in Hawaiʻi. (Rick Soehren)

trees in Hawai'i, producing fuzzy pink balls of flowers from May to August. The monkeypods along Pākī are pruned up to keep them off the road; you will see others in the park that have a more natural umbrella form. These trees have the unusual trait of folding up their compound leaves at night. These leaves are a hint that monkeypods are in the legume family; other legumes with similar compound leaves are the introduced *kiawe* and the endemic *māmane*.

Walk along Pākī in the Diamond Head direction. Scan the lawns for small birds, and especially look at areas that haven't been mowed for a while and have taller grass seed heads. The most common little brown seed-eating bird in the park is the common waxbill, its red-orange bill the color of old-fashioned sealing wax. It is a very tiny bird that can disappear in the lawn. These birds were introduced from Africa in the 1970s, probably as escaped cage birds. A slightly larger seedeater you'll see in the lawn is the distinctive Java sparrow, a native of Indonesia. These bold birds, black, white, and gray, with big pink bills, were

FIGURE 9.7 The common waxbill is common on O'ahu and becoming more numerous on other islands. (Jim Denny)

first introduced in 1867 and reintroduced in the late 1960s. Common waxbills and Java sparrows seem to be displacing the nutmeg mannikin, another introduced bird that used to be the most common bird of grassy areas. Introduced in 1867 from Southeast Asia, the nutmeg mannikin is a little brown bird with a black bill and a delicate scalloped pattern on the chest.

Near the Diamond Head end of the park you will pass the tennis courts on your left. To your right is a nice banyan tree, recognizable by its aerial roots that drop down out of branches to form extra trunks. Other big banyans flank the Waikīkī Aquarium and stand at the zoo entrance, near the end of your loop walk. Hawai'i has four species of banyan introduced from areas of tropical Asia ranging from India to China. These trees are members of the fig family, and each one is pollinated by its own species of fig wasp introduced in the 1920s and 1930s. The female wasps lay eggs in the banyan's fleshy flowers. The young wasps feed on the flower, grow up, and mate inside it, and the pregnant

FIGURE 9.8 The Java sparrow is common on Kaua'i, O'ahu, Maui, and the Big Island. (Jim Denny)

females emerge covered in pollen and look for a new flower that they'll pollinate as they lay their own eggs. Many banyan trees in Hawai'i are now dying from two introduced insect pests. Both were first seen in 2012. The only remedy is likely to be biocontrol: introducing insects to kill the insects.

Other prominent trees along Pākī Avenue include Moreton Bay figs from Australia and false kamani trees from the East Indies. Both trees have big shiny oval leaves and can have buttressing roots. The best way to recognize false kamani is to look for the two-inch, almond-shaped fruits with a fibrous husk that litter the ground beneath the tree.

Beyond the tennis courts at the Diamond Head end of the park there are many big *kiawe* trees, South American natives introduced to Hawai'i by way of Paris (see chapter 4). This part of the park, stretching around to the aquarium, is a good place to look for rose-ringed parakeets. These beautiful, adaptable sixteen-inch parrots are native to Central Africa and India but have gone feral in spots all over the world: California, Florida, and Europe from England south to Italy and east to Turkey. The parakeets are easiest to spot when they fly or move; otherwise their green plumage blends in with tree foliage.

At the tip of the park closest to Diamond Head and along the median of Kalākaua Avenue there are ironwood trees whose needle-like branchlets somewhat resemble pine. The term ironwood is used for various hardwood species around the world. In Hawai'i the term is used for two species of Australian trees in the genus *Casuarina*. These trees are able to grow in dune areas near the ocean, so they are fairly common beach trees in Hawai'i. Watch for yellow-fronted canaries feeding in these trees. These streaky yellow birds are native to Africa. You might also see white terns nesting in these trees or elsewhere in the park, especially between February and September. They are native, and urban Honolulu is the only place they nest in Hawai'i other than the remote islands of the Northwestern Hawaiian Islands.

As you head 'ewa along the ocean side of the park you will probably see red-crested cardinals from South America, the beautiful beggars of Hawaiian picnic areas. Other denizens of picnic areas include common mynas (figure 5.11) from India, zebra doves from Australia (figure 5.13), and the house sparrows that live almost everywhere humans live but are native to Europe. You may also see red northern cardinals from North America in the park.

FIGURE 9.9 The introduced *kiawe* tree is widespread in Hawai'i. (Rick Soehren)

FIGURE 9.10 The rose-ringed parakeet is common in Honolulu and on Kaua'i. (Rick Soehren)

FIGURE 9.11 The red-crested cardinal is common on all islands except the Big Island, where the similar yellow-billed cardinal takes its place. (Rick Soehren)

When you reach the Waikīkī Aquarium on your left, head over to the sea wall and beach walk behind the facility. From this vantage point you can see native black thin-shelled rock crabs scuttling on the rocks, and reef fish in the water (polarized sunglasses help). If the reef looks brown and shaggy, that's because it is covered with alien algae that were introduced intentionally in a failed attempt to grow them for production of carrageenan and agar. Hundreds of volunteers pick tons of the stuff off the reef every year. The zoo composts it for use in zoo gardens. Sans Souci Beach on the Diamond Head side of the Natatorium (an old enclosed saltwater swimming pool) is shaggier because it isn't cleaned as intensively. Despite the algae, Sans Souci is probably the best snorkeling spot in Waikīkī.

On the *mauka* side of Kalākaua Avenue there are many rainbow shower trees, the official tree of Honolulu. These medium-sized trees with compound leaves bloom profusely from April to November with flowers that range from dusty pink to orange, cream, and bright yellow. They are sterile horticultural hybrids of trees originally from Southeast Asia.

When you get to Monsarrat Avenue you can either follow it *mauka*

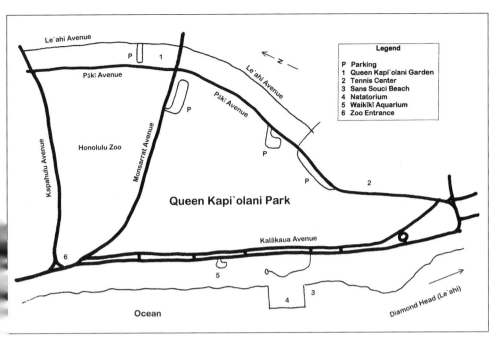

MAP 9.1 Kapi'olani Park is home to plants and animals from six continents.

back to your starting point, or pass the zoo entrance with its giant banyan, follow Kapahulu Avenue up to Pākī, then walk through the monkeypod tree tunnel back to the start of your walk. Either way, you have touched six continents and many nations on this field trip. The entire route is wheelchair accessible.

9.2 HOSMER GROVE. Just inside the entrance to Haleakalā National Park on Maui is Hosmer Grove, the remnants of a forest of introduced trees planted by Territorial Forester Ralph Hosmer starting in 1910. (You'll see other Hosmer plantings of Mexican weeping pine along the highway just before you reach the National Park entrance.) When Hosmer began his work, much of the Haleakalā forest had been grazed into a sorry state. Hosmer realized that the best thing for native forest was to keep "man and animals out," and he worked to establish forest reserves. But he also sought a local source of timber to reduce the need for imports from North America. He planted eighty-six species of potential timber trees gathered from around the world. What could possibly go wrong? Well, everything. Many of the trees just died. Other species developed shallow roots and blew over in the strong winds that can buffet the mountainside at this elevation of about 6,800 feet. Some trees grew too fast, producing weak lumber. And a handful spread, becoming invasive problem species and threatening the remaining native forest.

Today the National Park Service and the Nature Conservancy, owners of the adjacent Waikamoi Preserve, work to keep the alien species contained. You can see a mix of Hosmer's introduced trees and some native trees by taking the half-mile loop trail in the park. A much better option is to reserve space on a free guided walk into the Waikamoi Preserve. The Nature Conservancy offers monthly trips; sign up well in advance using their website. At press time, similar weekly walks led by the National Park Service had been suspended to prevent the spread of an introduced fungus that kills *'ōhi'a* trees. Call the Park Service to check availability. For more information on this area, see the **Field Trip!** description in chapter 5.

9.3 ALIENS TAKE OVER AT PU'U WA'AWA'A. Dry forests are among the rarest vegetation types in Hawai'i; they're almost all gone. Often introduced species have played a role in the destruction. At Pu'u Wa'awa'a on the Big Island, you can walk through a remnant dry forest and see a chilling example of devastation by aliens. But first, a little help with the pronunciation. Pu'u Wa'awa'a is one of those terms in which the *w* sounds like a *v* so it is pronounced POO-ooh VAH-ah VAH-ah. It means "grooved hill." Pu'u Wa'awa'a is one of the biggest and most visible of the many cinder cones on this part of the Big Island. It gets its name from the grooved pattern of erosion on the flanks of the big crater.

The area is located north of Kailua-Kona along the Hawai'i Belt Road or Māmalahoa Highway, Route 190. Between mile markers 21 and 22, Highway 190 makes an "S" curve on a steep escarpment near the tiny town of Pu'u Anahulu. Just before you climb the hill (if you're coming from Kailua-Kona) is the entrance road to Pu'u Wa'awa'a on the *mauka* side of the road, marked by a pair of odd white stucco pillars.

For the last 120 years or so, the dryland forest around Pu'u Wa'awa'a was off-limits to the public. The public land was leased and controlled by a big ranch of the same name. New grazing leases allow some public access, and two hiking trails are open to the public. The hours are limited: the gated area is open to the public only on weekdays from 6:00 a.m. to 6:00 p.m. It is still a working ranch, so open the gate, drive in, and close the gate behind you. You can hike all the way to the cinder cone and climb to the top if you want. It is about 8 miles round-trip with a 1,900-foot elevation gain. However, the level 1.1-mile Hala-pepe loop trail will take you by many of the dryland forest tree species found in the area and give you a good idea of the alien invasion taking place. Sign in at the first hunter check station, drive to the second. The trail starts to the left of the road. There may be trail brochures available, but you can print one out online ahead of time to make sure you have one. There is a link to the brochure on the website for the Pu'u Wa'awa'a volunteer organization.

The trail brochure text corresponds to numbered stops along the trail where native plants, some of them quite rare, still grow. The only trail maintenance is done by volunteers so unfortunately some of the numbered signs along the trail may be missing. This is a good place to see plants such as *'iliahi* (sandalwood), *wiliwili,* and *māmane* (figure 5.1). The *wiliwili* is easily recognizable with its rounded leaves, fat branches, orange flowers, and coral-red seeds. It is one of the rare

FIGURE 9.12 Endemic *wiliwili* trees have a distinctive thick-branched shape. They are threatened by many alien species. This one is along Waikoloa Road on the Big Island. (Rick Soehren)

Hawaiian endemics that has thorns. During the dry Hawaiian summer this tree conserves moisture by dropping its leaves. In the fall it blooms just before leafing out again. The *wiliwili* is often used in Hawaiian gardens. The dryland forest at Pu'u Wa'awa'a has a few of these trees. Another place to look for their distinctive thick-branched form is around mile 4 on the Waikoloa Road.

What's really noticeable along this trail is that you are surrounded by aliens. Alien insects, plants, birds, sheep. The *wiliwili* trees were being killed by an introduced gall wasp from Africa. In response, state officials turned to biological control. They found an African gall assassin wasp and introduced it. The strategy seems to be working; many struggling *wiliwili* trees are regaining their health.

Alien fountain grass grows everywhere here, with its feathery seed heads. The area is dotted with lantana bushes, a familiar landscape shrub. Introduced kalanchoe plants with weird fleshy spotted leaves send up stalks topped by bell-shaped red flowers. The silk oak and the black wattle, two of the healthiest tree species along the trail, were both intentionally introduced from Australia. The silk oak has dark green leathery leaves shaped like big feathers and bears big yellow-orange bottlebrush flowers in the spring. The black wattle has fernlike light green leaves and white pom-pom flowers.

Along the trail you will also see three yellow-to-green introduced birds. Most visible are the saffron finches, bright yellow with just a sprinkle of paprika orange on their heads. There are also yellow-fronted canaries—not the bright yellow of domestic canaries, but yellow with brown streaks. Finally, there are Japanese white-eyes in this woodland, tiny greenish birds with a prominent white eye ring (see figure 5.12).

You may see scruffy brown feral sheep, and they are at least part of the reason that the rare endemic trees described in the trail brochure are all old specimens. The sheep gnaw away any seedlings, preventing regeneration. These rare trees may be the last of their kind before this dry forest disappears.

9.4 NOISY NIGHT IN HILO. This field trip doesn't require much exertion. If you are in Hilo or almost any place south of Hilo in the Puna District of the Big Island, all you have to do is listen. An evening that would have been quiet in 1985 is now a cacophony of frog calls: little male coqui frogs singing their name, ko-KEE. In Hawai'i these little frogs are not bothered by their natural predators such as tarantulas, scorpions, owls, and snakes and can be found at five times the density they achieve in the forests of their native Puerto Rico. They eat a lot of endemic insects, and they compete with birds and other creatures that also rely on insects for food. Scientists fear that these frogs would provide a ready food supply for brown tree snakes if the snakes are ever introduced to Hawai'i. The frogs hide in foliage, so they're hitching rides on plants transported to the Kona side of the Big Island and the other main islands.

LEARN MORE

- George W. Staples and Robert H. Cowie, editors, *Hawai'i's Invasive Species* (Honolulu: Mutual Publishing and Bishop Museum Press, 2001). This book was written by a team of experts from the Hawai'i Biological Survey, a program of the Bishop Museum. At 116 pages, it describes only a selection of the worst invasive species but makes its point: invasive species are everywhere in Hawai'i and pose a huge threat to the environment and economy.
- H. Douglas Pratt, *A Pocket Guide to Hawai'i's Wildlife* (Honolulu: Mutual Publishing, 2014). This little guide isn't limited to introduced species, but many of the birds, reptiles, and mammals it describes are aliens.
- Almost any Hawai'i field guide is going to describe a lot of introduced species because that's what's out there. See *A Photographic Guide to the Birds of Hawai'i* (chapter 5) and *Hawai'i's Native & Exotic Freshwater Animals* (chapter 7).

10 Growth Potential
Agriculture and Culture

Start off the morning with a good breakfast: rice and eggs, with linguiça. Maybe half of a papaya, or some dragon eyes. Wash it down with Kona, medium roast. For a midmorning snack, a tasty malasada. At lunchtime, pass up the bento or plate lunch and go light with a bowl of saimin and a salad of Mānoa lettuce. By late afternoon when hunger returns pick up a musubi (Spam, of course) and some crack seed to munch on. For dinner, there's a *luau* at Auntie's house. She goes traditional: *poi*, *'ahi* poke with her own *limu*, *'opihi* that Uncle picked, *laulau*, *kālua* pig, chicken long rice. Relatives bring kim chee, manapua, and sweet bread. Plenty of apple bananas from family gardens. Top it off with *haupia* and a bit of *kūlolo*. The evening ends with entertainment: ukulele and slack key.

If you live in Hawai'i, this sounds pretty normal, maybe just a little belt busting. If you are a visitor or newcomer, it is nearly incomprehensible: you probably didn't recognize much at all after the rice and eggs and it seemed like the rice should have been served about two meals later. This remarkable day's menu is the product of a unique intersection of four factors: tropical island living, an ancient cultural heritage, a location with a history of big agriculture, and a population descended from agricultural laborers hired from all over the world. In Hawai'i, agriculture isn't just about growing stuff; it has shaped many aspects of island life.

It is easy to see how living on the tropical islands of Hawai'i would affect agriculture, food, and culture: chapter 7 mentioned some of the harvest from the sea, including *limu*, *'opihi*, and *'ahi*. The geography of the islands, with plenty of cooler high-elevation land, makes it possible to grow crops ranging from the tropical—sugarcane, pineapples, bananas—to the Mānoa lettuce developed by the University of Hawai'i and the Kula onions grown in cool upcountry Maui. Chapter 8 described the canoe plants that are still the foundation of many Hawaiians' diets.

Canoe plants and a range of climate zones help make Hawaiian agriculture diverse. The whole fabric of Hawaiian society is diverse, a legacy of commercial agriculture and the immigrants from around the world who came to work the fields. Their descendants make Hawai'i one of the most culturally diverse places on earth: no single racial or ethnic group makes up even a quarter of the population.

MAJOR CROPS

A hundred years ago Hawai'i was a major producer of the world's sugarcane and pineapple. Sugar came first. **Sugarcane** was one of the canoe plants brought to Hawai'i by Polynesians, but *kō,* as they called it, was a minor crop for the early Hawaiians. They had as many as forty different varieties, used it as a sweetener and, in times of famine, as a food. Westerners saw sugarcane as a cash crop. The first commercial sugar mills got a boost supplying the California Gold Rush in 1849. The American Civil War provided another boost when sugar supplies from the South were cut off. By 1866 thirty-two sugar plantations were producing nearly eighteen million pounds of sugar per year. Hundreds of thousands of acres of Hawaiian forest, already ravaged by grazing animals, were cleared for crop production.

Sugarcane is a member of the grass family. It can grow to a height of fifteen or even twenty feet, with a stalk up to two inches in diameter. It takes fifteen months to two years for a cane field to mature. By that time the leaves are drying out. The field is burned to get rid of the leaves, leaving behind the juicy stalks or canes. (If you visualize swarms of rats scurrying out of a burning cane field, you can understand the motivation for introducing mongooses.) The canes are then cut and the sweet sap in the stalk is extracted, reduced, and refined to make sugar.

Besides land, sugar production required a lot of water and a lot of labor. To get the water, planters diverted windward-side streams, tunneled through mountains, and built ditches to bring water to sunny leeward plantations. Lower stretches of many streams dried up completely, devastating endemic stream life. Many of the old water systems still exist today, but all the sugar operations have closed down and sugar production has moved to countries where labor is cheaper. Corporations that own the abandoned sugar plantations and still hold the old water rights envision a new cash crop: houses and development. Other people are fighting to return at least some of this water to streams where native fish and shrimp might be restored.

Labor was one of the biggest challenges for the sugar planters. Before modern equipment it took a lot of hand labor to plant, grow, irrigate, harvest, and process sugar. The work was hot, hard, and miserable. Some Native Hawaiians worked on the sugar plantations, but as the sugar industry was growing the population of Hawaiians was shrinking from disease and dislocation. Besides, planters believed that Hawaiian didn't work hard enough and were apt to go off in search of less wretched work.

So the sugar planters looked elsewhere for labor. They brought in laborers from China, Japan, Portugal, the Philippines, and at least half a dozen other nations. By 1865 there were more Chinese men than European men in Hawai'i. By the early years of the twentieth century, there were over 100,000 Japanese in the islands. By the 1930s the Japanese were joined by as many Filipinos. Most came as contract laborers. During their contract period, often five years, they were virtual slaves to the sugar planters. When their contracts were up some returned to their homelands, but many more stayed. From the melting pots of the sugar refineries came the melting pot of Hawaiian society.

Today commercial sugar production is gone from Hawai'i. The last Big Island mill closed in 1998, and sugar production on Kaua'i ceased in 2009. In 2016 the last remaining big sugar plantation, the Hawaiian Commercial & Sugar Company on Maui, announced it was ceasing operations. The future is not clear for 36,000 acres of cane fields and the company's 1901-vintage mill in the tiny town of Pu'unēnē on Maui's central isthmus. On other islands, most old cane fields lie fallow or have been converted to residences and golf courses. Only a small fraction of the acreage has been converted to other crops.

Hawai'i's other big commercial export crop was **pineapple**. Originally a South American plant, there are records of pineapple growing in Hawaiian gardens as early as 1813. Commercial production began in the late nineteenth century. In 1922 James Dole and the Hawaiian Pineapple Company bought the entire island of Lāna'i and turned it into the world's biggest pineapple plantation. Before long, Hawai'i was producing and exporting three-quarters of the world's supply of canned pineapple.

Farming *Koa*. One potential use for abandoned sugarcane lands, if they are fairly high and wet, is *koa* farming. *Koa* is a beautiful, valuable, and sought-after wood from an endemic tree. Cutting it out of native forest damages some of the rarest habitats on earth. So it seems like a logical idea to grow it plantation style. Some companies have established *koa* plantations, but it is a difficult business. It takes a lot of investment to get started, and you have to care for your *koa* trees for twenty or thirty years before you finally get a return on your investment. No company is at that point yet. Some companies are trying for early returns by selling carbon credits for the carbon sequestered in the *koa* trees. But right now, virtually any *koa* that you buy has been harvested from native forest, perhaps illegally.

The Hawaiian term for pineapple is *hala kahiki,* meaning *hala* from another land. Pineapples bear a superficial resemblance to fruits of the indigenous *hala* tree, but they are not closely related. Pineapple is a member of the bromeliad family. A pineapple with its surface of small geometric plates is not a single fruit but a cluster of small fruits that all grow together. Each little plate on the surface is a single fruit.

The prickly plants grow two to three feet tall. Each plant matures in twenty months to two years and usually produces one pineapple. When this mature pineapple is cut from the plant at harvest, workers also cut all but two branches from the plant. These branches will produce two more pineapples. Then the field is fallowed to enrich the soil, and the cycle starts again. New plants are started from the crowns of harvested pineapples. Pineapple production is on the same course as sugarcane: heading for tropical countries where land and labor costs are lower. In the 1990s the owners of Lāna'i decided it was more lucrative to grow luxury resorts than fruit, and they shut down pineapple production. Growers on other islands followed suit. Today, the only large-scale pineapple production is on O'ahu between Wahiawā and Hale'iwa, where about 2,700 acres of pineapple fields remain. Although the old pineapple fields are mostly fallow, the legacy of foreign labor remains. Even today, 45 percent of the people on Lāna'i are of Filipino descent.

Nearly all fresh pineapples in mainland grocery stores are a single variety. Most likely they came from Costa Rica and were picked a little on the green side because ripe pineapples bruise easily. In Hawai'i, at farmers' markets and even in grocery stores you may find other varieties that are sweeter and have lower acidity. They will taste better than mainland-purchased pineapples because they were riper when picked, golden or yellow outside, not green.

The decline of "cane and pine" has transformed Hawai'i from a territory that depended on agriculture to a state that derives just 1 or 2 percent of its economy from agriculture. But that doesn't mean farms are gone. In fact, Hawaiian agriculture is amazingly diverse. Significant crops include:

Macadamia nuts. Native to Australia, these nuts are popularly identified with Hawai'i for good reason: the islands supply between 70 and 90 percent of the world's commercial production. Mac nut orchards cover about 18,000 acres, mostly on the Big Island. The medium-size trees are evergreen, with long, narrow, oval, dark green leaves. The spherical nuts are notoriously hard to crack. Once out of their shell, they are dried and roasted to produce delicious nuts that are extremely high in oil content: 72 percent or more. Covering them in chocolate actually lowers the calories per ounce. Three places to see macadamia groves: around the 50-mile marker and between the 83- and 86-mile markers of the Māmalahoa Highway, Route 11, between Hilo and Kona; and along Macadamia Road east of its intersection with the Hawai'i Belt Road just south of Hilo near mile marker 4 on Route 11.

Coffee. Hawai'i is famous for its Kona coffee, grown on the leeward slopes of Mauna Loa and Hualālai where the mountains create perfect growing conditions (see chapter 4). This magical "coffee belt" is about twenty miles long and two miles wide, and ranges in elevation from seven hundred to two thousand feet. Its northern end is above Kailua-Kona, and it stretches south to the slopes above Pu'uhonua o Hōnaunau. Kona does not have a monopoly on Hawaiian coffee, however. About eight thousand acres of coffee grow on five islands. The Big Island's Ka'ū District on Mauna Loa's southern flank produces some very good coffee. A small amount of coffee is grown on Maui and on Moloka'i. Producers are now figuring out how to grow gourmet-quality beans on O'ahu. Kaua'i east of Hanapēpē is home to the largest and most mechanized coffee plantation in the world. It produces roughly a third of the state's output. This big mechanized farm is the antithesis of the small plots in Kona where the picking is done by hand to ensure the peak of ripeness and flavor. Coffee harvest peaks in the late summer and fall.

Papaya. Pity the mainland shopper stuck with expensive papayas that are hard and green, or bruised and overripe. One of the joys of island life is a trip to the farmers' market for abundant, inexpensive, ripe papayas. Of course, many Hawai'i residents don't need to go to a farmers' market, they just step out to the garden and pick their own heavenly fruits. For those without their own trees, Hawai'i has about two thousand acres of commercial papaya production. Papaya trees are unusual in many respects: they usually don't have branches, the fruit grows directly from the trunk, they grow quickly and can start to produce in a year. Production peaks in four-year-old trees, and by fifteen years they stop producing. The two main varieties are Rainbow, with yellow flesh, and Sunrise or SunUp, with red-orange flesh. Most of the papayas produced in Hawai'i are genetically engineered to resist a virus

FIGURE 10.1 Papaya trees have a single trunk without branches. The fruits grow from the main trunk. (Rick Soehren)

The GMO Issue in Hawai'i. Genetically modified organisms or GMOs are a big issue in Hawai'i. Of course, humans have been conducting genetic modification the old-fashioned way for thousands of years, saving seeds from outstanding plants and breeding domestic animals for particular traits. Modern genetic modification, sometimes called genetic engineering, involves inserting a gene from one organism into the genetic material of another organism. To create a papaya resistant to papaya ringspot virus, researchers at the University of Hawai'i inserted a fragment of genetic material from the virus into the DNA of the papaya.

A lot of the GMO controversy in Hawai'i is over big seed-production farms. These farms produce seeds of genetically modified strains of crop plants for use by farmers all over the world. Most of the seed production is for corn varieties that are modified to resist herbicides and to produce their own pesticides. Seed companies chose Hawai'i for their farms because the climate allows them to grow three or four crops of seed each year instead of just one. Also, the collapse of the sugarcane and pineapple industries left a lot of agricultural land vacant.

Concerns about GMOs include potential health impacts of ingesting GMO crops, escape of GMO genetic material into the environment, where it can contaminate non-GMO varieties and cause other problems, and heavy pesticide use by growers of GMO seed crops. Most Americans are already involuntary GMO guinea pigs; it is hard to avoid GMO corn and soy products. So far there is no published report of a direct link between ingestion of a GMO and a specific health problem. However, escape of genetic material is a very real concern. Growers of organic and non-GMO papaya are finding that the engineered virus-resistant genes are showing up in their plants. Growers of GMO seed use a lot of fertilizers, herbicides, and pesticides to produce their crops. Many people in Hawai'i believe these chemicals escape from the agricultural fields, causing environmental harm and human health impacts.

that virtually wiped out Hawaiian papaya farmers in the 1990s. Some nongenetically modified fruit is available at farmers' markets.

Bananas. If you think that the ordinary, commonplace banana could not hold any surprises, you would be so wrong. Consumers around the world are lulled into boredom because almost every market in the world offers the same variety, the Williams cultivar of the Cavendish banana type. It achieved its dominance more for its shipping and storage tolerance than its flavor. In Hawai'i there is a bit more variety: farmers' markets and even most supermarkets carry so-called apple bananas, actually a variety correctly called Brazilian dwarf. It has a firmer texture and an elusive taste that different people describe in very different ways, perhaps having the sweet-tart zing of some apples. These are just two among the hundreds of banana varieties in the world.

Banana plants can be thirty feet tall, but they are not trees and do not produce any wood. The trunk of a banana is made of whorled leaves. As they unfold, the leaves can be nine feet long. They tear easily in the wind, giving banana plants a ragged appearance. Many banana varieties have no developed seeds and are propagated from root sections called corms.

The early Hawaiians had as many as seventeen varieties of bananas collectively called *mai'a*, and had many rules governing banana use. Most notably, there were only a few varieties that women were permitted to eat. A woman's punishment for violating *kapu* and consuming the forbidden fruit was death. Most early Hawaiian varieties were not sweet but starchy, like the banana that Americans on the mainland call a plantain. Botanists still come upon old Hawaiian banana varieties growing untended deep in the forest. Today about 1,300 acres are planted for commercial banana production in Hawai'i, mostly to supply local markets. Many more backyard banana patches supply local households.

Miscellaneous. In addition to these tropical crops, there are some surprising agricultural categories in Hawai'i. The most valuable legal crop category in the state is now seed production, mostly corn (see the text box on genetically modified organisms or GMOs). Flower production, mostly orchids and anthuriums, is also important. Aquaculture is another significant category: perhaps most well known is the shrimp farming around Kahuku on O'ahu, but the most lucrative is algae production. See the field trip to NELHA in this chapter. There are small acreages of many specialty crops, including tropical fruits, vegetables, and spices such as ginger. *Kalo*, once the staple food of early Hawaiians, is planted to just 360 acres in modern Hawai'i.

AGRICULTURE'S LEGACY OF DIVERSITY

Most of the immigrants who came to Hawai'i to support the sugarcane and pineapple plantations were poor and arrived with very few possessions. But they could hang on to some of their cultural traditions, adapted by necessity to island conditions. Many of those cultural traditions related to food, and many of those beloved foods are still mainstays of island diets. The typical meals described at the beginning of this chapter draw from immigrant homelands all over the world.

A spicy Portuguese sausage called **linguiça** came to Hawai‘i with laborers from the Portuguese Azores Islands. (The little tail beneath the *c* is a diacritic called a cedilla. The *ç* in linguiça is pronounced like an *s*.) It has become a pretty standard breakfast meat in the islands. Often it is accompanied by **rice**, reflecting the Chinese and Japanese perspective that rice is an appropriate part of nearly any meal. These traditional breakfast choices aren't limited to insular ethnic groups; you can order linguiça, rice, and eggs for breakfast at fast food joints all over Hawai‘i. The **longan** is a Southeast Asian fruit related to lychee. Each fruit is a one-inch sphere with a thin outer shell-like bark, often harvested by cutting a small branch bearing several fruits. When the shell is peeled, the juicy white fruit looks like the English translation of longan: a **dragon eye**. Longans can sometimes be found at farmers' markets.

In addition to linguiça, the Portuguese brought other popular ethnic treats. The **malasada** is a donut without a hole that is fried in oil and coated in sugar. Sometimes malasadas are made extra healthful by filling them with flavored custard such as chocolate or coconut. They are best fresh from the bakery.

Meal options range from ethnic to uniquely local. The **bento** is a Japanese box lunch. Japanese field workers packed them for a midday meal. Today they are sold boxed to go or served in restaurants in a compartmentalized tray. They usually consist of a scoop of steamed white rice, a meat dish, and often a small salad or fruit. **Saimin** is derived from Asian noodle soup, but Hawai‘i has appropriated the dish as a healthful comfort food. The basics are a broth that can be chicken or another flavor with Asian noodles, usually topped with something to provide protein and visual appeal: char siu or Chinese roast pork, pink fish cake, sliced green onion, or yellow strips of omelet. Pick up the slippery noodles with chopsticks and slurp them in Japanese fashion. Use a ceramic spoon to drink the broth Chinese style.

A meal option that is uniquely Hawaiian is the **plate lunch**. The name is a bit of a misnomer, because a plate lunch is served to go in a foam box more often than it appears on a plate. A plate lunch almost always includes two scoops of steamed white rice, macaroni salad that sometimes includes potato and always includes lots of mayonnaise, and a meat dish that might be katsu, a Japanese-style cutlet of chicken or pork that is breaded and fried, or local fish.

Snack food can also demonstrate a strong Asian influence. The **musubi** is derived from another food packed by Japanese field workers. It is island evolution applied to a sushi roll: a big block of sticky white rice, almost invariably topped with a slice of Spam, wrapped in Japanese-style dried seaweed called nori. The natural habitat of the musubi is wrapped in clear plastic and piled under a heat lamp on the counter of a grocery or convenience store. **Crack seed** is an entire category of Chinese-influenced snack food, not a single item but an array of sweet or savory tidbits ranging from dried salted plums to rice crackers to sweet dried ginger. In the old days crack seed was sold in little specialty shops where each type would reside in its own big glass jar. A few of those shops remain, but today most crack seed is sold prepackaged in grocery or drugstores.

Finally, we attend the *luau* at Auntie's house. The cultural influences will come at us from all over the globe. Some traditional early Hawaiian foods are still popular today: *poi* is the quintessential staple consisting of cooked taro or *kalo* roots called corms that have been pounded into a paste with a little water added. After a few days it starts to ferment a bit, giving it a more complex flavor in much the same way that other cultures ferment milk into cheese or yogurt. Traditionally, *laulau* is a bit of pork wrapped in *kalo* leaves and cooked in the *'imu* or underground stone-lined pit for several hours. Today *laulau* is sometimes made with other meats including fish or chicken. Another traditional Hawaiian dish is **kālua pig**, covered and slow roasted in the *'imu* for many hours until it is smoky and tender. An old trick for keeping the meat moist is to put some wet banana stalks in the pit with the pig to make steam. Modern cooks roast it in the oven.

Other dishes traditionally served at a *luau* are borrowed from other cultures. You won't find salmon swimming in Hawaiian waters but **lomi salmon**, sometimes called *lomilomi* salmon, is a Hawaiian mainstay with Polynesian and Japanese influences. This dish is raw diced salmon mixed with salt, tomatoes, onion, and chili peppers. Far more popular today is **poke** (PO-keh). There are lots of variations but basic *poke* recipes include raw diced seafood such as *'ahi* (yellowfin tuna) or tako (octopus), sesame oil, *limu* (seaweed), green onion, and maybe ground *kukui* nuts. **Chicken long rice** is a Hawaiian adaptation of a Chinese food. There is no rice involved, and the chicken may be present only as broth. Long rice is a type of Asian noodle made from beans; they are sometimes called bean threads. The noodles are cooked in chicken broth, usually with ginger.

A **manapua** is similar to the Chinese bao, a bun that is filled with pork or other meat and steamed rather than baked. The name is said to be derived from the Hawaiian *mea 'ono pua'a* or literally "that tasty pork thing." **Kim chee** is a spicy Korean cabbage relish, a culinary relative

FIGURE 10.2 Breadfruit was a canoe plant brought to Hawai'i by voyaging Polynesians. A big tree is attractive and it can feed a family. (Rick Soehren)

Breadfruit: The Once and Future Food? One of the early Hawaiian canoe plants was breadfruit or *'ulu*, an important staple of the Polynesian diet. It never attained the same dietary prominence in Hawai'i. Like the pineapple, a breadfruit is actually many small fruits pressed together. It is usually oval or spherical, big (up to ten pounds), green, and grows on very attractive trees. As its name implies, it is starchy and only develops a touch of sweetness when very ripe. There are over one hundred varieties with varying taste and texture.

of sauerkraut. Look for jars of it in the grocery store refrigerator case. **Hawaiian sweet bread** is a clear descendant of Portuguese sweet bread. Early Portuguese immigrants built big wood-fired stone ovens to bake their beloved bread. You can do the same thing today; see the **Field Trip!**

Haupia and *kūlolo* are uniquely Hawaiian desserts. *Haupia* is similar to a coconut pudding, but stiff enough to be served in squares. *Kūlolo* is made from *kalo* or *poi,* coconut or coconut milk, and sugar. It often has the color and consistency of milk chocolate fudge. Look for it at farmers' markets on Kaua'i and sometimes on O'ahu.

The historic cultural influences of plantation-era immigrants have

In western cultures, the breadfruit is perhaps most famous for its association with Captain Bligh and the *Bounty.* In 1789, the specially outfitted British ship *Bounty,* her captain's quarters essentially turned into a greenhouse, was transporting breadfruit trees from Tahiti to Jamaica. The British hoped breadfruit could be cultivated as cheap, plentiful food for slaves. William Bligh was the *Bounty's* cruel and mercurial captain, commanding a crew that had just spent five months sampling the pleasures of Tahiti while they grew breadfruit cuttings to transportable size. It was a situation ripe for mutiny, and that's exactly what happened. Bligh and eighteen loyal crewmen were set adrift in a twenty-three-foot boat. Amazingly, they sailed more than four thousand miles in forty-seven days to reach the nearest European settlement in the Dutch East Indies, riding the Southern Hemisphere trade winds. Fletcher Christian and the rest of the mutineers returned to Tahiti before eventually settling on Pitcairn Island, where their descendants reside today.

Breadfruit is a potentially important food source. Recognizing this, the National Tropical Botanical Garden created its Breadfruit Institute in 2003, noting that more than 80 percent of the world's hungry live in tropical and subtropical regions. Farmers in the tropics need sustainable, low-input, nutritious crops. Nations with a total population of over two billion people have growing conditions suitable for breadfruit. And it is easy to grow. Most varieties are seedless and propagated by cuttings. Plant a shoot in the ground and within three to five years you can harvest your first fruit. Eventually your tree may produce one hundred or even several hundred breadfruits each year while providing shade and beauty.

The 'ulu isn't a major food plant in Hawai'i, but the intricate lobed leaf is a popular design in traditional Hawaiian quilting.

even touched Hawai'i's music scene. The instrument most associated with Hawai'i is the ukulele (oo-koo-LAY-lay) from the Hawaiian *'uku lele* or jumping flea. The fast-moving fingers of ukulele musicians inspired the name. The instrument is a four-stringed descendant of small guitars brought to Hawai'i by the Portuguese.

An important style of traditional music played on larger guitars is called slack key or *kī hō'alu* (loosened key), so named because one or more strings are loosened—made slack—so that the strings play a single chord. The style was developed by Hawaiian cowboys who learned about guitars from the Mexican cowboys brought to Hawai'i to help manage burgeoning herds of cattle. This distinctive tuning eventually led to the Hawaiian steel guitar.

Diverse cultural influences have helped to make Hawai'i's music scene much larger and more varied than you might expect from a population of just over a million people. Here's one measure of how huge the music scene is in Hawai'i: the Hawai'i Academy of Recording Arts bestows annual awards to the best musicians and music in the islands. They are called the *Nā Hōkū Hanohano* Awards. There are thirty-four categories. Just in Hawai'i. Every year.

FIELD TRIP!

Many of the field trips in this chapter are related to businesses and non-profit organizations. Their schedules, operating hours, and very existence can change suddenly. Be sure to check before you visit.

10.1 TO MARKET, TO MARKET. The old nursery rhyme starts out "To market, to market, to buy a fat pig." You probably can't buy the whole pig at a farmers' market in Hawai'i but you might get a plate of *kālua* pig, and just about anything else legally harvested in the state. There are over seventy markets on six islands where you can buy directly from the grower. Markets are held at various locations, various days of the week, various times. There's a wide range in market size and targeted customer base, too. The wildly popular Saturday morning market at Kapi'olani Community College just *mauka* of Diamond Head hosts more than seventy vendors and draws local residents as well as busloads of tourists from nearby Waikīkī. The residents buy salad greens, vegetables, and orchid plants. The visitors buy hot and cold prepared food by the plate,

FIGURE 10.3 The Saturday morning market at Kapiʻolani Community College in Honolulu is the largest in the state. (Rick Soehren)

fresh fruit, and packaged snack food suitable for consumption on the beach. You can combine a market visit with a Diamond Head hike.

The market held on Wednesdays and Saturdays in downtown Hilo isn't quite as large but makes up for it in diversity. I defy you to identify every plant product in the market without help from the vendors. At the other end of the spectrum are tiny markets with a handful of farmers selling a small selection of produce out of the back of pickup trucks.

For visitors, it is a revelation to taste tropical fruit that was picked ripe instead of green or half ripe. A ripe pineapple doesn't look or smell anything like the hard green things in mainland markets. If you're visiting Hawaiʻi for just a week, you don't even have time for grocery store papayas to ripen; get eat-it-now papayas from a farmer. Squeeze on a little lime juice to achieve perfection. Experience a ripe mango. Most grocery-store mangoes, even in Hawaiʻi, come from Mexico or Central America. Between May and October you might find super-flavorful ripe local mangoes at farmers' markets. Over five hundred varieties grow in Hawaiʻi, but commercial acreage is low, about three hundred acres. Most common varieties include Common (descended from the first seedlings imported in 1824), Pirie, Haden, and Mapulehu. Don't stop there; try a new fruit. Some of the larger markets include vendors of obscure fruits, often accompanied by helpful signage. Taste dragon fruit, star fruit, longan (also called dragon eyes), mamey sapote,

FIGURE 10.4 Farmers' markets like this one in Hilo are great places to sample unfamiliar fruits and other foods. (Rick Soehren)

sapodilla, lychee, or something else. If you don't know how to peel or eat any of them, just ask.

How do you find a market near you? The Hawai'i Farm Bureau sponsors about half a dozen markets, including the one at Kapi'olani Community College. Their website includes handy "tip sheets" that list the vendors at each market, giving you an idea of size and diversity. Farm Lovers Markets operates a handful of markets on O'ahu, including a big Saturday morning market at the Ward Gateway shopping center. *Edible Hawaiian Islands* magazine lists several markets on their website as well as farms that invite visitors. Or you can just do an Internet search for information.

10.2 Kona Coffee, Culture, and Cooking. It is easy and fun to spend a day in South Kona, taking in agricultural and cultural history. The Kona Historical Society does an excellent job of bringing history to life at their 1920s-era Japanese coffee farm, restored general store, and wood-fired Portuguese oven. Nearby you can take a tour of modern coffee facilities. Don't leave without some heavenly Kona coffee.

The Kona Coffee Living History Farm is located at mile marker 112 on the Hawai'i Belt Road, Route 11, about ten miles south of Kailua-Kona. Docents guide you through a small-scale coffee farm that is little changed from when it was operated by Japanese immigrants early in the twentieth century. On five acres of grounds you can get an up-close look at coffee bushes, macadamia nut trees, and other crops. There is an admission fee. For anyone interested in Hawaiian history, Japanese culture, or agriculture it is well worth it. Hours are limited: Monday through Friday, 10:00 to 2:00.

Two miles farther south near mile marker 110, the Kona Historical Society operates the restored H. N. Greenwell Store museum as this general store existed in the 1890s. Hours are very limited: Monday and Thursday, 10:00 to 2:00. Even more compelling is the weekly baking of Portuguese sweet bread in a wood-fired oven called a *forno* down in the pasture below the general store, every Thursday from 10:00 to 1:00. Guests can learn about the history of the Portuguese in the area, help form the rolls, watch as the bread is being baked, and then return a few hours later to purchase the heavenly result of their labor. The Kona Historical Society is a volunteer organization and hours of all activities can change; check their website for current information.

Adjacent to the restored Greenwell store is modern Greenwell Farms, offering free tours of a small commercial coffee-processing facility daily from 8:30 to 4:00. They have free tasting and coffee beans for sale. Several other farms in the region also offer tours and sell their beans.

South of Kona, the **Ka'ū Coffee Mill** in Pāhala offers tours at 10:00 and 2:00, and sells coffee and mac nuts. To get to the mill, watch for Kamani Drive between mile markers 51 and 52 on Route 11. Follow Kamani *mauka* through the town of Pāhala, turn right on Pikake, and follow the signs about two miles. The **Kaua'i Coffee Company** offers very informative tours, either guided or self-guided; there is a visitor center, museum, snack bar, and shop on Highway 540 between Hanapēpē and Kalāheo. An informative self-guided trail winds through coffee bushes, there are picnic tables on the grounds, and everything has excellent access for the disabled.

10.3 Nuts to You. The Big Island is home to most of Hawai'i's macadamia nut groves. A couple of nut companies operate visitor centers. One of the best places to see macadamia trees growing is along Macadamia Road just south of Hilo. The road stretches east for three miles from its junction with the Hawai'i Belt Road, Route 11, near the 5.7-mile point. Along Macadamia Road you'll pass one or two fields of papaya trees, but mostly it's macadamias: 2,500 acres, 250,000 trees. At the end of the road is the Mauna Loa Company's nut-processing plant, visitor center, and retail store. The visitor information is limited to a modest self-guided walking tour that leads visitors along windows into the processing plant. Stairways limit accessibility.

A more low-key experience awaits you on the other side of the island at the Hāmākua Macadamia Nut Company visitor center in Kawaihae, a few miles north of the Waikoloa resort area. There are no macadamia nut trees in this industrial neighborhood, but the staff is friendly, the videos are educational, and you have a view through big windows of the nuts as they are processed, roasted, and packaged. The center is a bit hard to find. It is on Maluokalani Street, a short loop road that runs parallel and *mauka* of the Akoni Pule Highway, Route 270, between mile markers 4 and 5.

10.4 Sweetened History. In a state once dominated by big sugar producers, today just the history of sugar survives. In 2017 the Hawaiian Commercial & Sugar Company, a subsidiary of Alexander & Baldwin, closed the last commercial Hawaiian sugar operation. It was in the tiny town of Pu'unēnē (hill of the *nēnē* or Hawaiian goose). The shuttered 1901-vintage sugar mill looks wildly out of place surrounded by former cane fields on Maui's broad central isthmus. The mill is closed, but the Alexander & Baldwin Sugar Museum is still open right across the road. The museum is housed in a 1902 plantation superintendent's house. Huge trucks and harvesters retired from the plantation are on the grounds. The displays are very well done, especially considering the small size of the museum. It is run by an independent nonprofit organization, but some bias in favor of its former benefactor Alexander & Baldwin does show. There are excellent displays describing the hard life of immigrant plantation workers, but little hint that many people in Hawai'i at the time disapproved of indentured labor and considered the plantation workers to be virtual slaves. Another display says of the company's nineteenth-century founders, "The partners were innovators and risk-takers." Competitor Claus Spreckels is described in less favorable terms: "Spreckels befriended King David Kalākaua. As a result of this royal connection, and the liberal and ruthless use of his wealth to influence Hawaiian politics, Spreckels obtained water rights, land, and desired legislation."

Despite the occasional bias, this is a nice educational little museum with a modest admission fee. Ramps for the disabled have been added to the old plantation home.

10.5 MEYER'S MILL ON MOLOKAʻI. During the latter part of the nineteenth century the Hawaiian sugar business was consolidating among a handful of big operators, but some small independent plantations still existed. One of them belonged to Rudolph Wilhelm Meyer, a German immigrant who came to Molokaʻi in 1850. In 1878 he built a mill that could produce fifty tons of sugar per year (the mill on Maui described above could produce up to two hundred thousand tons per year). The R. W. Meyer mill operated until 1889. For the next ninety-nine years it sat neglected but mostly untouched until energetic volunteers restored it to working condition. Today it is open to the public, a marvelous example of human ingenuity and resourcefulness. Staff at the adjacent Molokaʻi Museum & Cultural Center can provide a brochure for a self-guided tour.

The mill is located between mile markers 3 and 4 on the Kalaʻe Highway, Route 270, in the north-central part of the island.

10.6 COLD COMFORT ON THE KONA COAST. The oil embargo of the 1970s was a frightening event for Hawaiʻi, occurring at a time when virtually all the electricity in the islands was generated by burning oil. Today the most productive alternative energy sources in Hawaiʻi include solar, wind, and geothermal. But back then, a huge investment was made in a facility to generate power by using the temperature differential between ocean water at the surface and colder water thousands of feet deep. The coastline with the most abrupt drop in water depth is along the Kona coast, so that is where the facility was constructed, at Keāhole Point just south and *makai* of the Kona International Airport. The technology really wasn't ready for commercial power generation, and the State of Hawaiʻi was left with three big pipes, each about forty inches in diameter, drawing water up from a depth of two thousand to three thousand feet.

What does this have to do with agriculture? If life gives you lemons, make lemonade. If life gives you very cold clean ocean water, find businesses that can use it. Today the eight-hundred-acre facility is home to an assortment of businesses that can use this cold water. The Big Island Abalone Company farms abalone. Most of these single-shelled mollusks are shipped to Japan, but they are also for sale at the farm, in a few fish markets and restaurants, and at the Kapiʻolani Community College farmers' market in Honolulu. Other companies use the cold seawater to grow algae for the manufacture of nutritional supplements.

In 2015 the electricity generating system was finally connected to the power grid, producing enough electricity to supply 120 Big Island homes.

The facility has been known by several names. Some people call it OTEC (Ocean Thermal Energy Conversion). Others call the industrial park HOST Park (Hawaiʻi Ocean Science and Technology Park). The area is managed by a state agency, NELHA (Natural Energy Laboratory Hawaiʻi Authority). Finally, and most important for visitors, a group called Friends of NELHA (FON) schedules regular short informational lectures and tours of the facility and the abalone farm for a small fee. The abalone farm also offers stand-alone tours of its facility.

You can also enter the area on your own and drive around to take a look. Keāhole Point near the end of the road in the industrial park is the westernmost point on the Big Island. Be careful to read the signs at the entrance kiosk and note what time the gates are locked. The entrance is near the 94-mile marker on the Queen Kaʻahumanu Highway, Route 11, just south of the Kona airport.

10.7 POND TO PLATE. You can't get much closer to the source of your meal than this: visit one of the shrimp stands near Kahuku at the northern tip of Oʻahu. Enjoy a shrimp plate lunch while gazing out at the ponds where the shrimp were raised. Hawaiʻi's most visible aquaculture takes place in dozens of ponds along the Kamehameha Highway, Route 83, just north of the little town of Kahuku. The farms raise a species of freshwater shrimp called the Malaysian prawn.

There are many restaurants and food trucks on the north shore that serve shrimp, and driving there for a shrimp lunch is wildly popular.

In fact, the demand for shrimp is greater than the supply available from the shrimp farms. Some businesses serve imported frozen shrimp rather than the local product. To make sure you're getting crustaceans raised locally, visit one of the two stands located between the highway and the ponds.

The future of the shrimp farms is uncertain. The ponds are within the James Campbell National Wildlife Refuge and are leased to the shrimp farmers. The ponds provide some habitat for the wetland birds that the refuge was established to protect, but probably not under optimal conditions for the birds. In the future, the shrimp farmers may need to find a new home so that the birds have the space and conditions they need to survive. People can go someplace else for their shrimp, but the birds don't have any alternatives.

10.8 HANALEI VALLEY *KALO.* On the north side of Kaua'i, a national wildlife refuge coexists very nicely with commercial agriculture. The Hanalei National Wildlife Refuge was established to protect five species of endangered birds that rely on the Hanalei Valley for nesting and feeding habitat: the *ae'o* (Hawaiian stilt), *'alae ke'oke'o* (Hawaiian coot), *'alae 'ula* (Hawaiian gallinule), *nēnē* (Hawaiian goose), and the largest remaining population of the *koloa maoli* (Hawaiian duck).

The refuge is also home to 180 acres of *kalo* or taro, half the commercial production in the state. Each small field in the valley is surrounded by low dikes so the land can be flooded to grow wetland *kalo.* The flooded field is called a patch or *lo'i.* It turns out that the periodic staggered flooding and draining of these patches provides a variety of habitats for native wetland birds.

The refuge is not open to the public—too much human traffic interferes with breeding birds and the working farmers—but there are several ways you can see it. There is a sweeping view of the Hanalei Valley from the Hanalei Valley Lookout. It is a small roadside turnout just west of the Princeville Center shopping area. From the lookout you can see the Hanalei River winding through the valley below you, the bridge where the highway crosses the river, and *lo'i kalo* in various stages of growth. Some are drained mudflats, others have open water with widely spaced young *kalo* shoots, while others have mature patches with tall lush *kalo* plants nearly ready for harvest.

You can drive through the refuge on a narrow paved public road, but be careful to drive slowly and do not interfere with the farming operations. 'Ōhiki Road intersects Highway 560 just past the Hanalei River bridge. You can drive through the refuge for 0.7 miles to the trailhead for the public 'Ōkolehao Trail. There is a small parking lot on the left; the steep trail starts on the right side of the road and climbs 1,200 feet in less than 2 miles to the adjacent ridgetop. 'Ōkolehao is a liquor distilled from the roots of kī or ti plants. During prohibition kī plants were grown on the hillside for this purpose, and many are still growing in the area. The word means literally either "iron bottom," perhaps referring to the still in which the liquor was made, or "to fall forcefully on one's rear end," a likely effect of excessive liquor consumption.

It might be tempting to stop your car and stroll out along the grassy dikes, but don't do it. Off the pavement, refuge land is closed to the public, open only to refuge personnel and the kalo growers.

There is another way you can enter the refuge: by kayak. It can be a

FIGURE 10.5 A farmer and a Hawaiian stilt or ae'o coexist among kalo patches at Hanalei National Wildlife Refuge on Kaua'i. (Rick Soehren)

fun outing, but you won't see much of the refuge because the high banks of the river obscure your view. The dense thickets growing along sections of the riverbank are *hau,* a relative of hibiscus. The *hau* blossoms are bright yellow when they open in the morning and darken to red or orange during the day. By the next day they wither and fall from the tree. The arrival of *hau* in Hawai'i is a mystery. It has buoyant seeds that can float across oceans, but the species may have arrived as one of the canoe plants brought by Polynesian voyagers.

LEARN MORE

- Rachel Laudan, *The Food of Paradise: Exploring Hawaii's Culinary Heritage* (Honolulu: University of Hawai'i Press, 1996). Part cookbook, part cultural history, part memoir of exploring the Hawaiian ethnic food scene. In print for twenty years but still almost as relevant as the day it was published.
- Carol A. MacLennan, *Sovereign Sugar: Industry and Environment in Hawai'i* (Honolulu: University of Hawai'i Press, 2014). This award-winning book explores the complex relationships among the sugar industry, Hawaiian culture, and the environment of the islands.
- Carol Wilcox, *Sugar Water: Hawaii's Plantation Ditches* (Honolulu: University of Hawai'i Press, 1996). Sugar planters needed a lot of water to grow thirsty cane on the leeward sides of the islands. To get it there they built an extensive system of tunnels and ditches. This book chronicles their efforts in the context of the growth and eventual decline of the industry.
- Ronald Takaki, *Pau Hana: Plantation Life and Labor in Hawaii, 1835–1920* (Honolulu: University of Hawai'i Press, 1983). A scholarly but readable account of plantation life, written by the grandson of a Japanese immigrant who worked the sugar plantations.
- Angela Kay Kepler and Francis G. Rust, *The World of Bananas in Hawai'i: Then and Now* (Haiku, HI: Pali-O-Waipi'o Press, 2011). This big beautiful banana bible contains everything you ever wanted to know about bananas in Hawai'i. It covers cultural history, descriptions of 140 surviving varieties, even banana recipes, and includes 1,900 color illustrations in 610 pages. There is more to know about bananas than you realized.
- Diane Ragone and Craig R. Elevitch, *Ho'oulu ka 'Ulu Cookbook: Breadfruit Tips, Techniques, and Hawai'i's Favorite Home Recipes* (Hawai'i Homegrown Food Network and the Breadfruit Institute of the National Tropical Botanical Garden, 2012). Background information, cooking techniques, and recipes.

11 Heavens Above

Why Hawai'i Stargazing Is the Best

The first time my friend Loren and I drove over the high saddle between Mauna Kea and Mauna Loa at night, we thought we knew what to expect: lots of stars. It was the middle of the night on a summer evening. We stopped the car at a wide turnout along the dark, lonely road. I got out and looked up, and my heart sank. A big cloud stretched nearly across the sky, obscuring everything behind it. I was ready to get back in the car when Loren said, "Wait! That isn't a cloud. Those are stars." We were looking at the Milky Way.

If you live in a city or suburb with a lot of night lighting that drowns out stars or where smog often obscures the night sky, you will be amazed at the starry view from Hawai'i's tallest mountains. Even if you live in the countryside where the lights are few and the air is clear, you will be in for a surprise. When you're in a very dark place in the middle of a Hawaiian island, thousands of feet up, surrounded by the biggest ocean on earth, the view of the night sky is stunning. And the secret is out. Mauna Kea is acclaimed as one of the best places on the planet to put the biggest telescopes, and astronomers from around the world clamor to use them. The only place that comes close to the perfect viewing conditions in Hawai'i is the Atacama Desert in Chile. Chile is a lovely country, but even gushing travel guides describe the Atacama as a "parched wasteland." I'll take Hawai'i over the Atacama any day.

There are some places on other islands where you can escape night lighting and gaze at a nice dark sky (see the **Field Trip!** section), but this chapter focuses on the Big Island and, to a lesser extent, Maui. They best meet the conditions for excellent night sky viewing, and they are the locations of choice for astronomers' most sophisticated telescopes. For perfect viewing, all these factors must be just right:

Altitude. Clean air may seem transparent, but it is full of molecules. The nitrogen, oxygen, and trace materials in air will slightly obscure the view of the sky. At a height of 13,796 feet, the summit of Mauna Kea is above almost 40 percent of the earth's atmosphere. When you are striving for the clearest view possible, looking through 40 percent fewer molecules makes a difference. Don't worry—you will have enough air to breathe if you visit the summit of Mauna Kea or Haleakalā.

Dry Air. Obviously, clouds would obscure the view, but even water vapor or humidity can selectively absorb some wavelengths of radiation outside the visible spectrum and interfere with telescope function. Hawai'i's tallest peaks are above the inversion layer. Mauna Kea has very dry air and more cloud-free nights than almost any place on earth.

Clean Air. Hawai'i is far from most industrial sources of air pollution and most desert areas where winds can whip up clouds of dust. There are particles in the air, but fewer than almost anywhere else in the world. Occasionally erupting volcanoes produce huge amounts of ash and dust, but Hawaiian eruptions tend to be calm. Active Kīlauea is far below the observatories of Mauna Kea, and trade winds tend to blow volcanic pollutants away from the island.

Stable Atmosphere. Although the tallest island peaks are above a lot of the earth's atmosphere, they are still bathed in air. This air can impair a telescope's view, and turbulence in the air makes viewing even worse. The atmosphere in Hawai'i moves smoothly across thousands of miles of ocean and then lifts gently over the domed shape of the shield volcanoes, keeping turbulence to a minimum.

Dark Sky. City lights bounce off the atmosphere and make it harder to see the features of the night sky. Look upward on a clear moonless night from Waikīkī and you may see fewer than twenty stars. From a darker suburb like Kailua or Hawai'i Kai you might see as many as two hundred stars. Gaze at the night sky from the Saddle Road or higher points on Mauna Kea and you'll see two thousand, maybe as many as five thousand stars. Big Island skies are fairly dark at night because the population is relatively small, and Hawai'i County has had a "dark sky" ordinance since 1988. Most lights must be shielded so they shine only downward, and street lights have to be either low-pressure sodium (such as the streetlights that cast a yellow glow) or LED lights that have the easily scattered blue light filtered out. Maui County passed a similar but weaker ordinance in 2007 to protect the night sky above Haleakalā.

Resort owners successfully fought the mandate for low-sodium lighting. They said the yellow lighting would scare away tourists.

Support. It is a complex and expensive task to build and operate a world-class telescope. Such an undertaking requires at a minimum good harbors, airports, roads, telecommunication systems, support facilities, and living quarters for staff. Hawai'i has all these things. The combination of advanced infrastructure with remote darkness is very hard to find in the modern world.

Political Stability. The newest telescopes cost over a billion dollars to build, and they are not portable. The multinational consortiums that work together to build telescopes will not build in nations that face any threat of political instability. Chile, one of the most stable nations in South America, is home to a near-perfect place for big telescopes. Nevertheless, the European consortium that built telescopes there insisted on a "privileges and immunities" agreement with the government of Chile before it would build. The agreement gives the consortium sovereign authority over the telescope facilities.

Geological Stability. Physical stability is important, too. Mauna Loa is only 119 feet shorter than Mauna Kea, but it hosts one modest science facility while Mauna Kea has more than a dozen, including some of the biggest telescopes in the world. Mauna Kea is dormant, and Mauna Loa is still an active volcano. There are historical accounts of Mauna Loa's caldera glowing with lava, and it has erupted from its rift zones as recently as 1984. It would be foolhardy to build a billion-dollar telescope on Mauna Loa. Haleakalā is relatively stable but must be considered only dormant; it may have erupted as recently as 1790. Haleakalā is host to several science facilities but has the drawback of lower elevation than the Big Island volcanoes, and at 10,023 feet it has more cloudy nights than its taller neighbors.

Mauna Kea got its first telescopes in the late 1960s when NASA and the U.S. Air Force built optical telescopes on the mountain just in time for the 1969 moon landing. They were comparatively small reflectors with a diameter of 0.6 meters. About the same time, officials looking for economic activities to help the island recover from the devastating tsunami that hit Hilo in 1960 encouraged astronomy. By 1970, the University of Hawai'i completed a NASA-funded 2.2-meter optical telescope that produced stunning images. The world quickly took notice, and Mauna

What It Means to Be a Telescope. In 1609 the Italian scientist Galileo improved on a curious new device consisting of lenses mounted within a tube. It made distant objects—such as the previously invisible moons of Jupiter—appear closer. Today we call this a refracting telescope or refractor. In 1668 Sir Isaac Newton developed a telescope that used a curved mirror rather than a lens. It is called a reflecting telescope or reflector. The basics of these simple telescope designs haven't changed much for the last four hundred years: a user peers into the telescope and sees objects that appear much closer than they are.

The big telescopes in Hawai'i don't bear much resemblance to these early instruments. For one thing, scientists don't peer into telescopes anymore. Peering yielded to photography a century ago when astronomers began using their instruments more like the telephoto lenses on cameras and took permanent images to study. Today photography has been replaced by electronic sensors and computers.

Simple telescopes from the time of Galileo and Newton to the present are optical telescopes used to view a tiny part of the electromagnetic spectrum that we see as visible light. Modern scientific telescopes are built to detect electromagnetic radiation in different parts of the spectrum, including X-ray and ultraviolet telescopes, which detect wavelengths shorter than visible light; optical telescopes; infrared telescopes, which detect wavelengths longer than visible light; submillimeter telescopes; and finally microwave and radio telescopes, which detect the longest wavelengths. Most of these devices look more like satellite dishes than traditional telescopes.

Kea's reputation as one of the best locations for telescopes in the world was established. Today the state land atop the mountain is under long-term lease to the University of Hawai'i. The university, in turn, makes telescope sites available to other institutions.

With the mountain's popularity came controversy. Some Hawaiian people hold the mountain to be sacred, and they object to big construction projects erected near its peak. They argue that the scientists who develop and use the observatories have been dismissive of spiritual concerns. On the other side of the issue are those who believe that the astronomy conducted at the mountaintop is a modern extension of the ancient Polynesian wayfinding. The root of the issue seems to be two very different ways of knowing the world and existing within it. Many Hawaiians believe that the human, natural, and spiritual worlds are all connected, that the gods are their family, their ancestors. The scientists see an inert mountain, not a place of magic or spirituality. Native Hawaiians and astronomers can't come together because they live in different worlds.

The controversy erupted in 2015 when construction began on the Thirty-Meter Telescope (TMT), the largest in the world at the time. Protesters sought to protect the mountain by occupying it and blocking the access road. The governor stepped in and fashioned a compromise: construction on the new telescope could continue, but a quarter of the existing telescopes had to be removed, and the number of scopes was capped at the reduced number. In the future, any new telescope on the mountain would have to replace an older, less-advanced instrument. The compromise did not settle the controversy; in early 2018 the future of telescope construction was still uncertain.

The information on Map 11.1 will become obsolete as telescopes are removed or replaced. It is accurate as of early 2018. The telescopes are listed in Table 11.1 with information on wavelengths detected, size, sponsoring organizations, and "first light," or the year the telescope was put into use. Note that the diameter of the mirrors in the optical/infrared reflecting telescopes is given in meters because the metric system is the accepted standard in science. The University of Hawai'i's Institute for Astronomy maintains an excellent website with a current list and map of telescopes.

The **University of Hawai'i 2.2-Meter Telescope** is the oldest instrument on the mountain. It is small by modern standards. Coincidentally, this telescope is about the same size as the Hubble Space Telescope that was launched into space in 1990. Space is an even better—but more challenging—place than Mauna Kea to put a telescope because there is no atmospheric distortion and no absorption or blocking of certain wavelengths by the atmosphere.

Most of the Mauna Kea telescopes are used to study faint distant bodies, but the **NASA Infrared Telescope Facility** has a different purpose. It is dedicated largely to the study of bodies within our solar system, in support of NASA space missions. In a nice bit of symmetry, one program is the study of volcanic activity on Io, a large moon of Jupiter.

The **Canada France Hawai'i Telescope** was the first international collaboration on Mauna Kea. It is a small telescope by modern standards. Its operators have compensated with sophisticated instrumentation. One

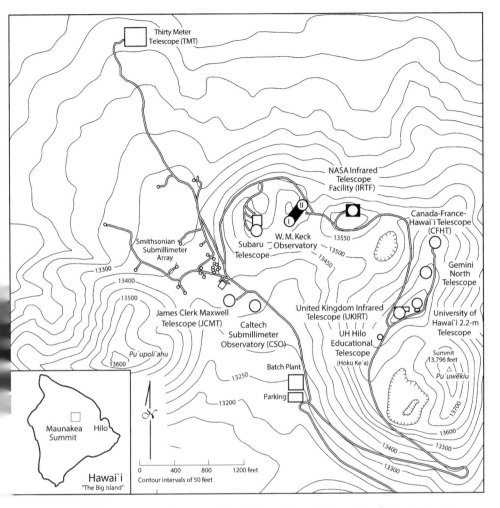

MAP 11.1 Telescopes near the summit of Mauna Kea. (University of Hawaiʻi, Institute for Astronomy)

example: in 2003 they built MegaCam, a digital camera with a mosaic of sensors to make it a 240-megapixel camera, at the time the largest in the world.

Many of the Mauna Kea telescopes work in both the optical and infrared wavelengths. The **United Kingdom Infrared Telescope** is the world's largest telescope dedicated solely to infrared. After thirty-five years of operation, the United Kingdom handed over ownership of the telescope to the University of Hawaiʻi in 2014. It is scheduled to be

Table 11.1 Telescopes of Mauna Kea

Name	Size in Meters	First Light
Optical / Infrared Telescopes		
University of Hawaiʻi 2.2-Meter Telescope	2.2	1970
NASA Infrared Telescope Facility	3.0	1979
Canada France Hawaiʻi Telescope	3.6	1979
United Kingdom Infrared Telescope (transferred to University of Hawaiʻi 2014)	3.8	1979
W. M. Keck Observatory 1 (Caltech, University of California)	10.0	1993
W. M. Keck Observatory 2 (Caltech, University of California)	10.0	1996
Subaru Telescope (Japan)	8.3	1999
Gemini Northern (USA, UK, Canada, Argentina, Australia, Brazil, Chile)	8.1	1999
University of Hawaiʻi Hilo Educational Telescope	0.9	2010
Thirty-Meter Telescope (US, India, China, Japan, Canada)	30.0	2024?
Submillimeter Telescopes		
Caltech Submillimeter Observatory (decommissioned 2015)	10.4	1987
James Clerk Maxwell Telescope (UK, Canada, Netherlands)	15.0	1987
Submillimeter Array (Smithsonian Astrophysical Observatory and Taiwan)	8 @ 6.0	2002
Radio Telescopes		
Very Long Baseline Array (National Radio Astronomy Observatory)	25.0	1992

decommissioned—disassembled and removed from the mountain—by 2022.

The twin **W. M. Keck Observatories** represent a clever way to overcome the technical challenges of building ever-larger telescope mirrors: build two smaller telescopes and link them electronically. Each twin has a ten-meter mirror that is a mosaic of thirty-six smaller hexagonal mirrors. As of 2018 they are the largest optical telescopes in the world. Larger telescopes have two advantages: greater light-gathering ability and greater resolution. The two linked Keck instruments have the resolution—although not the light-gathering ability—of an eighty-five-meter telescope.

FIGURE 11.1 The twin Keck telescopes and the NASA infrared telescope, with Haleakalā in the distance. Note automobile for scale. (Rick Soehren)

The **Subaru Telescope** is a marvel of Japanese engineering. Its 8.3-meter mirror is near the size limit for monolithic or single-piece mirrors and took seven years to manufacture and polish. It is the largest telescope in the world to have a camera mounted above the mirror, within the cylinder of the telescope itself. This allows the camera to record very faint objects. Even the shape of the building housing the telescope is revolutionary; instead of the familiar dome, it is a cylindrical building. Computer modeling showed that a cylinder would better prevent warm turbulent air from entering the building. Subaru is the Japanese name for the star cluster called the Pleiades or Seven Sisters. In Hawaiian it is the Makaliʻi.

The **Gemini Northern Telescope** is perfectly named (Gemini, a constellation of the zodiac, is Latin for "the twins") because this scope is one of a pair. Its twin is in Chile, where it can scan the southern skies. The U.S. National Science Foundation funded half of the twin instruments with an international consortium funding the other half. Astronomers from any of the supporting nations may apply to use the telescopes.

The **University of Hawaiʻi Hilo Educational Telescope** was a 0.9-meter instrument installed in 2010 that replaced an earlier 0.6-meter telescope, one of the first on the mountain. The new telescope was plagued with problems and never fulfilled its educational role. The university purchased a replacement telescope but as of 2018 has not installed it on the mountain because their telescope site may be abandoned as part of the agreement for construction of the Thirty Meter Telescope.

The **James Clerk Maxwell Telescope** observes wavelengths in the submillimeter or microwave range: from a little less than, to a little greater than, a millimeter in wavelength. These wavelengths are the most challenging to observe because they are readily absorbed by atmospheric moisture. The dry conditions on Mauna Kea make it a good place for submillimeter observation. Submillimeter wavelengths are emitted by dark places in the universe such as dusty star-formation regions and dark molecular clouds. The Maxwell Telescope is named after the nineteenth-century scientist who first explained electromagnetism. His namesake telescope is housed in a big cylindrical building, like optical telescopes, but the scope itself is a big dish structure. The building's viewing opening is covered by the world's largest sheet of Gore-Tex. It keeps out dust and sunlight but allows submillimeter waves to pass through.

The **Caltech Submillimeter Observatory** was taken out of service in the fall of 2015, the first of at least three facilities that are to be removed before the planned Thirty-Meter Telescope or TMT comes online. The Caltech dome will eventually be razed and the site restored or at least cleaned up so it looks like nothing had ever stood there.

The **Submillimeter Array** isn't a single structure but a cluster of eight dish antennas made of precision-machined aluminum. Each dish is six meters in diameter. The dishes can be moved among twenty-four foundations to produce different configurations; compact groupings are more sensitive, but broader arrangements of the dishes provide greater resolution. Each antenna weighs over forty-seven tons, and they are moved among the pads remotely, so don't get too close.

The **Very Long Baseline Array** is located well below the summit, at an elevation of about 12,200 feet. What you see on Mauna Kea is a single dish that is twenty-five meters in diameter and as tall as a ten-story building. It is called an array because it is one of ten similar dishes arrayed from the Virgin Islands in the east to the Big Island in the west. They operate as a single radio telescope, giving the array the best resolution of any telescope. An optical telescope with this resolution could read the cover of this book in Honolulu…from San Francisco.

Across the saddle from Mauna Kea there is a single science facility on Mauna Loa. The **Mauna Loa Observatory** measures atmospheric constituents such as carbon dioxide that may force changes in the earth's climate. At an elevation of 11,135 feet it is above the inversion layer and above nearly all the planet's atmospheric pollution, so it can produce consistent measurements of these atmospheric gases. (More about this facility in chapter 13.)

Across the 'Alenuihāhā (great billows smashing) Channel on Maui there are over half a dozen telescopes and related instruments near the summit of Haleakalā. Most of these are highly specialized for solar viewing or for military applications by the U.S. Air Force. One of the most intriguing is Pan-STARRS, the **Panoramic Survey Telescope and Rapid Response System**. It is a prototype wide-field imaging facility developed at the University of Hawai'i's Institute for Astronomy, and it uses the world's largest digital camera. A major goal of Pan-STARRS is to spot Earth-approaching asteroids and comets that might pose a danger to our planet.

And then there is the **Faulkes Telescope North**, a two-meter-class fully robotic telescope that teachers and their students can use for free.

FIGURE 11.2 The Faulkes Telescope North can be used remotely by students all over the world. (Edward Gomez, Las Cumbres Observatory Global Telescope Network)

It is part of the Las Cumbres Observatory Global Telescope Network, a collection of twelve robotic telescopes around the world that are available to educators over the Internet. The projects conducted using this telescope show what a wonderful opportunity it offers, and how impressive young minds can be: a class of tenth-grade students in Greece conducts a photometric study of the open cluster M25; two thirteen-year-olds in California study the age of stars and win a prize at the California State Fair for their work; an astronomy club in Ireland photographs a planet outside our solar system and wins a telescope at a county fair; students at the Sydney Girls High School determine the age of planetary nebula. Because of its ability to inspire young minds, Faulkes Telescope North may be the single most important telescope in Hawai'i.

Of course, you don't need a billion-dollar telescope to enjoy the night sky in Hawai'i. All you need is a spot where your view of the sky is not obstructed by trees, buildings, or bright lights. Binoculars help: you will be able to see ten times as many stars and pick out details like Jupiter's moons. There are helpful apps, books, and devices, too. See the **Learn More** section.

There are three sky sights that visitors to Hawai'i and novice observers ask about more than any others: the Milky Way, the Southern Cross, and the green flash. Here are some tips for seeing each of them:

The Milky Way. In many cases, modern explanations are far less exciting than Hawaiians' explanations for natural phenomena. A poorly understood hot spot pushing magma through the earth's crust probably doesn't fire the imagination as much as the story of Madame Pele. But where the early Hawaiians saw a cloudy wash of white across the night sky, we know that we are gazing up through the flat disk of stars that make up our spiral galaxy. The milkiness is untold numbers of stars, orbited by planets too numerous for us to imagine. And just maybe, somewhere up there, an astronomer or an adze maker or a flightless, island-bound bird is gazing back at us across the vast expanse of our galaxy. No myth or story could possibly be more humbling.

To get a good view of the Milky Way, you need to be looking at the right time of year. As the earth makes its annual orbit around the sun we see different parts of the night sky in different seasons; we are always looking away from the sun at night. That's why the constellations of the zodiac are associated with different months. From our solar system's position out on the edge of one of the spiral arms of our galaxy we look out from the galaxy into relatively dark space for part of the year. The stars we see are part of our galaxy, but they are pretty well dispersed. On summer nights, particularly July through September, we get a view looking toward the heart of our galaxy. There are so many stars in the center of our galaxy that when we face in that direction the night sky can look milky. Galileo was one of the first to train a telescope at the milkiness and discover that it was made of stars. His first telescope was 3×, magnifying objects three times, and he quickly made an improved 9× version. With modern binoculars, usually 7× to 10×, you can see the same celestial details as Galileo. The dark streaks obscuring some parts of the Milky Way are clouds of interstellar dust.

Light and pollution obscure the Milky Way. For the best view, get away from artificial night lighting, and try to pick a night when the moon is new or no more than a quarter full. A high-elevation vantage point is helpful but not essential. This is important: give your eyes time to adjust to the darkness. Avoid looking at any artificial light for fifteen to thirty minutes. It will make a big difference.

Makahiki. The early Hawaiians observed *Makahiki,* or the start of the Hawaiian year, at a carefully prescribed point in the calendar. To mark the start of the *Makahiki* season: first, wait for the star cluster of the Pleiades to rise at sunset, which occurs every year on November 17. Next, wait for the new moon that follows this sunset rising of the Pleiades, which will be one to twenty-eight days later. Finally, watch for the first visible crescent moon that follows this new moon. This marks the start of the *Makahiki* season dedicated to the god Lono, a time of celebration and peace, and the beginning of the Hawaiian year. In 1778 Captain Cook first sighted land on November 26. *Makahiki* had begun just a few days earlier, on November 20. The timing helped confirm early Hawaiians' initial belief that he was their god Lono.

The Southern Cross. Visitors to Hawai'i who come from more northerly latitudes often know only one constellation of the Southern Hemisphere sky: the Southern Cross, also known as Crux. In Hawaiian it is *Hānaiakamālama,* which means "to be cared for by the moon." It has been made famous in many ways: it appears on the national flags of several Southern Hemisphere nations, and it is mentioned in many popular songs. Mark Twain was excited to see it, too. In *Following the*

Equator, a book he wrote about his round-the-world lecture tour, he describes his anticipation and then his reaction upon seeing the constellation: "It is ingeniously named, for it looks just as a cross would look if it looked like something else."

That's part of the challenge of seeing the Southern Cross; you need a bit of imagination to perceive a cross. Twain said, "I would change it to the Southern Kite," because it is usually tipped a bit when we see it, forming more of a kite or diamond shape than a cross. It is only visible for a few hours each night from Hawai'i and only during spring (April to June or so) when the earth's axis is tipped to give the Northern Hemisphere the best view of that part of the southern sky. To make identification even more challenging, there is another group of stars nearby called the false cross that is sometimes mistaken for Crux. And finally, the constellation never gets very high in the sky, so you need an unobstructed view of the southern horizon and clear conditions to see it.

The best way to locate the Southern Cross is to use a sky map or star chart. The Bishop Museum's Planetarium web page publishes sky maps for each month of the year, making it easy to print out a chart of the constellations like Crux and location of the Milky Way any time you need it. More detailed star charts are posted on the Outreach page of the University of Hawai'i's Institute for Astronomy. Other sources are in **Learn More.**

The Green Flash. Ah, fabled phenomenon that follows the fading sun. If conditions are just right, you may be able to see a faint green flash above the horizon just as the sun sets below it. To understand what causes this phenomenon, we go back to topics mentioned earlier in this chapter: the visible portion of the electromagnetic spectrum and the effect of atmosphere on light. As the sun sets, we see our home star through a thick blanket of the earth's atmosphere. The atmosphere acts something like a prism, bending and separating different wavelengths of light that we see as different colors. As the light of the setting sun travels through the atmosphere, long red wavelengths are bent downward the most, and shorter green ones the least. As the sun dips below the horizon, the green light is the last to disappear. (Blue and violet wavelengths are even shorter, but air molecules tend to scatter the blue light and it doesn't beam straight toward us. Yellow and orange light is absorbed by water vapor so those colors tend to be diminished, too.)

This refraction alone can produce a very faint, very fleeting green flash, usually too faint for us to see. Under just the right conditions, a mirror image mirage of the setting sun forms in the atmosphere and magnifies the green flash, making it brighter and longer in duration—although it still lasts only a second or two. When the disk of the sun is halfway or more below the horizon and its edges appear notched or wavy on both sides or if it seems to form an omega shape (Ω) that gets much wider right at the horizon, this is a mirage interfering with your view of the sun. It's a good sign that the green flash is about to appear.

Hawai'i is a good place to see the green flash because the perfect viewing conditions are often in place. An unobstructed view of a distant horizon is necessary; a sun setting into the ocean with no clouds between you and the setting sun is perfect. The air has to be fairly clean with no dust, smog, or haze. The mirage effect is heightened when the water is warmer than the air, a condition that is more likely to occur in winter. The rising sun can also produce a green flash, but it is harder to see because you won't know exactly where to look before the sun appears.

Before you go running off to stare at the sunset, here's an important word of caution. The sun is very bright. Do not look directly at it before it is setting, or you run a high risk of permanently damaging your eyes. As the sun is starting to set, look elsewhere. When half or more of the sun's disk is below the horizon you can glance at it for just an instant. You should only look directly at the sun when there is just a sliver of it showing above the horizon. If the green flash makes an appearance, it will happen within seconds.

Looking for the green flash from a vantage point at Waikīkī? From mid-March to mid-September, the sun sets behind Barber's Point and you won't have an unobstructed view of the horizon. During winter the view is fine from Waikīkī but in spring and summer you'll need to find a more west-facing beach, such as Electric Beach (see chapter 7). At the height of summer, May through July, the sun is far enough north that the clouds over Kaua'i will spoil the view from O'ahu. Because the Hawaiian Islands are aligned southeast to northwest, a similar problem occurs from many vantage points on the islands during summer when the sun sets farthest to the north. The Kona coast of the Big Island is a good vantage point except during this summer period.

For visitors from higher latitudes, Hawai'i has one more celestial surprise. The state lies mostly within the tropics, that part of the earth that has the sun directly overhead for some part of the year. During the winter, people in San Francisco, Tokyo, or other northern cities see a sun that arcs low across the sky and provides a short day with little warmth. In Hawai'i the sun is only slightly lower in the sky than at other times of the year, so winter days are longer and warmer in Hawai'i. The sun always sets almost perpendicular to the horizon in the tropics, not at an angle, so darkness falls more quickly in Hawai'i, too.

FIELD TRIP!

The most popular astronomy destination in Hawai'i is Mauna Kea. You can drive to the Visitor Information Station, located at the Onizuka Center for International Astronomy, at an elevation of 9,200 feet. From there you can get all the way to the telescopes near the peak at 13,796 feet in one of three ways: on your own, on a guided Visitor Information Station tour, or on a commercial tour.

11.1 THE MAUNA KEA VISITOR INFORMATION STATION. The Visitor Information Station (VIS) is operated by the University of Hawai'i Institute for Astronomy and is run largely by volunteers. It is open from 9:00 a.m. to 10:00 p.m. 365 days a year. There are people to answer your questions, a small shop weighted toward astronomy, and free viewing through big portable telescopes on Tuesday, Wednesday, Friday, and Saturday evenings. At an elevation of 9,200 feet the VIS is usually, but not always, above the inversion layer. There are picnic tables out back, and an exclosure where you can walk around and get close-up views of Mauna Kea silverswords (see chapter 4). For those heading to the summit, spending thirty to sixty minutes at the VIS is a good way to acclimate the body to the high altitude and help avoid altitude sickness (see the cautions below).

The VIS is at the end of the pavement along Mauna Kea Road. Coming from either Hilo or Kona, take the Saddle Road to the 28-mile marker. This is roughly the crest of the Saddle Road, elevation about 6,500 feet. There is a crossroads of sorts with a hunter check station, Pu'u Huluhulu, and a parking lot to the south. Heading north is Mauna Kea Road. It is another 6.2 miles to the Visitor Information Station and 14.7 miles to the summit. Passenger cars can make it to the station, and most car rental companies now allow their cars to be driven this far. (Before the Saddle Road was widened, straightened, and improved, many car rental companies prohibited or discouraged driving on it. Those days are gone.) Driving times to the Visitor Information Station are 1 hour from Hilo and 1.5 hours from Kona under good conditions.

If you plan to visit the station at night for the telescope viewing, be sure you know in advance how to turn off your car's headlights. That way you can extinguish them quickly, before destroying the night vision of others. Similarly, it helps to have a small flashlight with a red filter because red light doesn't alter your night vision as much as white light. Red cellophane and a rubber band will do the trick.

As commercial tours of the summit have proliferated, the station has experienced severe crowding. Commercial tours stop at the station on the way up the mountain, and take advantage of its restrooms on the way down after dark. New rules are being considered to limit crowds at the VIS and the summit. My favorite way to avoid the crowds? After taking a peek through the telescopes, use a flashlight to make your way to the picnic tables at the back end of the parking lot. Take a rag or paper towel to wipe crumbs and lunch remnants off the tables. Lie down on a table in the peaceful darkness away from the crowds on the patio, allow your eyes to adjust, and gaze up at more stars than you can count.

11.2 THE MAUNA KEA SUMMIT TWO WAYS. It takes some advance planning and effort to get beyond the VIS. Why would you want to make a daytime visit to the summit? You will be on top of the tallest mountain on earth, and have a good view of the top of distant Haleakalā peeking out of the clouds. You will get a closer look at the collection of telescopes atop the mountain, and also be visiting a place of great spiritual importance in Hawaiian culture. Some people believe Mauna Kea is short for Mauna o Wākea or "mountain of the god Wākea." Wākea, sometimes translated as "sky father" is considered the deity from whom all things in Hawai'i are descended. The summit is considered a *wao akua* or sacred realm of the gods. It is the home of the snow goddess, Poli'ahu, one of a very few places in Hawai'i where there is ever any evidence of her presence. Hawaiian cultural practitioners recommend that you ask the mountain's permission before you visit the summit of Mauna Kea, and give thanks after your visit.

You can **drive to the summit** on your own if you have a suitable vehicle. From the VIS to the summit it is another 8.5 miles. The first four miles are gravel; this stretch can have washboard bumps and is rough, but it doesn't require off-road driving skill. The rest of the summit road is paved to minimize dust at the top. A 4WD vehicle is required, both for traction and so you can drive down the hill in a very low gear that will slow the vehicle down. Brakes overheat easily at this altitude because thin air is less efficient at cooling them. Most sport utility vehicles don't have a sufficiently low gear; you need a real 4WD. Nearly all the car rental agencies prohibit their vehicles, even the 4WD ones, from venturing beyond the VIS. Currently only one firm, Harper's, rents 4WD vehicles and allows driving off the pavement. You are asked to be on the summit only from a half hour before sunrise to a half hour after sunset. Vehicle headlights interfere with the observatories.

During limited hours you can enter some of the telescope buildings. The following information was accurate when this book went to press; check telescope websites for latest information. The Keck I Telescope has a visitor gallery and restrooms that are open from 10:00 a.m. to 4:00 p.m. Monday through Friday. There is a small viewing room where you have a limited view of the massive telescope itself. The Subaru Telescope offers 40-minute tours, usually on Tuesday and Thursday at 10:30, 11:30, and 1:30. Some are in English, some in Japanese. You can sign up for a tour on their website, at least a week in advance. They don't have public restrooms. If you sign up for a Subaru tour, allow plenty of travel time. Once you get to the Visitor Information Station you will need to stop for a while to acclimate. Nearly half of the remaining 8.5 miles to the summit is unpaved; allow at least 45 minutes.

The VIS used to offer free escorted summit tours every weekend, weather permitting. You would caravan from the VIS to the top of the mountain where a volunteer guide would point out various telescopes. The tour included entry to at least one of the scopes. You returned with the tour at around 4:30 or stayed on the summit for the sunset. You still needed to have your own vehicle with true 4WD. At press time, these tours were canceled indefinitely because controversy over the TMT led to demonstrations on Mauna Kea. You can check the University of Hawaiʻi Institute for Astronomy website to see if they have resumed. The ʻImiloa Astronomy Center (see below) still offers a similar tour, but only for Hawaiʻi residents.

If this is starting to sound like you can't get there from here, there are **commercial summit tours**. Several tour operators will pick you up at your hotel or other central location in Hilo or Kona in their 4WD van or small bus, lend you a warm parka and gloves, feed you hot snacks or a full meal, take you to the summit for sunset viewing and perhaps a telescope tour, then descend a bit where they can set up their own telescope. After a restroom stop at the VIS, there's the nighttime drive back to the coast. Expensive, but easy. Contact information for a list of authorized tour operators is on the website of the University of Hawai'i Institute for Astronomy.

No matter how you get there, some precautions are necessary for a visit to Mauna Kea. Altitude sickness is a real concern; some people feel it, while others seem immune. Be sure to stop to acclimate at the VIS. Symptoms of altitude sickness include rapid pulse, hyperventilation, or a pounding headache. Do not go up the mountain if you have been SCUBA diving in the last twenty-four hours (snorkeling is OK). Wait forty-eight hours if you dived below one hundred feet. Otherwise you could get a fatal case of the bends, with dissolved gases coming out of solution to form bubbles in your bloodstream. Be prepared for virtually any weather condition from bright burning sun to howling wind to bitter cold. Maybe all three. At this altitude, there is much less atmosphere to block ultraviolet rays; sunglasses and sunscreen are important. In the winter, snow is a possibility. Start your trip with a full tank of gas. The VIS shop is the only retail facility of any kind on the mountain. They sell bottled water, snacks, sweatshirts, but not gasoline. Drink plenty of water in the dry air. Standard health advice is that certain groups should not venture higher than the VIS: women who are or may be pregnant, anyone under sixteen, and anyone who is severely overweight, unsteady, or has heart or respiratory problems. Avoid gassy foods like beans, cabbage, and onions. Gas expands at high altitude and could be painful. Don't let any of this scare you away; just be prepared and enjoy the visit.

11.3 ʻImiloa Astronomy Center. This modern facility in Hilo, at the University of Hawai'i Hilo campus, is a museum, a planetarium, a hands-on learning activity center, and a respectful showcase for Polynesian voyaging, ancient and modern. An hour or two spent at ʻImiloa will enhance your subsequent visit to the Visitor Information Station partway up the big mountain, your stargazing from high elevations on the Big Island, or your trip to the summit. You will learn a lot about Polynesian voyaging as well as astronomy. The facility was originally called the

Mauna Kea Astronomy Education Center. Later the name was changed to 'Imiloa (distant traveler) and the tagline is "where astronomy meets Hawaiian culture."

'Imiloa has the world's first 3-D planetarium show, and it is dazzling. The architectural design of the building features three titanium-covered cones representing Mauna Kea, Mauna Loa, and Hualālai. On the grounds is an extremely tidy native plant garden. There is an admission fee. The center is closed Mondays and some major holidays. Wheelchair access is good.

11.4 THE RAINY DAY MUSEUM CRAWL IN HILO. On a rainy day in Hilo you can stay dry, educated, and entertained by making the rounds of local museums. Hilo holds the title for rainiest city in the United States, an average of over 120 inches per year. (If you want to quibble, Ketchikan and Yakutat in Alaska receive more annual rainfall, but I wouldn't call those tiny burgs cities.) Hilo residents will tell you that most of their rain falls at night so it really doesn't cause any inconvenience. But sometimes it does rain during the day. All. Day. Long. When that happens, take time to visit the town's museums. In addition to 'Imiloa you can check out the Mokupāpapa Discovery Center (see chapter 12), the Pacific Tsunami Museum, and the Lyman Museum and Mission House. The biggest attraction at Lyman is the Mission House. It is the oldest wood-frame house on the island, built by New England missionaries David and Sarah Lyman in 1839. Among its famous guests were Mark Twain and Isabella Bird, whose writings are highly recommended (see chapter 1). The adjacent museum houses some good displays on the natural and cultural history of Hawai'i, plus oddly out-of-place collections of seashells and minerals from around the world. If you're planning visits to several museums, the nonprofit organization Destination Hilo sells a pass that will get you discounted admission to eleven museums on the Big Island.

11.5 SUMMER NIGHT MAGIC ATOP HALEAKALĀ. The summit of Haleakalā is a lot easier to visit than Mauna Kea. You will be at an altitude of only ten thousand feet or so, not quite as lofty as Mauna Kea, and sometimes the inversion layer is high enough to put you in dense clouds. But when it is clear, and it usually is, there are compensations. The night view down into Maui's isthmus and the lights of towns far below you is unforgettable. There are a few small tour operators who are starting to bring telescopes to Haleakalā, but you'll avoid the huge crowds of the VIS on Mauna Kea; often you will have a crater overlook all to yourself at sunset. During the summer there will be the sight of the brightest part of the Milky Way and the singing of the ʻuaʻu or Hawaiian petrel. Spending a chilly summer evening on Haleakalā is one of the most magical experiences a nature lover can have. See chapter 5 for a full Haleakalā itinerary.

LEARN MORE

Just as there have been huge advances in telescope technology in recent years, there have also been huge advances in information technology to enlighten people about visible celestial bodies. Today, there are inexpensive smartphone apps that can show you constellations, planets, even satellites. Download one before you head up the mountain; you'll need Wi-Fi to download the app, and you'll want time to learn its features. Be sure to check what the app can do for you when there is no Wi-Fi or cell signal.

Want a low-tech approach? Get a planisphere, a simple star chart consisting of two disks attached by a central pivot. The bottom disk has a star chart, and the upper disk has a window of visible sky. You rotate the upper wheel according to the current time and date, and it shows you the constellations—but not planets—that are visible. If you live far from tropical Hawaiʻi, you probably can't pick one up in a local shop near home. Planispheres are calibrated for latitude, usually in ten-degree increments. For Hawaiʻi you need one that is accurate between latitudes of 20° and 30° north, providing accurate coverage for most of the state. The shop at the VIS sells them.

Want free information that is detailed and specific? Star charts can be printed from the websites of the Bishop Museum's Watamull Planetarium and the University of Hawaiʻi Institute for Astronomy Outreach page.

- Leslie Lang and David A. Byrne, *Mauna Kea: A Guide to Hawaiʻi's Sacred Mountain* (Honolulu: Watermark Publishing, 2013). A good concise overview of history, natural history, cultural significance, and telescopes as they existed in 2013.

12 Early Departure
Extinction and Why It Matters

She was wandering alone on the slopes of Mauna Loa. She picked at herbs and flowers, tearing them off with her stout beak. The lava terrain was hilly with deep crevices, hard for a fat flightless goose to traverse. A sudden shift in the wind caught her by surprise and showered her with volcanic ash from a nearby eruption on the mountain's southwest rift zone. With gritty ash in her eyes she stumbled and fell into a deep crack in old *pāhoehoe.* More ash rained down. She tucked her head under her wing for protection but it was not enough. Overcome by volcanic gases, she slipped out of consciousness and lay very still as more ash covered her. And she remained there for nine thousand years.

The drilling crew was hard at work on the flank of Mauna Loa above Pāhala, tunneling through solid basalt under lava flows one hundred feet thick. They were working to put a water tunnel through a ridge on a mountain the locals called Kaumaika'ohu (hill where the mist rests). Suddenly they punched through into softer material, a deposit of volcanic ash. What they found next surprised them so much that they stopped work and called for the foreman. When he arrived, the crew showed him the bones of a goose: fragile, stained, cracked, cooked goose bones. The bone fragments were sent off to the United States National Museum, where a perplexed technician could not readily identify the species. The bones were labeled and tucked away. The year was 1926.

By 1943 the museum had amassed skeletons of geese from all over the world. Confident that an identification could now be made, scientists at the museum took another look at the old bones from Hawai'i. The goose had been similar in size to the Cape Barren Goose living in southern Australia, but its stout leg bones were more like those of an extinct goose from New Zealand. Still puzzled, the museum concluded that these definitely were not the bones of a *nēnē*, the Hawaiian goose, but some unknown extinct species. The ancient bird was given a Latin name. The bones were boxed up carefully and put away for another thirty years.

In 1971 an inquisitive woman by the name of Joan Aidem was strolling along the windy beach at Moʻomomi on the northwest coast of Molokaʻi. During the last ice age when the coral reef along this shore was exposed by lower sea levels, the persistent wind ground away at the dead coral heads and turned them to sand. Sand dunes accumulated along the beach. Over time, rain dissolved the tiny bits of coralline limestone and the dunes lithified, turning into fragile sandstone and encasing all the detritus that one expects to find in beach dunes.

But what Aidem found protruding from the weathered edge of a dune was not expected. She found bird bones—no surprise there. But Aidem was something of an amateur archaeologist, and she knew her birds. She suspected that these well-preserved bones were not the bones of any bird alive on earth, and she was right. They were similar to goose bones, but from a bird that was huge and stout and clearly incapable of flight. Later when the bones were compared to the old fragments from the Big Island, there were distinct similarities between the two. But the puzzle only grew more mysterious. Similar flightless birds on two islands separated by nearly one hundred miles of water and the islands of Maui, Lānaʻi, and Kahoʻolawe. What was going on here?

During the mid-1970s the puzzle pieces finally started to fall into place. People were finding more old bones in other parts of Hawaiʻi. Collapsed lava tube skylights had trapped any flightless birds that were unlucky enough to tumble into them. Other lava tubes held the bones of birds that could fly, and the shells of ancient land snails, and the remains of bats. On Oʻahu the unique geology of ancient reefs lying above sea level formed sinkholes. These underground chambers held the biologists' equivalent of a mummy's tomb: a jumble of old bones just waiting to be identified and pieced back together.

Storrs Olson and Helen James, a couple of archaeologists from the mainland, took on the overwhelming task of excavating and identifying tens of thousands of bird bones. They made some surprising discoveries. There was evidence that birds like the *ʻiʻiwi* and *palila*, now restricted to high-elevation refuges, once ranged down to sea level. They found bones from big flightless ducks and geese, matching those from Kaumaikaʻohu and Moʻomomi. The flightless ducks were so different from anything alive today that Olson and James coined a new term for them, *moa nalo*, lost fowl. Eventually they pieced together a reality that shocked, amazed, and horrified them. They found the remains of thirty-two fantastic bird species that were completely unknown to science, and partial skeletons that suggested perhaps twenty more: hawks and eagles and owls, a variety of seabirds, flightless ibises, and the remains of so many new honeycreeper species that they outnumbered all the living species in the islands. The more they looked, the more they found. And these were just the birds that happened to be caught in sinkholes and lava tubes and dunes, whose bones had been preserved. There probably had been others whose remains did not survive the ages.

Just how old were these mysterious bones? That was perhaps the most astonishing part. These were not fossils that had turned to stone over millions of years. Olson and James called them subfossils. They were in fact just old bird bones. Some were ten thousand years old, from species that may have gone extinct before the arrival of early Hawaiians. Others were mingled with fishhooks and other artifacts of the early Hawaiians from a few hundred years ago.

And then in the archaeological record the species started dropping off. Dozens of these astonishing bird species were completely gone by the time the first western naturalists described and drew the birds of Hawai'i. Roughly thirty more, their portraits lovingly painted by early artist-naturalists, have since joined their fellow species in oblivion. Sometimes only their feathers remain. Figure 8.3 shows one of the last examples of Hawaiian featherwork that used bright yellow feathers from endemic birds. This cloak contains the feathers of a species of 'ō'ō, an extinct black and yellow Hawaiian honeyeater.

It turns out that the fragile, wondrous species that evolve on islands do not coexist well with late-arriving humans. And not just modern humans with their golf courses, condos, hotels, freeways, and hungry grazing animals. Most of the wondrous bird species that evolved in Hawai'i over millions of years had perished by the time early Hawaiians first saw Captain Cook's sails rising over the horizon, and the list has grown since then. Countless plants and invertebrates, even a mammal (a bat species), have disappeared. The islands that we treasure as a biological wonderland are actually more like a mummy's tomb after it has been plundered by looters. What's left is still a treasure, but we can only imagine—and grieve—for what once existed.

It is fair to ask, "How can this possibly be true? The early Hawaiians were famously good stewards of the land. And even today, there is some fairly undisturbed country left for Hawai'i's birds and plants and land snails and everything else." The answer is complex. Most significantly, living things that have evolved on islands may lose their competitive edge. No sense putting energy into defense mechanisms that aren't needed. For example, flightlessness apparently evolved over and over again among geese, ducks, rails, and ibises in Hawai'i. A flightless bird faced little risk on an island without terrestrial predators, so it would not expend energy growing big wings it didn't need. When hungry Polynesians arrived, with dogs, those wings would have come in handy.

By the time western naturalists started to catalog Hawaiian birds, just a single flightless species remained on the main islands: a small, secretive rail, relative of the Hawaiian coot and gallinule. The old bones tell us it was one of ten or twelve flightless rails in the main islands, among at least two dozen flightless bird species. Nobody has seen a Hawaiian rail since 1884 when one was spotted between Hilo and Volcano. About the same time, mongooses were multiplying and spreading to that part of the island. The Laysan rail existed in the Northwestern Hawaiian Islands for much longer, surviving introduced rabbits that ate their food and cover, cats that ate them, storms that killed them. Rats hopped off a U.S. Navy landing craft in 1943 and most likely devoured the last of their kind.

And the rats that had hopped off Polynesian voyaging canoes a thousand years earlier did damage far out of proportion to their diminutive size. They nearly wiped out the only genus of endemic Hawaiian palm trees by eating palm seeds. And they may have been responsible for the disappearance of land snails from many parts of the islands. They probably also started the long decline of forest birds by robbing nests of eggs and chicks.

Island species are more vulnerable than those on continents or in oceans because their numbers and their range are necessarily limited. A localized catastrophe such as a forest fire or tornado will kill a lot of animals on a continent but will rarely destroy the entire range of a species. One big fire on the dry grassy slopes of Mauna Kea could wipe out the *palila,* an endangered honeycreeper that exists only on its high southern slopes. When Hurricane 'Iniki made a direct hit on the high forests of Kaua'i the birds had no viable option: many of those that stayed in high forest were killed by the two-hundred-mile-per-hour winds or starved shortly afterward; many that came down to lower elevations for protection or food were killed by avian malaria spread by lowland mosquitoes, or were eaten by rats and cats. The tsunami generated by the 2011 Fukushima earthquake in Japan swamped nesting seabirds on Midway; someday rising sea levels will similarly obliterate many low islands favored by seabirds already in peril from a variety of human impacts.

Sometimes the path to extinction is harder to trace. Why have the 'i'iwi and 'apapane and 'amakihi survived when dozens of related species perished? We don't know. It may be that these surviving birds are generalists when it comes to diet and habitat needs. They have lost some of their range to disease-carrying mosquitoes and some of their food to forest-eating goats and sheep, but they have managed to find alternatives.

Sometimes the species that perishes is unknown to us, but we discover that it provided services that are now lacking. Coevolution—two species changing and evolving together—is common on islands. Tragically, it often means that when one member of the coevolved pair dies out, the other likely is doomed. Botanists from the National Tropical Botanical Garden monitor a few surviving individuals of the extremely rare plant *Brighamia insignis* or *ālula* growing on almost sheer Kaua'i sea cliffs where the plants have avoided being eaten by goats. These weird-looking plants almost never set seed by themselves. Whatever used to pollinate them—probably an endemic Hawaiian moth—is gone forever. The *ālula* survives only because dedicated botanists rappel down the cliffs to pollinate the flowers by hand with tiny brushes or pipe cleaners. On the Big Island, only a few wild specimens of *Kokia drynarioides* are left, a tree related to cotton that has evolved big red flowers that look like outsized hibiscus flowers. When University of Hawai'i ecologists compared the flowers with old bird bones, they found the shape and size of the blossom to be a perfect match for the beak of a bird called a *kioea*. The last time anybody saw one of these birds alive? Shot in 1859.

These grim stories and dozens more like them reflect Hawai'i's status as the extinction capital of the United States, with more than 270 species known to have vanished since western contact. The tiny island state has nearly 500 threatened or endangered plant and animal species. The other 49 states—all of them together—have about 1,000.

And despite our greater knowledge today, species continue to go extinct. In 1975 a young biologist by the name of Rob Shallenberger was part of a team that took cameras and bulky sound recording equipment into the Alakaʻi Swamp, one of the wettest places on earth. They were headed for the last refuge of the Kauaʻi ʻōʻō or ʻōʻō ʻāʻā (small ʻōʻō bird, or perhaps small flower piercer), lone survivor among five species of Hawaiian honeyeaters that included four species of ʻōʻō and the *kioea*. These birds' ancestors lived in Hawaiʻi for at least fourteen million years, first arriving before any of the current inhabited islands emerged from the sea, when tiny islands of the Northwestern Hawaiian Islands were larger and higher. They evolved and island-hopped down the archipelago as new islands formed. Shallenberger and the team returned from the swamp with the best color photographs ever taken of the ʻōʻō and

FIGURE 12.1 The Kauai ʻōʻō was the last Hawaiian honeyeater to survive. This ʻōʻō was photographed in the Alakaʻi Swamp on Kauaʻi in 1975. By 1987 the species was extinct. (© Robert Shallenberger)

very good sound recordings of its haunting, flutelike song. The last time anyone heard that song was in 1987 when the ʻōʻō population had fallen to one, a male that called in vain for a mate. Then he, too, disappeared. These birds had survived everything that nature could throw at them on erupting, subsiding, eroding Pacific islands for fourteen million years. But two centuries of contact with modern humans did them in.

The loss of the ʻōʻō ʻāʻā and its relatives is especially tragic for another reason. These birds were long thought to be descended from the honeyeaters of Australia and Asia, birds that the "Hawaiian honey-eaters" closely resembled. No one had questioned the assumption since the time of Captain Cook. Then in 2008 clever scientists analyzed DNA from old museum specimens. The birds weren't true honeyeaters at all. They were more closely related to very dissimilar birds like North American waxwings. It was a case of convergent evolution: the development of similar traits in distantly related organisms because they faced similar conditions that caused the traits to evolve. The so-called Hawaiian honeyeaters were so unique they made up their own now-extinct taxonomic family.

During my lifetime the Kauaʻi ʻōʻō and the *poʻouli* have been definitely lost forever, and it is likely that several other rare and secretive bird species disappeared as well. We just don't know enough about them to be certain. Most Hawaiian ecologists would probably bet that for each charismatic and (relatively) easily observed bird we've lost, the islands have lost several insects and plants, some never even described by science.

After reading eleven chapters of this book you know that Hawaiʻi is full of amazing plants and animals that are endemic to these islands, and the diversity is rounded out with a lot of beautiful introductions. There is still a lot of exquisite island life to see. And you know that Hawaiian islands inevitably sink back below the waves after a life of twenty or thirty million years or so. Most of the unique plants and animals that evolved in Hawaiʻi are destined to be drowned in a few million years along with their island homes. Why should we exert ourselves to save struggling species that are on evolutionary dead-end roads? Why restrict human activities when there are plenty of birds, insects, plants, fish, and other creatures to go around? It turns out there are quite a few reasons, and they resonate whether you care about these Hawaiian endemics or not.

Perhaps the most persuasive reason is unknown consequences. Nature is complex. The familiar refrain of this book is "we don't know." When we remove one species from nature's mix, we don't know what consequences there might be. The biologist Aldo Leopold put it this way: "If the biota, in the course of aeons, has built something we like but do not understand, then who but a fool would discard seemingly useless parts? To keep every cog and wheel is the first precaution of intelligent tinkering." John Muir, Scottish naturalist and cofounder of the Sierra Club, put it even more eloquently: "When we try to pick out anything by itself, we find it hitched to everything else in the Universe." Sometimes we can see the effects of removing a species: catch all the tasty parrotfish on a reef, and the living coral may be overwhelmed by algae growth. Other times we don't know what we've got till it's gone: the *kioea* and *Kokia*, the *ālula* and an unknown moth.

Another reason to preserve species is to preserve their genetic diversity. Our world's climate is changing rapidly. The more adaptable a plant or animal is, the more likely it will survive coming changes. The Hawaiian honeyeaters were able to cope with an astonishing variety of habitats. They first arrived in Hawai'i fourteen to seventeen million years ago, probably dwelling in the forests of Gardner Island, now eroded to barren pinnacles. The honeyeaters survived the "break in the conveyer belt" of islands when Gardner eroded away, surviving on lower, more barren islands. When the high islands of today's Hawai'i emerged from the sea, the genetic diversity of the ancestor honeyeaters allowed them to evolve into five new species of forest birds. After surviving at least fourteen million years of radical environmental change, we managed to kill them off in the blink of an eye. First to go was probably the *kioea* before 1860. The last, a Kaua'i 'ō'ō, died in 1987 while building a tidy nest and singing in vain for a mate that no longer existed. What genetic traits enabled the honeyeaters to evolve their way through so much change? What killed them all so quickly once westerners arrived in Hawai'i? This would be good information to have as we enter an age of climate change.

A more selfish reason to prevent extinction is that we might develop a very personal need for a particular plant or animal. Physicians often conclude that if we live long enough and avoid all the other perils of life, some kind of cancer will eventually kill most of us. When scientists discovered that bowhead whales may possibly live for more than two hundred years, they suspected that these whales' genetics may offer some kind of cancer-fighting mechanism. They are now splicing whale genes into laboratory mice to test the theory. Some corals may offer similar medicinal hope. Scientists at Hawai'i Pacific University have found that a substance found in some soft corals may have double benefits: blocking the growth of cancer cells and helping preserve brain cells after a stroke.

Here's another reason, and it is an embarrassment for our conservation efforts. When we fail to protect our own endangered species, we forfeit the moral authority to tell others that they should protect theirs. Take the *palila*, for example (see text box). We are allowing this amazing little bird to go extinct so that a few thousand vocal hunters can have a little more space to hunt. Are we forfeiting our right to tell the Japanese they shouldn't slaughter whales for "research"? That commercial tuna boats shouldn't cast their nets on dolphins? That Sumatra should stop converting orangutan habitat to palm-oil plantations? Funny how it's harder to see our own failures here at home.

And then there's the lesson most of us learned before kindergarten: don't take something that doesn't belong to you. Powerful economic interests, greedy anglers, or vocal hunters don't have the right to

The *Palila*: Next to Go?   One of the less common honeycreepers—in fact one of the most endangered birds in the world—is the *palila*. This little gray, yellow, and white bird isn't doing as well as some of its generalist relatives because its diet is very specific: it uses its conical finch-like bill to feed almost exclusively on green seed pods of *māmane*, a shrub or small tree of cool, dry, high elevations. The *palila* used to occur on O'ahu, Kaua'i, and a large part of the Big Island. Now its range consists of a single dry area of endemic *māmane* and *naio* trees on the southwest slope of Mauna Kea.

This area has been ravaged by sheep and mouflon for a long time. The feral ungulates eat the *māmane* trees so voraciously that new trees can't regenerate and big old trees die. Back in the 1930s the State of Hawai'i built a fifty-five-mile fence around state lands on the upper slopes of Mauna Kea to protect the forest reserve, but mouflon had no trouble getting through or over it. By the 1960s the *palila* was listed as an endangered species, and it became clear that a better fence was needed. The State of Hawai'i resisted clearing the mountain of hungry exotic sheep because they were popular quarry for take away species or habitats or ecosystems that belong to all of us. We should be vocal with our outrage when they try.

There are, however, some success stories for Hawaiian endangered species. A century ago the *nēnē* was headed straight for extinction. It still faces threats, but today the birds are plentiful on Kaua'i and surviving on the Big Island and Maui. The predator-proof fence at Ka'ena Point has allowed nesting Laysan albatross to stage a comeback on the main Hawaiian Islands. These big birds are not endangered—there are over a million nesting on Midway—but multiple nesting colonies will give them greater resilience against events like hurricanes, tsunami, or sea-level rise. The weird little *ālula* plant may never be able to flourish in the wild, but enterprising botanists have saved it from extinction.

And that's the best we will be able to do. We can't "keep every cog and wheel" because sometimes the mechanisms of extinction are already in place. Introduced species that compete with endemics or harbor disease can't be completely removed. Climate change will reduce available habitat beyond a survivable minimum for some species even if we stop carbon emissions tomorrow. But ingenuity and perseverance and dedicated biologists and botanists and people like you can make a difference and help preserve some of the wonders that Hawai'i has to offer.

hunters. Eventually public interest groups went to court; yet the state continued to resist despite three court orders to remove the feral ungulates and protect the *palila*.

The *palila* certainly needed protection. As recently as 2003 there were more than 6,000 of them, but by 2011 their numbers had declined sharply to fewer than 1,400. The State is finally taking its protection responsibilities a little more seriously, removing sheep and goats from *palila* habitat and improving the old fence. Bird numbers are rebounding slightly. Still, state officials acknowledge that the new fence won't be completed for years to come.

Since 1979 when courts first ordered the State of Hawai'i to take protective action for the *palila*, a lot has changed in the world. We've invented personal computers and built the Internet, created cell phones and smartphones and put them into the hands of more than half the people in the world. We've launched space telescopes and an international space station, and driven vehicles on Mars. We've eradicated smallpox. But the State of Hawai'i could not build a fence to save one of the rarest birds on earth.

FIELD TRIP!

Many of the field trips in this book take you to places where endangered species can be seen, where struggling plants and animals are holding their own or making a comeback with a little human help. Visit Kaʻena Point on Oʻahu to see Laysan albatross and wedge-tailed shearwaters nesting in dunes where dogs, cats, and rats used to regularly eat eggs and kill birds young and old. Now the birds are protected behind a predator-proof fence (see chapter 5). More happy, protected seabirds are at the Kīlauea Point National Wildlife Refuge on Kauaʻi. You can see strange *ālula* plants and many other endangered plants at the gardens of the National Tropical Botanical Garden on Kauaʻi (see chapter 4). You can even gaze upon the feathers of species that are gone forever. Visit the Hawaiian featherwork displays at the Bishop Museum in Honolulu (see chapter 8). To see a diverse Hawaiian forest in nearly undisturbed condition, take a guided walk into the Nature Conservancy's Waikamoʻi Preserve (see chapter 5). Want more?

12.1 MOKUPĀPAPA DISCOVERY CENTER. The remote Northwestern Hawaiian Islands are protected as the Papahānaumokuākea Marine National Monument. The monument isn't open to the public but its visitor center, the Mokupāpapa Discovery Center, is a good place to learn how the refuge protects species and ecosystems. The national monument itself is huge, encompassing about 583,000 square miles of Pacific Ocean. That's larger than Washington, Oregon, California, Idaho, and Nevada put together. There are vast expanses of healthy coral reef that continue to be dominated by big predatory fish that have mostly been overfished in other areas. There are huge colonies of nesting seabirds. The monument is a stronghold for green sea turtles and Hawaiian monk seals. There are programs to remove introduced predators like rats and cats, and efforts to remove the tons of marine debris such as fishing nets and plastics that wash ashore. In short, it is a place where we are taking a strong stand against extinction.

You can learn about the national monument at its visitor center, paradoxically located at the extreme opposite end of the archipelago in downtown Hilo on the Big Island. There are murals, artifacts, videos, interactive displays, life-sized wildlife models, an aquarium, and friendly staff. After you've learned about the national monument, take a moment to appreciate the century-old building that houses the center. The staircase is made of *koa,* and the hardwood flooring is *ʻōhiʻa.*

The Mokupāpapa Discovery Center is at 76 Kamehameha Avenue at the corner of Waiānuenue. Admission is free and the center is open Tuesday through Sunday.

12.2 MAKAUWAHI CAVE RESERVE. Most of the archaeological digs harboring ancient bird bones, snail shells, and Hawaiian artifacts are off-limits to the public, their locations sometimes carefully guarded to prevent looting or accidental damage. But there is one fascinating site that you can visit. The Makauwahi Cave Reserve near Poʻipū on the south shore of Kauaʻi is open to the public on a limited basis.

The cave is unusual for volcanic Hawaiʻi. It is not a lava tube and not even volcanic in origin. About four hundred thousand years ago, huge sand dunes began to form along this shore. Over time they lithified into a sandstone/limestone rock. Then groundwater flowing seaward from the rainy mountains of the interior created caves in the stone. When the last ice age ended the sea began to rise, and about seven thousand years ago seawater entered the cave system. The sloshing seawater eventually dissolved and eroded the ceiling of the cave, and a big round section collapsed, creating a skylight into the cave system. The collapse mostly blocked off the sea, and the opened cave became a freshwater or brackish pond at the bottom of a big hole. For the next seven thousand years the peat sediments of the pond accumulated and preserved bird bones, land snail shells, pollen, seeds, tsunami debris, and bits of wood. Then about a thousand years ago new specimens were deposited: the bones of rats and dogs, *kukui* nuts, coconuts, charcoal, and carved fishhooks. In the recent layers of sediment there are no more big flightless birds, no bird-catching owls, no seeds of the endemic palm *loulu,* no more native land snails.

Eventually a nearby stream was rerouted by local farmers, and the pond dried up. When amazing subfossils were being discovered all over Hawaiʻi some scientists explored the sediments of Makauwahi Cave. They found one of the richest deposits of preserved specimens in the state. Thirty feet of sediment yielded a nearly ten-thousand-year record of life at the site. The archaeologists call it a "poor man's time machine."

Today much of the pond area has been excavated or sampled, but work continues at the site. It is easy to safeguard despite the proximity

FIGURE 12.2 Makauwahi Cave near Po'ipū on Kaua'i holds a treasure trove of ancient bones, pollen, and artifacts. (Rick Soehren)

of homes, farms, and resorts because of its unique configuration. The ancient pond has nearly sheer cliff walls. The only way to enter without rappelling down a cliff is to crawl through one short cave passage that connects the dry pond area to the outside world. An iron gate at this passage protects the treasures that remain inside.

The nonprofit Makauwahi Cave Reserve organization manages the cave, organizes tours of the cave site, and conducts native plant revegetation projects on the surrounding land. Unfortunately, the future of this amazing site is not as secure as it should be. The land is owned by Grove Farm Company, a former sugar plantation that has morphed into a development company. The Makauwahi Cave lies squarely in the path of resort development along the Po'ipū shore.

At press time you could visit the cave Wednesday, Friday, Saturday, and Sunday each week between 10:00 and 2:00 when a docent is present to show you around the site. Check the cave reserve website for current information. To reach the cave, you will travel east on Po'ipū Road past a string of resorts until the pavement ends and the road becomes Weliweli Road. This rough red-dirt road is passable in a passenger car in dry weather, although some rental car contracts may prohibit driving on unpaved roads. Follow this road for one to two miles to reach parking areas to the south or north of the cave. Maps and trail brochures can be downloaded from the cave reserve website, with detailed driving instructions at the "contact" link. This field trip offers a lot: an exciting cave, a nice little hike, native plants, great ocean views from the bluffs, and an informative tour of a world-class archaeological site.

12.3 IN PURSUIT OF *PALILA.* The *palila* is one of the most endangered birds in the world, yet it is still possible to see this species on the high, dry southwestern slopes of Mauna Kea. Experienced birders who do their homework can search for the *palila* on their own. Want homework? learn to recognize the bird by sight and by its call, and recognize *māmane* and its green seed pods. Use a high-clearance 4WD vehicle to get from the paved road on the saddle up to the area on the mountain where *palila* population densities are highest (or least low, since there aren't many of these birds anywhere). None of this is really too daunting because color photographs and sound recordings are available on the Internet. But once you do all this, you still might not see the birds. They tend to be rather localized so you could be in *palila* critical habitat and miss them.

If you come to the Big Island with the goal of seeing *palila,* a safer bet is to book a commercial tour or hire a guide. Tour operators or guides can help you identify all the birds and plants you encounter. In a single day's birding, they can take you to several different habitat types where you have a fair chance of seeing several endemic bird species and loads of endemic plants. On a really good day you might add ten endemic birds to your life list. You can visit some birding areas along the saddle road like the Puʻu ʻŌʻō Trail and Kīpuka 21 on your own. Other spots like Hakalau Forest National Wildlife Refuge and *palila* habitat are harder to visit solo. The website for the Hakalau Forest National Wildlife Refuge maintains a list of reputable commercial guides.

EARN MORE

- David A. Burney, *Back to the Future in the Caves of Kauaʻi: A Scientist's Adventures in the Dark* (New Haven, CT: Yale University Press, 2010). A very personal account of the formation, exploration, and restoration of the Makuawahi Cave area by the man who knows the story best.

- Alvin Powell, *The Race to Save the World's Rarest Bird: The Discovery and Death of the Poʻouli* (Mechanicsburg, PA: Stackpole Books, 2008). Perhaps the most painful Hawaiian extinction story. The *poʻouli* was a primitive honeycreeper that wasn't even discovered until 1973, in the rugged rain forest of windward Haleakalā. The last known individual perished in 2004.
- Robert J. Cabin, *Restoring Paradise: Rethinking and Rebuilding Nature in Hawaiʻi* (Honolulu: University of Hawaiʻi Press, 2013). An easy-to-read account of hopeful stories of ecological restoration in Hawaiʻi today.
- Elizabeth Kolbert, *The Sixth Extinction: An Unnatural History* (New York: Henry Holt/Picador, 2014). This book takes a global look at modern extinctions and was awarded the Pulitzer Prize.
- David Quammen, *The Song of the Dodo: Island Biogeography in an Age of Extinction.* See the listing in chapter 3.
- E. O. Wilson, *The Diversity of Life.* See the listing in chapter 3.

13 Is It Hot in Here?

Climate Change and How It Threatens Islands

In the late afternoon of March 10, 2011, the eighty-one scientists, caretakers, and visitors on Midway Atoll received alarming news: Japan had experienced a devastating earthquake, and a tsunami likely was headed east toward Midway, the rest of the Hawaiian Islands, and even the west coast of North America. The atoll's human inhabitants knew just how to prepare: take everything valuable and transportable to high ground (or at least the highest bit of land the atoll offered, a mere forty feet above sea level) and huddle together on the top floor of the three-story bunkhouse.

Midway's other inhabitants—reef fish, seals, turtles, and millions of nesting seabirds—had no early warning system. When the tsunami arrived just before midnight, it pulverized coral reef and flung it on to the island's airport runway, deposited schools of fish on land, and carried turtles far ashore and stranded them there. But it was the birds that fared the worst. Hundreds of thousands of albatross chicks sat innocently on the ground, unable to fly and unaware of what was to come. Bonin petrel chicks were even worse off, enjoying false security in the underground burrows their parents had dug to protect them.

The devastation was heartbreaking. Over a hundred thousand birds were drowned or buried in their burrows. Many more were injured and died a slower death. All the human inhabitants of the atoll survived and labored valiantly to rescue wildlife and minimize the environmental catastrophe. The task was overwhelming, and only a relative handful of affected birds could be saved.

The disaster that occurred on Midway was not due to climate change. It was caused by a sudden shift in tectonic plates. This shift displaced an immense quantity of water and generated waves that pushed all the way across the Pacific. But the disaster provided a peek into the future and offered a glimpse of one of the ways that a changing climate might affect the natural world on Pacific islands.

The tsunami that caused such devastation was a little less than five feet high when it hit Midway. That doesn't seem like much, but about a third of Midway—including areas where several hundred thousand seabirds take refuge and nest—sits at an elevation of five feet above sea level or less. At the rate our seas are warming and rising, the oceans may be more than six feet higher by the end of the century. Extreme tides and storms will push seawater even farther ashore. Nesting seabirds will be crowded on to smaller islands and will be subjected to more frequent overtopping surges. As on Midway, humans with adequate resources will survive amid devastation. Meanwhile, wildlife will perish and habitats will be destroyed.

Predicting the effect of climate change on a system as big and complex as our planet is somewhat inexact: we don't know how much humans may change their behavior over the next few decades to reduce our effect on the climate, we don't know how much additional buffering the planet may be able to provide, we don't understand all the feedback loops. But the basics are pretty well understood. Human activity is releasing a lot more carbon into the atmosphere now than was held in the atmosphere before the widespread use of fossil fuels. Most of this carbon is in the form of carbon dioxide, CO_2, that is released when oil or coal is burned. Before we added so much carbon to the atmosphere, there was a happy balance between heat from the sun's rays that fell on earth and heat that radiated back into space. Carbon dioxide and other forms of carbon, such as methane, act as greenhouse gases, holding more heat in our atmosphere and allowing the planet to get warmer.

One of the first scientists to predict this phenomenon, and the one who developed an accurate way to measure atmospheric CO_2, was C. David Keeling. He searched for a location away from continental pollution and above the inversion layer where he could measure the carbon in clean, unpolluted air. He established his sampling station atop Mauna Loa in 1958, and it is still operating there today. He quickly found that the planet "breathes." That is, there is a regular annual rise in carbon dioxide that peaks in May, and then a seasonal reduction as Northern Hemisphere plants take up carbon dioxide. Over time, another pattern emerged. Figure 13.1 shows the alarming trend revealed by

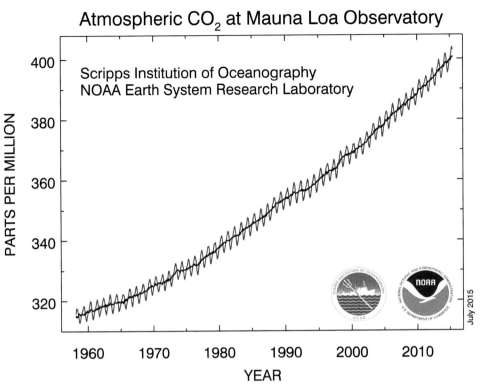

Atmospheric CO$_2$ at Mauna Loa Observatory

Scripps Institution of Oceanography
NOAA Earth System Research Laboratory

July 2015

FIGURE 13.1 The Keeling Curve shows a steadily rising concentration of the green-house gas CO$_2$ in the atmosphere atop Mauna Loa. (Earth System Research Laboratory, NOAA)

his careful monitoring: the amount of carbon in our atmosphere has climbed steadily since Keeling's measurements began. When Keeling first turned on his sampling instrument, there were 315 parts of carbon dioxide per million parts of air; by 2015 the number had climbed past 400. This graph of Mauna Loa readings is called the Keeling Curve.

Based on this rise in atmospheric carbon it is not unreasonable to assume that seas will rise a little more than six feet (two meters) by 2100. What happens to the Hawaiian Islands in that case? The Northwestern Hawaiian Islands are utterly transformed. Nesting habitat on Midway and Laysan shrinks considerably, leaving hundreds of thousands of birds with nowhere to lay their eggs and rear their young. Even worse, Pearl and Hermes Reef and French Frigate Shoals—ancient islands with names that evoke the days of sailing ships—will nearly

Climate Science and Uncertainty. Climate science is complicated. Just imagine trying to predict the effect of a warming planet, something totally outside human experience. Some consequences seem obvious: ocean water expands as it gets warmer, and ice melts faster in a warmer world. Both cause sea levels to rise. But sometimes we don't see the changes we expect because the planet *buffers* change. For example, the oceans have absorbed more than half the CO_2 we've pumped into the atmosphere, slowing the rate of warming. (But that added CO_2 has made the seas more acidic, which hinders creatures trying to build shells or coral heads.) When a buffer is exhausted, such as when the oceans can absorb no more excess CO_2, a *tipping point* may occur. That's when the effect of some process suddenly becomes much worse. Finally, there are *feedback loops:* mechanisms that accelerate or intensify effects of warming. One example: as the planet warms, frozen tundra in the arctic will thaw. Plant material in the

disappear beneath the waves. Monk seals will lose the beaches where they bask and nurse their young. For a species already on the verge of extinction, this loss may herald the end of their ancient lineage. Green sea turtles—whose kind have nested on these islands for millions of years—will arrive to find their ancestral beaches gone. There are green sea turtles in other seas that may carry on, but the Hawaiian population may perish. And remember, turtles live a long time. Young turtles you see while snorkeling could easily live to a time when the island of their birth is underwater. And for birds that depend on the Leeward Islands, there are no good alternatives. Likely doomed to extinction under a scenario of rising seas: black-footed albatross, Laysan albatross, Bonin petrel, Laysan duck, Laysan finch.

And that's not all. The remote Northwestern Hawaiian Islands, protected as the Papahānaumokuākea National Monument, serve as nursery and refuge for much of the wildlife that eventually finds its way down to the main islands. More than a million Laysan albatross breed in the northwestern islands. Their progeny have repopulated protected areas on the main islands, like Kaʻena Point on Oʻahu and Kīlauea Point on Kauaʻi. Ninety percent of the green sea turtles in Hawaiʻi nest at French Frigate Shoals, then make their way down to the shores of the main islands to feed. The pattern is similar for monk seals: 80 percent of the population resides among the Leeward Islands. That's why Kauaʻi, northernmost of the main islands, sees more monk seals than the other tundra will decompose when it thaws, releasing the greenhouse gas methane and accelerating the warming effect.

There is uncertainty, not about whether the planet is getting warmer—we are already witnessing that—but uncertainty about just how much the planet will warm and how bad things will get for all its inhabitants. Thus, predictions of sea-level rise range from the rather conservative 2014 projection of the Intergovernmental Panel on Climate Change or IPCC (between 10 inches and 2.7 feet by year 2100), to suggestions of top scientists like Jim Hansen (10–13 feet by 2100, with more rapid rise thereafter). The United States' National Climate Assessment recommends planning for a rise of at least 6 feet if there is "a low tolerance for risk." If you own a beachfront hotel at Waikīkī or you are an albatross and the survival of your species depends on the existence of nesting grounds in the Northwestern Hawaiian Islands, you have a low tolerance for risk.

FIGURE 13.2 These nesting Laysan albatross or *mōlī* on Midway Atoll are part of a leeward breeding population of over a million birds. Most of their nest sites would be underwater—with no alternative nesting location—if sea level rose six feet. (Forest & Kim Starr)

main islands. There are only a handful of seals along the shores of the Big Island at the southern end of the island chain. The impact may even extend to fish: some biologists believe the Northwestern Hawaiian Islands are an important spawning ground, producing the larvae that provide the next generation of fish and invertebrates around the main islands.

The low, sinking atolls of the Leeward Islands will see the worst effects of climate change, but no island will be spared. The main islands are much higher than the ancient atolls and pinnacles to the northwest, but they will suffer too. Sandy beaches will be inundated. Many corals will die in water that is deeper, warmer, and more acidic. Predicting changes in weather patterns is very difficult, and climate scientists are not sure whether Hawai'i will experience wetter or drier conditions. Ironically, it may be both: winter drought combined with summer hurricanes that are more powerful and more frequent. Figure 13.3 depicts a simulation of the new Honolulu coastline when the ocean is six feet higher. Say good-bye to low-lying Waikīkī.

The highest elevations will be affected, too. A 50 percent decline in silversword numbers on Haleakalā over the last thirty years is attributed to a warmer, drier climate on the mountain. At this rate of decline, the silvery *'āhinahina* could be extinct in the wild by 2100.

Sometimes it is the little things that get you. The mosquitoes introduced to Hawai'i by whaling ships in the 1820s are tropical species, limited to elevations below 4,500 feet or so. Over time they have adapted to cooler weather. They've been able to slowly expand their range upslope, carrying avian malaria and avian pox with them. A warmer climate will accelerate their spread. The only two refuges for endemic forest birds lacking immunity to these introduced diseases are the high forests on Maui and the Big Island. These high forest refuges will shrink as mosquitoes move upslope, reducing the birds' populations and making them more vulnerable to other threats. Add to your climate change extinction list endemic forest birds such as *'i'iwi, akiapōlā'au, 'ākepa, 'ōma'o 'ākeke'e, 'akikiki, puaiohi, 'anianiau, 'ā'kohekohe, 'alauahio*, Hawai'i creeper, and Maui parrotbill. The abundant *'apapane* may survive. The species groups of *'amakihi* and *'elepaio* show some resistance to avian disease, which may save them.

This all sounds like a bad dream. It makes us hope that we'll wake up and the problem will be gone. Or maybe climate change isn't really happening. There are some very big multinational corporations that fervently wish it weren't happening, and some of them would like us to believe it isn't a problem. Energy companies are holding trillions of dollars in reserves of coal and oil. If the world decides to stop consuming so much coal and oil, decides to try to save the Laysan albatross and the *ʻiʻiwi* and ten thousand other species that might be wiped out by climate change, those trillions of dollars are mostly off-limits, worthless. Among scientists of the world, there is overwhelming consensus about the basics of climate change. We are not dreaming.

There is some uncertainty surrounding climate change predictions. Wouldn't it be terrible to act based on incorrect information? What if the doubters are right, and human energy consumption is not causing a buildup of greenhouse gases and a warming planet? There are two ways to look at it. If climate change skeptics are right and we curtail the burning of fossil fuel based on faulty information, the result is massive investment of funds and job creation in renewable energy industries, cleaner air and water, and the safeguarding of finite fossil fuel reserves for future generations. On the other hand, if climate scientists are right but we don't take action, then sea levels rise, coastal cities flood, species go extinct, and your children or grandchildren curse you because you didn't act. In other words, the choice for humanity should be an easy one, even in the face of uncertainty.

And the longer we wait to take action and stop producing so much of these greenhouse gases, the harder it will be to preserve a comfortable planet. All the CO_2 we have already put into the atmosphere is going to stay there for hundreds of years and continue to build up atmospheric heat all that time. Even if everyone on the planet stopped using all fossil fuel today, the planet would continue to heat up for a long time. We have only just begun to feel the growing effect of our past fossil-fuel use. Some leading scientists believe that if we don't take drastic worldwide action in the next few years, we will have set a course for irreversible, intolerable climate change that won't dissipate for thousands of years.

In Hawaiʻi there is direct evidence, in the form of exposed ancient coral, that the world's oceans have been as much as one hundred feet higher than today, and the shared plants and animals of the islands of Maui Nui, suggestive of previous land bridges, are circumstantial evidence that sea level was once nearly four hundred feet lower. These wide swings in sea level suggest wide swings in atmospheric carbon, but that isn't necessarily the case. Scientists estimate that atmospheric carbon today is the highest it has been for a couple of million years. What's going on? Several factors seem to be involved. First, the sun's energy output is not constant but varies on an eleven-year cycle. In addition, astronomers believe that the gravitational force of other planets creates slight changes in the earth's orbit around the sun. This can draw us closer to or pull us away from our solar heat source. Also, the tilted axis of our planet—the tilt that gives us seasons—can wobble a bit, affecting global temperatures. Each of these phenomena seems to recur in cycles that can last twenty thousand to four hundred thousand years. Depending on how these factors coincide, the planet's climate can change slowly, with long periods that are warm or cold. And these periods can be stoked by feedback loops. The result? Very warm times when polar ice melts and seas rise, or ice ages that draw lots of seawater into polar ice and cause water levels to fall. Today we are layering a new factor on top of all the others, pushing our atmosphere to extremes never before seen by humans. (The **Field Trip!** section tells you where to see evidence of past sea levels.)

Two Critical Numbers.   There are two numbers that show up frequently in climate change information: 350 and 2. An atmospheric carbon level of 350 parts per million is widely believed to be a safe target for maintaining a livable planet. From the Keeling Curve above, you can see that we passed that concentration a little before 1990. It will take a lot of effort to get back to that level. The other number is 2° Celsius or centigrade (that's 3.6° Fahrenheit). Many climate scientists believe that a global temperature rise of that amount, averaged over all locations and all seasons, is the most our planet can take without experiencing catastrophic effects. Since 1900 global temperatures have already climbed about a degree centigrade.

The grim scenarios of extinction and suffering are enough to make lots of people want to take action, but reversing the climate trends of a planet is a huge task, not something an individual can tackle alone. Climate change is a global problem, and it has to be attacked globally or at least nationally. Unfortunately, that is not happening. To be sure, the leaders of the Pacific island nation of Kiribati have taken action. They bought five thousand acres of high ground on Fiji. Why? Because Kiribati's main island and national capital, Tarawa Atoll, has a maximum elevation of ten feet. It will be the first national capital to be submerged. Sea-level rise is already making some farm fields on Kiribati too salty to grow crops, so the new land on Fiji will help ensure a food supply for Kiribati. Later, the land on Fiji just might be the new home for one hundred thousand residents of Kiribati when their nation is overwhelmed by rising seas.

Most of the rest of the world has not been so proactive. Reversing our trends of energy consumption will produce distinct winners and losers in the world, and politicians don't like to turn powerful multinational corporations into losers. It is becoming clear that—if the world wants to avoid a future worse than any science fiction we can imagine—individuals have to lead their politicians.

Residents of the United States are among the top producers of CO_2 in the world, whether measured by total output or per person. It is virtually impossible for individuals in modern society to reduce their carbon footprint to zero; the best we can do is to reduce it at the personal level and to work for planet-transforming change at the national or international level. There are three categories of action that almost anyone can take: use less energy, demand change, and share knowledge. Our politicians are tragically unwilling to take sufficient action, so all of us need to lead the effort. Here are some ideas on how you can fight climate change:

Use less energy. There are a lot of ways individuals can reduce their "energy footprint." You've heard all these before, and you may already be doing many of them. Insulate and weather-strip your house. Install photovoltaic panels to generate your own electricity. Use a clothesline instead of a clothes dryer. If your homeowner's association objects, politely fight back. Take mass transit, or bicycle, or walk whenever you can. Get an efficient car, perhaps hybrid or electric, for those times when the alternatives won't do. Combine errands, or eliminate some trips. Reconsider whether driving an SUV is really the best way to protect your kids. Conserve hot water. Replace lightbulbs with LEDs. Upgrade to efficient appliances. Use a solar cooker. Buy less stuff, because it all takes energy to make and ship. Eat more locally produced food, and waste less. We should all be doing these things right now.

What about Flying to Hawai'i? Commercial air transportation uses less than 2 percent of the United States' annual energy budget, one tenth what we use in our personal cars. Most of us don't fly every day, but a single long flight can add a huge amount to a person's annual carbon footprint. To see how much carbon is generated by each of your daily activities such as home heating and cooling, driving, and jet travel you can use an online carbon footprint calculator. Each calculator uses its own assumptions, so results may vary. Still, they give you a good relative idea of how each activity contributes to your carbon output. As this book goes to press, the U.S. Environmental Protection Agency or USEPA has a very good calculator that provides tips on how to reduce your carbon footprint, but it doesn't allow you to factor in any air travel. The Nature Conservancy has a calculator that allows you to include jet travel in your energy budget. Their website even allows you to buy carbon offsets for your CO_2 output: your contribution allows TNC to preserve forest or avoid carbon production in some other way so you can fly with a cleaner conscience.

Swimming with a sea turtle, watching the courtship dance of an albatross, or seeing an 'i'iwi foraging among blooming 'ōhi'a trees makes us stronger advocates for the planet. But the uncomfortable reality is that jet travel produces a lot of atmospheric carbon and harms the natural wonders of the world. Perhaps the best strategy is to increase the duration of your vacations and reduce their frequency. Then take other actions to fight climate change.

Demand change. Personal energy conservation is important but to make a real difference soon enough, changes in energy use will have to be dramatic and global. Unfortunately some individuals and governments will never conserve energy until they must meet requirements set by law. That's why political leaders have to be involved. Communicate with your elected representatives at the national, state, and local level. Let them know that climate change is an important issue, to you and to your children. Sell off the oil and coal company stocks in your retirement fund, or communicate with your fund managers and ask them to divest. Support organizations and political candidates that advocate change.

Economists believe a simple and effective way to curb the planet's appetite for fossil fuel is a carbon fee. It would work like this: energy producers such as oil companies and coal mines would be charged a fee based on the amount of CO_2 generated by their products. This would make oil and coal more expensive than alternatives such as solar and wind power. The fee would be rebated to households; if you use little or no fossil fuel, you could make money. Few politicians will advocate such a fee, so their constituents will have to demand it.

Share your knowledge. Today it's easy to be complacent because the magnitude of the problem is not apparent. By the time the worst effects of climate change are apparent, it will be too late to take meaningful action. So do what you can to fight this inertia by helping others to understand the problem and the solutions. Explain to others why you are taking action. Don't be afraid to repeat yourself. Repeating a message helps to reinforce it.

FIELD TRIP!

Do you want to see evidence of sea levels that were much higher than today? Field trip 7.1 describes two Oʻahu snorkeling spots where you can see massive exposed reef: **Kahe Point Beach County Park** (also known as Electric Beach) on the southern Waianae coast and **Pūpūkea Beach County Park** (better known as Shark's Cove) on the north shore just north of Waimea. Both have big rocky outcroppings that are actually ancient reef formed when sea levels were as much as thirty feet higher.

13.1 Maui Nui at a Glance. About 120,000 years ago there was much more seawater locked up in polar ice caps, lowering ocean levels by more than two hundred feet. At that time three islands of Maui Nui—Maui, Molokaʻi, Lānaʻi—were all connected. During earlier times Kahoʻolawe was also part of the big ancient island, before island subsidence allowed water to flood low areas and divide the landmass. The biological evidence of past connection remains today; these islands share more species than they would if they had never been joined.

You can see Molokaʻi, Lānaʻi, and Kahoʻolawe from many places along the Lahaina waterfront, which might help you visualize the ancient island of Maui Nui. My favorite spot to enjoy this multi-island view is at Puʻunoa Point, a quiet little beach north of downtown and *makai* of the Cannery Mall. From downtown Lahaina, head north on Front Street. Where the road curves, turn *makai* on Ala Moana. (There is also an access road for the boat launch ramp and dilapidated wharf at this junction. Keep left on Ala Moana.) At the end of the road you'll see the Jodo Mission Buddhist Cultural Park on your left (you can see the ornate temple, massive temple bell, and huge statue of Buddha from outside the fence), and an old cemetery on your right (where the graves are being reclaimed by dunes). From the modest beach park you can look behind you to see the West Maui Mountains, right to see Moloka'i, straight ahead to see Lāna'i, and left to see little Kaho'olawe in the distance. At one time you could have walked to Moloka'i or Lāna'i across an isthmus reminiscent of the valley that bisects Maui today.

The water at this beach is very shallow and very calm, thanks to a protective reef offshore. Many Lahaina children get their introduction to the ocean at this "baby beach." There is some shade from big *kiawe* trees. Showers and poorly maintained restrooms are available next door at the boat launch ramp; to reach them, walk up the beach toward the old wharf, then follow the entrance road.

13.2 Hawai'i, Year 2100. This final field trip is the easiest and the hardest in the whole book. It involves nothing more than strolling down to the beach at Waikīkī, this guidebook in hand. If you're on an island other than O'ahu, just go to a nearby beach and use your imagination a bit. Look around until you spot a baby in a stroller or in a parent's arms. Maybe it is your own child. Now, take a look at figure 13.3. It shows how a rising sea will alter the coastline by the time that baby is elderly: beach eroded, resort hotels flooded and abandoned, homes inundated, people displaced. The truly scary thing is that it may be too late to avoid this level of calamity. We have created a global atmosphere that still seems pretty comfortable but is headed for trouble. It is like paddling out to sea in a boat with a slow leak. Things don't seem too bad right away, but pretty soon you're bailing water out of the boat like mad and wondering if there are sharks nearby.

Remote islands like Hawai'i are some of the most fragile and vulnerable environments on earth. The forests and beaches and reefs and oceans have always needed our care, our *mālama*. Now they need it more than ever.

FIGURE 13.3 (facing page) (*a*) This aerial photo shows Waikīkī as it exists today. (Data provided by University of Hawai'i School of Ocean and Earth Science and Technology); (*b*) This simulation shows how a six-foot rise in sea level would affect Waikīkī. (Simulation courtesy of NOAA Office for Coastal Management; data provided by SOEST)

LEARN MORE

The science of climate change is advancing so quickly, and the planet's climate is worsening so rapidly, that most traditional books on the subject become obsolete very fast. Trusted Internet sources will provide more current information. As this book goes to press, some U.S. government websites are being dismantled by newly appointed climate change skeptics. New federal policies may continue to reduce, change, or eliminate dependable information from these websites in the future, but there are plenty of other good sources of information. The United States Environmental Protection Agency, or **USEPA**, formerly maintained a useful website and still posts some good information. The National Oceanic and Atmospheric Administration, or **NOAA**, maintains a site that helps distinguish between weather and climate. Thirteen federal agencies operating as the U.S. Global Change Research Program or USGCRP have sponsored a website called **GlobalChange** devoted to global change, both human-caused and natural. They also produced the **National Climate Assessment**.

The University Corporation for Atmospheric Research or **UCAR**, a consortium of over one hundred colleges and universities, has a good website. The Intergovernmental Panel on Climate Change, or **IPCC**, publishes exhaustively documented consensus reports on climate change. The **Pacific Islands Regional Climate Assessment** (PIRCA) is a collaborative effort to assess climate change effects and adaptive capacity of Hawai'i and other Pacific islands. Its website describes research and provides information to help predict effects of climate change on island resources and develop coping strategies.

Among nongovernmental organizations, the **Climate Reality Project** offers a website with basic information and opportunities to take action. Even more action-oriented is an organization called **350.org**. You can guess their website address. The Center for Climate and Energy Solutions or **C2ES** has a site loaded with information and news. The **Climate Institute** has a site with good background information and a lot of news links. The **World Resources Institute** maintains a website called the Climate Analysis Indicators Tool or **CAIT** Climate Data Explorer that makes it easy to dig into climate data. The **Citizens' Climate Lobby** advocates for a carbon fee. And don't forget the carbon footprint calculators offered by USEPA, the Nature Conservancy, and others.

Appendix
Field Trips by Island

This table shows field trips by island so that you can plan an island trip or decide which island you want to visit. For each field trip the table shows what natural topics are evident on the trip, not all the topics that are discussed in the field trip description itself. For example, the text for field trip 10.8 to Hanalei Valley describes *kalo* (taro) culture in the valley. You would have to read other chapters of this book to fully appreciate the great examples of evolution, native plant life, and endemic birds that can be seen in the valley. The accessibility column shows whether the field trip is fully accessible (x) or partially accessible (p) to a wheelchair user.

Field Trips by Island	Geology	Evolution	Plants	Birds & Others
Kaua'i				
2.11 Waimea Canyon	X		X	X
2.12 Hā'ena Caves and the Nā Pali Coast	X			
3.4 Any Big Lawn, August through April				X
4.4 A Silversword Relative	X	X	X	X
4.8 McBryde and Limahuli Gardens		X	X	
5.1 Kīlauea Point National Wildlife Refuge	X	X	X	X
5.8 Birding at Kōke'e State Park	X	X	X	X
6.2 Watching Whales from Shore	X		X	X
6.5 Spotting the Elusive Monk Seal	X		X	X
7.6 Snorkeling Kaua'i				
8.2 Canoe Plants			X	
8.6 Kaua'i Cultural Sites	X			X
10.1 To Market, to Market				
10.8 Hanalei Valley *Kalo*		X	X	X
12.2 Makauwahi Cave Reserve	X	X	X	X
O'ahu				
2.8 Diamond Head	X		X	X
2.9 Pali Lookout	X		X	
2.10 Ancient Reefs	X			
3.2 Lāna'i Lookout	X	X		X
3.4 Any Big Lawn, August through April				X
4.5 Koko Crater Botanical Garden	X	X	X	
4.6 Lyon Arboretum			X	X
4.9 Indoor Koa in Honolulu	X	X	X	X
5.3 Ka'ena Point	X	X	X	X
5.6 Native Plants and Snails above Honolulu		X	X	X

Marine Mammals	Reef Life	Hawaiian Culture	Introduced Species	Agriculture	Astronomy	Extinction	Climate Change	Accessibility
			x					p
								p
								p
		x	x	x				
x								x
			x			x	x	p
x								x
x								p
x	x							
		x	x	x				p
		x		x				p
				x				x
		x		x				x
x		x	x			x		
			x					
			x					x
	x							
x								
								x
		x	x					
		x	x					
x	x	x	x	x	x	x		x
x			x			x		
			x					

(*continued*)

Field Trips by Island	Geology	Evolution	Plants	Birds & Others
Oʻahu (*continued*)				
6.2 Watching Whales from Shore	X			X
6.4 Observing Dolphins at Their Resting Bays	X		X	X
6.5 Spotting the Elusive Monk Seal	X		X	X
7.1 Snorkeling Oʻahu	X			
7.7 Aquariums			X	
7.10 Coral from Shore				X
8.1 Bishop Museum	X	X	X	X
8.2 Canoe Plants			X	X
8.3 Oʻahu Cultural Sites		X	X	X
9.1 Kapiʻolani World Tour	X			X
10.1 To Market, to Market				
10.7 Pond to Plate				X
13.2 Hawaiʻi, Year 2100	X			
Maui				
2.4 Haleakalā National Park	X	X	X	X
2.5 ʻĪao Valley	X		X	
2.6 Cape Kīnaʻu	X		X	
3.4 Any Big Lawn, August through April				X
4.7 Maui Nui Botanical Gardens		X	X	
5.4 Birds and More at Haleakalā National Park	X	X	X	X
5.5 Keālia Pond National Wildlife Refuge				X
6.1 Listen to the Whales				
6.2 Watching Whales from Shore				
6.3 Whale Watching by Boat				
6.6 Special Events, Cetacean Style				
7.2 Snorkeling Maui	X			

Marine Mammals	Reef Life	Hawaiian Culture	Introduced Species	Agriculture	Astronomy	Extinction	Climate Change	Accessibility
X								p
X								p
X	X	X					X	
X	X		X				X	
X	X	X						X
	X	X	X					X
X	X	X	X	X	X	X		X
		X	X	X				
		X	X					p
	X		X				X	X
				X				X
			X	X				X
						X	X	X
			X		X	X		p
								p
X	X	X						
								X
		X	X	X				X
			X		X	X		
X	X		X					X
X	X							
X								X
X								
X								p
X	X	X	X					

(continued)

Field Trips by Island	Geology	Evolution	Plants	Birds & Others
Maui (*continued*)				
7.7 Aquariums				
7.10 Coral from Shore				
8.2 Canoe Plants				
8.5 Cultural Sites of Maui Nui				
9.2 Hosmer Grove		X	X	X
10.1 To Market, to Market				
10.4 Sweetened History				
11.5 Summer Night Magic Atop Haleakalā	X	X	X	X
13.1 Maui Nui at a Glance	X	X		
Moloka'i				
2.7 Subtraction and Addition on Moloka'i	X			
3.4 Any Big Lawn, August through April				X
6.1 Listen to the Whales				
6.2 Watching Whales from Shore				
7.4 Snorkeling Moloka'i				
8.5 Cultural Sites of Maui Nui	X			
10.1 To Market, to Market				
10.5 Meyer's Mill on Moloka'i				
Lāna'i				
3.4 Any Big Lawn, August through April				X
6.1 Listen to the Whales				
6.2 Watching Whales from Shore				
6.4 Observing Dolphins at Their Resting Bays				
6.5 Spotting the Elusive Monk Seal				
7.3 Snorkeling Lāna'i				

Marine Mammals	Reef Life	Hawaiian Culture	Introduced Species	Agriculture	Astronomy	Extinction	Climate Change	Accessibility
x	x	x						x
	x		x					x
		x	x	x				p
		x	x	x				
			x					
				x				x
		x		x				x
			x			x		p
x							x	
		x						
								x
x	x							
x								p
	x							
		x	x					
				x				x
		x		x				
								x
x	x							
x	x	x	x					
x	x		x					x
x	x	x	x					
x	x		x					

(*continued*)

Field Trips by Island	Geology	Evolution	Plants	Birds & Others
Lāna'i (*continued*)				
8.5 Cultural Sites of Maui Nui				
10.1 To Market, to Market				
Big Island				
2.1 Hawai'i Volcanoes National Park	x	x	x	x
2.2 Ahalanui Warm Springs	Destroyed by lava flows in 2018			
2.3 Kaūmana Cave	x	x	x	
3.1 The Big Island's Loneliest Spot	x			
3.3 Mountaintop to Mountaintop	x	x	x	x
3.4 Any Big Lawn, August through April				x
4.1 Big Island Vegetation Zone Driving Tour	x	x	x	x
4.2 Endemic Plants in Hawai'i Volcanoes National Park	x	x	x	x
4.3 Eat an Endemic Plant			x	
4.10 Indoor Koa on the Big Island			x	
5.2 Saddle Road Birding Sites	x	x	x	x
5.7 Butterflies and Native Plants at Kīpuka Puaulu	x	x	x	x
6.2 Watching Whales from Shore				
6.4 Observing Dolphins at Their Resting Bays				
7.5 Snorkeling the Big Island				
7.8 Swim with Mantas				
7.9 Big Fish from Shore				
8.4 Big Island Cultural Sites	x		x	x
8.7 Hula	x		x	x
9.3 Aliens Take Over at Pu'u Wa'awa'a	x	x	x	x
9.4 Noisy Night in Hilo				
10.1 To Market, to Market				

Marine Mammals	Reef Life	Hawaiian Culture	Introduced Species	Agriculture	Astronomy	Extinction	Climate Change	Accessibility
x	x	x	x					
				x				x
x		x	x					p
					x			
x		x						
			x		x			p
		x	x			x		p
		x		x				
		x						p
			x		x	x	x	
			x			x		
x		x						p
x	x	x						p
x	x	x	x					
		x						
	x							
x	x	x	x	x				p
		x						p
			x			x		
			x					x
				x				x

(*continued*)

Field Trips by Island	Geology	Evolution	Plants	Birds & Others
Big Island (*continued*)				
10.2 Kona Coffee, Culture, and Cooking				
10.3 Nuts to You				
10.6 Cold Comfort on the Kona Coast				
11.1 The Mauna Kea Visitor Information Station	X	X	X	X
11.2 The Mauna Kea Summit Two Ways	X		X	
11.3 'Imiloa Astronomy Center			X	
11.4 The Rainy Day Museum Crawl in Hilo	X	X	X	X
12.1 Mokupāpapa Discovery Center	X	X	X	X
12.3 In Pursuit of *Palila*	X	X	X	X

Marine Mammals	Reef Life	Hawaiian Culture	Introduced Species	Agriculture	Astronomy	Extinction	Climate Change	Accessibility
		x		x				
				x				x
	x			x				p
		x	x		x			x
		x			x			
		x			x			x
x	x	x						p
x	x	x	x			x	x	p
			x			x		

Index

Page numbers in **bold** refer to illustrations.

endemic species: at Puʻu Waʻawaʻa, 275; defined, 54, 73
epiphytes, defined, 83
evolution, 52–56; coevolution, 324; convergent, 326
exotic species. *See* introduced species
extinction, 57–58, 320–334; and climate change, 340; reasons to prevent, 326–329; statistics, 324

F

FADs (fish aggregation devices), 204
fairy tern (white tern), 125, **125**
farmers' market, 290; in Hilo, 291, **292**; at Kapiʻolani Community College, 290, **291**
featherwork, 236–238, **237**, 322
feedback loop, 342
ferns: *ʻamaʻu*, 69; *hāpuʻu*, 70, 81; *uluhe*, 70, **70**
fish aggregation devices (FADs), 204
fish: freshwater, 206–207; marine, 182–194. *See also individual species*
fishpond, early Hawaiian, 231; Heʻeia, **232**; Kaloko, 244; on Molokaʻi, 248
flash floods, 65
founder species, 56
freshwater fish, 206–207

G

Gardner Pinnacles, 28, 57, **57**
geckos, 256; gold dust day, **256**
genetically modified organisms (GMOs), 284
glaciers, 88
GMOs (genetically modified organisms), 284
goatfish, 183, **183**
gray francolin, 126–128, **128**
great frigatebird (*ʻiwa*), 112–113, **113**
green flash, 312–313
green sea turtle, **2**, 194–198; at Hoʻokipa Beach Park, 197; at Kaloko-Honokōhau National Historical

Park, 245; at Puʻuhonua o Hōnaunau National Historic Park, 245
guides, listed on website, 333
gulls, 114, 139
gyres, 48; North Pacific, 48

H

Hāʻena State Park, 43
Haleakalā, 13, 24, 62, 66, 83, **307**; visiting at night, 318–319
Haleakalā National Park, 35–36, 137–138; Hosmer Grove in, 273–274; introduced species at, 273
Halemaʻumaʻu Crater, 20, 22, 30
halfbeaks, 188
hammerhead shark, 199–200
Hanapēpē Salt Ponds, 251
Hanauma Bay, 25, 40, 208–210
hāpuʻu, 70, 81; at Kaūmana Cave, 86
hau, 33, 299
haupia, 289
Hawaiian coot (*ʻalae keʻokeʻo*), 121, 139; at Hanalei on Kauaʻi, 297
Hawaiian duck (*koloa maoli*), 122
Hawaiian gallinule (*ʻalae ʻula*), 121; at Hanalei on Kauaʻi, 297
Hawaiian green sea turtle. *See* green sea turtle
Hawaiian Islands Humpback Whale National Marine Sanctuary, 151–152, **151**
Hawaiian language, 4–6; alphabet, 5, 238; plurals, 116; pronunciation, 5
Hawaiian monk seal, 159–161, **160**; observing from shore, 164–165
Hawaiian petrel (*ʻuaʻu*), 116–119, **117**, 138; on Haleakalā, 319
Hawaiian sovereignty, 239
Hawaiian stilt (*aeʻo*), 121, 139, **298**; at Hanalei on Kauaʻi, 297
Hawaiian sweet bread, 289; baking, with Kona Historical Society, 293
Hawaiʻi Ocean Science and Technology Park (HOST), 295–296

Hawai'i state fish, 187–188, **188**
Hawai'i Volcanoes National Park, 20–22,
    30–33, 141; endemic plants at,
    90–93; ferns at, 81; Friends of, 33;
    goats in, 257; petroglyphs in, **4**
hawksbill turtle, 198
hazards. *See* safety
heiau, 231–232; Pi'ilanihale at Kahanu
    Garden, 247, **247**; Pu'u Koholā,
    243–244; Pu'u o Mahuka, 242; at
    Wailua, 249; at Waimea Valley, 243
honu. See green sea turtle
Hosmer Grove, 137, 273–274
HOST (Hawai'i Ocean Science and
    Technology) Park, 295–296
hot spot, 12–14, 27
house finch, 128
house sparrow, 128
Hualālai, 13, 22, 24, 83
hula, 238, 251
Hulihe'e Palace, 100
Hulopo'e Bay, 213
humpback whales, 144–153, **146**, **149**;
    observing from boats, 164; observ-
    ing from shore, 133, 162–163;
    singing, 162; special events, 165;
    whaling in Hawai'i, 152
humuhumunukunukuāpua'a, 188, **188**
hunakai (sanderling), 59, 139
hurricanes, 68

I

'Īao Valley, 36
'i'iwi, 108–109, **109**, 134–135, 137; used
    in featherwork, 237; subfossil, 321
'iliahi (sandalwood), 79–80, 83; at Pu'u
    Wa'awa'a, 275
iliau, 93–94
'Imiloa Astronomy Center, 317
indigenous species, defined, 73
introduced species, 73, 253; birds,
    103; cattle egret, 125, **125**, 262;
    coqui frog, 276; in Kapi'olani Park,
    266–273; mongoose, small Indian,
261, **262**; mosquitoes, 260, 340;
    mouflon sheep, 259, **259**; number
    in Hawai'i, 254; partial list, 254; at
    Pu'u Wa'awa'a, 274–276; snail, giant
    African, 263, **263**; transport on
    shoes, 3
invasive species, defined, 253
inversion layer, 65–66
'Iolani Palace, 99
ironwood, 74
island life cycle, 17–27, **18**
isolation of Hawai'i, 9, 45, 59–61, 191
'iwa (great frigatebird), 112–113, **113**

J

Japanese white-eye (*mejiro*), 126, **127**
Java sparrow, 126, **269**

K

Kā'anapali Beach, 212
Ka'ena Point, 135–137
Kahalu'u Beach County Park, 214
Kahanu Garden: 241; heiau at, 247, **247**
Kahe Point Beach County Park: 42, 210;
    and sea level rise, 345
Kaho'olawe, 11, 29
kāhuna, 232
Kaimana Beach, 212
Kalahaku Overlook, 138
Kalalau Trail, 43
Kalaupapa Peninsula, 38
Kalāwahine Trail, 140
Kalij pheasant, 141; at Kīpuka Puaulu,
    90
kalo, 71, 231, 287; acres planted today,
    285; farms at Hanalei on Kaua'i,
    297; at Limahuli Garden, 98; at
    Maui Nui Botanical Gardens, 97
Kaloko-Honokōhau National Historical
    Park, 244
Kalōpā State Recreation Area, *'ōhi'a* at,
    81
kālua pig, 287
kama'āina, defined, 6

Southern Cross, 311–312

South Point, 59–61

species: defined, 50–52; transport, 46–48

spider: ballooning 46; Hawaiian happy face, **46**, 129; no-eyed big-eyed hunting, 131–132

spinner dolphins, 153–157, **154**; observing from shore, 133, 164; swimming with, 157

spotted dolphins, 158

squids, 177

subfossil, defined, 322

subsidence, 23–24

sugarcane, 279–280; historic mill on Moloka'i, 295; at Maui Nui Botanical Gardens, 97; museum, 294–295

sunscreen, 3

surgeonfishes, 185–187, **186**

sweet potato, 71, 230

symbiosis, 171, 172, 176

T

tangs, 185, 187; convict, **186**; sailfin, **2**; yellow **175**

taro. See *kalo*

taxonomy, 50–51

telescopes: conditions for siting, 301–302; Faulkes North, on Haleakalā, 309, **309**; on Mauna Kea, 302–308, **307**; Subaru, 307, 316; types, 303; visiting, 315–317; W. M. Keck, 306, **306**, 316

thorns, on Hawaiian plants, 84

threats to native species, 105, 131, 323–324; aquarium trade, 187; disease, 105, 108, 109, 138; garbage, 115; habitat loss, 120; to marine mammals, 161–162; night lighting, 118–119; pesticides, 132; predation, 112, 117, 134, 136; wind turbines, 132

Thurston Lava Tube, 31

tiger shark, 200–201, **202**

trade winds, 39, 47, 64–65

tree molds, 32, 90

triggerfishes, 187–188, **188**

tropics: of Cancer and of Capricorn, 10; defined, 10; sun position in, 313–314

trumpetfish, 188–189

tsunami, 15; at Midway Atoll, 335

tuff, defined, 17

tuna, yellowfin (*'ahi*), 204–206, **205**, 218

turkey, 128

turtle. *See* green sea turtle; hawksbill turtle

Twain, Mark, 8, 20, 21, 253

Two Step, 214

U

'ua'u (Hawaiian petrel), 116–119, **117**, 138; on Haleakalā, 319

uhu (parrotfish), 192–193; bullethead **192**

'ūlili (wandering tattler), 59, 139

'ulu (breadfruit), 288, **288**

uluhe, 70, **70**

urchin, sea, 179–180; rock-boring, **168**; slate-pencil, **168**; spiny **180**

V

vegetation zones, 69, **73**, 72–86

Volcano House, 20, 31

W

Wai'ale'ale, 43

Waikamoi Preserve, **6**, 138, 258, 274

Waikīkī, 39; and sea level rise, 346, **347**; snorkeling at, 211–212

Waimea Canyon, 24–25, 42–43

wana (spiny sea urchin), 179–180, **180**

wandering tattler (*'ūlili*), 59, 139

wedge-tailed shearwater, 133–134, 135–136

West Maui Mountains, 36, 346

whales, 155, *See also* beaked whales; humpback whales

About the Author

Rick Soehren is a consulting zoologist with extensive experience in natural resource conservation, environmental restoration, and interpretation of natural sciences for the general public and for technical audiences. He has worked in Hawai'i and California, and is the author of *The Birdwatcher's Guide to Hawai'i*.